PERGAMON INTERNATIONAL LIBRARY
of Science, Technology, Engineering and Social Studies

*The 1000-volume original paperback library in aid of education,
industrial training and the enjoyment of leisure*

Publisher: Robert Maxwell, M.C.

Human Behavior and Public Policy:
A Political Psychology

(PGPS-41)

————— Publisher's Notice to Educators —————

THE PERGAMON TEXTBOOK
INSPECTION COPY SERVICE

An inspection copy of any book published in the Pergamon
International Library will gladly be sent without obligation for
consideration for course adoption or recommendation. Copies may
be retained for a period of 60 days from receipt and returned if not
suitable. When a particular title is adopted or recommended for
adoption for class use and the recommendation results in a sale of
12 or more copies, the inspection copy may be retained with our
compliments. If after examination the lecturer decides that the
book is not suitable for adoption but would like to retain it for his
personal library, then our Educators' Discount of 10% is allowed on
the invoiced price. The Publishers will be pleased to receive
suggestions for revised editions and new titles to be published in this
important International Library.

PERGAMON GENERAL PSYCHOLOGY SERIES

Editor: Arnold P. Goldstein, *Syracuse University*
Leonard Krasner, *SUNY, Stony Brook*

The terms of our inspection copy service apply to all the above books. A complete catalogue of all books in the Pergamon International Library is available on request.

The Publisher will be pleased to receive suggestions for revised editions and new titles.

ii

Human Behavior and Public Policy:
A Political Psychology

Marshall H. Segall
Syracuse University

PERGAMON PRESS INC.

New York / Toronto / Oxford / Sydney / Frankfurt / Paris

Pergamon Press Offices:

OXFORD	Pergamon Press Ltd., Headington Hill Hall, Oxford, England
U.S.A.	Pergamon Press Inc., Maxwell House, Fairview Park, Elmsford, New York 10523, U.S.A.
CANADA	Pergamon of Canada Ltd., 207 Queen's Quay West, Toronto 1, Canada
AUSTRALIA	Pergamon Press (Aust.) Pty. Ltd., 19a Boundary Street, Rushcutters Bay, N.S.W. 2011, Australia
FRANCE	Pergamon Press SARL, 24 rue des Ecoles, 75240 Paris, Cedex 05, France
WEST GERMANY	Pergamon Press GmbH, 6242 Kronberg/Taunus, Frankfurt, West Germany

Library of Congress Cataloging in Publication Data

Segall, Marshall H
    Human behavior and public policy.

    (Pergamon general psychology series ; 41)
    Includes index.
    1. Political psychology. I. Title.
[DNLM: 1. Social behavior. 2. Politics. JA74.5 S454h]
JA74.5.S44   1976   320'.01'9   75-35631
ISBN 0-08-017087-0
ISBN 0-08-017853-7 pbk.

Printed in the United States of America

288882

Contents

About the Author

Marshall H. Segall (Ph.D. Northwestern University) is Chairperson of the Graduate Interdisciplinary Social Science Program in the Maxwell School of Syracuse University. As Professor of Social and Political Psychology at Syracuse, he directed that university's Program of Eastern African Studies for several years.

An early participant in the development of cross-cultural psychology, Professor Segall has spent many years in Africa where he founded the psychology program at Makerere University in Uganda and conducted research projects reported in numerous journal articles and in the co-authored volume (with Donald Campbell and Melville Herskovits), *The Influence of Culture on Visual Perception*. His other publications include *Visual Art: Some Perspectives from Cross-Cultural Psychology, Becoming Ugandan: The Dynamics of Identity in a Multi-Cultural African State*, and a fieldwork manual for cross-cultural research on communication via facial expression (with Carolyn Keating and Allan Mazur). He is now completing a textbook on cross-cultural psychology.

Professor Segall is an active member of the American Psychological Association, the Society for the Psychological Study of Social Issues, the International Association of Cross-Cultural Psychology, the Society for Cross-Cultural Research, and the International Studies Association.

Preface

My aim in this book is to stimulate academic psychologists and their students to consider whether knowledge of the hows and whys of human behavior matters to anybody else. Should persons outside the academy care about psychological data and theories? Conversely, should psychologists attend to what non-psychologists need to know? In short—is psychology, and ought it be, relevant?

I am convinced, as are many (but by no means all) of my professional colleagues, that the facts and theories that have been generated by psychological research comprise practical knowledge of potentially great value. I view much psychological knowledge as worth acquiring for reasons other than passing courses, earning degrees, and attaining comfortable status in the world-after-college.

That world—the "real world" as many academics half-jokingly dub it—is the psychologist's ultimate laboratory. It is the origin of all questions that peak the psychologist's curiosity and the only place in which his/her tentative answers may meaningfully be put to the test. The classroom, the scholar's study, and the specially contrived psychological laboratory are intellectual sanctuaries into which selected stimuli are allowed to flow and distractions are screened out. The best of these sanctuaries are *not* built of ivy-covered stone; the walls of those that function best are transparent and porous. Many psychological sanctuaries are of this loose-weave variety. Inward through their walls have streamed questions that cause wonder wherever human lives are lived and outward have trickled some answers that could enhance those lives.

This book, I hope, will demonstrate that the products of psychological research, both the findings that are already extant and those that we are equipped to uncover, contain guidelines for all who seek not only to understand but to improve the way humans relate to their environment and to each other. I have tried to make this book a testament to the proposition that the criterion against which psychology ought be judged is its contribution to the search for a better world. Material included in this book was selected because of its relevance to this search. As clearly as I could, I have tried to make that relevance explicit.

What I have called "the search for a better world" is, of course, not without controversy. Indeed, the search may best be characterized as a weighing and sifting of public policy alternatives, all of which have something to commend them. Policy dilemmas are inherently normative conflicts that are ultimately resolvable only in the political arena. Moreover, their resolution requires multiple contributions from all branches of enquiry—scientific, social scientific, and humanistic. Thus, public policy *cannot* be shaped exclusively by psychology nor can policy dilemmas be resolved by psychologists. But to the degree that public policy dilemmas involve disputes over what the lay person likes to call "human nature," the policy makers, whoever they are, need the best information psychologists can provide them. It is my conviction that most policy dilemmas involve psychological disputes and that, for many of those dilemmas, psychological disputes are central.

Examining knowledge about *human behavior* for its applicability to *public policy* dilemmas is an ongoing enterprise that I call *political psychology*. This book, then, and the scholarly pursuits which I hope it encourages, comprise an operational definition of "political psychology." This phrase has been used by others to mean other things—the psychology of politicians and voters, for example—but I would hope that the study of political behavior will come to be seen as part of the much larger enterprise which I am here calling political psychology. Knowledge of voting behavior and theories about the personalities of political elites surely constitute significant aspects of what we need to know as we continue to strive to reshape society into a better home for our psyches. But so is information about socialization practices in different cultures (or for different persons within single cultures), and so are theories about the factors that influence human abilities and skills, and so are the findings of experiments on aggression, on obedience, and on teachers' expectations regarding their pupils. Indeed, all of these kinds of data and theories may be more central to the enterprise I am calling "political psychology" than is research on political behavior *per se*. Hence, this book deals not with political psychology as the political behavior students define it, but rather with a panoply of somewhat more "basic" psychological issues that have political implications.

If one of the by-products of my definition of political psychology is a blurring of the distinction between basic and applied psychological research, all the better. For, as much of the book attempts to show, that is a pseudo-distinction, an effect of which has been to cause us to overlook much that is already known and useful. Many of today's policy errors might have been avoided had some of yesterday's "basic" information been employed by the policy maker.

I wrote this book in the hope that it would be used in interdisciplinary social science courses, in courses concerned with public affairs, and in psychology courses taught by the increasing number of academics who either share my bias that psychology is and ought to be relevant or who wish to explore that premise with their students. I know that most of their students, like most of mine, wonder whether psychology *is* relevant, and many of them wish it were. Some academics, I know, have been distressed by the clamors of their students for "relevance." In the Sixties, many university teachers, psychologists among them, deplored student challenges to "knowledge for its own sake" and resisted their demands that all intellectual inquiry be bent toward sociocultural change. In the Seventies, those teachers are confronted by a neo-relevance movement, marked by demands that the curriculum become more vocationally oriented. Aspects of these calls for relevance are distressing but I see no satisfactory defense for "knowledge for its own sake." Neither do I see any need for drastic changes in what research we do, how we do it, or in what we teach about what we have learned from that research. What ought to be changed is *how* we teach, and this book constitutes my efforts to facilitate that change.

Rather than teaching psychology as a list of topics that happen to have interested psychologists (e.g., perception this week, attitude change the next), we can expose students to what we have learned in ways that make clear how that information pertains to issues that concern them. College students, preparing for lives and careers, just might find that information worth learning.

It has been my experience at Syracuse that this approach to the teaching of psychology—the approach I have dubbed political psychology—reaches student and, in their vernacular, turns them on. It turns them on to learning much that psychologists have learned, some of it of a rather technical nature and much of it methodological as well as substantive. They do so, I believe, because they see easily why they ought to learn it—because it matters.

To teach psychology in this way is not to pander to anti-intellectualism, to naive revolutionary aspirations, or to renascent Babbitry. On the contrary, properly done, it can engender respect for the efforts of the intellectual and awareness that his vineyard is the same one in which the most action-oriented, practical, socially aware among us toil. The university then is seen as a part of the world, not apart from it.

As is often asserted in the following chapters, human behavior is not a random process; it is orderly. It has "causes" and the means to discern those causes are at hand. My own behavior in writing this book and, earlier, in formulating the attitudes that are reflected in it, has been caused by numerous forces. Among them, of course, were social forces—influences derived from other persons. To many, I owe intellectual debts; to others, I owe other kinds of debts, for (often unknown to them) they helped to create a social environment which set the stage for the particular developmental path along which my life has evolved.

Three psychologists, more than any others, have caused me to become a political psychologist. Donald Campbell must, however much it may embarrass him, be designated my mentor. He taught me, as he has taught many others, that there is virtually no question pertaining to human existence that might be ducked by the psychologist. He has shown and continues to show the less creative among us how we might reinterpret what we already know in order to see how it might apply, and, best of all, he has taught us how to revise and sharpen our methodologic and analytic skills to work on problems the solutions of which have thus far escaped us. My intellectual debts to Donald Campbell will be obvious to the reader throughout this book.

Leonard Doob has served preeminently as a role model for me. How much I have emulated him and how great the gap between model and follower will be apparent to any who have read his pathfinding works in political psychology—on propaganda, on culture-change in Africa, on the psychology of nationalism, and on efforts to resolve international conflicts.

To Otto Klineberg, I owe another significant debt. It is to this pioneer social psychologist, who dared to study intergroup relations in the United States and among nations in the world at a time when academic respectability demanded obeisance to "pure science," that I and all other political psychologists must attribute our courage. We need so little because he displayed so much.

To Dean Alan Campbell of the Maxwell School of Citizenship and Public Affairs at Syracuse University must be credited the maintenance of an intellectual atmosphere that encourages all social scientists, psychologists included, to apply themselves to the policy dilemmas of the city and the world. And the founders of the Maxwell School must be noted for their wisdom, some 50 years ago, in creating the chair of Professor of Social and Political Psychology and placing in it Floyd Allport. This book has been written mostly in my Maxwell School office, which I will always think of as Floyd's.

Numerous colleagues at Syracuse—among them Arnold Goldstein, Sidney Arenson, and Clive Davis—and many students—including Walt Shepard, Susie Kelman, Sharon Dyer, Carrie Faupel-Keating, Robert Feldman, David Giltrow, Geri Kenyon, Maire Dugan and Jane Steinberg—bore with me during the years this book germinated and took shape. They all contributed to its completion. The perseverance and skills of Sarah LaMar and Penny Andreas, who transcribed my notes and prepared the manuscript, were beyond all reasonable expectation. And two first-rate executive secretaries—Gloria Katz and Ann Hayes—relieved me of burdens that would have kept this book an unrealized ambition. To all—my thanks.

Marshall H. Segall

Acknowledgments

We are grateful to all authors and publishers for use of quoted materials in our book including:

Doob, Leonard W. The analysis and resolution of international disputes. *The Journal of Psychology*, 1974, 86, 313-326.

Doob, L.W. (Ed.) *Resolving Conflict in Africa: The Fermeda Workshop*. Yale University Press, New Haven, 1970.

Doob, L.W. The impact of the Fermeda Workshop on the conflicts in the Horn of Africa. *International Journal of Group Tensions*, 1971, 1, 91-101.

Doob, L.W. and Foltz, W.J. The impact of a workshop upon grass-roots leaders in Belfast. *Journal of Conflict Resolution*, Vol. 18, No. 2 (June 1974) 237-256, by permission of the Publisher, Sage Publications, Inc. (Beverly Hills/London).

Etzioni, A. The Kennedy experiment. *Western Political Quarterly*, 1967, 20 (2), 361-380.

Firestone, S. *The Dialectic of Sex: The Case for Feminist Revolution*. Morrow, New York, 1970.

McClelland, D.C. Testing for competence rather than for 'intelligence'. *American Psychologist*, 1973, 28, 1-14.

Excerpts from *Sexual Politics* by Kate Millett. Copyright (c) 1969, 1970 by Kate Millett. Reprinted by permission of Doubleday and Company, Inc., New York, and Rupert-Hart-Davis, Granada Publishing, Ltd., London.

Myrdal, G. *An American Dilemma*. Copyright (c) 1944, 1962 by Harper & Row, Publisher, Inc., New York.

Osgood, C.E. *An Alternative to War or Surrender.* University of Illinois Press, 1962.

Scarr-Salapatek, S. Race, social class and IQ. *Science*, Vol. 174, 1285-1295, 24, December 1971. Copyright 1971 by the American Association for the Advancement of Science.

Skinner, B.F. *Beyond Freedom and Dignity.* Alfred A. Knopf, Inc., 1971.

Zimbardo, P.G. The tactics and ethics of persuasion. In B.T. King and E. McGinnies (Eds.) *Attitudes, Conflicts and Social Change.* Academic Press, New York, 1962.

1
Psychology's real-world relevance

By the latter half of the 20th century, psychology could claim to
have become a productive science. From meager beginnings toward
the end of the 19th century, marked by the accomplishments of a
few philosophers and physiologists like Wundt in Germany and
Sechenov in Russia and self-declared psychologists like James and
Titchener in the United States, the scientific study of human
behavior has grown steadily. In the brief course of 100 years,
psychology has become a thriving intellectual enterprise involving
thousands of researchers in many hundreds of centers throughout the
world.

Each month, in dozens of different periodicals, there appear
reports of new empirical research findings, as well as conceptual
articles in which earlier findings are interpreted in the light of various
psychological theories. The sheer quantity of behavioral facts (not to
mention the varieties of competing interpretations which the facts
have spawned) that line the library shelves exceeds the ability of any
single reader to digest them. So, it may confidently be asserted, a
very considerable body of psychological information has accumulated during psychology's first century as a science.

Certainly, the time has come to ask whether all this information
adds up to knowledge. And, if it is knowledge, whether it is useful.
What have psychologists learned about human behavior and what
difference would it make if more people knew what the psychologists have learned? Have they, in fact, learned anything coherent

about human nature in a century of effort to develop a science of behavior? Is what they've learned of any value to those who would attempt to improve the quality of human life?

Questions like these have influenced the writing of this book. Admittedly, however, the questions are rhetorical; the book has been written with the conviction that considerable information *is* available about the hows and whys of human behavior and that this comprises a form of knowledge that *does* have implications for public policy. The intent of the book, then, is to review some examples of psychological knowledge and to consider some of their policy implications.

It is, thus, a book with a definite point of view. Some readers might label this a bias or a prejudice, since, at the very outset of the book, before any evidence could possibly be marshaled to support it, a bold assertion is being made: to wit, *there are significant insights latent in the findings of scientific psychology which could enhance general understanding of social problems and guide the formation and implementation of policies to ameliorate them.*

A claim such as this cannot go unchallenged. Many people doubt its validity, and for more than one reason.

To begin with, there are many who challenge the very premise that psychology is scientific, or can ever become scientific. These people, impressed by the dazzling variety of behavioral patterns which humans display, bewildered by the array of environmental events which comprise the context in which behavior occurs, and confronted by the phenomenological "evidence of wilful control over their own actions, conceive of behavior as essentially unpredictable." As B.F. Skinner has commented, "It is easy to conclude that there must be something about human behavior which makes a scientific analysis . . . impossible" (Skinner, 1971, p. 7).

Those persons who cling to the view that behavior is just the outward manifestation of self-regulating, free-willed, autonomous beings, functioning haphazardly, are not even likely to read this book. Why not? Because people tend to expose themselves to information that supports the beliefs they hold and to shun communications that challenge them.

The principle of selective exposure to attitudinally relevant information may be derived from cognitive dissonance theory (Festinger, 1957) and has received empirical support from many studies (e.g., Erlich *et al.*, 1957) which showed that recent car buyers read more advertisements about cars they had already chosen than about cars they had rejected. Freedman and Sears (1965) also demonstrated an implication of the selective-exposure process by showing that warning people that they would be subjected to some attitudinally discrepant information increased their resistance to an attitude-change attempt.

Dissonance theory, to be precise, predicts a combination of seeking and avoiding attitudinally discrepant information. One study (Rhine, 1967) revealed a complex pattern of selection of political pamphlets by Johnson and Goldwater supporters during the 1964 U.S. presidential election, which resembled the process that the theory predicted. Another study (Feather, 1963) showed that smokers expressed more interest in information linking smoking and lung-cancer than did non-smokers. This is another kind of selective exposure process.

Although dissonance theory may not fit the real world perfectly (see Chapanis and Chapanis, 1964, for a critique), the hypothesis of selective exposure is tenable. Under many conditions, people do shun attitudinally discrepant communications.

It being the case that those who are reading this book are probably already disposed to accept a deterministic approach to human behavior, we shall not belabor the point. Having acknowledged the existence of persons who reject the deterministic orientation of modern psychology, we shall, on the contrary, simply accept it as a fundamental "given" of the enterprise. The fact is, of course, that the enterprise is thriving—with some 30,000 or more psychologists in the United States alone, many of them professionally devoted to conducting scientific research on the assumption that order underlies the apparent chaos.

Still other critics ask, "Isn't the panoply of human behavior so complex and the variables which influence it so numerous and intertwined, that the effort to understand it must fail? Isn't the goal of psychology, which is to discover the forces that shape behavior so that behavior might be predicted and understood, a goal that will forever elude us?" It is, admittedly, an elusive goal, but it will be one of the burdens of this book to demonstrate the progress that has already been made toward it.

Human behavior *is* very complex and the variables that influence it comprise a complex network of interrelated forces. To determine what the relevant variables are, how they operate, and how they interrelate, is what psychological research is all about. To do research that produces satisfactory answers to such questions has proven to be a difficult, but not impossible, task.

In Skinner's review of various impediments to a true science of behavior, he implied that he believes psychologists have not yet tried hard enough to overcome them. "It can always be argued that human behavior is a particularly difficult field. It is, and we are especially likely to think so because we are so inept in dealing with it. But modern physics and biology successfully treat subjects that are certainly no simpler than many aspects of human behavior. The difference is that the instruments and methods they use are of commensurate complexity" (Skinner, 1971, p. 6).

In a similar vein, Sigmund Koch, editor of a massive, long-range study of the field of psychology, has called attention to many of psychology's failures to live up to the standards of the physical sciences. Koch, however, faults psychologists for having tried too hard to emulate science, thereby failing to develop a discipline capable of studying man. In this regard, then, Koch exemplifies those who doubt that psychology can succeed as a science (Koch, 1959-1963).

In the century since psychologists declared their independence from philosophy and adopted the methods of science, they have made many false starts, have claimed discoveries that no one could subsequently replicate, and generated theories for which little or no empirical support could be mustered. In that same century, however, they have learned much about the application of the scientific method to the study of behavior. They have devised techniques for the measurement of behavioral events, thereby quantifying phenomena previously considered non-quantifiable, and they have gradually accumulated some genuine principles of behavior, many more than some people think.

Therefore, another assumption latent in this book is that the orderliness inherent in human behavior is very much discoverable. However ingenious we may have to be in designing methods to delineate it, that ingenuity is not beyond us. We may yet have a long way to go, but we have already come a long way.

So we can—and do—assert that human behavior is properly, and with probable success, subject to scientific inquiry. We *do* know something about human behavior and we are capable of learning much more.

Having asserted this, we must now consider the other part of the question asked at the start of this chapter: what difference would it make if more of us knew what psychologists have learned? As was said earlier, the point of view from which this book is written holds that psychological knowledge has important implications for public policy. This assertion is also subject to challenge. Many people do challenge it and, again, the challenge rests on more than one ground.

First, there are those who say that psychology *can't* be applied to the solution of real-world problems; second, there are those who insist that it *shouldn't*.

Those who argue that psychology cannot be used to guide the resolution of public policy dilemmas take a position similar to that taken by the critics who said psychology couldn't be scientific. Their basis for doubting the applicability of psychology to public policy analysis is the apparent ease with which mutually contradictory policies are claimed to rest on psychological knowledge. It thus appears to these critics that psychology doesn't yet have its scientific house in order. Its own handbook seems to contain contradictions. How then could we search in it for the key to resolving policy dilemmas?

All of us have probably heard a particular public policy advocated on the grounds of some behavioral fact only to discover another "fact" that appeared to support a diametrically opposed policy alternative! It is all too true, given the present state of psychological knowledge—lots of facts and little unifying theory—that psychological "evidence" can be marshaled in support of almost every conceivable policy. (Given the political motivations of many policy advocates, the evidence is not always even accurately depicted, but that's another story.) This does not mean, however, that psychology can't be *better* employed than it has been as a basis for choice among alternative policies. We shall argue in more detail below (see Chapter 2) that although psychological facts cannot serve alone to determine policy choices, they can be made more rationally if psychological facts, fairly and cautiously interpreted, are employed as input to the decision-making process. This procedure we shall call *political psychology*.

For the moment, however, we state merely that the existence of so many facts that competing policy advocates can claim psychological "proof" is hardly good ground for arguing that psychology can't be relevant. Quite the opposite. What we need to do, of course, is to sharpen our critical skills so that all these bits of fact might be properly sifted. Then psychology could be honestly used, rather than ignored—or worse, abused—by policy makers.

Those who argue that psychology *shouldn't* be applied to public policy issues implicitly admit that it could be. It is perhaps understandable, then, why this position is often found among psychologists themselves. Perhaps better than others, they know the relevance inherent in their science, but seem often reluctant to encourage its realization.

Another category of persons who oppose the application of psychology to social issues are those who fear various alleged consequences such as a loss of freedom and other forms of erosion of what is often referred to in the United States as "the American way of life." This opposition implies that the potential relevance of psychology is very great indeed! However unrealistic, such fears relate to very serious and important issues bearing on behavioral control in the social engineering sense.

Throughout most of the 20th century, as psychology witnessed the proliferation of laboratories and university teaching departments, the dominant ethos of the discipline remained that of a "pure science." Prestige and acclaim, if not money, which served as incentives to psychological research workers, flowed mainly to those who shunned the real world in favor of the rarified atmosphere of the laboratory.

Modern scientific psychology, which developed mainly in America, took shape partly in reaction to an earlier European tradition of political and social philosophy. Through many centuries up to the present one, theories of human nature have been spawned by succeeding waves of theorists, each with personal axes to grind, either a particular *status quo* to be maintained or a singular version of revolution to be advocated. As an attempted corrective to such value-laden armchair psychologizing, "objective research" becomes the means (and, for some, the end) of modern psychology. Generations of academic psychologists were taught, and in turn taught others, that their discipline was, and ought to continue to be, "value free." In spite of the general pragmatism that prevailed in America, psychologists attempted to characterize their discipline as a "disinterested inquiry," a pursuit of knowledge for its own sake.

As a result, many psychologists developed an allegiance not only to science but to what may be termed *scientism*.[1] Many considered the potential applicability of their research to real-world issues not as a matter of pride, but almost of shame. The efforts of these few psychologists who rejected the dominant *Zeitgeist* and directed their attention to real-world settings were left, until recently, outside the mainstream of psychological literature.

Since the 1930s, the American Psychological Association has had a division called the Society for the Psychological Study of Social Issues (SPSSI). The existence of the SPSSI attests to the fact that some psychologists have for long been concerned with the need to relate psychology to policy issues. At the same time, the fact that the SPSSI had to be created at all, and as a separate division of the APA, testifies to the marginal status generally given to political psychology by American psychologists.

SOME CALLS FOR A RELEVANT PSYCHOLOGY

In recent years, not incidentally during the turbulent decade of the 1960s, psychologists, like other social and natural scientists, have been challenged by appeals for relevance. While many Americans generally felt helpless in the face of the seemingly never-ending war in Indochina and the continuing failure to achieve racial and other domestic harmony, many others began to critically assess the nation's institutions, including its universities and research centers. In other countries, some of the same institutions (although for different reasons) also came under a similar scrutiny. As only one aspect of the very pervasive reassessment of values and practices of Western society during the 1960s, psychology's tradition of disinterested scientific inquiry was for the first time effectively challenged.[2]

A rather dramatic example of such a challenge was presented at the 1969 meeting of the American Psychological Association by a philosopher, Bernard Baumrin. In his address he asserted that conducting scientific research merely ". . . for the sake of science *is likely to be* immoral, and that justifying that activity in terms of its benefit to mankind, or some portion of it, *is* immoral" (Baumrin, 1970, p. 73, italics in original).

Baumrin's thesis was that the conduct of disinterested research (studies designed not to prove a socially meaningful point but merely to find out how something or someone functions) diverts scarce manpower and resources from sorely needed attempts to solve pressing problems. He reminded his listeners that science could equally well "be pursued for the sake of what it can do," which I take to mean for the practical and applicable knowledge that might emerge from research. A more immoderate view, which Baumrin himself acknowledged as "radical," was that those psychologists who spurn such efforts and justify the pursuit of pure knowledge "by reference to future hypothetical beneficial results" are in fact contributing to "avoidable deleterious consequences" (p. 74). This latter is, perhaps, a poorly thought-through accusation, but it serves to illustrate the intensity of feeling that permeated the neo-pragmatism of the Sixties.

In a very interesting argument, Baumrin distinguished the pursuit of *knowledge* for its own sake from the pursuit of *science* for its own sake. The former activity, he allowed, is benign; the latter, he insisted, can never be, for scientific facts always have practical consequences. They are always, he argued, potentially useful, or, as seems so often the case, capable of being misused. So, he concluded, society must support research that is openly practical, done by scientists who acknowledge the relevance of what they are doing. Society must favor, according to Baumrin, the research projects "that promise to be more beneficial to society-at-large than others" (p. 81).

There are difficulties with Baumrin's thesis, one of which derives from the ambiguity of the concept "relevance" when used in the present context. He asserted that scientific research "is relevant so long as the foreseeable consequences of its successful prosecution make headway in solving substantial extant problems facing man" (p. 81). Many scientists would reply that it has seldom been possible to foresee the consequences of a particular piece of research. Moreover, some of the most important practical consequences of scientific research have been unforeseen.

This perplexing problem notwithstanding, Baumrin stated a clear position that is being taken up, at least in part, by increasing numbers of psychologists. Many who would not embrace Baumrin's immoderate language would at least agree that science is seldom, if ever, value-free. They would admit that scientific research is never done in an ideological vacuum and that most of the alleged objectivity of the recent past was grounded in unrevealed value-premises. These values were reflected even in the problems selected to be studied. Thus, the purposive avoidance of applied research in favor of "pure" research was itself an act with social consequences.

Is this argument particularly pertinent to psychology? At the 1969 meeting of the American Psychological Association, a high-ranking federal government official told the psychologists assembled in the nation's capital that they have "a special role in explaining to the American public the whys and wherefores of those manifestations of prevalent American social diseases and in seeking to alleviate, if not cure, them" (Kramer, 1970, p. 34). He cited "many American dilemmas that cry out for psychological explanations, but that have been unfortunately ignored" (p. 34). While the main thrust of Kramer's plea was for psychologists to become more vocal and activist, his comments were consistent with Baumrin's insistence that psychologists choose to do research on problems of current social concern.

At the same Washington meeting, the former science advisor to the late President Kennedy called for participation by psychologists in an enterprise labeled "social engineering" (Weisner, 1970). (Significantly, he also called for more federal funding for socially relevant psychological research.) Like Kramer, Weisner spoke of "an American dilemma," in this case the book by that title written years earlier (Myrdal, 1944). By citing this classic work on America's race problems, Weisner underscored both the long-standing concern of social scientists with such problems and the inadequacy of efforts over a 30-year period to solve them. Weisner accordingly suggested "that we must develop a mechanism for fostering reasoned and continued examination of these social problems and controlled experimentation,[3] so as to prevent the present almost totally blind and almost completely random decision-making process from ultimately leading to our destruction" (Weisner, 1970, p. 89).

Still another call for relevance was issued to the psychologists meeting in Washington, this by the 1969 President of the APA, George A. Miller, who urged them to communicate and interpret what their research had already uncovered. Miller stressed that psychologists must learn to "give away" their knowledge; "Psychological facts should be passed out freely to all who need and can use them" (Miller, 1970, p. 15). His reason for urging this was that, in his view, the most urgent problems society confronts are, at base, psychological problems. "They are human problems whose solutions will require us to change our behavior. . . " (p. 5). Miller further argued that for many of these human problems, partial solutions are already at hand. At least, he said, "more is known than has been used intelligently" (p. 5).

Miller also rather dramatically asserted, ". . . scientific psychology is one of the most revolutionary intellectual enterprises ever conceived by the mind of man" (p. 8). In support of this claim, he reviewed only a few of the problem areas in which potentially relevant psychological knowledge already exists. These include how to prevent and resolve conflicts and how behavior may be shaped through the control of reinforcing stimuli, to cite only two. (We will be concerned with these and others in later chapters.) However, even more significant than these technological potentialities, according to Miller, is the "new and different public conception of what is humanly possible and what is humanly desirable" (p. 10).

Indeed, the impact of Freud during the first half of the 20th century and the (likely) impact of Skinner during the second half may well lie more in their concepts of human potential than in the instruments and techniques for influencing behavior that these two psychological giants devised. Because of Freud, people generally have become aware of how much our behavior reflects non-obvious influences; because of Skinner, many now comprehend how much behavior is controlled by those who can manipulate our environment. With the spread of these insights will come a new definition of "human nature" which could foster the application of psychology, either for good or for evil. Accordingly, Miller called on psychologists to participate actively in the task of advancing psychology "as a means of promoting human welfare" (p. 21). This is an arena in which some have already done much, but many must do more.

Taken together, these four recent calls for psychological relevance epitomize an ideology that impacted forcefully on the academic world at the end of the 1960s. The ideology emphasizes (a) that society is confronted by man-made problems, which only appear to be intractable, (b) that their solution lies in changing the behavior of the men who made them, (c) that while psychology has already begun to change man's conception of his potential, psychological knowledge requires extension, dissemination, and application, and (d) for psychologists *not* to participate actively in efforts to improve the quality of life is just as political an act as doing so.

Psychology was not the only discipline confronted by impassioned calls for relevance. No part of the academic enterprise escaped, because all disciplines, to one degree or another, were vulnerable to the charge of having favored purity over involvement. At the same time, some disciplines, particularly the physical sciences, were being attacked for *lack* of purity, with their critics characterizing them as willing handmaidens of the military-industrial complex.

For a time during the Sixties, on campuses and at professional meetings of scientific and social-scientific societies, the normal business of research was occasionally (and noisily) interrupted by debates over just how relevant research could or should be. At some future time, aided by historians, we shall perhaps be better able to understand the forces in Western society that produced these debates, but surely they reflected widely felt frustrations stemming from society's apparent inability to end obviously fruitless wars, or to solve problems of poverty and discrimination, or to create a lifestyle that would satisfy more legitimate urges than merely the desire to possess and consume.

Increasingly, as larger numbers of young Americans and Europeans participated in higher education, the discrepancy between what could be and what was became painfully obvious. In the universities they could see vast resources, material and human, being directed to the pursuit of knowledge but it was hard to detect much impact of that knowledge on our societies' problems.[4]

This was, in my opinion, a good thing. This is not to say that the attacks on psychology and the reactions of the psychologists constituted an unmixed blessing. But if a major result of the time-consuming, sometimes acrimonious debating is a reasoned reassessment by psychologists of what they do and why, psychology can only be the better for it.

There is another point to be made about the demands made on psychology to become relevant. Imbedded in some of them were attacks that were unfair and, more important, misleading. They exaggerated the degree to which psychology was "irrelevant." Unless one reads carefully the calls for relevance like those issued by Baumrin, Kramer, Weisner, and Miller, one might fail to note that they were implying that psychology was *already* relevant, in spite of some appearances and tendencies to the contrary.

THE NON-OBVIOUS RELEVANCE OF PURE RESEARCH

However much it appeared to many students that most psychological research focused on questions of little interest to the non-specialist, and however true it may be that psychologists thought they were serving the gods of "pure science," psychological research has always been *potentially* relevant. The relevance of research designed expressly to deal with a salient social problem is, of course, obvious. Most psychological research, however, has not been of that kind; its relevance, therefore, is non-obvious.

The non-obvious relevance of "pure" psychological research is a feature that needs to be stressed. One of the unfortunate consequences of the argument over relevance has been a creeping anti-intellectualism among university students—the very persons best equipped to carry on intellectual endeavors. For students to turn away from psychological research because it appears to them to be irrelevant would delay attainment of the very goal they have espoused—the enhancement of human life via the application of knowledge of behavior. This paradoxical consequence might be prevented if it could be demonstrated that the alleged irrelevance of pure psychological research is more apparent than real.

Another assumption underlying this book, then, is that most of the research done by psychologists, including all of those studies done by persons who had no real-world problems in mind when they did them, has yielded findings and generated theories that contain insights of potentially great practical value. As a corollary of this assumption, it is asserted that our society might well be much further along toward the solution of some of its problems had attention been paid to psychological facts gathering dust in the library. Indeed, many of today's problems might well have been prevented had some of yesterday's been attacked by persons armed with the outputs of so-called pure, disinterested research.

We are already familiar with examples of society's ignoring social scientific forecasts of increasingly complex problems that would result from a failure to deal with their precursers on the basis of the best available knowledge of the day. Weisner, in 1970, had to remind us that Gunnar Myrdal "spelled out the shame of our race problem 30 years ago, and Sigmund Freud even before that, in *Mankind and his Discontents*, forecast . . . our failure to adjust psychologically and politically to the new world of technology" (Weisner, 1970, p. 88). Now, the words of Myrdal and Freud were avowedly relevant; they were conscious efforts to deal with society's ills. It is, therefore, very striking that such works have had so little impact. It is perhaps of greater significance that the far larger body of psychological research—the thousands of studies that have yielded bits and pieces of information about behaviors that just happened to interest the psychologists—has been ignored only because its potential relevance has gone unnoticed!

It takes little reflection to realize that every social issue probably has a psychological dimension. Social issues are controversies concerning policies that will influence human behavior. How we shall educate, house, and otherwise care for our citizens are issues that relate to questions about human needs, wants, and capabilities. How we should tax is an issue that relates to questions about incentives and their impact on human performance. How we shall control crime is an issue that relates to theories of the etiology of aggression, to ideas about socialization, and to theories of punishment. Although all policy dilemmas entail matters of ethics, values, and political ideologies that must guide efforts to resolve them, all policy dilemmas also have a psychological component. This, too, must be entered into the equation.

Some additional reflection can lead to the realization that all psychological facts probably have implications for social issues. (This is the converse of the position articulated in the preceding paragraph.) Although few people would immediately perceive it to be so, a finding from a pigeon experiment (e.g., the frequency of the bird's key-pressing in the absence of tangible rewards was determined by the pattern of previous rewards) possesses wide-ranging implications for educational and training policies! So do the results of studies of how people make friends, how infant monkeys acquire affection for cloth-covered (but milkless) surrogate mothers, and how rats learn to attack other rats who had never attacked them.

In short, it matters very little, perhaps not at all, whether the scientists who designed the studies revealing such "hows" and "whys" of behavior were themselves concerned with the social implications of their discoveries. Social implications do not have to be actively sought in order to be present in psychological research.

It should now be clear that this position contrasts with Baumrin's definition of "relevant" research, wherein relevance was linked to *foreseeable* consequences. I am suggesting that the foreseeability of consequences is of no import. (Or, as I am tempted to say, it is irrelevant!) It doesn't matter whether research has been designed with a social consequence in mind. All research can have a social consequence; if it does, then it is relevant research. By insisting on this, we have purposely blurred the distinction between *basic* and *applied* research, for there is potential social relevance in all psychological research.

Accordingly, if the recent crescendo of calls for psychological relevance is taken as justification for ignoring what has already been learned, a great disservice would be done both to psychology and to society.

As the book proceeds, we shall deal mostly with psychological facts and theory. What shall be notably missing from our discussion of social policy dilemmas is consideration of the rather obvious economic and political forces that impinge upon those dilemmas. As the president of the Society for the Psychological Study of Social Issues, Albert Pepitone (1974) has asserted, "It doesn't take special powers to perceive the economic and political origins of the many social problems that SPSSI members think about and do research on. . . . Who can doubt the plausibility of . . . arguments that the economic system is the root cause of many 'social issues.' . . . Nor is it an original insight that political power is the handmaiden of economic interests." Like Pepitone, I see little that psychologists, as such, can add to "this familiar, ideological line of thinking," but much that they can do by supplementing it with "fine-grained sociocultural analysis." Certainly, economic, political, and ideological analyses of social issues are not hard to find; psychological analyses have been far less common. Much rarer than ideological pronouncements have been efforts to develop empirically based psychological theories concerning sociocultural phenomena.[5] Such efforts comprise the central thrust of this book.

This thrust constitutes an operational definition of "political psychology." I take that phrase to mean an ongoing enterprise whereby knowledge of human behavior is examined with a view toward its applicability to social policy dilemmas.

The various ways that psychology can be applied to the analysis of social policies are discussed in Chapter 2. In Chapters 3-8, six issues of contemporary concern are examined, and in Chapter 9 an example of a design for research on still another real-world issue is explored. As a whole, the book deals, then, with a panoply of psychological topics, all of which have social and political implications.

Let us turn now to some models for a political psychology.

NOTES

[1] As Bass (1974) succinctly put it, "Theory for theory's sake is scientism, not science." His article is further testimony to the proposition that the psychologist ought to find his research problems in the real world and, ultimately, test his theories there.

[2] Although "relevance" became a clarion call of the 1960s, it is worth noting that some of our most preeminent behavioral scientists have from time to time been concerned with applying their work to the solution of social problems. Skinner is merely one among many psychologists who have occasionally done applied psychological work. However, while such a concern was the theme of his 1971 book, *Beyond Freedom and Dignity* (see Chapter Two), earlier, the applicability of his work was at best an ancillary feature of it. This was also true of many of his predecessors. An example is Kurt Lewin, who was primarily a seminal contributor to social psychological theory but who also dared, long before it was fashionable, to attempt the development of a technology that would modify social behavior.

[3] In Chapter 2 we shall discuss a particularly interesting version of an experimental approach to public policy making—Donald T. Campbell's "experimenting society."

[4] See reports by Kenniston (1965, 1967) of psychological research which led to some enlightening analyses of "student unrest." See also Foster and Long

(1970), Miles (1971), and Peterson and Bilorusky (1970) for discussions of student activism and protest movements of the 1960s.

[5] Some difficulties inherent in such efforts are discussed in a number of recent articles. The interested student should consult Archibald (1970), Becker (1967), Caplan and Nelson (1973), Coleman (1972), Hawkes (1973), London (1972), Myrdal (1973), and Viteles (1972).

2
Applying psychology to public policy analysis: Three alternative models

In Chapter 1 it was asserted that psychologists already know much about human behavior that could be used to help shape a better world, or, as a former presidential science advisor put it, to make "a better home for our psyche" (Weisner, 1970, p. 86). We will test this assertion in the chapters that follow by viewing several contemporary social issues in the light of psychological information which seems to bear on them.

As a prelude, the present chapter is devoted to a discussion of various models for the application of psychology to public policy analysis. This allows us to confront, in advance, some sticky questions that are likely to be provoked by our attempts to apply psychology. The very idea of applying psychology in this way, which we are calling "political psychology," is itself controversial.

Few people are sanguine about such notions as the conscious use of *behavioral technology*, the development of *social engineering* programs, the creation of an *experimenting society*, and other rubrics that appear in discussions of political psychology. Notions like these seem to generate rather anxious reactions in many people.

I recall once having used a particular elementary psychology textbook (Keller and Schoenfeld, 1950) in an introductory psychology course at a major American university. The text, and the course which was built around it, were heavily oriented toward a "pure science" approach. As the book unfolded, each succeeding chapter revealed to the student an increasingly complex array of basic principles of behavior, with illustrative material derived mainly from laboratory studies of the behavior of pigeons and rats. The emerging picture of psychology which the book reinforced was that of a very rigorous and highly abstract discipline—in short, a science. At the very end of the book, however, there appeared a brief epilogue in which the question was tentatively raised as to whether it might some day be possible to apply principles of behavior to the improvement of human society. One student,on encountering this epilogue on the last day of class, exploded in tears of anger, charging that she had unwittingly been led through a Communist-inspired brainwashing experience! The mere hint that techniques for social control, which were inherent in the scientific principles she had learned, might actually be used (and that some psychologists might actually advocate using them!) frightened and repelled her.

While her reaction was extreme (probably more so than it would have been had the hint been dropped earlier), the reaction was genuine and expressive of some profound concerns. They reflect ethical and ideological questions that must be confronted by those who advocate applying psychological techniques to the control of human behavior. We shall raise them in the present chapter, for they are questions that deserve a priority position rather than being treated as an afterthought.

One way to discuss these vexing questions is to consider the possible forms that an applied, political psychology can take.

THREE MODELS FOR POLITICAL PSYCHOLOGY

Psychology's contributions to public policy analysis can take several forms. In this book, we shall advocate three approaches, which will be presented as "models." Although together they comprise complimentary and overlapping approaches to political psychology, they should also be thought of as independent alternatives.

Model One: The psychologist as "expert witness"

In this, the simplest model, the psychologist merely offers what he knows to those who could apply it. If it is acknowledged merely that psychological facts ought to be brought to bear on policy dilemmas, then policy makers, either elected officials or their appointed administrative agents, could be encouraged to seek interpretations of existing psychological facts from psychologists. The judgment as to the relevance of such facts and their implications for a particular policy dilemma would be exercised by the policy makers themselves.

Presumably there will occur instances in which the expert testimony of the psychologists would contain contradictions. Under such circumstances, although Model One leaves the responsibility for resolving them to the policy maker, he might press the psychologists to clarify matters, for their expertise includes practice in determining the circumstances under which one principle applies rather than an apparently contradictory one.

In the final analysis, however, the policy maker has both the right and the responsibility to select from the testimony what he considers to be the most relevant arguments and to base his choice of policy on a combination of those arguments and whatever moral, ethical, or ideological values he considers pertinent. While this model advocates considerable input from the psychologist, an essential feature of the model is clearly that the ultimate choice of policy remains in the hands of the policy maker/administrator. This model involves, then, no shift in power since society's usual agents remain free to use or reject whatever psychological information is made available to them.

To illustrate Model One, I cite a paper in which one psychologist argued, "We [psychologists] do have a serious respect for data [and] . . . As psychologists . . . we do have some special knowledge . . ." (Guttentag, 1970, p. 40).[1]

Guttentag offered some compelling examples of psychological facts, which social welfare program administrators might choose to keep in mind. For example: To be a "helper" is to be prone to some pertinent perceptual distortions concerning those whom one is helping. One such distortion is the tendency to see the helped as responsible for their own plight. The basis for this generalization rests in several recent pieces of research by psychologists (e.g., Berkowitz, 1969; Kaufman and Zenar, 1968; Pepitone, 1969).[2] To the degree that this perceptual distortion is manifest, social welfare agents could well become prey to hostile attitudes and behaviors toward those whom they are mandated to help. At the very least, then, people in positions of helpers ought to be informed of the likelihood of this tendency so that they might guard against it. Since that is not an easy thing to achieve (as much other psychological research has shown), a more promising policy recommendation which follows from a consideration of the helper-distortion principle would be to try to remove the helper from the social welfare scene.

This could be accomplished by minimizing the directness with which assistance is given, thereby impersonalizing it. For example, we could retire the present system (which requires a case worker to dispense aid in specific amounts to a particular person in response to specific, documented needs) and substitute for it a negative income tax program.

In addition to this example, Guttentag cited several other psychological principles that have social-welfare policy implications and she asserted, as we do here, that still others exist which "psychologists can provide to help the decision makers" (Guttentag, 1970, p. 43). Clearly, she was urging that psychology be called upon and that psychologists volunteer to offer their expertise, but only in the form of guidance. This exhortation exemplifies Model One: Testify, but allow the policy maker to accept or reject the testimony.

This hardly seems revolutionary. In fact, this model has been in operation for some time. However, while experts from the natural sciences and from a few of the social sciences (primarily economics) have regularly given "testimony," psychologists have done so only to a very minor extent. It is still necessary to call, as Guttentag did, for the more frequent application of this model. Psychologists have so seldom behaved as expert witnesses to government that the occasions on which they have done so are both notable and well known.

The single best-known example involves the 1954 U.S. Supreme Court decision that racial segregation in public schooling was unconstitutional. With this action, the Court reversed the Plessy vs. Ferguson decision of 1896 which, for so many years, had, in effect, sanctioned segregation. When, in 1954 the Court ruled against segregation, it did so as much on the basis of psychological evidence as on legal precedent.

Among the psychological findings cited by the Court in its 1954 decision were those produced in studies by Clark and Clark of various psychological impacts of prejudice and discrimination on American Negro children (Clark and Clark, 1958).[3] These impacts have been summarized by Kenneth Clark as "the effects of adverse, persistent social negatives on the distortion of personality and the impairment of psychological effectiveness of the victims of persistent rejection" (Clark, 1971, p. 1049). [4]

On the basis of such psychological facts as these, the Court once and for all demolished the long-standing concept of *separate-but-equal* by asserting the psychological contradiction inherent in that concept. The 1954 Court agreed that the research had shown that enforced separateness *per se* produces a sense of inequality.

This was truly a landmark decision, not only for society at large but also for the discipline of psychology. It was a rare and dramatic instance of psychology's serving as expert witness, thus exemplifying Model One. Given this example, it ought to be clear that the Model has implications that are not at all inconsistent with contemporary humanitarian values. It may, therefore, be hoped that the Model will be employed far more often in the future than it has been in the past.

Model Two: The psychologist as policy evaluator

Imagine, if you can, "an honest society, committed to reality testing, to self-criticism, to avoiding self-deception. . . . It will be a scientific society in the fullest sense of the word 'scientific.' The scientific values of honesty, open criticism, experimentation, willing-ness to change once-advocated theories in the face of experimental and other evidence will be exemplified." This noble vision was the creation of Donald T. Campbell, eminent psychological method-ologist and recipient in 1970 of the Distinguished Scientist Award of the American Psychological Association and in 1975, the president of the Association. Campbell's words serve well to introduce our second model, which advocates that psychologists contribute their research tools to help policy makers determine the effectiveness of their social programs.

In contrast with Model One, wherein the psychologist contributes existing empirical findings, Model Two is concerned only with the psychologist's methodological expertise, his ability to ask answerable questions about variables which might influence human behavior. At the same time, as Campbell himself made clear, Model Two shares with Model One the important feature that ". . . the conclusion drawing and the relative weighting of conflicting indications must be left up to the political process" (Campbell, 1971, p. 8).

One of Campbell's basic arguments regarding social programs as presently constituted in the United States and elsewhere is that it is difficult to say not only what *is to be* done but also what *has been* done. Particularly when programs have been introduced without a preplanned effort to assess them, their evaluation is an extremely complex process, calling for exacting methodological skills. These typically require a degree of sophistication that is possessed by relatively few people who have been trained, as have research psychologists, in the twin arts of statistical inference and research design.

Assessment and evaluation are difficult even under the best of conditions, but the problem of arriving at valid assessments of actual social programs is exacerbated by several conditions which prevail in most societies. These conditions were reviewed by Campbell in a 1969 paper. In it he noted, "It is one of the most characteristic aspects of the present situation that *specific reforms are advocated as though they were certain to be successful*" (Campbell, 1969, p. 409, italics in original). Typically, a reform program advocate, in order to obtain funding for the program from those who control the purse strings, feels himself compelled to assure them of the program's likely (if not guaranteed) success. Once having committed his position and career to that particular program, he is likely to "prefer to limit the evaluations to those the outcomes of which [he] can control" (p. 409).

An even more unfortunate ramification of present conditions surrounding program evaluation is that hardly ever is there more than one program in any given arena to be evaluated! Comparison, which is the *sine qua non* of evaluation, is seldom possible.

To deal with such difficulties, Campbell has carried what is in effect our Model Two to its logical conclusion by proposing the creation of an "experimenting society." In his terms, this would require a shift "from the advocacy of a specific reform to the advocacy of persistence in alternative reform efforts" (1969, p. 410). In other words, in the Campbellian concept of the experimenting society, policy makers would typically seek funds to establish several alternative pilot projects, which could be conducted either simultaneously or in programmed sequence. Their relative effectiveness would be assessed and the best features of each retained. With modifications as indicated by the assessment, a pre-tested program would emerge.

Although the experimenting society is a visionary idea, its basic premise is not altogether foreign to men in government. Consider, for example, a position taken early in 1972 by U.S. Senator Ribicoff *vis-à-vis* proposed legislation for "welfare reform." Although he generally supported an overall approach that had been proposed by the President, Senator Ribicoff called for the implementation of small pilot projects prior to commitment to any particular program.[5]

Nonetheless, it should be very clear that there does not presently exist, anywhere in the world, a society that conforms to Campbell's prescriptions for an experimenting society. There are, however, many nonexperimenting societies with social programs that very definitely require evaluation. When the conditions of an experimenting society do not prevail, evaluation is just much more difficult but certainly no less necessary.

This is not to say that program evaluation would be an easy matter even if the pilot-project approach of the experimenting society were implemented. (The pilot-project approach would probably enjoy, however, the incidental advantage of encouraging far more evaluation than presently takes place.) Evaluative research presents so many methodological challenges that the utilization of pilot projects could not alone guarantee valid evaluative conclusions. Validity depends on the appropriateness of the design of the evaluation study, be it a pilot study or an after-the-fact assessment of a full-scale program.

Indeed, an important part of Campbell's advocacy of a role for psychology in the evaluation of social programs is his inventive contribution to the design of real-world experiments and "quasi-experiments" (e.g., Campbell, 1957, 1963, 1969; Campbell and Stanley, 1963). These teachings on how to design research are valuable whether the evaluation research is to be done within an experimenting society of the future or in the "special interests" world of today.[6]

Any research, even an experiment done under laboratory conditions, with maximal control by the experimenter of variables that could influence the outcome of his experiment, is subject to invalidity.[7] When research is done outside the laboratory, with the likelihood that numerous influences have been left free to vary, the threats to the validity of conclusions drawn by the researcher are much more intense. Since evaluation studies must be done in real-world settings, they are particularly subject to invalidity threats.

Campbell has distinguished two classes of threats to the validity of an evaluation study. The first includes any circumstance which makes it likely that an obtained "effect" of a program was not really a result of that program but a result of some unknown or uncontrolled variable. These are referred to as *internal validity threats*. The second class, *external validity threats*, includes any circumstance that casts doubt on the representativeness or generalizability of the research outcome. Some examples of both kinds follow.

1. *Some internal validity threats*

Whenever a researcher asserts that his experiment demonstrated that a particular treatment (some experience provided by the experimenter to persons whose behavior he is studying) resulted in some behavioral effect, there is always the possibility that events other than the experimental treatment, coterminous in time with that treatment, were in fact responsible for the alleged effect. Any event that could affect all persons in the study—like a marked change in economic conditions, a hard-fought election campaign, or the like, if relevant to the behavior under study—could make a "treatment" appear more or less effective than it really was. If some such external events occurred, then the effect could really be due to what Campbell calls "history" (1969, p. 411).

There is also the possibility that the people on whom the treatment impinged had changed in some way that has nothing at all to do with the treatment itself. For example, they might simply have aged, become fatigued, or acquired some coincidentally relevant enthusiasms over the period of time during which they also happened to be exposed to the treatment. To some unknown degree, the treatment would have been irrelevant. In such a case, the cause of whatever behavioral changes might have occurred would have to be attributed in part to what Campbell calls "maturation."

History and maturation, then, both constitute internal threats to validity.

As a final example of a threat to internal validity (selected from a list of nine such threats discussed by Campbell), there is the possibility of "regression artifacts." These are changes in scores that are due merely to regression to the mean, a very common statistical artifact which, as we shall see, has plagued some well-known efforts to evaluate social programs. Whenever individuals are *selected* into a study on the basis of their having *extreme* scores (i.e., scores that deviate very much from the average scores of the population to which they belong), these individuals will, usually, as a group, when they are re-tested obtain a mean score that is closer to the population average than was the mean of their original scores. So, if they had been selected originally *because* they had low scores, a subsequent test will give the impression of improvement. Regression to the mean is a change in score toward the population average, which change can occur *whether or not* any treatment intervened between the two testing sessions.

Hence, obviously, the cause of an apparent improvement in scores among persons who were initially selected *because* they were extreme scorers cannot be attributed simply to a treatment to which they happened to have been exposed. Consider, for example, a program designed for persons who perform poorly in some measurable task, with the program open *only* to such persons. After the program is completed, they will, on the average, perform better. But since part of the "improvement" must be attributed to regression, it would be invalid to credit the program with all of the improvement.

As Campbell has pointed out, threats to internal validity (of which history, maturation, and regression artifact are illustrative examples) are usually avoided in true experiments by random assignment to experimental and control groups. ("True" experiments are the kinds of studies done typically in psychological laboratories.) Precisely because program-evaluation research nearly always falls short of the requirements of a true experiment, evaluators must be wary of the internal validity threats that impinge on their research.

2. *Some external validity threats*

No less serious are threats to external validity. Even when an evaluator can conclude that a given treatment had a particular effect in a particular study, there exist several sources of doubt about the generalizability of that conclusion. Would the same results obtain in a different setting or with slight variations in the treatment? Would the same effect appear if different measuring instruments were used, or even the same ones applied at different times?

Threats to external validity include any condition which makes the research setting atypical of the real-world setting in which the treatment under study will regularly be applied. Such conditions include any selection of persons who might happen to be more (or less) responsive to the treatment than people for whom the program is intended. Another such condition would be the use of a treatment in the study which varies in some way from the treatment that subsequently will be employed in the full-scale program.

Still another threat to external validity is inherent in the frequent practice of testing people before *and* after they are exposed to a treatment. This is because pre-treatment testing often has a sensitizing effect, making those tested more (and sometimes, less) responsive to the treatment than they would have been had they not been exposed to the test. Thus, any treatment effect that has been demonstrated to hold for a pre-tested sample of people may not hold true for a non-pre-tested population. This threat, which Campbell labels "an interaction effect of testing" is a subtle but extremely potent constraint on the generalizability of many experimental research results.

We have reviewed here only a few of the sources of invalidity which plague program-evaluation researchers. Perhaps these few suffice to underscore the need for evaluation research to be designed by professional psychologists, knowledgeable about validity threats and with experience in overcoming them. As matters presently stand, this is surely not the case. The typical evaluation of a social program would appall a beginning student of research design.

Most often, in fact, the effectiveness of a social program is gauged by a one-group, pre-test post-test design, that Campbell has referred to as "a casual version of a very weak quasi-experimental design" (1969, p. 142). With H.L. Ross, Campbell has illustrated the ways in which threats to invalidity plague such a study (Campbell, 1969; Campbell and Ross, 1968; Ross and Campbell, 1968). In these papers they examined a program enacted in Connecticut in 1955 under the leadership of then Governor Ribicoff in an effort to reduce the number of fatal accidents on the highways of that state. In the initial evaluation of the program, the pre-test measure was the 1955 traffic fatality figure of 324 persons; the treatment was a new law which established unusually severe sanctions against speeding (e.g., revocation of drivers' licenses); and the post-test measure was a traffic fatality figure in 1956 of "only" 284. The temptation to credit the law with the saving of 40 lives was great; not surprisingly, the governor could not resist the temptation.[8]

It was easily shown, however, that the decline of 40 persons in the traffic fatality statistics could not, in the absence of additional information, confidently be attributed solely to the new law. The evaluation as originally carried out was subject to several of Campbell's sources of invalidity, both internal and external.

More important, Campbell also showed how some very slight variations in the evaluative research could have eliminated those threats to validity, thereby approaching the possibility of drawing a valid conclusion about the effectiveness of the speeding law.

For example, merely by transforming the study of the Connecticut speeding law from a pre-test post-test study to an "interrupted time series design" (Campbell and Stanley, 1963), in which fatality figures were examined for several years both before and after the law was introduced, it became possible to determine whether the 1955-1956 change was at least significantly different from the changes that occurred in other years. [9] As it turned out, incidentally, the 1955-1956 decline was significant in this respect (Glass, 1968). So, this exercise had the additional virtue of demonstrating that an improvement in evaluative research design need not produce a result that embarrasses the program advocate! To some degree, at least, in this case the more rigorous evaluation supported the initial optimistic conclusion.

In any case, we have now seen enough in this brief extract from Campbell's work to buttress our assertion that the psychologist has something to offer the program evaluator. What is offered is simply a knowledge of how to do research on the effectiveness of a program designed to change human behavior, which knowledge reflects a healthy respect for the pitfalls inherent in such research. This, then, is our second model for applying psychology to the real world. As was the case with Model One, Model Two can hardly be characterized as revolutionary, nor is it likely to be terribly threatening to any who might fear a brave new world under psychological domination. Model Three, which we are now ready to discuss, might be a different matter altogether.

Model Three: The psychologist as social engineer

In Chapter 1 I quoted an assertion by a recent president of the American Psychological Association (George A. Miller) that psychology is a revolutionary intellectual enterprise, which can produce a new public conception of what is humanly possible and desirable. I also reported a plea by a recent science advisor to the President of the United States (Jerome Weisner) for federal financial support for "social engineering." Together, these ideas reflect the essence of our third model for political psychology. In effect, this model says, "We have a new way of understanding human behavior which should be applied toward the maximization of occurrence of socially desirable behavior."

Implied in this model is the notion that our new understanding of behavior consists of a fairly detailed awareness of how human behavior is controlled. Hence, the application of psychology that is called for in Model Three boils down to the intentional use of techniques of behavioral control. In other words, since we know how behavior is controlled, we, rather than someone else, may control it; so let's do so rationally and, of course, for good ends.

There can be little doubt that this model is attractive to many and anathema to many others. It is clearly the only really controversial one of the three models being advocated in this chapter. I have found that whenever it is proposed it provokes vigorous, sometimes angry, discussion.[10] Among the first questions asked whenever the concept of conscious behavioral control is raised are these:

Do psychologists really know enough about how behavior is controlled?

Who will decide which behaviors are socially desirable?
Won't social engineering lead to a totalitarian society?
Who will have the power to control behavior and how, if at all,
  will they themselves be controlled?

Often, such questions are asked rhetorically; the questioner doubts
that they can satisfactorily be answered. Nevertheless, they are
legitimate questions, pertaining to issues of considerable importance,
and they deserve answers. Even if their being asked is a disguised
attack on this model of political psychology, those who advocate the
model must try to answer them.

The single best-known effort to date to deal with such questions is
by B.F. Skinner in his book *Beyond Freedom and Dignity* (1971). It
is a carefully reasoned effort by this eminent experimental psychologist to summarize some basic principles that reveal how human
behavior is shaped and controlled by environmental forces (both
natural and man-made) and to argue that this knowledge should be
employed to produce pre-planned social change. Obviously, then,
Skinner's book exemplifies Model Three; it therefore deserves our
careful consideration.

Skinner's ideas will be summarized here largely in his own words,
not only because it is difficult to improve upon them, but also
because his ideas have so often been misrepresented. Let's try here to
look at what Skinner really says.[11]

1. *What does Skinner advocate?*

Skinner proposes the use by our society of "a technology of
behavior . . . which would . . . reduce the aversive consequences of
behavior . . . and maximize the achievements of which the human
organism is capable" (Skinner, 1971, p. 125). Like any technology, it
would be based upon a science. In this case, since it is a *behavioral*
technology which is being advocated, obviously the *sine qua non* for
its development is the prior existence of a *science of behavior*.

Skinner asserts that presently ". . . a behavioral technology
comparable in power and precision to physical and biological
technology is lacking . . ." (1971, p. 3) because ". . . the methods of
science have scarcely yet been applied to [the study of] human behavior" (p. 7). In other words, we don't yet have a very rich behavioral
science on which to build a behavioral technology. On the other
hand, "although no one knows the *best* way of raising children . . . it
is possible to propose better ways than we now have and to support

them by predicting and eventually demonstrating more reinforcing results" (p. 145).

Skinner clearly urges us to do so. He is willing to urge it, even though he admits that we don't yet know all of the best ways to do much of anything, because we *do* know something much more fundamental from which might be derived not only guidelines for child-rearing but lots of other educational procedures as well. That fundamental something is the product of our science.

2. *What are the scientific underpinnings of behavioral technology?*

What is in fact known to the behavioral scientist is the basic generalization that behavior is shaped by external events. This is to say, behavior can best be explained by taking into account the environmental conditions under which it occurs. The most critical environmental events for the shaping of an individual's future behavior are those that occur contingently following each occurrence of a response. In short, the probability of a future occurrence of a given response is strengthened if it is followed by positive consequences and weakened if no positive (or aversive) consequences occur. Thus, behavioral dispositions are modified by behavioral consequences.

As Skinner states it, "Behavior is shaped and maintained by its consequences" (1971, p. 18). From this principle, the following line of argument emerges: If the contingent consequences of behavior shape behavior, then the ability to influence behavior intentionally is available to anyone who has the power to control environmental consequences. And, as Skinner admonishes us, whether we like to admit it or not, we must face up to the fact that "the environment can be manipulated" (p. 18). A moment's reflection is all that is needed to recognize that, in any society, massive control over the world in which we live has always been exercised by someone or other. Mankind must have, since ages past, understood what Skinner has now merely made explicit.

That behavior is shaped and maintained by its consequences is, of course, the explanatory keystone of Skinnerian psychology—the study of operant behavior. That enterprise, (the results of which are reported in hundreds of journal articles and several summary volumes[1][2]) has focused on the contingent environmental consequences of behavior, analyzing in great detail relationships between the strengths of various behaviors on the one hand and the pattern of events that are contingently linked to them on the other. The findings that have accrued from these analyses constitute impressive support for the proposition that a satisfactory explanation for behavioral change must be based on a consideration of that behavior's contingent consequences. In short, and somewhat paradoxically, the causes of behavior reside in its consequences. As the environment is molded, so is shaped the behavior of those in it.

3. *What does this "environmentalist" view displace?*

Traditionally, of course, explanations for behavior were sought elsewhere—notably, as Skinner has pointed out, in some hypothetical inner force, sometimes conceptualized rather literally as "an inner man" and often called "human nature." Although physics and biology long ago moved away from personified causes (such as internal impulses, purposes, vital forces, the *nature* of the object, etc.) in their attempts to understand the *actions* of objects which they study, the behavior of persons, Skinner reminds us, "is still attributed to human nature . . . . traits of character capacities, and abilities. Almost everyone who is concerned with human affairs . . . continues to talk about human behavior in this pre-scientific way" (1971, p. 9). "Unable to understand how or why the person behaves as he does, we attribute his behavior to a [hypothetical, internal] person we cannot see . . ." (p. 14).

According to Skinner, "modern" psychologists object to this traditional "mentalistic" strategy of explanation mainly because when it is pursued, as it has been for centuries (and still is by nearly all lay persons, as well as some psychologists), ". . . the world of the mind steals the show. Behavior is not recognized as a subject in its own right . . . things a person does or says are almost always regarded merely as symptoms . . . [or] as the expressions of ideas and feelings . . . [or] as the material from which one infers attitudes, intentions, needs, and so on . . . only recently has any effort been made to study human behavior as something more than a mere by-product [of such inner states of mind] " (1971, p. 12).

4. *Why is the mentalistic view so tenacious?*

Skinner identifies two reasons for the popular espousal of the mentalistic tradition and the concomitant resistance to an environmentalistic conception. The first consists of the historical link between mentalism and a primary Western value, dating at least from the Greeks, to the effect that man is autonomous. The second is based on the simple fact that the mechanisms whereby the consequences of behavior shape it are not at all obvious. There is much phenomenological and existential support for the concept of autonomous man and for the related notion that man's behavior is controlled from inside. On the other hand, there is little in everyday experience that encourages us to perceive that it is the external result of an act that shapes that act.

Concerning the concept of autonomous man, Skinner argues that by postulating an inner man as "a *center* from which behavior emanates . . . we say that he is autonomous . . ." (1971, p. 15). This conception, according to Skinner, helps to preserve the idea of man's divinity. It is also an intuitively compelling notion since ". . . the outer man whose behavior is to be explained could be very much like the inner man whose behavior is said to explain it. The inner man has been created in the image of the outer . . . [and] the inner man seems at times to be directly observed" (p. 15). Therefore, this hypothetical inner man, whether he be thought of as a homunculus, or a soul, or a mind, or a set of internal traits, habits, attitudes or whatever, ". . . has not departed gracefully . . . he can marshal formidable support . . . [from the] tremendous weight of traditional 'knowledge' " (p. 19).

That behavior is shaped instead by its consequences is not at all obvious, but neither is it obvious that genetic mutations, and hence evolutionary changes in behavioral propensities, are affected by *their* consequences. Skinner reminds us that evolution is a process by which ". . . the environment acts in an inconspicuous way [to produce, not serve merely as a passive setting for, varieties of organisms] ; . . . it does not push or pull, it *selects*" (1971, p. 17).

In other words, in coming to understand evolution, we have learned not to invoke any intentional purposive tendencies within organisms to change for the better, and we have come to realize that we need not be teleological. Analogously, we may understand the behavior of individual organisms. "The environment not only prods or lashes [as Pavlov showed us occurs via classical conditioning], it *selects* [via the process of operant conditioning]." It is this latter process which is analagous to "natural selection, though [it occurs] on a very different time scale. . ." (Skinner, 1971, p. 18). Modern psychologists, via the study of operant behavior under laboratory conditions, are able to detect the ways in which the contingent environmental consequences of behavior shape, or select, behavior. At the same time, the casual observer of behavior hardly ever notices it.

So, the mentalistic view hangs on and, in the course of its being defended by well-intentioned supporters who see it as the only truly "humanistic" view, vigorous objections to behavioral technology are raised. We have seen that these objections stem largely from pervasively learned ideologies. By rejecting the evidence of external control of behavior, some cherished concepts of what man *is* are sustained. Moreover, since the fact that the social environment shapes behavior is far from intuitively apparent, few see any reason to question the traditional "explanations" of human behavior, whereby it is seen as emerging from the inside, flowing outward.

5. *To what extent is behavior socially controlled?*

Of course, the argument which was just developed would be irrelevant if behavior were not externally controlled. What evidence have we that it is? One eminent student of the processes of persuasion and attitude change, Philip Zimbardo, has recently pointed to some diverse threads in social psychological research, all of which make quite clear how very susceptible we are even to mild persuasive efforts. Referring to the burgeoning literature on conformity, on compliance, and on attitude-change, Zimbardo states, "Research from many disparate areas clearly reveals how easy it is to bring behavior under situational control. Hovland (1959) has noted that it is almost impossible *not* to get positive attitude change in a laboratory study of attitude change. Orne (1962) despairs at being able to find a task so repulsive and demeaning that experimental subjects will *not* perform it readily upon request. Milgram (1963) shows that the majority of his subjects engage in extremely aggressive behavior [administering what they believe to be painful shocks to a peer] in a situation which psychiatrists had believed would have only a weak effect in inducing blind obedience" (Zimbardo, 1972, p. 83).

Since the persons who served as subjects in these various research programs were "just people like you and me," people who are likely to believe in their own autonomy, the prevailing findings reviewed by Zimbardo are provocative. That the typical subject in these experiments was so pliable and conformist must induce some agonizing reappraisal among those who stubbornly deny the power of environmental control.

With regard to just this argument, it is ironic that so many people *do* resist attempts by psychologists to convince them that they are persuasible when they seem so unable generally to resist persuasion!

Perhaps this is less ironic and contradictory than it seems at first glance. For, as Zimbardo has indicated, it is not attempts at persuasion that we typically resist; rather, it is the recognition of the fact that we have been persuaded. In Zimbardo's opinion, and in mine, we are persuaded far more often than not. "We comply, conform, become committed, are persuaded daily in the endless procession of influence situations that we enter, yet each of us continues to maintain an illusion of personal invulnerability" (Zimbardo, 1972, p. 83). Might not this stubbornness, then, be related to our need to maintain a sense of personal freedom and dignity? Skinner certainly thinks so.

One of the most provocative aspects of Skinner's *Beyond Freedom and Dignity* is his discussion of the implications for both behavioral science and behavioral technology of the two value-concepts which appear in the title. At some length, Skinner shows how the mentalistic approach to analyzing behavior depends on and, in turn, supports the values of freedom and dignity. Moreover, he readily admits that these values are forced into question by the research findings of the behavioral scientist. "By questioning the control of autonomous man and demonstrating the control exercised by the environment, a science of behavior also seems to question dignity or worth" (Skinner, 1971, p. 21). Skinner further admits that this science throws into question the notion of responsibility, whereby man "may be justly blamed . . . [or] be given credit" (p. 21). Most of us would give up such ideas only with great reluctance, partly because the values of freedom and dignity, as Skinner acknowledges, have led to much that is admirable in human behavior. Nevertheless, Skinner argues that both the "literature of freedom" and the "literature of dignity" (by which phrases he means the rhetoric surrounding the concepts) have outlived their usefulness and by now serve mainly to impede essential new developments in human society. The impedance results mainly from the fact that these literatures help to mask the facts of behavioral control.

The literature of freedom, according to Skinner, encourages us to lose sight of the fact that we often "choose" to behave in ways which allow us merely to avoid undesirable consequences placed in front of us by other people. The literature of dignity encourages us to feel that we deserve credit for behaving in socially acceptable ways when, in fact, such behavior leads to contingent positive consequences which, again, are controlled by others.

The literature of freedom, Skinner maintains, deals. mostly with avoidance of aversive stimuli imposed by other people and it errs in "defining freedom in terms of states of mind . . . [so that] it has therefore not been able to deal effectively with techniques of control which do not breed escape or revolt but nevertheless have aversive consequences" (1971, pp. 42-43). The illusion of freedom may not, after all, be such a good thing.

As Skinner sees it, in our insistence that we are free, we have overlooked many kinds of controls to which we are regularly subjected, but of which we are not usually aware. Freedom as a state of mind is often no freedom at all because, "Freedom is a matter of contingencies of reinforcement, not of the feelings the contingencies generate." An advertising campaign can result in our "needing" and, hence, buying a sled with a motor on it for a price equal to several months' rent, and feeling that the decision to buy the sled was "freely" taken. A federal tax ruling which grants an increase in deductions for dependents can affect the highly personal matter of procreation, while reinforcing the illusion that we are free to make babies or not. In short, Skinner suggests that one of the consequences of current techniques of behavioral control, which are embedded in the context of an ideological ambiance stressing "freedom," is actually to control our behavior while making us believe that we are not controlled.

If this analysis is valid, then the *status quo* is not very moral; it involves a very profound duplicity on the part of the controllers. Furthermore, to the degree that it is valid, the analysis makes clear that what Skinner is advocating is not the introduction of controls where none exist, nor any net reduction in our freedom. Quite the contrary, what would be reduced by the adoption of Skinner's program is the ease with which our freedom, through subterfuge, is constrained behind the facade of an ideology that purports to sustain it.

It cannot be denied that throughout history some men have manipulated the environment in order to shape other men's behavior. From time to time, one set of leaders or another has redesigned various cultural institutions, usually with some ill-defined behavioral aims in mind. As Skinner puts it, "For a long time men have introduced new practices which serve as cultural innovations [innovations in government, education, psychotherapy, etc.] and they have changed the conditions under which practices [i.e., behaviors] are selected. They may now begin to do [so] with a clearer eye to the consequences" (1971, p. 208). Thus, Skinner is not advocating the introduction of behavioral control, but he is pleading that the social environment be more rationally designed than it ever has been before so that its impacts on personality could become predictably consonant with positive social values.

6. But who selects the values, shapes the environment and controls?

Skinner himself raises these obvious questions. "As the emphasis shifts to the environment, the individual seems to be exposed to a new kind of danger. Who is to construct the controlling environment and to what end?" (1971, p. 22). Moreover, Skinner acknowledges that some very fundamental value judgments must be made before such questions may be answered. Still, he is willing to answer them; those people who are most knowledgeable about the way in which environmental consequences shape behavior are those on whom we would rely to guide us in the design of our environment.

Just as, centuries ago, Plato proposed the *philosopher-kings*, is not Skinner proposing *psychologist-kings*? Skinner is not prepared to go to such lengths. Acknowledging that to rely on psychologists for guidance is tantamount to granting considerable power to a knowledgeable elite, he insists on the necessity for this elite's behavior itself to be under surveillance and control. With confidence (and some complacency, perhaps) Skinner asserts that it is inevitable that the controllers' behavior will itself be controlled, because everyone's behavior, even that of a society's leaders, is subject to contingent consequences. Thus, "To prevent the misuse of controlling power, . . . we must look not at the controller himself but at the contingencies under which he engages in control" (1971, p. 168).

In other words, Skinner is saying that the political system must retain the ability to react, to sustain, or to reject any given leader.

To some readers at least, this last idea will appear to beg the question of how the controller himself is to be controlled. The notion that his introduction of contingent consequences for others is under the influence of its own contingent consequences appears to involve an infinite regress. Thus, one can ask next, "Who arranges the contingencies which impinge on the controller's behavior?"

With regard to this apparent dilemma, Skinner is rather cavalierly optimistic. He deals with it by asserting what he calls, the *reciprocity of control*, noting that it is inevitably true that "the child [controls] the parent, the patient the therapist, the citizen the government" (1971, p. 169). Again, with an optimism bordering on faith, Skinner opines that "the ultimate improvement [in culture] comes from the environment which makes them [the controllers] wise and compassionate" (p. 171).

Throughout this particular aspect of Skinner's argument, there runs the thread of a characteristically American faith in the democratic process. Noting that "in a democracy the controller is himself found among the controlled" (p. 172), Skinner implies that the controller will prudently implement his policies since they will necessarily impact on himself as well as on others. At the same time, Skinner's faith is tempered by his acknowledgement that it will be a "great problem . . . to arrange effective counter-control and hence to bring some important consequences to bear on the behavior of the controller" (p. 171).

Although great, the problem seems not insurmountable to Skinner. Somewhat ironically, near the end of his book, Skinner calls upon the two values of freedom and dignity (which, earlier, as we saw, he charged with the responsibility for *retarding* the development of behavioral technology) as the safety valves that would prevent the misuse of behavioral technology. He thus suggests that there is, after all, still something worthwhile in the literatures of freedom and dignity. They are seen by Skinner as fostering the role of "the individual as an instrument of counter-control" (p. 213). Apparently advocating individual vigilance, Skinner asserts, "Attacking controlling powers is, of course, a form of counter-control. It may have immeasurable benefits if better controlling practices are thereby selected" (p. 181).

Thus, what Skinner seems after all to be advocating is increased application of the principles of behavioral modification (in the most general sense of this phrase) through control of the social environment, so that *both* control and counter-control, both of which already exist, might be more rationally employed. Put in these terms, Skinner's proposal seems a small step forward.

It is, nevertheless, a departure. Although late in the book Skinner appears to resurrect the literatures of freedom and dignity, he still lays at their feet the responsibility for some of the most negative aspects of the *status quo* in Western societies. Notably, he blames them for the continuing widespread reliance on punishment and the concomitant reluctance to try promising alternatives to punishment as a means of social control. So, although he is not apparently advocating the abandonment of the values of freedom and dignity, he is clearly urging, as his title makes explicit, that we go *beyond* them to a more enlightened stage of civilization.

7. Won't this produce a totalitarian society of automatons?

By no means does Skinner advocate a totalitarian state. He explicitly labels this condition "morally wrong" (1971, p. 174), implying that he would wish to avoid such a state of affairs. At the same time, however, he is compelled to remind us that presently many other moral wrongs exist, including economic and social exploitation (as in the manipulation of workers' output via piece-work wages), vengeful punishment, the distribution of harmful drugs, and many other practices that are generally deplored but "freely" tolerated. Such practices Skinner roundly condemns, not only because they are inconsistent with prevailing humanitarian values but because they have demonstrably aversive consequences, as much psychological research attests.

For all that is wrong with society in its present form, however, Skinner would not substitute another moral wrong, such as a totalitarian state. But would not what he proposes lead inadvertently to totalitarianism? He insists that the technology which he has proposed "is ethically neutral" (1971, p. 150) but one that could, if properly implemented, encourage the design of reinforcement contingencies for the good of others. To accomplish this, he says, "we must look to the contingencies that induce people to act to increase the chances that their cultures will survive" (p. 158). In effect, this is a call for a quantum leap in social consciousness, marked by an unprecedented concern for the species and its future.

With this emphasis on an essentially unselfish concern for *cultural* survival, what will happen to the individual? Won't he become less significant and lose his uniqueness? Skinner believes not. "No intentional culture can destroy that uniqueness, and any effort to do so would be bad design" (p. 209). Nor does Skinner fear that a more rationally designed culture will make men more machine-like. After all, he reminds us, ". . . while man himself may be controlled by his environment . . . it is an environment which is almost wholly of his own making" (pp. 205-206).[13]

To Skinner it is a sad fact indeed that man still continues to construct an environment for himself and his fellows that is full of aversive consequences. For example, man provides more rewards to other men for producing cars than for behaving in ways which might reduce the pollution that cars produce. Many similar reinforcers, of our own rather thoughtless design, today conflict with the kinds of reinforcers that would induce people to behave in ways that would enhance the survival potential of their culture while simultaneously enhancing the quality of their lives.

For these reasons, and for many more which space does not permit our reviewing here, Skinner explicitly and boldly calls for more "intentional control, not less . . ." In sum, his position epitomizes a plea for social engineering, based on a science of behavior which acknowledges the key role of environmental consequences in shaping behavior. This science—behaviorism—is today poorly understood by most lay persons, and the notion that it be transformed into a technology is very threatening to many of them. Skinner knows this and says so; ". . . those who do not find the very possibility ridiculous are more likely to be frightened by it than reassured" (1971, p. 3).

Just how frightened some have become is obvious in the tenor of some recent public reactions to behaviorism. In both its scientific and technological shapes, behaviorism has been called "un-American" in the Congress of the United States and scorned as "characteristically American" by some of that country's shrillest critics. Skinner himself has been branded a Marxist/Pavlovian ideologue *and* a neo-Fascist! One critic recently referred to behaviorism as a "monumental triviality" and another called it responsible for the assassinations of John and Robert Kennedy.[14]

This Skinnerian ideal is, nevertheless, a striking example of our Model Three—the psychologist as social engineer. In its dramatic Skinnerian version, this model has stirred controversy for many years, long before Skinner's 1971 book appeared. Some readers will recall the debate published 15 years earlier between Skinner and Carl Rogers, the eminent clinical psychologist.[15]

More recent critical analyses of the basic Skinnerian view of man also call into question Skinner's attempts to derive a behavioral technology from that view. A very reasoned analysis was offered by Albert Bandura in his 1974 Presidential Address to the American Psychological Association (Bandura, 1974).

One of his central criticisms of the behavioristic conception of how humans learn and thus modify their behavior is that this conception probably exaggerates the degree to which external consequences *per se* are responsible for behavior change. According to Bandura, empirical facts preclude treating external consequences as either the sole determinants of behavior or as automatic in their operation. Bandura sees external consequences as very influential because they serve several cognitive and motivational functions, including the imparting of information about the appropriateness of various behaviors and about anticipated benefits of future behaviors. In his view, reinforcement works not by mechanically strengthening a response made by an organism whose consciousness is irrelevant but by informing and motivating an aware human being.

Moreover, merely by observing consequences accruing to other people's behavior, an observer can profit, storing the information gained in the observation and applying it to his own behavior on some subsequent, apparently appropriate, occasion. And, the human being has high capacity to produce his own reinforcements to his own actions, as well as engage in a dazzling variety of perceptual distortions that may obscure relationships involving his own behavior and the effects it produces. For these and other reasons, Bandura warns that a behavioral technology based on a mechanistic form of behaviorism will either not work or, as was the case in early behavior modification efforts, have as net effect "a tedious shaping process that produced, at best, mediocre results in an ethically questionable manner."

Despite all of this criticism, Bandura must be counted as an advocate of behavioral technology, albeit an enlightened version thereof. As such, Bandura is more a reinterpreter of Skinner than an opponent. Like Skinner, he doubts the efficacy of restraints of conscience as a controlling force to ensure moral conduct. He perceives, with approval, that "reinforcement practices are being increasingly used to cultivate personal potentialities and humanistic qualities" (p. 863). And he notes, again approvingly, that psychologists are increasingly coming to realize that "they must apply their corrective measures to detrimental societal practices rather than limit themselves to treating the causalities of these practices" (p. 863). Going beyond Skinner, and placing greater emphasis than he might on the human ability to self-reinforce, Bandura applauds a version of behavioral control whereby the external agent merely creates a situation via social contracting whereby the learners arrange their own enviornmental inducements for their own performance, which they themselves evaluate and reward as and when they see fit.

While Bandura offers many criticisms of several of Skinner's assertions (see, especially, Bandura's discussion of the relationship between determinism and freedom and his skeptical treatment of the Skinnerian view of awareness as a countervail to exploitative controls), Bandura—like Skinner—advocates behavioral technology. Hence, Bandura's ideas also exemplify our Model Three. More concerned than Skinner with existing power differentials, Bandura is nonetheless optimistic in that he sees power as beginning to diffuse more broadly in American society, setting the stage for.an enlightened application of behavioral modification techniques. With the stage thus set, Bandura sees the Model Three role of the psychologist not as telling people how they ought to live their lives but providing them "with the *means* for effecting personal and social change" (italics added). A clearer statement of Model Three would be impossible to construct.

As dramatic as the Skinnerian version and Bandura's refinement of it might be, there is another instance of a Model Three proposal that could be more shocking. In 1971, newspapers in the United States, in reporting Kenneth Clark's Presidential Address to the American Psychological Association, zeroed-in on a section wherein he suggested "psychotechnological intervention" in the conduct of government. By this catchy phrase, Clark had in mind the application of such techniques as brain stimulation, the use of behavior-controlling drugs, and other biochemical procedures among men who happen to enjoy the power to lead us in order to ensure that they lead us well (Clark, 1971). In contrast, Skinner's position seems tame and unimaginative!

That Clark dared to go as far as he did in his proposals underscores how strongly he feels mankind's need for some rational constraints on self-destructive tendencies. In words similar to Skinner's, Clark warned, "Man can no longer afford the luxuries of a leisurely, trial-and-error, trivia-dominated approach to the behavioral sciences . . . the psychological and social sciences must enable us to control the animalistic, barbaric, and primitive propensities in man and subordinate these negatives to the uniquely human moral and ethical characteristics of love, kindness and empathy" (pp. 1054-1055).

With these words ringing in our ears, we can bring to a close our discussion of Model Three, noting thereby that it possesses some idealistic (almost utopian) characteristics which, it is hoped, will counter its threatening aspects for the more timid among us. Let us also note that the proposal to apply what we know, even when the proposal takes dramatic shapes as in the versions offered by Skinner, Bandura, and Clark, is a reasonable response by men of goodwill who refuse to believe that the world as we know it is the best we can hope for.

Let us also recall that Model Three is the most extreme of the three models discussed. When one advocates applying psychology to real-world problems, one does not necessarily have Model Three in mind. To urge the practical application of psychology is by no means necessarily to call for chemical control of individual behavior (a la Clark) nor even to advocate the degree of intentional control of the environment that Skinner advocates. One can share the basic premise of both these psychologists that the contemporary world needs some new directions. One can also admit that we haven't yet properly applied what we already know about the shaping of human behavior. One can do both of these without, at the same time, granting any power to the psychologist (beyond what he may already enjoy) to affect social change.

On the other hand, it seems beyond argument that if we grant that the world needs help and that the psychologist may be armed with relevant tools and information that have so far largely gone unused, we ought to encourage their use. In response, the psychologist ought to at least publicize what he knows (Model One) and offer assistance in the evaluation of other people's programs of social improvement (Model Two).

By devoting considerable space in this chapter to a discussion of Model Three and, particularly, by looking closely at what Skinner and Clark have said, we were at least forced to consider the present state of society, to discover the kinds of controls that are already in effect, to take account of the behaviors that our present controllers are encouraging, and to think a bit about the techniques that might be implemented to bring about a more desirable state of affairs. Thus, without endorsing all that Skinner and Clark have said, we have probably performed a useful exercise.

It matters little that Model Three engenders caution in many who confront it, for it is not the only way in which psychology may be applied. What does matter is whether those who shape our environment will take into account what we know about human behavior. If Skinner is right *only* when he says that a more rationally designed culture is "essential if the human species is to continue to develop," (1971, p. 175) and if Clark is right *only* when he, too, links our survival to our knowledge of human behavior, then psychologists who have the professional responsibility to acquire such knowledge, have also, as members of the human species, the moral responsibility to offer the products of their best labors to the world outside their laboratories and libraries. If conditions are at all as Skinner and Clark see them, psychologists have no moral alternative to making this offering and to pressing it doggedly if policy makers resist it. At the same time, as Bandura has urged, "psychology must also fulfill a broader obligation to society by bringing influence to bear on public policies to ensure that its findings are used in the service of human betterment" (1974, p. 869).

So, in the chapters that follow we shall engage unabashedly in political psychology, attempting to apply a small portion of what is collectively known by psychologists to a very few real-world problems. Most often, we shall function as in Model One—"giving away psychological knowledge." Occasionally, we shall see what can happen when Model Two is implemented—by critically assessing, with some of the research tools employed by psychologists, some prototype programs intended by their sponsors to be socially beneficial.

Instances of *bona fide* psychological engineering are still quite rare,[16] so Model Three will have few examples in the forthcoming chapters. Perhaps some day Model Three will be commonly implemented, but surely not before psychologists have demonstrated that they can make welcome contributions by implementing the two less radical models. Let's see, in the chapters that follow, if that demonstration has begun.

NOTES

[1] Guttentag singled out two ways in which psychological knowledge could be put to use: (a) by employing known facts to guide the administration of ongoing social programs and (b) by applying the research skills of psychologists in program evaluation. Actually, we will limit our concern here to Guttentag's first way, since the application of known facts is the essence of Model One, while evaluation is the essence of Model Two.

[2] Helping behavior—or altruism—is not a well-studied topic. However, what few data are available are consistent with a proposition that may be derived from various psychological theories that stress cognitive consistency—namely, "If I perceive that he needs help and I can provide it and if I am capable of providing it, he must be less able than I. Unless I attribute my own abilities to good fortune, I am unlikely to attribute his lack of abilities to back luck. Therefore, his needs likely reflect his inadequacies."

[3] The research of Clark and Clark and related studies by others will be discussed in Chapter 5.

[4] Appropos of the argument presented in Chapter 1 concerning the relevance of "basic" research, Clark in 1971 said, "It may be of some value to point out that the earlier studies of the development of self-identification and evaluation in children with Mamie Clark were not motivated by or conducted with any direct concern for their applied or policy implications and consequences. The fact that the United States Supreme Court . . . cited these findings : . . was a gratifying illustration of the possibility that . . . what is called 'pure' research can sometimes have some direct social policy and applied social change effects" (p. 1049).

[5] Ironically, a traffic control program implemented but not pre-tested by Senator Ribicoff when he was Governor of the State of Connecticut was the object of a critical reanalysis by Professor Campbell and one of his colleagues. See p. 26.

[6] A contemporary, realistic treatment of evaluation research possibilities may be found in the work edited by Riecken and Boruch (1974).

[7] See, for example, the work of Zimbardo and Ebbeson (1969) for an application of the Campbell and Stanley (1963) discussion of validity threats to experimental research in attitude change.

[8] In pointing out misinterpretations by Governor Ribicoff, Campbell commented, ". . . we criticize Ribicoff's interpretation of his results, from the point of view of the social scientist's proper standards of evidence. Were the now Senator Ribicoff not the man of stature that he is, this would be most unpatriotic, because we would be alienating one of the strongest proponents of social experimentation in our nation." In summarizing the critique, thereby giving it additional exposure, I must echo Campbell's sentiments. Senator Ribicoff's recent endorsement of a pilot-project approach to welfare program reform, discussed above, has added to his stature as a friend of rigorous evaluation.

[9] With change scores available for a number of years, one can employ a statistical test of inference that, in effect, compares one change with a series of others (Box and Tiao, 1965).

[10] The Spring 1974 issue of the *Maxwell Review* was devoted to a symposium, the theme of which was "Social Science and Public Morality." Using a discussion of Model Three as a springboard, contributors to the symposium tended to limit their discussions to most obvious misuses of science—e.g., the employment of aversive electric shocks to modify prisoners' behavior (Weissman and Rosenthal, 1974) and the notorious Tuskegee syphilis study (Dawson, 1974). That a discussion of Model Three provokes such reactions demonstrates an awareness that somebody is already exerting behavioral controls, and often at very high cost to the relatively powerless. Not inappropriately, this awareness generates skepticism and vigilance regarding any proposal pertaining to behavioral technology, even when the proposer explicitly opposes such misuse of power. It is clearly necessary, however, to search for the promising versions of behavioral technology, just as it is to search out the exploitative perversions of it.

[11] This account will, necessarily, be brief. It cannot satisfactorily substitute for Skinner's own account. His book should be read by anyone who would claim to be educated with respect to contemporary American psychology. Furthermore, whatever one's predilections regarding the ethical and political issues

touched on in *Beyond Freedom and Dignity*, reading Skinner's treatment of them is a provocative experience.

[12] See, especially, Keller and Schoenfeld (1950), Skinner (1938), Skinner and Ferster (1957), and almost any issue since 1940 of any journal devoted to experimental psychology, as well as any modern psychology textbook, for examples. Note also that the study of operant behavior began before Skinner gave it that name in the late 1930s. See, for example, the pioneering work of E.L. Thorndike (1933). Finally, see Skinner's more recent attempt to summarize his behavoristic system, *About Behaviorism* (1974).

[13] Skinner even takes issue with those who blame the industrial revolution and the age of computers for dehumanizing man. He claims, in one of the more provocative assertions in his book, that the more machines we make for man to use, the less machine-like he needs to be.

[14] Skinner himself reports some of these reactions in *Beyond Freedom and Dignity* (1971).

[15] See Skinner and Rogers (1956).

[16] Of course, psychologists and others have participated in a variety of efforts to shape human behavior, especially in education, psychotherapy, advertising, and political campaigning, to mention only a few arenas in which systematic efforts to modify behavior have occurred. What I have here called *bona fide* psychological engineering, however, differs from such efforts in that it demands a public, rather massive program of environmental manipulation—the judicious employment of reinforcements to a degree never before attempted openly.

3
The intellectual capacities of human groups

Of all the contemporary social issues on which psychologists have something to offer (either as expert witnesses or policy evaluators or even as behavioral engineers) probably the most basic one concerns different manifest levels of ability among human groups. By *human groups* I mean populations defined by nationality, ethnicity, race, or any other socially significant, ascribed category label. What is *believed* to be true about differential abilities among such social entities influences and sustains some very important social policies.

Throughout history, human groups aware of their distinctiveness have, far more often than not, related to other human groups in ways that reflected beliefs about superiority and inferiority. The maintenance of unequal power relationships has consistently been justified on the basis of putative inequalities in ability, merit, and other generally assumed-to-be inherent characteristics. Many forms of international colonial domination and of sociopolitical discrimination within multi-ethnic nations have been sustained by the belief that while some peoples were capable of mastery others deserved slavery.

In the United States, the most striking (but by no means only) manifestation of this phenomenon has been relations between Blacks and Whites. These relations have periodically been punctuated by debates over the intellectual capacities of Blacks relative to Whites. These debates concern alleged Black intellectual inferiority, its presumed causes, and whether or not educational "remedies" are possible. Similar debates take place elsewhere, for men everywhere have perceived "good reasons" for believing in their own superiority vis-à-vis others. Christians and pagans, Protestants and Catholics, Gentiles and Jews, Jews and Arabs, Europeans and Asians—all such pairings have involved beliefs about ability differences, and relationships have been characterized by intergroup confrontations that reflected those beliefs.

In much of the world, colonialist domination and slavery are on the wane. Still, more subtle forms of domination by one people over another are very much with us and these, too, reflect and are "justified" by prevailing beliefs in differential abilities. Arguments in the United States over the need for and promise of "compensatory education" for the so-called "culturally-deprived" is a case in point. Some who oppose any such educational effort predict its failure on the grounds that its target group is inherently unable to benefit from it. Those opposed to efforts at equalizing opportunity argue that environmental intervention on behalf of a group whom they perceive to be suffering from deficits could not possibly overcome the genetic limitations, so they counsel doing nothing.

For example, during President Nixon's first term, one heard talk of a policy of "benign neglect" for American Blacks. This policy proposal was reportedly formulated as a strategy for preventing violent protest by restraining government spokesmen from suggesting to the underprivileged that more was possible than could really be achieved. (See the discussion below, in Chapter Five, of ghetto rioting and the theory of rising expectations.) Some critics of this notion, however, saw just under the surface at least a hint of the long-standing conservative Euro-American belief in African inferiority. Of course, this implication was denied by the policy's advocates. Indeed, it must be admitted, the notion of "benign neglect" is consistent with the broader Nixonian doctrine, which can be paraphrased, "Ask not what your country can do for you; ask, instead, what you can do for yourself." (In these words, reminiscent of John F. Kennedy's genuinely lofty call in his inaugural address, a writer for the French newspaper Le Monde satirized Nixon's second inaugural speech.) The benign neglect concept, thus, could have been merely a reflection of a general, laissez-faire, individual-effort political philosophy. But there is no doubt that it is also consistent with the belief that any special effort to provide assistance would likely be wasted, since the target population is thought of as unable to improve its status.

Compensatory education and cultural deprivation are controversial not only with regard to the issue at hand, but in other ways as well. For example, Cole and Bruner (1971), although taking an empiricist view of performance differences across cultural groups, worried that the popularity of the cultural deprivation concept may have led psychologists ethnocentrically to interpret as deficits many behavioral differences that should be seen *only* as differences. This warning is consistent with the rejection by some Blacks of compensatory education on the grounds that their own subculture does not need compensation. So, it is not only those who believe that Blacks can't benefit from compensatory education who oppose it.

Nevertheless, perceiving those who may display performance deficits (relative to some core-cultural norm) as "culturally deprived" at least has more optimistic policy implications than does concluding that they are inherently and immutably "inferior."

The anticipated success of educational intervention clearly depends on beliefs about human ability and on beliefs about its determinants. So this issue is a fundamental one. It is also an issue for which the relevance of psychology is very apparent, even to the relatively unsophisticated. The assessment of ability is popularly known to be a psychological activity. Generally, when people say "psychology" they think "testing" and, more specifically, IQ testing. Moreover, it is often thought that IQ is a measure of inborn intelligence.

The measurement of diverse human traits and characteristics, especially those which imply abilities, has long been a keystone of psychology. Psychometrics—the assessment of individual differences in behavioral potential—has a long history in psychology. Thus, no discussion of intelligence and how it is determined can overlook the findings of the psychometric research tradition in psychology. Not surprisingly, then, here is an issue for which the public generally looks to psychology for some guidance.

Moreover, psychology transcends psychometrics and concerns itself with several other topics that are also pertinent to the issue of human capacity. One of these is the interest shown by psychologists since Freud in early experience as a determinant of human personality. As we shall see, the early experience postulate bears directly on beliefs about factors responsible for intergroup differences in performance, since "early experience" comprises a rival explanation to genetic determination.

Closely related to the early experience doctrine is the prevalent concern in contemporary psychology with the learning process. Many psychologists, like Skinner (some of whose views were discussed in Chapter 2), place considerable emphasis on the influence of environmental consequences of behavior. Certainly, the environmentalist orientation of modern psychologists has displaced the earlier instinctivist bias exemplified by MacDougall.[1] With the onslaught on the instinct doctrine by Watson in 1912 and with the work of several generations of post-Watsonian learning theorists, the classical view of man as a pre-programmed complex of instincts has been replaced by a view of man as a flexible, responsive organism with a behavioral potential far greater than any single man's behavior would suggest.

Together, the notions that early experience is critical and that man is very flexible comprise a point of view that predisposes most psychologists to doubt that *observed* performances reveal the genetically determined *limits* of capability. Most psychologists would view any behavioral act by any particular organism as a complex and end-product of genetic potential interacting with some unique pattern of that organism's experiences. Therefore, these two notions —experience and learning—which represent important modern trends in psychology, are also very pertinent to the issue of intergroup differences in intelligence.

Still another psychological arena that impinges on this issue is the tradition in social psychology known variously as "culture and personality," "national character," and "psychological anthropology." Common to all these labels is a concern with characteristics shared by members of a designated human group, which characteristics might serve to distinguish them from other human groups.

An immediate precursor of contemporary research on what might be thought of as "group psychology" was *Volkpsychologie* as practiced in German universities near the end of the 19th century. The German folkpsychologists urged the accumulation of behavioral ethnographies as documentation of the characteristics of various subgroups of mankind. Of course, concern for the psychology of various peoples antedated the 19th century; throughout history one finds tales by travelers impressed with exotic behaviors attributed to the "nature" of the peoples encountered.

Subsequent to the German tradition there developed research activities by social psychologists and anthropologists who not only documented behavioral customs but sought explanations for them in cultural forces. From this Volkpsychologie-anthropology tradition of Western social science there thus derives the notion that groups of people share behavioral traits because they first share *culturally* determined experiences. This notion, quite obviously, also bears on the issue at hand.

We have seen, then, that various aspects of psychology—psychometrics, learning theory, and cross-cultural social psychology—bear on the issue of what determines observable intergroup differences in intellectual performance. In what follows in this chapter, we shall see applied to this issue various concepts and findings that are germane to one or another of these aspects of psychology. However, it is psychometrics research and theory that is central to the issue, so it is to psychometrics that we turn first.

WHAT IS INTELLIGENCE AND HOW IS IT MEASURED?

The concept *intelligence*, which denotes general ability and specific (albeit related) skills, undoubtedly predates by many centuries the technical developments used by psychologists during the 20th century when they began to measure it. As a result of this ancient history, there coexist several ways of conceptualizing intelligence.

There is, first of all, the traditional awareness that individuals differ from each other in general capability and that this difference manifests itself in performance differences rather consistently over a variety of tasks. Those who consistently perform well are generally acknowledged to be "more intelligent" than those who do not. Thus, traditionally, intelligence has been defined as the "capacity" to exhibit skillful performance. The circularity of this notion—residing in the fact that "capacity" is inferred from performance, which is then attributed to capacity—usually goes unnoticed.

Secondly, with the availability and use of standard IQ tests, a technical meaning of intelligence has developed. While the technical definition retains much of what "intelligence" has traditionally meant, psychometricians prefer to define intelligence as *whatever it is that IQ tests measure*. This kind of definition is also circular, but it is a perfectly adequate—indeed, necessary—definition for those scientists who have adopted the philosophical position known as "operationalism." As applied to psychometrics, the position results in the assertion that any hypothetical trait, like intelligence, personality, etc., can *only* be defined by the "operations" performed to measure it. In this case, the crucial operations happen to be the IQ tests that were invented to measure intelligence. When intelligence is defined in this fashion, its hypothetical nature (the fact that it is not directly observable, but inferred from observed performances) is underscored.

Thirdly, and somewhat ironically, the widespread use of standard intelligence tests has contributed to a popular reification of the concept of intelligence. Many people have come to think of intelligence as not only what an IQ test measures but also some almost real substance inside people. It is as if intelligence is some "stuff" of which the "inner man" is composed so that his IQ score is considered merely an imperfect reflection of the amount of stuff he possesses. Perhaps because the word intelligence is a noun, it seems difficult to resist the temptation to reify it.

To most psychologists, however, the word *intelligence* is primarily a short-hand way of expressing the *level* of performance of an individual on an IQ test, *relative* to that of other individuals. Such performances are of more than theoretical interest, of course, because an IQ test is some standard sample of tasks that have been rather painstakingly assembled on the basis of evidence that performance on these tasks predicts performance on certain socially significant, real-world tasks. The class of real-world tasks that IQ test performance best predicts is, simply, performance in school. More correctly, IQ test scores predict performance in schools that are designed in accordance with Western, primarily middle-class values and concepts of education. The psychological anthropologist, Robert LeVine, in a review of studies which sought in vain to ascertain cross-cultural differences in general ability, reminded us that "standard intelligence tests measure [only] the current capacity of individuals to participate effectively in Western schools . . ." (LeVine, 1970, p. 581).

From the very beginning of scientific concern with intelligence, this has been true. Binet and Simon, in 1905, constructed the first successful IQ test *in order to* discriminate between children likely to succeed or fail in the Paris school system. All subsequent IQ tests, to varying degrees, reflect the same practical concern. This is not to say that IQ test scores predict *only* school performance. Since school success relates to success in some other enterprises, IQ predicts success in those enterprises also. However, IQ best predicts (but does not necessarily *cause*) school performance and that is what it was meant in the first instance to predict.

This is also not to say that IQ predicts school performance *perfectly*. In fact, from a large number of studies with large numbers of children, it appears that IQ scores typically correlate no better than .7 with school grades, which is the equivalent of saying that IQ scores predict about 50 percent of the variance in school performance.[2] Obviously, performance in school reflects factors other than the kinds of individual abilities involved in IQ test performance.

Moreover, in referring to *ability* underlying IQ test performance, it must be kept in mind that ability is *inferred* from performance and that the test performance *per se* reveals little or nothing about the determinants of that so-called ability. Some of the determinants of test performance are situational, some reflect degree of experience of various specific kinds, and some reflect the essentially fortuitous co-mingling of genetic factors, which occurred at the instant of the individual's conception. All of these interact to produce an individual's performance on an IQ test. Disentangling these interacting determinants is an extremely difficult analytic task that can never be perfectly accomplished. One can only estimate the relative contributions of these determinants and then only for populations, not for individuals. This must be kept in mind, for the degree to which ability as inferred from IQ test performance reflects genetic factors is the core of the issue to which this chapter is devoted. There is considerable disagreement (and misunderstanding) on this very point.

Before it can adequately be dealt with, there is a bit more about the definition and measurement of intelligence that must be understood. Psychometric measurement always involves assumptions about the psychological characteristic being measured. A basic assumption made about intelligence is that it is *normally distributed.* In other words, it is a trait dimension along which entire populations are dispersed, with most people near the middle of its range and with decreasing numbers at increasing distances from the middle. The resulting distribution is the familiar bell-shaped curve of the statistician. This is a reasonable assumption, since many characteristics of living things that involve chance determination are distributed in this way. Once having made this assumption, however, those who construct instruments to measure intelligence are constrained to refine their instruments *so that* they will yield, for a large population of persons, a distribution of scores approaching normality. This is precisely what the psychometricians have done.

Thus, an IQ test is an instrument which, *by design*, yields a normal distribution of scores, a distribution wherein decreasing proportions of people earn scores of increasing deviation from the average score. The test is built to ensure that outstanding scores will be rare. Now this is not as circular as it sounds, for if whatever it is that IQ tests measure were *not* normally distributed in nature, repeated applications of IQ tests would not yield normal distributions of scores. But they tend to, so the assumption was an appropriate one to make. Perhaps it is best to think of the process as circular, but appropriately so. The circularity exists in the fact that the tests are built, refined, and modified so as to yield normal distributions of scores meant to reflect a hypothetical population trait that is itself assumed to be normally distributed.

With this behind us, it becomes easy to understand an IQ score. During the early days of IQ testing, performance was converted into "mental age" and then IQ was calculated as the ratio of mental age to chronological age. Since mental age had to be determined by examining the proportions of persons of various ages who performed certain tasks successfully, it became apparent that there was no need for a concept of mental age. What is essential is simply that a given individual's performance be compared with the typical performance of some appropriate standard sample of other persons. In short, a record of performance need only be compared with norms to be converted directly to an IQ score.

For example, if an individual's performance is typical of the normative sample with which he is being compared, his IQ is set at 100, the number arbitrarily assigned to the exact middle of the IQ distribution. If his performance happens to be exceeded by, say, 84 percent of the normative sample, his IQ is set at 85. This is so because in normal distributions 84 percent of all cases fall above the minus-one standard deviation point; in the normal distribution for IQ, the mean arbitrarily has been defined as 100 and a standard deviation is 15. In this example, the individual's performance fell at the point that is 1 standard deviation below the mean (or, 100 - 15 = 85).

This somewhat laborious digression into psychometrics was designed to underscore the fact that an IQ score is merely a short-hand expression for *relative* performance on a kind of test designed with certain constraints that reflect some very specific assumptions. We have also seen that the practical value of an IQ score resides simply in the fact that it is a good, but imperfect, predictor of success in school. It should be quite clear what IQ is—and what it isn't.

As a statement of relative standing along the continuum of probable success in school, IQ is the best known hypothetical construct ever invented by a psychologist. Nearly everyone has heard of it and practically everyone imbues it with great importance. Unfortunately, most laypersons, even those who in recent years have grown wary and suspicious of IQ testing, tend to think of IQ as both fixed and genetically predetermined. (Most attacks by laypersons have been directed to *testing* and not to IQ *per se*; when the testers are accused of failing to measure IQ validly, it is implied that IQ is "there" to be measured in some fairer way.) It may seem to many that the trouble undergone in attempts to measure IQ testifies to its real existence. It is a simple enough extrapolation from thinking of it as existing to thinking of it as immutable; if people *have* IQs, then IQs must be substantive quantities that are possessed for a lifetime. A lifetime implies from birth onward, so the ultimate implication is that IQ is genetically determined. This is a deceptively persuasive chain of arguments. IQ is only hypothetical stuff, and although it is inferred from a score that changes little in the course of a typical lifetime,[3] that score reflects much more than what has been bequeathed to the individual by genetics.

We are now ready to treat the question of the degree to which IQ is genetically determined. This question is central to the controversy over intergroup differences in ability.

THE HERITABILITY OF IQ AND THE JENSEN CONTROVERSY

How often have we heard the query, "Is intelligence inherited *or* is it a product of experience?" This question as worded is naive and misleading. No human behavioral characteristic is one *or* the other; all traits involve both genetic and experiential determinants. The question, therefore, may appropriately be framed only as a search for the *relative* contributions of heredity and environment.

Even when properly stated, the question is of dubious significance; yet it is frequently posed. It is often asked because its answer seems to many people to bear heavily on another question; to wit, do identifiable human groups differ in their intellectual *capacity* as fixed and determined by genetics.

In the United States, the question has most often been applied to Black/White comparisons. Interest in this question has peaked and waned but it regularly recurs. Although there have been times when little attention was paid to it, there have been periods when professional associations of scholars have felt it necessary even to issue proclamations asserting a position.[4] Whenever the issue has become salient, as it did in the United States in the late 1960s, debate has tended to be acrimonious.

Recent interest peaked in 1969 with the publication in the *Harvard Educational Review* of an article by Arthur R. Jensen entitled, "How Much Can We Boost IQ and Scholastic Achievement?"[5] The article added fuel to the long-simmering controversy and provoked considerable criticism—much, but not all of it, valid.

In his article, Jensen dealt primarily with three sets of issues. One had to do with whether or not compensatory education is likely to succeed. Another is whether the reliably established differences between mean IQ scores of black Americans and white Americans are mostly genetic or experiential in origin. The other was the more basic question of the heritability of IQ generally. Although these three issues are related, they are separable; the answers to one issue do not predetermine the answers to the others. They must be examined separately.

In fact, we will not treat the question of compensatory education until the next chapter. In this chapter our primary concern is with intergroup *differences* and *their* degree of heritability. To treat this issue properly, we must begin with the question of the heritability of IQ generally. This happens to be the one question that Jensen answered reasonably well in his paper (cf. Jensen, 1969, pp. 28-59), so the account that follows is consistent with his. (We will see later, however, that it is necessary to question both Jensen's answer *and* the application of his answer to the issue of group differences.)

How heritability is assessed

Once man isolates any aspect of the appearance or behavior of his fellows and decides that the aspect is socially or otherwise significant, there are reasons for measuring it and seeking its determinants. The list of human aspects that have been deemed significant is finite but numerous.

Some of them are physical and, as result, may be measured simply by the application of standard, multi-purpose, measuring instruments. For example, human height is measured by the same gadgets that measure the dimensions of dining room tables and distances along superhighways. Many other human aspects are not so easily measured; they are non-physical and can't be measured with generalized instruments. Intelligence, as we have just seen, is such an aspect. Like other "personality traits," intelligence exists only by inference, and it is "measured" by instruments designed to measure only its presumed manifestations.

In spite of this important difference, IQ shares one very significant feature with the more tangible, physical aspects of persons. It is, to some degree, heritable, just as height is. These two human characteristics, along with many others, are influenced by the fortuitous co-mingling of parental chromosomes. Both of them, however— height and IQ—are also influenced by non-genetic factors. The assessment of degree of heritability of both height and IQ therefore involves the same logic. Let us consider this not-popularly understood activity of geneticists—the assessment of heritability—as it may be applied to any human aspect.

If one begins with a definition of genetic inheritance, a number of consequences for observable characteristics flow from it. As any student of biology knows, the key concept in inheritance is probability—the chance occurrence of possible pairs of genes. From this concept may be derived a whole series of predictions concerning the proportion of particular phenotypes in filial generations, the shape of the frequency distribution of phenotypic scores, and, most significantly for our immediate concerns, correlations in phenotypic scores among various pairs of people of differing degree of biological relationship, from identical twins to unrelated strangers.[6]

It may be stated with complete confidence that if height (to use a simple trait) is genetically influenced, then the correlation in height between pairs of identical twins will be higher than the comparable correlation for siblings. This latter in turn will be higher than the comparable correlation for pairs of unrelated persons. Moreover, if height were completely *determined* by genetics (which, of course, it is not) one could specify that the identical-twin correlation for height would be perfect, or *unity* (+1.00), while the correlation for a randomly selected sample of unrelated persons would not depart significantly from zero. Under these conditions, the difference between the correlations would be maximal. So, it should be clear, the greater the difference across the correlations, the more genetic influence there must be.

The formulation just described is somewhat oversimplified. In actual practice, geneticists employ refinements in the technique of assessing heritability. They must, for example, always allow for the possibility that non-genetic factors (diet, exercise, health history, etc.) influence height even within pairs of identical twins. Therefore, they would find it very useful to compare correlations between identical twins who have been reared together with correlations between identical twins reared apart. When so doing, they would assume that separate rearing makes differential experience within twin pairs more likely. In such a comparison, and with this assumption operative, the *smaller* the difference in these two correlations, the greater the genetic influence. Whatever the refinement of technique, however, the essence of heritability assessment is a comparison of correlations across pairs of persons of known degree of relationship.

It is standard practice for geneticists to summarize heritability estimates in terms of a statistic "h^2" which means, technically, the proportion of phenotypic (i.e., observed) variance that may be predicted from genotypic (i.e., theoretical) variance. It follows from this that the square root of h^2 (or h) is, by definition, the correlation between genotype and phenotype (see footnote, 2, p. 74). However, since genotypes are not observable or measurable, it is not possible actually to *calculate* a correlation between genotypes and pehnotypes. The geneticist can work only with phenotypes, so whatever he does results at best in an *estimate* of h^2. As we have already seen, a basic way of making this kind of estimate is to examine patterns of correlations involving phenotypes of persons of varying degrees of interrelatedness and then to assign proportions of the total variance to different theoretical components of variance. (The statistically sophisticated reader will guess that what is here being described is an application of analysis of variance.) The proportion he assigns to genetics is his best estimate of h^2.

Jensen's estimate of the "h^2" of IQ

Enough has been said about the assessment of the heritability of any trait to make clear that it involves some educated guesswork. However, if it is a guessing game, it is one played according to generally accepted rules. Fortunately, when the game is played with characteristics like height, a phenotype that may be measured reliably and validly, the outcome of the game tends to be the same, no matter who is playing it. With height and similar characteristics, there is seldom controversy over how to assign phenotypic variance to its several components. With IQ, far more controversy is inevitable.

Nonetheless, the procedure for estimating the heritability of IQ is identical to that employed for height. There are difficulties inherent in the application of the procedure, not the least of which reflects the possibilities of unreliable or invalid IQ scores. Still, the attempt can be made. The best known recent attempt is Jensen's, whose estimate, based on what appears to be a very cautious application of the procedure, was that IQ's heritability is about .8 (Jensen, 1969, p. 51). In other words, according to Jensen, about 80 percent of IQ variance is genetically determined.

After examining relevant studies enabling him to compare various sets of correlations, Jensen arrived at the estimate that $h^2 = .8$ for *people in general*. It is important to note this qualification, for as

Jensen himself admits (pp. 64-65) any particular sub-population might have to be assigned a different h^2 (either higher or lower). In this regard, it is particularly noteworthy that at the time Jensen performed his estimation analysis, the only correlations available were based on studies done with white samples only. We shall find it necessary to return to this point, for it is of considerable significance for the issue of the determinants of racial *differences* in IQ. For the moment, however, we can tentatively accept Jensen's conclusions about the *general* heritability of IQ. Although one could easily quibble with the actual numerical value of Jensen's estimate, the available evidence supports the conclusion that IQ as measured among white American schoolchildren reflects a significant contribution of heredity.

Some selected facts support this conclusion well.[7] For example, for 14 separate studies of identical twins reared together, the median correlation between IQ scores was .87. (Recall that if h^2 were unity, the correlation, theoretically, would be 1.) In four studies of identical twins reared apart,[8] the median correlation was .75. (That it is less than .87 shows that experience counts; that it is not very much less than .87 indicates a potent genetic component.) For siblings reared together, the correlation was .55; for siblings reared apart, .47. Some 25 sibling studies contributed to the last two cited median correlations. Finally, from four studies of unrelated children reared apart (who share neither heredity nor experience), the IQ correlations were not significantly different from zero. This kind of evidence should convince anyone that whatever it is that IQ tests measure, IQ *scores*, although obviously experientially and situationally influenced, also reflect genetic factors.

Some psychologists, however, caution against accepting this conclusion uncritically because of possible faults in the studies analyzed by Jensen in the course of his estimation of heritability. Kamin (1973, 1974), for example, specifically has challenged the twin studies and studies of foster parent/child pairs, studies that are crucial to Jensen's analysis. Kamin has reminded us that there are, first of all, very few such studies that have been done and among them there exist ambiguities even with regard to the ways in which IQ scores were determined.

Two technical points made by Kamin (1974) suffice to cast doubt on these studies. The first concerns all studies employing twins who, by definition, are of the same age. It happens that there is a correlation between age and IQ, which appears in studies employing a number of pairs of twins of different ages. Given this age and IQ correlation, the correlation of IQ between members of twin pairs must be considered partly (and to an unknown degree) an artifact of the age/IQ relationship. The implication of this is that the correlation of IQ across pairs of twins may appear higher than it would be if the age variable could be factored out. That would be possible if studies were done employing a large sample of twin pairs, all of the same age. Unfortunately, this has not been the case.

The second technical point made by Kamin concerns foster home studies, which have revealed relatively low correlations between foster parents and their non-biologically related children. This fact tends to weaken the "nurture" position in this controversy and, by implication, to support the "nature" position. However, according to Kamin, in those few foster home studies in which it was possible also to examine IQ score correlations between the foster children's scores and the scores of their biological parents, it appears that those correlations are only slightly higher than the foster parent/child correlations. Apparently, then, the IQ scores of children reared by adults other than their own parents, while not very predictable on the basis of their foster parents' IQs, are neither very predictable on the basis of their true parents' IQs. So, the data from foster home studies are not as supportive of Jensen's conclusions about heritability as those data were interpreted by him to be.

Other psychologists might still accept Jensen's conclusions about the degree of "heritability" of whatever it is that is reflected in IQ *scores* but would nevertheless caution against thinking of IQ as an index of general ability. No one, after all, has ever seen this ability and certainly no one has ever distinguished the genes that could possibly produce it.

David McClelland, a psychologist who is best known for his careful studies of achievement motivation (another hypothetical trait that predicts success in school and in other enterprises), has cogently expressed the fears of some psychologists that there may not be any such thing as intelligence if that be taken to mean *general ability to succeed in whatever endeavor.* Acknowledging that IQ and other aptitude test scores predict success in the classroom, McClelland reminded us, "The games people are required to play on aptitude tests are similar to the games teachers require in the classroom. . . . So it is scarcely surprising that aptitude test scores are correlated highly with grades in school" (McClelland, 1973, p. 1). The really important question then becomes to what degree do *either* IQ scores *or* grades in school contribute to real-world performances. The answer to this question may well be *Not at all*! If they appear to, it may be the result of certain artifacts. After reviewing the relevant research, McClelland concluded that there isn't even any good evidence that grade point average in school is related to anything other than doing well on tests, nor, conversely, that doing well on tests is related to anything other than grades in school.

What *does* relate to success-in-life is the *level* of schooling attained. Since IQ scores relate to school-level attainments (perhaps only because IQ scores are employed by school admissions officers as a selection criterion), it can easily appear to the unwary that success in life *depends* on (i.e., is causally related to) "intelligence." But IQ scores, school grades, amount of schooling attained, and real-world accomplishments *all* relate to socioeconomic background, so McClelland felt compelled to remind us that the key variable in this whole complex of interrelationships may be a social class-linked *credentials* factor rather than an inherent ability factor.

A person of high socioeconomic background has during childhood what McClelland termed, "easy access . . . to the credentials that permit him to get into certain occupations. Nowadays, these credentials include the words and word-game skills used in Scholastic Aptitude Tests" (McClelland, 1973, p. 6). The same credentials, of course, permit him to enter educational programs and to perform the tasks for which his teachers reward him with good grades. He also has access to the kinds of attitudes, aspirations, and expectations (as well as the money) that pave the way to higher levels of education, which in turn provide him with the degree (more "credentials") and the social contacts that lead to high-status occupations.

The person of low socioeconomic background lacks *all* of these advantages. Accordingly, the well-established relationships involving (a) social-class and IQ score, (b) IQ score and educational level attained, and (c) educational attainment and success in life, had all better be recognized as subject to more than one interpretation. The traditional and popular interpretation *assumes* that there is such a thing as native intelligence and goes on to assert quite naively that poor people are poor because they lack intelligence, that their children inherit their parents' low levels of intelligence and then neither do well in school nor succeed in life *because* of their own, inherited, low levels of intelligence. What McClelland has pointed to as an equally plausible interpretation is that because some parents are poor, their children will be relatively unlikely to learn what has to be learned (skills, attitudes, etc.) in order (a) to do well on tests *or* in school, (b) to advance to higher levels of education, and (c) to end up happily placed in a satisfying occupation.

Certainly, McClelland's "credentials" interpretation fits all the relevant evidence as well as the inherent abilities interpretation. If McClelland should be right, then the very concept of intelligence, as it has traditionally been defined, will have to be discarded, and Jensen's seemingly painstaking effort to estimate its heritability will be discarded with it. If, after all, instead of *general ability* there is only a complex set of learned behaviors (the learning of which is linked to opportunities that vary across families)—all of which behaviors show up in IQ test scores, success in school, *and* success in life—then all the sophisticated estimates of the heritability of intelligence will turn out to have been seriously misleading. The estimates will, after all, have only established that more closely related persons resemble each other more on a particular set of behaviors than do less closely related persons, not *because* they share more similar genes but because they share more similar degrees of access to learning opportunities.

So, even the part of Jensen's analysis which he is generally considered to have performed best—his estimate of the general heritability of intelligence—must not be considered the last word on that subject. As bizarre as it may seem, he may have emerged with a heritability estimate for a non-existent trait!

Let us now return to the social issue to which the question of heritability relates—racial *differences* in intelligence. It can be shown that in regard to this issue, Jensen was clearly wrong. Even *if* we were to accept his conclusions about the heritability of intelligence, there would remain some very good reasons for disputing his conclusions pertaining to the causes of racial differences in IQ test performance.

JENSEN'S ERRONEOUS CONCLUSIONS ABOUT RACIAL DIFFERENCES

With regard to this very crucial question of group differences, Jensen argued that racial variations in measured intelligence cannot be accounted for by differences in environment, and therefore may have to be attributed at least partially to genetic differences. Moreover, he implied that the genetic contribution to racial differences was higher than popularly acknowledged, and he further implied that the magnitude of the genetic contribution to racial differences was somehow related to the magnitude of the genetic contribution to IQ scores generally. It is here that we must strongly take issue with him.

It easily may be demonstrated that the degree of heritability of a trait in any or all populations (the magnitude of h^2 for that trait) has *no necessary* implication for between-populations differences in that trait. Even if h^2 is extremely high for *all* groups (and with regard to IQ we don't know that it is) between-group differences could actually be totally determined by environmental factors! Astonishing as this may seem, a state of affairs familiar to agriculturalists and described recently by Scarr-Salapatek (1971a) makes it very apparent that within-group heritability and between-group heritability are totally independent concepts: "Draw two random samples of seeds from the same genetically heterogeneous population. Plant one sample in uniformly good conditions, the other in uniformly poor conditions. The average height difference between the populations[9] of plants will be entirely environmental although the individual differences in height within each sample will be entirely genetic." (Scarr-Salapatek, 1971a, p. 1286).

There are reasons why this agricultural example is not a perfect analogy for the situation that pertains with regard to racial differences in IQ. As Scarr-Salapatek herself noted, "racial groups are not random samples from the same population, nor are members reared in uniform condition within each race" (p. 1226). This does not, however, detract at all from the point being made, which is simply that the two heritability estimates (within and between) are completely independent of each other.

Note that Scarr-Salapatek is not drawing the analogy in order to argue that h^2 for intelligence *is* high, while h^2 for between-group differences *is* low. Rather, she is reminding us that even if h^2 for IQ *were* very high, this alone provides no basis for concluding that any observed intergroup difference in IQ has to be, as a consequence, genetically determined. As in the plant example, h^2 generally could even be unity (+1.00) with no consequence for intersample differences. The determinants of any between-group difference represent a separate question, which has to be answered with data of quite a different kind from the data yielding estimates of h^2 *per se*.

As Scarr-Salapatek's plant analogy suggests, what must be taken into account if one is to determine the factors that contribute to intergroup differences in any trait, whatever its h^2, are all the similarities and differences in environments surrounding members of isolated samples. To ascertain the determinants of between-group differences in IQ, research must be done wherein all possible determinants are allowed to vary, so that their effects might be noted. Since "all possible determinants" are many indeed, no single study, nor even a good number of studies, will provide definitive answers. Since many of the possible determinants of intergroup differences in IQ are confounded with each other, disentangling them is no easy task. Hence, approaching a satisfactory answer to this question has required the accretion of bits and pieces of fact culled from many different studies, which in turn require careful synthesis. A final, definitive answer is not yet at hand, but as the data accumulate, a consensus is emerging as to how they might best be synthesized. The consensus departs markedly from Jensen's conclusion.

To most psychologists, what appears to be a racial difference is really an "environmental advantage" difference. How do we arrive at this conclusion?

We must begin by acknowledging that there is a very reliable average difference in IQ scores between Whites and Blacks. This average phenotypic difference (which has been manifest typically as a 15 IQ-point spread in favor of Whites) is, by itself, not evidence for either genetic determination *or* for environmental determination. It is simply an empirical fact, a phenomenon requiring explanation. And, as we have already seen, the fact that heritability of IQ may be high among Whites is irrelevant.

To explain this phenotypic difference, there are two competing (albeit mutually compatible) hypotheses, which Scarr-Salapatek has dubbed the environmental disadvantage hypothesis and the genotype distribution hypothesis. With regard to the former, environmental disadvantages include any factors associated with poverty, including those that have biological impacts (like malnutrition) and those that involve deficits in social-learning opportunities (See Birch and Gussow, 1970; Deutsch, Katz, and Jensen, 1968).

As McClelland's argument, summarized earlier in this chapter, has reminded us, there is considerable evidence that experiential factors associated with poverty relate statistically to IQ scores. If such factors impinge *differentially* on Whites and Blacks, it might be those factors that are responsible for most if not all of the average difference in IQ scores between Whites and Blacks.

Not surprisingly, then, most attempts to find an explanation for phenotypic differences in IQ between Whites and Blacks in the United States (which have involved simply comparisons of samples drawn from both "racial" groups) are considered by psychologists to have produced ambiguous findings.

In short, because race and social class[10] are confounded, they are difficult to disentangle in research. However, unless one tries, research findings defy interpretation. If, for example, one merely compared IQ scores across samples drawn from different socio-economic classes, what could one make of mean differences in scores? If IQ scores varied with social class, this finding would, of course, establish that there *are* differences in IQ attributable to social class, but since the races would be disproportionately represented in the social class samples, the "social-class difference" in IQ could partly have been produced by "race." So this paradigm is not very satisfactory. (It is ambiguous for the same reason, of course, that a first-order comparison across races, with social class ignored, is always ambiguous.)

Fortunately, there are ways to disentangle race and class, at least partially. In one approach, one compares samples drawn from different social classes *within* racial groups. Even here, however, there are difficulties, for social class designations within one racial caste may be functionally quite different from the same designations in another racial caste. So, a middle vs. lower class comparison among Blacks is not likely to mean the same thing as a middle vs. lower class comparison among Whites. But precisely for that reason, should the interclass differences turn out to be similar in both races, this finding would strongly support an environmental disadvantage hypothesis.

Another approach is to attempt to hold social class constant while making interracial comparisons. In other words, to compare Black and White average IQ scores for groups of similar social class background. Here, too, there are problems, for it is relatively difficult to find middle-class Blacks to compare with middle-class Whites, and relatively difficult to find lower-class Whites to compare with lower-class Blacks. But if one can overcome them, and succeed in controlling for social class in a biracial comparison, to the degree that one can reduce the phenotypical difference in IQ scores between races (from 15 to something closer to zero) one will have demon-strated that apparent racial differences could well be social class differences.

In research done over the years employing one version or another of these two research paradigms, the findings have consistently supported the environmental disadvantage hypothesis.[11] That is to say, the research outcomes have satisfied most psychologists that one need not postulate racial differences in genetically determined capability to account for observed racial differences in IQ test performance. Enough of that difference is accountable by experi-ential factors that there is hardly any difference left to be explained in any other way. And the fact that there is any left to be explained at all is most likely a result of the impossibility of completely disentangling the confounded factors of race and social class.

Incidentally, it is only with regard to this left-over difference that Jensen quarrels with the psychologists. After reviewing numerous studies of IQ scores of Blacks and Whites in which attempts were made to control for social class, Jensen merely noted that a Black-White difference was still there and concluded that it obviously could not be explained away as a social class difference (*since* social class had been controlled.) But, after reviewing some of the very same studies in 1963, Klineberg[12] remarked how much of the original difference disappeared and how little was left to be explained. The argument reduces to a matter of judgment. Which is more impressive, the amount of the "racial" difference which *must* be attributed to "class" or the part that still remains to be explained? Is it not likely that the residual can also be explained in terms of "class," even though the research findings don't force this conclusion?

Let us next try to establish just what is clear and what is ambiguous, and then try to decide what to do with the ambiguity. To do so, consider the following simplified, hypothetical, but not inaccurate, picture of the state of affairs that prevails as regards phenotypic IQ scores. We shall employ hypothetical versions of the research paradigms just discussed in order to create a more concrete picture.

If one were to test a sample of black children and a sample of white children, with no attention paid at all to social class or related factors, the white sample might earn a mean score of, say, 100, and the black sample a mean of 85. This is represented in Fig. 1a.[13] But, as we know, there is mostly ambiguity in this pair of distributions, because "race" and "social class" are confounded and no attempt has been made to dis-confound them.

(Similarly, as was suggested earlier, if one were to test a sample of higher-class children—say, above the median—and a sample of lower-class children, with no attention paid to race, the former sample might earn a mean of, say, 105, and the latter, 90. Again, since race and class are confounded, the picture is highly ambiguous.)

Now, if one were to test *two* white samples, one above and the other below the social class-index median, one might obtain test means of, say, 108 and 91, as in Fig. 1b. Similarly, when testing two black samples, also selected in terms of the same social class index, the means might be, say, 97 and 83, as in Fig. 1c. In these two studies, represented in Figs. 1b and 1c, an effort would have been made to disentangle race and class. As a result, much of the ambiguity would have been reduced.

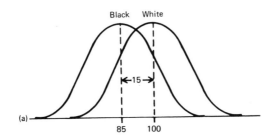

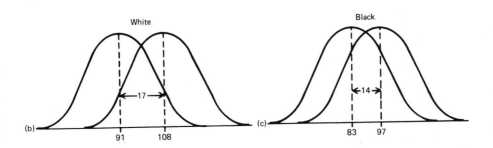

Fig. 1 Hypothetical distributions of IQ scores illustrating how class could account for apparent "racial" differences.

On the basis of the information shown graphically in Figs. 1b and 1c, the situation represented by Fig. 1a becomes considerably more interpretable. Because, as Figs. 1b and 1c show, social class relates to IQ scores in *both* races, with low scorers in both sharing low social class standing, the most parsimonious explanation for depressed IQ test performance is simply social class (and all that the phrase signifies).

The only remaining ambiguity rests in the fact that among children of higher social class standing, there are proportionately more Blacks than Whites with lower IQ scores. This fact shows up in Figs. 1b and 1c, where we find a difference of 17 points between the two white "classes" and one of "only" 14 points between the two black "classes." Another reflection of it in these hypothetical sets of scores is that the white upper-class mean is 11 points higher than the black upper-class mean while the white lower-class mean is 8 points higher than the black lower-class mean. These last calculations, of course, mean first of all that what once appeared as a 15-point "racial" difference has been reduced to something between 8 and 11 points. But it is not yet zero. It is precisely (and only) these residual differences in black and white mean scores, after attempts to control for class, that are ambiguous and generate arguments as to their most appropriate interpretation.

Jensen asserts that the mere fact that there is a residual forces him to conclude that black-white differences cannot be explained totally as the result of social class factors. At first glance, this assertion seems compelling. Jensen also expresses the opinion that the residual difference is most likely a reflection of genetic factors. This opinion is obviously subject to argument. In fact, I shall now argue that Jensen is probably wrong on *both* counts.

First, be reminded that a large portion of what originally appeared as racial differences in IQ scores has been *shown* to be parsimoniously interpreted as social class differences. Secondly, recall that in studies in which one *attempts* to dis-confound race and class (as in our hypothetical examples), the attempt is almost sure to fall short of complete success. Because of the direction of the race and class confound in the United States, any failure to dis-confound is much more likely to have an adverse effect on black scores than on white scores. (The facts that lower-class Blacks are more disadvantaged than lower-class Whites and that a single social class index cannot with equal validity be applied to the two races are similarly relevant to this issue.) So, the residual that Jensen asserts *cannot* be explained away by social class factors certainly *can*, merely by taking into account the extreme likelihood that in all the relevant studies, the social class factors have not been completely controlled.

The argument just developed summarizes the views of many of Jensen's psychologist-critics, all of them in general accord with the views expressed by Klineberg so many times since 1935. Most psychologists agree that most, if not all, of the racial difference in IQ scores is due to inequalities in experience. Despite the popularity of this line of argument, however, it might be wrong. At least, its popularity *per se* doesn't prove it. Science is not a matter of referendum. Besides, the position is not, strictly speaking, a finding; it is what is generally believed to be the most logical *interpretation* of a set of ambiguous findings. Furthermore, the popularity of the line of argument may also reflect an egalitarian value that is widely held by American, and other, social scientists.[14] So, for all these reasons we must ask what if the popular argument is wrong? What if the residual ought *not* be attributed to uncontrolled experiential factors?

Even if it were wrong (and I believe it is right), one still need not accept Jensen's opinion that the residual is best explained in terms of genetics. There is still another well-known experiential factor that is very relevant to the small residual difference in observed black and white IQ scores. This is, simply, the fact that IQ tests are culturally biased. Blacks, like all other non-white Americans, are likely to earn scores that are depressed as a direct result of the built-in biases of the IQ tests themselves. A recent account of the unfairness of tests may be found in the work of Loeblin, Lindzey, and Spuhler (1975). The evidence for IQ test bias against minority samples is enormous; in his 120-page monograph Jensen ignored all of it, saying only that he doubted that cultural biases in the tests could account for the performance of Blacks relative to Whites!

It is hardly a new discovery that IQ tests are biased against any persons whose cultural background differs from that of the test's original normative sample. In 1927, the anthropologist Melville Herskovits (who, like Klineberg, was a student of Boas at Columbia) commented:

> Environmental background, cultural as well as natural, plays a tremendous part in whatever manifestations of innate intelligence an individual may give us through the results from the application of standardized tests to him. Thus it has been found that the American Indians usually rate somewhat lower in psychological tests than whites, and that this holds true when the tests are of non-language variety, where the use of words is reduced to a minimum. But the consideration of the fact that the tests ordinarily used have been constructed by persons of a background different from that of the subjects is usually overlooked; and were there to be presented, for consideration as to what is wrong with a given picture, a six-clawed bear rather than a net-less tennis court, one wonders whether the city-dwelling white might not be at a loss rather than the Indians. (Herskovits, 1927, p. 3)

Over the decades since Herskovits warned that intergroup differences in IQ test scores might tell much more about the tests than about the groups, psychometricians have come gradually to acknowledge that this is so. Several attempts have been made to produce "culture-free" or "culture-fair" IQ tests, but none of these has been totally successful. Clearly, culturally mediated experience interacts with test content to influence test performance. Accordingly, any attempt to assess IQs of non-core-cultural groups is highly likely to result in performance depressions which have to be attributed to deviations in fit between culture and test content. Even on the basis of this fact alone, Jensen's conclusion about the genetic contribution to intergroup IQ differences is clearly unwarranted.

DeVos and Hippler (1969), who reviewed many cross-cultural studies, have made it clear that the once so-called culture-free tests, like the Raven Progressive Matrices and the Goodenough Draw-A-Man test, are unavoidably biased in favor of urban, advantaged Western peoples. As educational and economic conditions anywhere come to resemble those characteristic of the West, test scores reach Western norms (e.g., Husen [1967] showed this to have happened in Japan). For some examples from Africa, see McFie (1961), Price-Williams (1961), and Vernon (1965, 1967); for a comprehensive discussion of the interrelationships between culturally mediated experience and features of testing, see Biesheuvel (1949). All these writings refer to one or another of the many ways in which the testing situation, the tester, his materials, and even his demeanor are likely to elicit performances from non-advantaged Westerners that will yield invalidly low scores.

The kind of evidence that convinces us that IQ tests are culturally biased includes that produced by studies cited years ago by Klineberg which showed, for example, that among northern, urban-dwelling Blacks who had been born in rural southern settings there was a positive correlation between length of time in the less deprived environment of the North and IQ scores (e.g., Lee, 1951). Clearly, the more exposure to the kind of culture in which the tests were first developed, the better the performance on the tests.

To cite one recent study that illustrates the contribution of culture to test performance, there is the very careful comparison by Lesser, Fifer, and Clark (1965) of four ethnic groups in New York City, each divided into social class subgroups, all of whom completed a battery of aptitude tests. A major finding of this study was that the social class variable was a better predictor of IQ score than was ethnic group membership (which fact is consistent with the major argument of the present chapter). More pertinent to the immediate point was the fact that each ethnic group in the study had a unique *pattern* of subgroup scores. For example, Chinese-American children excelled in arithmetic subtests, black-American children excelled in some of the quantitative subtests, and so on. The most parsimonious interpretation of these findings is that each subculture features experiences that are more conducive to performance of certain kinds of tasks than of others.

At this juncture, a minor digression may help propel our argument. Because, as we have just seen, all tests are biased, one can easily conceive of a situation in which black/white comparisons of IQ scores would appear to reveal Black intellectual superiority *vis-à-vis* Whites. One need only employ an IQ test composed of content and test procedure that fits black cultural experience better than it fits white cultural experience.

The fact is, however, that just so long as IQ-testing is employed to predict school performance, it is just as well to continue to use existing tests, since they do that quite well. (They would not do as well, of course, if the procedures and content of schooling were significantly changed.) In fact, as Scarr-Salapatek has recently asserted, "The hypothesis of cultural differences in no way detracts from the predictive validity of aptitude tests for the scholastic achievement of black children. The correlations between aptitude and achievement are equally good in both racial groups" (1971b, p. 1294).[15] At the same time, it should be clear that the tests should not be used in attempts to assess the genetically determined general capacity of *any* groups, especially all those for whom the tests are negatively biased. The results of any such assessment attempts can only be misleading.

A few more words on IQ test bias are necessary. Because IQ tests are designed expressly to predict success in a school system which itself reflects particular cultural biases, the tests *must* be biased in the same way. So, IQ test bias is justified; it is not the result of a deliberate attempt to embarrass particular groups. The bias has negative implications only when a test is used improperly, for any reason other than that which inspired its original construction. This must be kept in mind when one considers the fact that IQ scores predict success in school for Blacks as well as they do for Whites. It does so because the test content resembles school content. But neither success-in-school *nor* test performance reflect genetically determined capacity to the same degree for Blacks as for Whites. And we aren't even sure that genetic *capacity* is involved at all, for anyone!

Let us now take another look at the concept of heritability and relate it to the discussions that have filled the past few pages. Recall that earlier we accepted, despite some objections, Jensen's estimate that h^2 for IQ among white Americans is about .8, but we have seen that this would provide no basis for estimating h^2 among other populations. We also showed that h^2 within a group had no implication for the degree to which group differences might be genetically produced.

Recently, Scarr-Salapatek reported some new research among black children which supports the conclusion that "genetic variability is important in [relatively] advantaged [Black] groups, but much less important in the disadvantaged. Since most Blacks are socially disadvantaged, the proportion of genetic variance . . . [for aptitude scores of Blacks] . . . is considerably less than that of the white children . . . (1971b, p. 1294).

Another way to say this, of course, is that Black IQ scores are more reflective of extra-familial environmental factors than are White IQ scores. As a result, enhancing the environments of Blacks should improve their average performances more than a similar environmental enhancement would improve White performance.

Moreover, no matter how high h^2 may be for a particular population, if that population *also* suffers from unfavorable environmental conditions, improvement in those conditions would raise its mean phenotypic IQ. Even if h^2 were unity, the mean would go up even as the distribution maintained its shape and the persons whose scores are plotted retain their standings *vis-à-vis* each other. The only set of conditions that would make environmental intervention ineffective is a combination of high heritability and *already favorable* environment. Since we know that *neither* part of this combination prevails for black Americans (nor probably for many other groups in our society), the mean phenotypic level of IQs in that population is highly susceptible to enhancement as a result of any program that would provide access to environmental conditions already available to the more favored among us.[16]

What we have just made clear, then, also shows that the great to-do over the heritability of IQ, to which Jensen devoted so much effort in his famous paper, was really much-ado-about-nothing. The fact that h^2 for white IQs may presently be assessed at .8 has no real implication for h^2 among other populations, nor for the question of why one population has a higher mean score than another population, nor even for the consideration of possible social policies. All that we know from a judicious examination of all the relevant research is that environmental influences, both long term and situational, are so important that improvements in environmental conditions will positively affect test performance and the real world accomplishments which test performance predicts.

Accordingly, the mere fact that Jensen did what he did with h^2 may have serious social consequences. While he may have dealt with a complex technical issue (heritability) in a technically competent way, he also drew some dubious implications. His technical competence may have protected him from criticism, even when he dealt with issues beyond his technical specialty. Most important, given that there is so much evidence to support the environmental disadvantage hypothesis, it appears to some social scientists that Jensen was irresponsible to have asserted that genetic, racial differences are *necessary* to account for existing population differences in IQ. As Scarr-Salapatek has put it, ". . . to assert, despite the absence of evidence, and in the present social climate, that a particular race is genetically disfavored in intelligence is to scream 'Fire!' . . . I think, in a crowded theater." (1971a, p. 1228)

SUMMARY AND SOME FINAL OBSERVATIONS

Because the ages-old belief in the inherent inferiority of disadvantaged groups dies hard, this entire chapter has been devoted to an analysis of intergroup differences in intelligence. Both psychometrics and sociocultural psychology were employed in the analysis. It focused on the particular question of the determinants of observed differences in test performance between black and white Americans, primarily because this particular issue is such a socially significant one at this moment in history. This particular manifestation of the group differences controversy was chosen for discussion also because it was the subject of the single best-known recent example of attempts to revive the genetic-determination hypothesis—the work of Arther Jensen.

Jensen's work was shown to be dangerously misleading. His discussion of the concept of the heritability of IQ scores was the strongest part of his work but even that discussion was flawed. As McClelland dramatically suggested, there may even not be any such thing as intelligence to *be* inherited. But even if there were, Jensen's opinions concerning the factors responsible for intergroup *differences* in IQ were found to be indefensible.

Among the reasons developed in this chapter for rejecting Jensen's position on racial differences were:

1. The heritability of intelligence within a given population has no necessary implications for explaining interpopulation differences.

2. IQ may well be more influenced by environmental factors among black Americans than among white Americans.

3. The environmental factors that are known to *depress* IQ scores are far more prevalent in black American subculture than in white American subculture.

4. Negative biasing factors inherent in IQ tests themselves apply far more to black Americans than to white Americans.

A consideration of all these factors leads to the conclusion that Jensen succeeded no better than previous exponents of the racial-inferiority school in his attack on the environmental-disadvantage hypothesis. This hypothesis still stands, supported by several decades' output of psychological research. Whatever may presently be the case, it is entirely feasible that environmental interventions will obliterate phenotypic group differences in performance.

If Scarr-Salapatek was right in saying that Jensen did a disservice to society by providing apparent comfort to the enemies of equality-of-opportunity, perhaps he also served society by inspiring social scientists to offer expert testimony. Of all the attacks on the environmentalist position that have ever been mounted, Jensen's was probably the most sophisticated and most extensively reported by the popular press. As such, it demanded the best effort the social scientists could mount to defend their position. If the position has survived Jensen's attack, as I clearly believe it has, perhaps we will all be spared the redundant recitation of facts that by now should be well known and understood.

There is a final point to be made about the competition between the genetic and environmentalistic hypotheses concerning group differences in IQ. Although the psychologists' evidence says the difference is perhaps entirely environmentalist and Jensen says it is to a significant degree genetic, in the final analysis, for the question of how human beings ought to be treated, it wouldn't matter one bit even if Jensen were right. I quote:

> If a society completely believed and practiced the ideal of treating every person as an individual, it would be hard to see why there should be any problem about race *per se.* . . . The full range of human talents is represented in all the major races of man and in all socio-economic levels. Therefore, it is unjust to allow the mere fact of an individual's racial or social background to affect the treatment accorded him. All persons

rightfully must be regarded on the basis of their individual qualities and merits and all social, educational and economic institutions must have built into them the mechanisms for insuring and maximizing the treatment of persons according to their individual behavior.

The author of this statement is Arthur Jensen.

If society treated every person as an individual. . . . The sad fact is, of course, that few societies do. Worse, when the individual's group membership is employed as a basis of decision as to how he should be treated, inaccurate beliefs about his group's general characteristics often cloud the issue. Treating a person as a member of a particular group is not necessarily irrational behavior. But discrimination based on myth is.

So, fairness of treatment probably *does* depend (even though Jensen agrees it shouldn't) on what is generally *believed* about the reasons for the presently observable characteristics of any individual's group. Whether or not a society will even try to ameliorate the plight of disadvantaged groups (by, for example, a policy of compensatory education) is probably related to beliefs and attitudes about the potential efficacy of such a policy, which, in turn, is related to beliefs about the determinants of behavior, personality, and ability.

In the next chapter, we will discuss compensatory education. We shall see there that Jensen's ill-founded opinions are relevant. We are not yet finished with our analysis of the nativist vs. environmentalist controversy that Jensen's dubious scholarship forced us in this chapter to consider at such length.

NOTES

[1] MacDougall's 1908 textbook *Social Psychology* (the first, along with a text by E.A. Ross in the same year, to be called that) was essentially a laundry list of supposed human instincts. See Beach (1955) for a demonstration of how the roots of the instinct doctrine lie in ancient Western philosophy and theology and how it relates to the concept of an internal force exerting behavioral control. (Recall Skinner's discussion, summarized in Chapter 2, of this same tradition in Western thought.) In Beach's paper he asks, "Why is it that the instinct concept has survived in the almost complete absence of empirical validation?" Later, in Chapter 6, we shall see that it has certainly survived, at least in the works of some popular writers concerned with human aggression.

[2] It should be recalled that correlation is a mathematical summary of the degree to which two sets of scores co-vary. A correlation coefficient can range from 0 (i.e., two sets of scores are independent) to 1 (i.e., knowing several individuals' scores in one set, their scores in the other are also known). The amount of the variance in one set that is predictable on the basis of the other set is the square of the correlation coefficient. Thus, $.7^2 = .49 \cong 50\%$.

[3] The most complete survey of research pertaining to the stability of IQ scores over age within individuals (Bloom, 1964) leads to the conclusion that after age 4, IQ is about as stable as height. As children age, they of course grow taller, but tend to maintain *relative* position on the height dimension *vis-à-vis* each other. So it is with IQ. Only in this sense is there anything "fixed" about IQ.

[4] For example, The American Anthropological Association in 1961 proclaimed, ". . . there is no scientifically established evidence to justify the exclusion of any race from the rights guaranteed by the Constitution of the United States." During the late 1960s and early 1970s, various associations passed resolutions designed to counter assertions of biologically determined racial differences in abilities.

[5] Students would do well to read this article as reprinted in a subsequently issued volume entitled *Environment, Heredity and Intelligence* (Harvard Educational Review Reprint Series, No. 2, 1969). This volume contains numerous replies to Jensen's article, which serve to place it in context.

[6] Note that such predictions exclude statements about the characteristics that will be manifest in any *particular* individual. The predictions all refer to proportions among aggregates.

[7] These facts are drawn from Jensen (1969, p. 49, Table 2).

[8] Nearly everyone appreciates the fact that studies of identical twins reared apart are particularly informative. That there have been so few such studies simply reflects the fact that this phenomenon is rare.

[9] Scarr-Salapatek might better have said *samples*, rather than populations, but the thrust of her example still holds.

[10] I am here using "social class" as a short-hand label for all background variables that the term connotes (income, quality of housing, neighborhood facilities, etc.) Other background variables relevant to a discussion of IQ scores include rural/urban residence, region of origin, proportion of life spent in particular environments, etc. "Race" is also a short-hand term used to refer here to the social castes, Black and White. In the U.S., "Whites" and "Blacks" are not really races in the biological sense of the term.

[11] In this chapter, no attempt will be made to review these studies. They are numerous and have been frequently reviewed, by, for example, Klineberg (1963) and Scarr-Salapatek (1971a, 1971b). It is, therefore, unnecessary to review them here. Instead, in order to make what could be a complicated argument as coherent as possible, it will be developed without the frequent pauses that would be needed in order to cite the relevant studies.

[12] Klineberg's paper is subtitled, "A new look at an old problem." For that scholar, it is indeed an old problem; he has been attending to so-called racial differences in intelligence since the 1930s (see, for example, *Negro intelligence and selective migration*). With all due respect to Klineberg, he has often reiterated his position over a period of 40 years, seldom saying anything new. However, this redundancy was called for. He was correct from the beginning and had merely to reassert well-known facts because other writers, disposed to argue that races are differentially endowed intellectually, either distorted or failed to cite Klineberg's facts. His 1963 paper was just such a needed reaction to Shuey (1958). Klineberg was forced to repeat his argument still one more time (see Klineberg, 1971), this time in response to Jensen.

[13] Although it may not be immediately relevant, it ought to be noted in Fig. 1a that even with a one-standard-deviation difference in means, the two distributions overlap tremendously. As shown in this figure, despite the mean difference, there are many individual Blacks who earn scores higher than those of many Whites. This is a simple and obvious observation, but one that is often lost sight of in discussions that focus only on mean differences.

[14] For evidence that investigators' own attitudes may influence their interpretations of intergroup intelligence comparisons see Sherwood and Nataupsky (1968), who examined the predictability of interpretations on the basis of the interpreters' region of origin.

[15] There are, nonetheless, some good reasons to consider abandoning the widespread use of IQ test scores as selection criteria for educational institutions. As McClelland recently put it, "Why keep the best education for those who are already doing well at the games?" (1973, p. 2). We shall take up this issue in Chapter 4 where compensatory education is discussed.

[16] Some readers may recall that in 1972, the psychologist, Richard Hermstein predicted that if society should succeed in providing equal opportunities to all, the result would be that achievement would become a product solely of genetically determined abilities. Many of his readers were disturbed. The implication seemed to be that our society would become a genetic meritocracy, with status determined at birth. Given what we have learned about h^2, it ought to be clear that whatever Hermstein may have been implying, his prediction was just a tautological consequence of the relationship between the herita-

bility of any trait and its environmental influences. Of course, h^2 must go up as environmental variation decreases. But, as we have just seen, if h^2 goes up as a result of equalizing opportunities, that same program also results in an enhancement of the IQs of the heretofore disadvantaged. So there is no reason to fear that the resultant "meritocracy" would freeze existing Black/White discrepancies in achievement. Contrary to what some of Hernnstein's readers may have thought, his views on the enhancement of h^2 do not constitute a satisfactory argument against environmental intervention.

4
Compensatory education: Can we better educate those who need it most?

"Compensatory education has been tried and it apparently has failed." With these words, A.R. Jensen began his well-known 1969 paper. In that paper, he argued (a) that intelligence is largely a genetically determined trait, (b) that racial differences are also mostly genetically determined, and (c) that therefore compensatory education was doomed to fail. In Jensen's opinion, the relatively low and, in his view, fixed IQs of the disadvantaged would prevent them from benefiting from whatever help might be directed their way.

In the preceding chapter, we saw that Jensen's technical efforts at estimating the heritability of IQ test scores was perhaps wasted effort, especially if his conclusions are taken to mean that intelligence is genetically caused. It may "run in families" to the high degree that it does simply because intrafamilial experiences are more alike than interfamilial ones. In that same chapter we also saw that Jensen was clearly incorrect in concluding that Black-White *differences* in IQ scores were genetic in origin. Hence, on the basis of our earlier discussions in Chapter 3, it is already apparent that there is no logical reason to conclude that compensatory education can't work. It probably could, and there are good reasons to expect that it will. Compensatory education should not only improve school performance, it should also bring about an enhancement of test scores (which, by the way, shouldn't matter as much as some people think). Still, it remains a legitimate empirical question to ask whether and how well particular varieties of educational programs do work. In this chapter we shall discuss this question. By so doing we shall dispel at least two illusions perpetrated by Jensen—one, that compensatory education has been tried enough to give it a fair test; the other, that it has failed.

To accomplish this, we shall have to discuss what compensatory education is, who its targets are, what its goals are, what varieties have been attempted, and what kinds of assessments of them have been performed. We shall also consider carefully what is meant by the popular phrase, *culturally deprived*. Finally we shall consider the very sticky problem of selection of students for places in our educational programs, compensatory and otherwise.

THE BASIC PREMISE OF COMPENSATORY EDUCATION

Many psychologists who have studied the learning process, beginning with Watson and extending through Skinner, have drawn conclusions that are incompatible with the opinions of Jensen as to how competence is acquired. Psychologists, in contrast to Jensen, do not view the child as a vessel with limited capacity into which only so much knowledge may be poured. Rather, they see an active, striving organism, capable of processing an incredible variety of experiences, constantly reconstructing a world-view, a conception of reality, a lifestyle and a set of competences all of which reflect his/her particular complex pattern of experiences. While they acknowledge that all the skills and habits developed by each person reflect both genetic and experiential factors in complex, unique interaction, psychologists consider the experiential factors as far more limiting than the genetic ones.

Jensen himself argues (1969, p. 60) that environment acts like a threshold variable on intelligence. He admits that environmental betterment would improve IQ scores wherever environment presently stunts intellectual development and prevents IQ from reaching its genetically determined limit. Most psychologists see environmental factors as hurdles; indeed, for most psychologists it is these hurdles that are the significant ones. In this regard they differ very much from Jensen. Whereas he is explicitly pessimistic about possible gains from environmental manipulation, most psychologists are quite optimistic. One's degree of optimism about the possible impact of environmental improvement probably reflects one's judgment concerning the quality of existing environment. Jensen seems to believe that few children in the United States reside in truly deprived environments; many psychologists, on the other hand, doubt that any but a few have yet been reared under conditions that maximize intellectual growth. In this sense, most of us are culturally deprived, with some far more so than others. (See the discussion on cultural deprivation in this chapter.)

The policy implications of the environmentalist view are clear enough. To maximize intellectual growth, we must provide more intellectually enriching experiences. Because some have suffered more than others from inadequate environmental stimulation, the "more deprived" must be the primary recipients of "intellectual enrichment" programs. In mounting these efforts, we need not be constrained by existing distributions of IQ scores, nor need we worry because existing data lead to high heritability estimates for IQ. These are facts, but they are facts which merely *describe* present conditions. They say little, perhaps nothing, about what is possible. Existing patterns of IQ scores across various social groups, if *properly* interpreted, tell us that many children have not yet been provided with the kinds of life-shaping experiences which encourage or even permit them to acquire the competence of which they are capable.

This is the basic premise underlying the prescription of compensatory education. As employed here, the prescription applies potentially to *all* children. In practice, however, special efforts would be prescribed for those who, as a result of historical patterns of socioeconomic discrimination, have been prevented from escaping life settings which singularly impede the realization of their potential. For such children, special educational efforts are needed, not to take the place of fundamental social change but to facilitate it by providing the disadvantaged with the tools needed to break loose from the vicious cycle of poverty and unrealized competence.

Obviously, a basic assumption in this line of argument is that the roots of individual failure reside in the social structure. The competition for available rewards is unfair, since many have been prevented from acquiring the skills needed for this competition. As a first step in remedying this state of affairs, the compensatory education advocates would attempt to provide the victims of this unfair treatment with the prerequisite experiences.

To become skilled, they must be exposed to experiences that induce skills acquisition. As Martin Deutsch has put it, "an emphasis on potential environmental influence of intellectual level would promote an educational approach whose aim would be the fostering of intellectual growth . . ." (1970, p. 53). Most psychologists, as we saw in Chapter 3, do emphasize the environmental determinants of intelligence, as opposed to the genetic determinants. Accordingly, they favor educational efforts and expect them to succeed. On the other hand, much of the public and many of its elected officials remain skeptical. As a result, as Deutsch sees it, efforts to mount programs of compensatory education have been impeded by "the residual vitality of the old-fashioned assumption that intellectual level has a low susceptibility to enhancement by environmental means" (p. 53).

The Jensen article must surely have given comfort to the conservatives, who saw it as giving new life to the intelligence-is-fixed assumption. But as Deutsch has noted, new data contrary to that assumption are continually being amassed and "some of the rigidity of the concept of fixed levels has begun to give way" (p. 53). As the old assumption fades, efforts at experiential enrichment via new forms of education for the disadvantaged are being undertaken, but not without difficulty; society so far has seemed reluctant to finance the effort.

Even if psychologists were not as sure as they are that intellectual growth is subject to environmental enhancement, it would be worth experimenting with enrichment programs. Merely by setting aside the fixed-level assumption—neither accepting nor rejecting it—we at least become free to formulate programs that *might* foster cognitive development and investigate which ones, if any, actually work. The compensatory education movement is presently in such an experimental stage. However, it is an experiment that is being conducted in a difficult political atmosphere. There are those who hope its findings will be positive; there are others convinced they cannot be. There are even those who may try to sabotage the experiment, lest its outcomes challenge the view that the status quo is God given. Accordingly, the efforts to date to put the environmental enhancement hypothesis to a practical test must be examined very carefully. It will not be easy to discern the facts, since they are, as we will see later, hard to come by, and many are difficult to disentangle from the attitudes surrounding them.

SOME BASIC FEATURES OF COMPENSATORY EDUCATION ATTEMPTS

Deriving from the psychologists' emphasis on environmental influences on human potential is an emphasis on programs designed to foster cognitive development of children from birth onward.

Inherent in this emphasis is the widely held psychological notion that early experience must be granted a key role in human development. In fact, the notion that the effects of human experience are cumulative permeates the psychological theories that underlie the formulation of compensatory education programs. As applied to compensatory education, the prescription becomes: the earlier a child is directed toward growth-enhancing experiences the better. As one noted developmental psychologist has put it, "... the hope of the future is in the education of the very young" (Kessen, 1970, p. 200).

If that hope is to be realized, the basic premise of compensatory education must be translated into specific strategies based on psychological research findings concerning what can and need be learned by young children as a foundation for subsequent learning. These strategies must also take into account what we know about which aspects of the social environment are most feasibly and fruitfully manipulated.

Accordingly, the first feature of most compensatory education programs is that they provide very young children with training in skills that are believed to be the basic building blocks of more complex skills. Most programs focus on cognitive and motivational responses which specialists in developmental psychology (e.g., Bruner, Piaget, Kessen) have shown to be basic, fundamental prerequisites of competence. The cognitive responses include linguistic habits, concept formation and discovery tasks, and simple sensory-motor responses like those involved in pattern recognition and manipulation of small objects. It is no accident that such skills resemble those that are tested by intelligence and aptitude tests. Neither is it coincidental that these are the skills that teachers reward their pupils for displaying. For these are the skills that earn one points on IQ tests and grades in school, and are the very credentials, in McClelland's sense of that term (1973), that provide entry to society's reward structure.

The motivational responses that are taught in compensatory education programs are also those that our society seems to prefer. These include such acquirable motives as the need to achieve and the searching after praise. Children in these programs are also given practice in performing for delayed, sometimes symbolic, rewards as opposed to immediate, concrete ones.

These happen to be the kinds of skills and motives that the dominant core-cultural group in the United States consistently rewards; children who belong to this group tend to learn these skills pretty much as a matter of course. For children from other cultural backgrounds, opportunities to learn them are very limited. In that sense, such children are culturally deprived.

It is another feature of compensatory educational programs that they are intended primarily for culturally deprived children. Since the concept of the culturally deprived child is subject to possible misinterpretation, a digression to examine the concept closely is in order at this point.

The concept of cultural deprivation

Earlier in this chapter it was suggested that all children are culturally deprived to varying degrees since it is unlikely that any child is provided with the maximum possible enrichment. Education at its current best surely falls short of what is possible. But as popularly employed, the concept of cultural deprivation applies primarily to children of non-core-cultural subgroups and in recent years in the United States it has been applied almost exclusively to black American and other non-White children. Because race relations remains a highly emotional issue in the United States, the practice of labeling non-whites as culturally deprived has been seen by many observers as another in a long series of racial slurs. The term, in fact, does seem to carry the connotation that anybody's culture other than that of the dominant White majority is a deficient culture. This is a most unfortunate and, I believe, unintended connotation.

However unintended, the connotation is there, and some special effort must be made to ensure that the concept is not misused. It is also desirable that the term, *culturally deprived*, not be *overused*—we must not prematurely label all cultural differences ethnocentrically, so that every time a non-White behavioral characteristic is noted it is interpreted as an index of deficiency.

Two eminent developmental psychologists have recently issued this warning in very explicit terms (Cole and Bruner, 1971). They have noted, not without disapproval, that the cultural deficit hypothesis to account for intellectual performance differences between ethnic groups has generally replaced the genetic determination hypothesis. The positive implication of the deficit orientation is, according to Cole and Bruner, precisely what we have argued here is its positive implication; it leads to an early-stimulation intervention recipe based on the faith that the original effects of cultural deficits are reversible and that later potential effects are avoidable.

Since the cultural deficit hypothesis is such an improvement over the discredited and obviously racist biological view, there is the possibility, as Cole and Bruner see it, that the cultural deficit hypothesis will be accepted too uncritically by well-intentioned social scientists, who might inadvertently perceive deficits even where none exist; in such cases, they would—albeit unwittingly—be behaving ethnocentrically. (And, for the victims of racism, it matters little whether the racism they encounter is intentional or unconscious.)

Cole and Bruner note that much social science literature of the 1960s called attention to such characteristics of Black and other non-White subcultures as fatherless homes, stereotyped linguistic interaction among the subculture's members, minimal parental guidance, and the like. These characteristics were often written about in negative terms, and summarized as "failures to provide essential stimulation for cognitive growth." Similarly, there was a tendency to label all the performances of children from these subcultures *whenever* they differed from the performances of white children, as deficient performances since they were taken as the products of deficient experiences.

It is with respect to this tendency that Cole and Bruner urge particular caution. In their article they aired the suspicion that the perception of deficit in many cases is ethnocentric. Indeed, one of the general lessons of anthropology and cross-cultural psychology has been that one of the most common manifestations of ethnocentrism is precisely the tendency to perceive somebody else's way of doing something as less good than one's own way. So they ask us to ask ourselves whether the language spoken by ghetto residents is truly less rich than the language spoken in the suburbs or whether the solutions black children offer to problems they are presented with on a standard IQ test are any less inventive than the solutions keyed by the test-makers as "correct."

A particularly telling point made by Cole and Bruner is that the present state of the art in psychometrics is such that the only real *deficiency* may reside in the tests' ability to measure competence among non-core-cultural peoples. Reviewing many of the arguments presented earlier in Chapter 3, Cole and Bruner concluded that our testing methodology itself may *exaggerate* the degree of difference between "their" behavior and "ours." To the degree that this is so, our error would be compounded. We would not only be identifying "deficiencies" when they ought merely to be treated as differences, we would sometimes be evaluating differences that aren't even differences! Cole and Bruner derive from their analysis of the deficiency of existing aptitude tests some very interesting arguments about what needs to be done if one really wishes to measure competence in diverse cultural groups. For example, they note that one can probably find, for any cultural group, a task on which it will excel, relative to other groups. To find it, the psychologist may have to try many variations of tasks until he can specify which tasks, presented under which conditions, are the ones which elicit "best" performances. Until that has been accomplished, the psychologist cannot claim to be in a position to infer competence. This strategic suggestion is compatible with arguments presented in Chapter 3.

I think the points made by Cole and Bruner are important, and their warnings about unconscious ethnocentric interpretations ought to be heeded. We must be wary about labeling every apparent difference in behavior as a deficit. On the other hand, we ought not abandon the cultural deficit hypothesis, because its policy implications are so much more desirable than those that flow from the genetic determination hypothesis. Besides, there is one sense, at least, in which the cultural deficit hypothesis is probably an excellent statement of fact. Since history cannot be reversed, it must be recognized that we are presently living in a world in which certain values and lifestyles are dominant, with reward systems linked to these values, and certain behaviors are demanded if the rewards are to be obtained. The people who have learned to emit these behaviors earn the rewards; those who have not, don't. Those who do possess power in its most fundamental sense. Those who don't are relatively powerless. As a result, behavioral *differences* become functional *deficits*. Until or unless there is a fundamental change in the power structure, those who lack the skills and habits generating rewards *are* de facto culturally deprived.

Cole and Bruner come very close to saying this themselves when they note that there are "application rules," culturally determined, which govern the display of knowledge in any society. There are also, according to them, certain superficial behaviors, as in the case of verbal habits, which are "amplifiers," permitting the display of competence in ways that are intelligible to those who judge it.

For the present, at least, the judges in society tend to be the testers, teachers, and employers, most of whom use themselves as the standard models of competence against whom all comers are evaluated. It is in relation to them and to the cultural tradition from which they spring that the culturally deprived are deprived.

Those who are culturally deprived in this sense may some day rebel. Many are already rebelling. Others are at least expressing their resentment at being so labeled. But there is considerable reason to believe that over much of the world, not in the United States alone, a good number of the aspirations of the oppressed are consistent with the value systems of their oppressors. Just so long as, and to the degree that, the have-nots aspire to what the haves possess, the have-nots are culturally deprived. If they want a share of what is presently available, and the means exist to help them get it, then those who can provide the help ought to do so. This is the ultimate defense of the compensatory education movement and the ultimate justification of the concept of cultural deprivation. For all of its negative implications, the concept is valid and useful.

Let us return now to our discussion of the basic features of compensatory education.

We have seen that the programs are designed primarily for those who in the normal course of events lack exposure to the kinds of experiences that generate "competence" and lead to "credentials," it being understood that both competence and credentials are socially defined. We have also seen that the programs seek to reach children of very young ages and teach them skills and behavioral styles that are believed to be primary and prerequisite to later cognitive and motivational development.

The last general feature that can be discerned in many compensatory educational programs is the employment of techniques and tactics which, there is reason to believe, might be more efficacious than traditional classroom teaching methods. These include the use of computer assisted instruction, teaching machines, television and other audio-visual devices, and sometimes the involvement in the program of the target children's siblings or parents in an effort to have some impact on the social environment in which the child finds himself during his after-program hours.

In short, then, compensatory education is a class of efforts to provide, in the most effective manner possible, enriching experiences early in life to children who need them the most. Let us now examine two examples of programs that possess some of these characteristics.

TWO EXAMPLES OF COMPENSATORY EDUCATIONAL PROGRAMS

One program that displays some of the features described in the preceding section of this chapter was undertaken during the 1960s by the National Laboratory on Early Childhood Education. It has been described in a psychological journal by the Laboratory's director (Miller, 1970). Having noted that IQ score discrepancies between black and white children in the United States have been found actually to *increase* with age throughout childhood, Miller and his colleagues properly inferred from this that environmental inadequacies comprise the primary causal factors responsible for the depressed performances of black children. Because the effects of these environmental inadequacies appear to be cumulative and progressive, Miller's team chose early childhood as their point of intervention. Their target group was composed of three-year-old children.

In accord with the general philosophy of compensatory education, the program was built upon an environmental intervention. The aspect of the child's environment attended to in the program was what Miller labeled the *instrumental environment*, "those significant others who mediate between the child and the objective environment . . ." (p. 180). Since at age three the instrumental environment comprises primarily the family and, more particularly, the mother, mothers were identified as the primary instrumental agents. The total program, then, was composed of two interrelated curricula—one for the children, the other for their mothers.

The content and pedagogical techniques of the children's curriculum reflected goals that were articulated by the Laboratory team members on the basis of their interpretation of various relevant research findings. Taken into account were studies showing that particular ethnic groups appear to impart different emphases on particular skills (e.g., Lesser, Fifer, and Clark, 1965; see review in Chapter 3), that language patterns vary with social class (e.g., Bernstein, 1961), that lower-class children typically learn to prefer concrete rewards (e.g., Terrel, Durkin, and Wiesley, 1959) while more advantaged children learn early in life to work well for abstract rewards (e.g., Zigler and de Labrey, 1962) and many other published studies that reveal characteristic performance differences across groups of differing ethnicity and social background.

Accordingly, for example, one of the program's goals was a modification of the children's reward expectations. This goal was sought by employing a procedure where concrete rewards were employed early in the program but were gradually eliminated as abstract rewards were substituted for them. This programmed reinforcement change was applied to the training of a variety of skills, including the recognition of sets, discrimination of rough and smooth objects, and a number of other basic discriminatory behaviors which involved imposing a linguistic order on things in ways that would enhance the child's ability to perceive order and predict future occurrences on the basis of that perception. The justification for this kind of curriculum was, in Miller's words, "As predicting skills increase the child enhances his opportunity for innovative and creative solutions to the problems which confront him. This is the essence of competence" (1970, p. 188).

Mothers, in turn, were taught techniques that could be expected to stimulate the child to engage in the kinds of behavior he himself was learning. For example, mothers were encouraged and taught to read to their children. The emphasis in the mothers' phase of the program was as much on motivational and emotional response patterns as on particular cognitive skills.

The mother-child pairs enrolled in the program were recruited from low-income families living in an urban housing project. The typical measured IQs of the mothers was 85, and most of them were employed as domestic servants. The program lasted for about two and one-half years, until the target children entered the first grade of elementary school.

A critically important concomitant of this program was a fully integrated research project. Indeed the program itself was an experiment, planned in advance, with the research design dictating some of the program's features. These included the use of four groups of children who were differentially treated. In only two were mothers involved in the manner described above. Another interesting research-design feature was the employment of the target children's younger siblings as the focal group in whom cognitive performance improvements were sought. This search for "vertical diffusion of competence" was a most intriguing aspect of the pre-planned evaluation of Miller's program. Later in this chapter, we shall examine some of the findings of this evaluation. For the present, we are concerned only with its content and strategy, in which respects it is an exemplary program, one which its designers characterized as "a comprehensive development curriculum to foster socialization for competence" (Miller, 1970, p. 184).

Another example of a compensatory education program is one

built around computer-assisted instruction, which, its designers were convinced, "offers a mode of instruction ideally suited for students from educationally deprived areas" (Suppes and Morningstar, 1970).[1] By 1970, the Institute for Mathematical Studies in the Social Sciences at Stanford University had designed and implemented numerous computer-based tutorial programs in mathematics, logic, and foreign languages for college, high school, and elementary school students at various sites. Programs undertaken by the Institute which fit our definition of compensatory education include some in a California elementary school in which more than 80 percent of the pupils were from non-White subcultures, and some in schools in New York City and in McComb, Mississippi. The computer programs employed in these various tutorial efforts were described as having been based on "psychological variables known to have a positive effect on learning" (p. 223).

The crucial variable affecting learning, of course, is the reinforcement schedule. Typically in the computerized curricula employed by Suppes and his colleagues, reinforcement in the form of praise and permission to proceed was programmed to be consequent upon success, while the withholding of such reinforcement was the typical consequence of failure. For example, the first time a student failed to produce a correct response, that failure produced the message from the computer, "NO, TRY AGAIN." A second failure produced "NO, THE ANSWER IS (whatever it is). TRY AGAIN". Note that via this program, progress by the student is impeded by failure, but not stopped. As Suppes and Morningstar describe the student-computer interaction, it includes the following characteristics:

"(a) An active response mode
 (b) Immediate knowledge of whether the response is correct
 (c) An opportunity to correct an incorrect response
 (d) An opportunity to respond correctly after the correct response has been supplied
 (e) Total time per problem controlled by the student, and
 (f) Provision of a permanent copy of the problems and a summary of the student's performance which he may take and use as he pleases. . ."

That such features are likely to contribute to learning, whether the learner be from a culturally disadvantaged background or not (and whether the teacher be a computer or merely [sic] a wise human being) is a prediction that may confidently be derived from empirical research on the learning process that has accumulated in psychological journals since the days of Watson and Thorndike, who preceded the present writer by four professional generations! But does it work for disadvantaged children? There is, of course, no reason why it shouldn't. And, indeed, pre-test post-test comparisons of both treatment and control groups available to Suppes and his colleagues led them to conclude "that CAI computer-assisted instruction is an advantageous tool for compensatory education" (p. 227). We shall see later whether this evaluation was valid.

From what we have seen in these two examples, compensatory education is no more or less than the application of the best available knowledge of how basic cognitive skills and supportive motivational patterns are instilled in children who, in the normal course of events, are not likely to have competence-enriching experiences, particularly early in life when they need them the most. From all that we know about teaching and learning, compensatory education should work, and many who have tried it believe they have shown that it does. But evaluation is a difficult matter, and it is to evaluation of compensatory education that we now turn.

EVALUATION OF COMPENSATORY EDUCATIONAL PROGRAMS

A newspaper editorialist once reminded a President of the United States who led an effort to scuttle federally assisted social programs that if one man drowns because he has been thrown a rope too short to reach him, it is not very logical to conclude that more lives would be saved by telling all men henceforth to sink or swim for themselves.

Assistance programs might appear to fail merely because they have not been given a fair test. (They might also appear to succeed for the same reason.) What constitutes a fair test is a very complex matter indeed, involving all of the issues we first discussed in Chapter 2 when considering the role of the psychologist as evaluator. The issues are those of internal and external validity.

The parable of the drowning man and the too-short rope has an *external* validity moral. A life-saver that can't possibly reach a stricken swimmer is hardly representative of the "treatment" that the advocates of life-saving have in mind. All ill-funded, poorly staffed and otherwise inadequately realized programs are likely to fail. To generalize from *their* failure to the likelihood of failure of full-fledged programs that have never been tried is sheer folly, and it is either stupid or shameful for persons in authority to do so.

But this is obvious; at least it should be, for it is so simple. More complex, of course, are the evaluation problems that exist even when a program is just what its advocates intended it to be. These are problems in research design, some of which are rather complex ones that plague efforts to evaluate compensatory education. As an illustration, we will now consider how regression artifacts are likely to invalidate evaluative research in this field.

In Chapter 2 we referred to the possibility of regression artifacts as internal validity threats to evaluation research. We learned in that chapter that the term *regression artifact* refers to changes in scores that are due merely to test-retest unreliability, which necessarily results in extreme scorers on one administration of a test being likely to earn less extreme scores on another administration of that same test. Since this phenomenon constitutes a threat to efforts to evaluate compensatory education programs and has, in fact, invalidated more than one such effort, we must review here what we know about regression artifacts and how they might be avoided. Then we can examine one example, an evaluation of a compensatory education program known as Headstart, wherein regression artifacts almost certainly made the program look less successful than it may really have been, and another example, an evaluation of the Sesame Street TV program, wherein regression artifacts could have made the program look more successful than it really was!

The single best treatment of regression artifacts as a threat to evaluations of compensatory educational programs has been provided in a study by Campbell and Erlebacher (1970). In it they make several basic facts very clear. First, they point out that regression to the mean is, under certain conditions, inevitably a property of two or more distributions of scores. Consider the following:

1. A test is administered twice to the same sample of people.
2. The correlation between the resultant two sets of scores is less than perfect, as shown in Fig. 2, which is a scatter-plot. Each point in the plot represents the two scores of a single person in the sample. In the hypothetical case depicted in this figure, the mean score on Test administration #1 is 5 and on administration #2 the mean score is 6. (Any pair of means would do, even one in which the means are identical, but for simplicity let us assume that a small average improvement in scores occurred from the first to second administration.) If everyone in the sample scored one point

higher on second testing than he did on first testing, the two sets of scores would have been perfectly correlated and all points in the plot would have fallen along the solid diagonal line that appears in the figure. But in this hypothetical example, as practically always in reality, this doesn't happen. Instead, the dotted line in the figure, known technically as the "regression line of testing 2 on testing 1" which connects the average score on testing 2 of people who earned various scores on testing 1, summarizes the degree of correlation—actually obtained. As drawn here, it indicates a positive correlation that is clearly greater than zero but to some extent less than plus-one.

3. Because the test-retest correlation is less than perfect, the regression line falls, as it does in Fig. 2. If one examines the regression line, it will become apparent that persons who scored either very low or very high on the first testing, *on the average, score closer to the mean on testing 2 than they did on testing 1.* Moreover, this "regression to the mean" is proportional to the extremity of scores on the first testing; i.e., it is greater for people who were extreme scorers on the first administration of the test than it is for people who scored near the mean on that test administration. This feature of the situation is shown clearly by the vertical arrows in the figure.

4. It should now be clear that whenever two measurements are made and these measures are not perfectly correlated, there will be some regression to the mean. It is more marked for those persons who obtain the more extreme scores on one of the tests. None of this is magic; it is pure mathematical necessity, inherent in correlation.

Now, be sure to understand that what has just been described is *regression to the mean*, an inevitable phenomenon in two or more distributions of scores that are less than perfectly correlated. This phenomenon becomes an *artifact* only when the regression to the mean is misinterpreted as evidence for some real change in the trait being measured.

A particular kind of research design which many evaluation researchers have found tempting to use is particularly susceptible to this artifact. The research design in question is one in which subjects are selected for a program (and into its evaluation study) *because* they possessed extreme scores prior to the program.

To make this a bit more concrete, look again at Fig. 2 and consider the following:

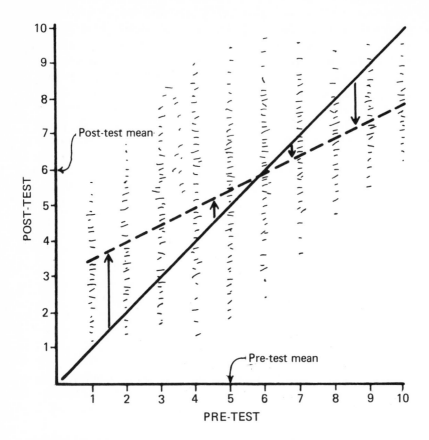

Fig. 2 Pre-test–post-test scatter plot illustrating regression-to-the-mean. Extreme scorers on the pre-test tend to be closer to the post-test mean (see text for explanation).

At a particular moment, which we may call Time 1, we administer an abilities test to a sample and select from it those individuals who score relatively low—say below 3 on the first administration of the test; these scores are now plotted in Fig. 2. We then attempt to teach them something over a period of time and retest them at the end of the period, Time 2. We find that, on the average, the sample shows a statistically significant gain in score from Time 1 to Time 2. However, since the two administrations of the test are not perfectly correlated, some of the gain shown by those who had extreme scores at Time 1 must reflect regression to the mean. If we complete our research design by adding a group of *non*-selected persons (who may resemble in some respects members of the experimental group, but whose scores at Time 1 ranged both below and above 3), it should be clear that our experimental group would be more subject to regression to the mean at Time 2 than the control group. If, at Time 2, the between-administrations improvement in average score for the experimental group was greater than that for the non-experimental group, we might be tempted to conclude that our teaching program was responsible for some of the experimental group's improvement. However, the degree of apparent success of the program, as indicated by whatever difference in improvement between the two groups shows up, would be an overestimate. That difference would have been inflated by the regression to the mean among the experimental group scores. Such a study clearly involves a regression artifact.

Consider another example. Suppose we recruited people from a given population into a program without regard to their pre-test scores but knowing that they were all from a population that had a relatively low mean score. Then suppose we constructed a control group by selecting people from another population known to have a higher mean score, but with only low scorers selected in order that our control group matched our experimental treatment group. In this set of circumstances, the control group would be more subject to regression to the mean than the treatment group, and our research would once again be invalidated by a regression artifact. This time, however, the control group would appear to improve more than it really did, and the real difference between the two groups would be masked. As a result, the obtained group difference would be an underestimate of the treatment's efficacy.

It should now be apparent that regression to the mean can produce artifacts in evaluation research with resultant errors of interpretation in *either* direction. If either of two groups being compared is more subject than the other to regression to the mean, the differential regression will comprise an artifact.

There is another way to say this. If the two groups being compared in fact have different true means to begin with, the scores in each group will be regressing toward different means. When we compare groups we think we have matched (but have actually selected extreme scores in one group but not in the other), we have differential regression to the mean and, therefore, an invalid study.

THE REGRESSION ARTIFACT IN SOME COMPENSATORY EDUCATION EVALUATIONS

Operation Headstart

Campbell and Erlebacher (1970) have shown how a regression artifact very likely invalidated the Westinghouse/Ohio University evaluation of the Headstart Program of the 1960s. The evaluation resulted in findings that suggested that the program was actually deleterious! This appeared to be so because a "matched control group" of children who did not participate in the program scored higher on some relevant tests than did a group of children who did participate in the program. Part of this better performance of the so-called matched control group, however, was probably a reflection of the fact that they were selected from a population that, on the average, was more able than the treatment group. Thus, the control group was more subject to regression to the mean than the experimental group, and this differential regression constituted an artifact.

In contrast to the hypothetical examples we just discussed, the research design employed in this evaluation study did not include pre-testing. So, it must now be made clear that the phenomenon of regression to the mean does not require actual pre-testing. As was noted earlier, *whenever* we compare groups, only one of which is composed of selected extreme scorers, we will have differential regression to the mean. It is easier to understand the concept of regression by reference to actual pre-test post-test comparisons, but even individuals who are only tested once can obviously be thought of as having some level of potential performance before they are tested, and the population of which they are a part obviously has some true mean score even if it is not ascertained by an actual pre-test. If people from the same population are selected because they resemble in some ways persons from *another* population with a lower true mean, these selected persons, whenever tested, will probably score higher than they were expected to. Why? Because they would in effect be regressing to a mean higher than the mean of the population of the group with which they were supposedly matched.

In the Headstart evaluation study, the control group was composed of children very painstakingly searched out by the researchers, because they matched program children in sex, socioeconomic status, and racial-ethnic background. The researchers obviously expected that these children would have scored as low as the program children had the two groups been tested with neither being exposed to any treatment. In any event, the researchers assumed that they were comparing two groups from the same population after the program was finished, who differed from each other only in that one group had participated while the other had not. But the matching technique probably did not succeed in creating two equally able groups from the same population. Instead, it most likely resulted in a control group that was a *selected* subsample of a more able population than the population of which the treatment group was a sample. Therefore, part of the enhanced performance of the control group reflected the fact that it was composed of persons from a more able population than that of the treatment group. It must be concluded, therefore, that the study was invalidated by a regression artifact. Its findings, accordingly, are ambiguous.

To properly evaluate Headstart, all children who qualified for entry into the program should have been randomly assigned to treatment and control groups. Such randomly created groups would have been equally subject to regression to the mean, since they would have been samples from a single population. No regression artifact could then have resulted. Instead, as we have just seen, the control group was composed of selected persons, while the treatment group was not.

In fact, the research design employed was one of the weakest possible. Called an *ex-post-facto* design, it should probably never be used (see Campbell and Stanley, 1963 for a critique), since it yields uninterpretable results if one is trying to determine the effectiveness of a treatment. Therefore, to use it is to create the illusion of scientific evaluation when in fact there has been none. Worse, when the ex-post-facto design is employed as it was in the Headstart evaluation—a comparison of post-treatment scores with the scores of an untreated sample drawn from a more able population—the outcome will have the extremely serious consequence of making the program look deleterious. Unfortunately ex-post-facto designs are still widely used. A most desirable outcome of efforts by psychologists like Campbell to broadcast their research design talents would be the enlightened avoidance of this research design by program evaluators in the future.

A recent review of several studies designed to evaluate compensatory education programs (McDill, McDill and Spreke, 1969) showed positive outcomes for all studies involving random assignment to treatment and control groups; in studies without random assignment only one in five showed significant positive effects. It is most encouraging that compensatory education's efficacy was demonstrated with the research design that all researchers advocate as the one that is least subject to threats of invalidity, and it is noteworthy that the "failures" of compensatory education appear in evaluations that were very much subject to invalidity threats. Indeed, the studies reviewed by McDill *et al.* in which random assignment was not employed were probably all invalidated by the use of a superior control group (Campbell and Erlebacher, 1970, p. 195). The faulty evaluation of Headstart, then, was not an isolated event. Quite generally, it appears, the evaluation of compensatory educational programs has been plagued by regression artifacts that serve to mask their effectiveness. In the better studies, the effectiveness is obvious. What a waste it would be if we were to abandon beneficial programs because we had failed to evaluate them fairly. Indeed, in the long run, a society wastes more that way than by investing in programs that don't work. Inventing something efficacious only to fail to demonstrate its efficacy can be a most serious setback. The likelihood of its being reinvented must surely be dampened by its apparent failure.

In societies led by persons drawn from the relatively advantaged there are likely to be strong forces of resistance to programs that would benefit the relatively disadvantaged. If those who lead are given evidence that the programs they don't wish to fund are "not working," they are very apt to cite that evidence in support of their decisions not to fund similar programs. Since most societies are led by the relatively advantaged, it seems politically realistic to expect that compensatory education efforts will not gain a firm toehold, even on an experimental basis, so long as attempts to evaluate them fail to show how good they are. Indeed, the political cards are probably stacked against them even when they are shown to be efficacious. It is therefore particularly compelling that those who evaluate them give them a fair evaluation.

It is also true, of course, that evaluators ought not err in the opposite direction. Societal harm of a different kind could also result from the raising of false hopes. Since those who advocate compensatory educational programs obviously want them to succeed, there is the danger that they will perceive more success than really exists. The political atmosphere surrounding various programs for the poor was optimistic in the United States during the 1960s. It was a time of considerable innovation in attempts to foster cognitive development of children of pre-school age. Did the optimism of the day somehow make those innovations look too good? Let's examine one of them.

Sesame Street

The most glamorous compensatory educational program launched during the optimistic years of the Johnson Administration in the United States was the television series known as Sesame Street. In many respects it was a model program, and it certainly reached more children than any other single attempt at teaching basic skills to those likely not to learn them elsewhere. In its first year of televising, Sesame Street's one-hour program segments were shown five days per week for 26 weeks on 170 television channels across the United States. On some channels the daily segments were shown several times each day. The audience numbered millions.

The content of the program segments was jointly planned by educators, media experts, and development psychologists (see Lesser, 1970, 1974) so that the program might complement other kinds of early childhood education available to children between the ages of three and five years. The planners made special efforts to provide the kinds of experiences that less fortunate children in American society would not be likely to receive elsewhere. Thus, the prime target population was composed of the relatively disadvantaged—e.g., the 80 percent or so of American three- and four-year-old children who were not in nursery school. A strategically significant fact about this population was that the children who comprised it practically all had access to a television set and were already quite used to watching it. If ever a medium seemed to have some intrinsic attraction for children, TV surely did in the 1960s. So it was decided to employ this medium in a nation-wide effort to reach the disadvantaged.

It was also known from audience analyses that TV watching by children was not altogether independent of program content. Among the most gripping materials that filled the tube and speaker were commercials—the ubiquitous, repetitive, short stories designed to make one product appear to stand out from its competition. For whatever reason, these fairy tales attracted and held the attention of pre-schoolers at least as much as any other content on TV.

Accordingly, Sesame Street segments were rapidly paced, commercial-like units, each devoted to teaching a single element. The content of the segments was chosen in accordance with findings that had been accumulated in research on basic cognitive processes (object recognition, shape discrimination, concept discovery, and the like). Thus, the planners and sponsors of Sesame Street hoped, and had reason to expect, that the program would be watched, attended to, and enjoyed by a large audience who would also learn and learn how to learn to a degree not previously possible.

By 1970, it was possible to complete an evaluation of Sesame Street's short-term effects. This evaluation, conducted by the Educational Testing Service (a private, non-profit enterprise), yielded a positive pronouncement. The evaluators declared Sesame Street "a success in terms of its own goals—to teach some simple and complex skills to children of pre-school age" (Carnegie Corporation, 1971, pp. 5-6). Was it really? Might not the evaluation have been biased by over-enthusiasm? In view of the difficulties of evaluation with which we have been concerned in this chapter, ought we not examine this study very skeptically? Let's look at it.[2]

Before the Sesame Street program was begun, tests were designed to elicit performance of the various skills—recognizing, naming, sorting, classifying, etc.—that were the targets aimed for in the bulk of the program. These tests were administered to about 1,000 children before and after the 26-week program was telecast. With such a pre-test post-test design, which necessarily involved children with different television-watching habits, various confoundings and other threats to validity were possible. And, as any reader of this chapter must be aware, a regression artifact could cloud the interpretation of any findings that might result from a before-and-after study, depending, of course, on how it was done and what precautions were taken either to avoid it or assess it. A key consideration in this regard is, as the reader should already know, the manner of selection of children whose performances were assessed and compared.

For example, if Sesame Street were to have been evaluated by comparing performances of its "graduates" from particular neighborhoods with performances of children from similar neighborhoods who seldom or never watched the program, the bias in such a comparison would be in the direction of artifactually enhancing Sesame Street's efficacy. Why? As Campbell and Erlebacher argue, "In any given neighborhood, it will be the more competent homes that know of the program's existence, and make certain that their children get to see it" (Campbell and Erlebacher, 1970, p. 203).

In fact, the evaluation of Sesame Street by the Educational Testing Service was subject to this methodological problem. The degree of watching could not be controlled by the researchers; they could only compare the performances of children whose degree of watching was under their own or their parents' control. Whatever variables relate to decisions to watch, were therefore confounded with actual watching.

However, this state of affairs was unavoidable, given the simple fact that the program was broadcast. The research design therefore simply had to accept this fact and make the most of it. What the researchers did was to make their basic comparisons across four groups of children, divided into quartiles according to how much they watched the show. Those in the first quartile watched rarely or never, while those in the fourth quartile watched an average of more than five hours per week (which is equivalent, in effect, to exposure to the total program); children in the intervening quartiles (the second and third) watched for intermediate amounts. For the sample as a whole, and for those identified by the researchers as disadvantaged and relatively advantaged children examined separately, one very clear finding emerged: those who watched the most performed the best on the post-test.

For example, among the disadvantaged children, those in Quartile One answered, on the average, 14 percent of test questions requiring the identification of letters of the alphabet, while those in Quartile Four answered 62 percent correct. This difference, and others like it, was statistically significant, so the investigators could conclude that the amount of viewing of Sesame Street was positively *related* to performance. But, of course, significant differences like this one would not, by themselves, justify a conclusion that the superior post-test performances of the watchers was *caused* only by the fact of their having watched the program. If the children in Quartile Four were somehow more competent to begin with than those in Quartile One, the superior performance of the former group could not be attributed solely to the fact that they watched more of Sesame Street.

In this particular instance, the researchers would have been in a quandary if they had *not* had pre-test scores. Fortunately they did, and these scores showed that watching Sesame Street was related to levels of competence prior to watching. For example, on the relevant pre-tests for the two groups mentioned in the preceding paragraph, Quartile One averaged eight percent correct on letter identification and Quartile Four averaged 19 percent correct. So, the watchers were more competent to begin with, which meant that watchers and non-watchers were not truly comparable. But this was known, thanks to the pre-test scores, and therefore it could be taken into account in the interpretation of the post-test differences. And indeed it was. With all of the data we have now mentioned arrayed in the following table, it should be clear that the investigators could conclude, as they did, that children who watched Sesame Street the most "started out ahead, ended up ahead, and gained the most in-between" (Carnegie Corporation, 1971).

	Before	Percent Correct After	Gain
Watchers	19	62	43
Non-Watchers	8	14	6

There is no reason not to be impressed by the difference in gain scores, which is so obvious in these data. It is particularly impressive that those children who started higher gained more. Surely one must credit Sesame Street with some impact. On the other hand, the same array of data in our little table makes it evident that (1) the impact of the program varied with the initial competence of the viewers, and (2) watching *per se* cannot be taken as the sole reason for improvement in relevant skills.

It appears, then, that the most prudent conclusion from data such as these is that watching Sesame Street, a worthwhile activity for all, is particularly valuable for those who by age three have already acquired some of the very skills which Sesame Street stressed. Moreover, even that conclusion must be tempered by the following observation: since watching itself is correlated with pre-program competence, those who watch more are also likely to be exposed more to experiences *other* than Sesame Street which have similar positive impacts. Hence, the marked difference in gain scores shown in the table cannot safely be attributed *solely* to the Sesame Street program.

This should be apparent just as soon as we consider what we know and what we don't know about watchers and non-watchers. We know from the pre-test scores that watchers are better performers than are non-watchers. What we *don't* know about either group is what other personal characteristics may have contributed to their watching patterns. Were the children in Quartile Four more highly motivated, more responsive to stimulation, more subject to parental encouragement, more practiced in verbalizing? Any one of these factors could make them *both* more responsive to Sesame Street and more likely to respond to *other* experiences (not a part of the Program at all) in ways that would result in performance gains over the 26-week period that intervened between testings. That we know them to have been relatively competent before this period makes it very likely that to some degree at least they were also as we have just described them. Accordingly, we have to emerge with a somewhat qualified conclusion from the Sesame Street evaluation: better informed and more skilled pre-schoolers who, for whatever reason, watched more of Sesame Street, displayed larger gains in relevant performance areas than did less well-informed and less skilled pre-schoolers who, for whatever reason, watched it less. While all the measured gains cannot be attributed solely to the program, watching it produced some gains for all, more for those who watched it more (who were also more competent to begin with), and watching it certainly did no harm to anyone.

However qualified this conclusion is, it still follows that if ways could be found to transform non-watchers into watchers, they would benefit. Accordingly, our analysis of the Sesame Street evaluation permits us to conclude on a positive note.

Before we truly conclude our analysis, we had better check one more possible bugaboo—the possibility of a regression artifact. There was, after all, some matching involved in the evaluation design, and didn't we see earlier that matching of subjects is a research design feature that can open the door to regression artifacts?

The matching in this study involved socioeconomic characteristics. Watchers and non-watchers (self-selected in this regard) were from matched neighborhoods, but, as we have already seen, they were differentially able individuals. Given this state of affairs, a regression artifact could easily have crept in to invalidate the whole study. Had, for example, the watchers been compared with a *selected* sample of non-watchers, selected *so that* their pre-test scores matched the pre-test scores of the watchers, a regression artifact would surely have resulted. Knowing what we do know about non-watchers—that they come from a population with a lower mean pre-test score than the watchers—selecting relatively high scorers from that population would have produced a control group that would have been particularly subject to downward regression to the mean. The end result would have been an artifactual enhancement of the post-test difference between groups.

Fortunately, as we know, this was not the case. While the research design that was used did not avoid the confound between watching and initial competence, it did escape the possibility of regression artifact. It is, however, instructive for us to notice how easily a regression artifact could have invalidated the Sesame Street evaluation, had the evaluators employed a version of the design used in the Headstart evaluation. It is also interesting to recognize that while the regression artifact in the Headstart study made it look less effective than it really was, the same artifact, had it been present in the Sesame Street evaluation, would have made Sesame Street look better than it really was.

So, we have now seen that the Sesame Street study avoided regression artifact. We have also seen that motivational and experiential differences between the groups actually compared were probably partly responsible for the superior gains made by the watchers. On balance, it is probably safe to conclude that the Sesame Street evaluation was well done and that it showed a degree of superiority in gains by watchers compared to non-watchers that demonstrates that the program must be credited with some positive impact. While differential characteristics of watchers and non-watchers were present, they were measured and obvious, and could be taken into account when the gains were assessed, as we have done in our analysis of the study. Thus, the Sesame Street evaluation results, tempered by the qualifications here suggested, are quite impressive. It is a program that has been shown to be effective.

This judgment is reinforced by a number of subsidiary findings reported by the evaluators. For example, the basic finding to which we have referred several times—that among disadvantaged children, the more watching, the greater the test-score gains—was replicated several times in different regions of the United States, including urban centers in Massachusetts, North Carolina, and Arizona, and a rural area in California. The regional generality of the finding increases our confidence in it, as does the fact that the same finding was obtained for a sample of relatively advantaged children in suburban California.

A remarkable substudy was one involving 43 Spanish-speaking children in the southwestern United States. This group, which happened to be a sample of high watchers, actually surpassed the average score on the post-test of the advantaged suburban sample just referred to. And the gain scores of the Spanish-speaking sample were among the highest recorded, the consequence, of course, of very low pre-test scores and very high post-test scores. In this case, the most significant knowledge transmitted by Sesame Street to these children was probably knowledge of English, the language of the program and the tests. With this in mind, one must acknowledge that this sample's low pre-test scores were an obvious result of test bias. Still, the finding of significant, large gains is impressive.

Finally, some age comparisons make the basic finding look quite solid indeed. Although Sesame Street was aimed at four-year-old children, in the evaluation study samples of three-, four-, and five-year olds were tested, both before and after. The division into amount-of-watching quartiles was done separately for each age group, which resulted in some very provocative findings. For example, on the post-test, the highest watching (Quartile Four) three-year olds had higher average scores than three-fourths of the four-year olds (those in Quartiles One, Two and Three) and higher than one-half of the five-year olds (those in the first two quartiles). Those same three-year olds had earned lower scores than any of the older groups of children on the pre-test. So now we have a comparison showing not only greater post-test and gain scores for a group that watched more of Sesame Street; this time the higher gain scores were earned by children who started out with lower pre-test scores.

Putting all of this together makes a quite impressive package. The initial evaluation of Sesame Street's first season was competently done, not altogether free of design complications, but probably free of regression artifact, and it yielded results that may safely be taken as evidence that watching it helped children improve their competence in areas measured by most so-called aptitude tests.

We have now completed our examination of two efforts to evaluate particular compensatory educational programs. Both evaluations were subject to internal validity threats; in one they were largely avoided, while in the other they were not. Sesame Street's evaluation was planned before the program started, Headstart's was not. With pre-planning, it was possible to avoid regression artifact, even though recruitment into the Sesame Street program was such that a small slip by the evaluators would have introduced the artifact. It did invalidate the Headstart evaluation, which prompts the plea that pre-planning of evaluation become a regular feature of such programs. Without it, evaluators rely on an ex-post-facto design, for which there is no defense.

The second lesson inherent in our analysis of these two evaluations derives from the fact that the invalid evaluation made the program look bad, while the well done one revealed the program's benefits. This suggests that when evaluation is carried out properly, compensatory education will probably be shown to be effective. Whether or not that is the case, we ought to give compensatory education the fairest evaluation of which we are capable.

SHOULD COMPENSATORY EDUCATIONAL EFFORTS BE CONTINUED?

Our lengthy exploration of methodological difficulties inherent in program evaluation research has shown, I think, that a cautious reading of the available evidence supports the view that compensatory education can work. Admittedly, not many well-funded, well-designed programs have been implemented by the 1970s, and the attempts to evaluate them have not been altogether satisfactory. But what little we know about the programs that were tried should encourage further experimentation. Unless the egalitarian rhetoric of democracy is only rhetoric, unless the democratic ideal of providing equal opportunity is not one to which society truly aspires, educational intervention among disadvantaged children is clearly called for. The little evidence we have, based on the few attempts we have made, is justification enough for a sincerely democratic leadership to sponsor more and better attempts.

The political psychologist has at least two roles to play in this effort. As expert witness, he/she must testify about the implications of all that we already know about the cumulative effects on cognitive development of early stimulation, effects that clearly indicate that well-designed compensatory education *will* work. As policy evaluator, he/she must insure that the programs actually undertaken are given a chance to demonstrate their effectiveness. If the political leadership still condemns compensatory education to the mounting pile of untried social welfare programs, that leadership must bear the burden of guilt. Perhaps the political psychologist can help to make that burden too heavy to bear.

A POSTSCRIPT:
COMPENSATORY EDUCATION FOR EVERYBODY?

Earlier in this chapter it was stated that cultural deprivation is a relative thing. Unless we are prepared to argue that the educational system we have already developed is the best of all possible systems, we should acknowledge that no children yet receive all they could receive to enhance their competence to contribute meaningfully to society's enterprises and to derive maximum benefits from its available rewards. Thus, all may be said to be culturally deprived, some more than others, of course, but all to some degree.

This line of argument leads to the suggestion that compensatory educational innovations ought be tried not only for the effects they might produce among the most disadvantaged but also for the insights that might emerge as guidelines for educational innovations throughout the system. In short, and for example, computer-assisted instruction might prove to be worth trying for all our children.

When one begins to speculate on possible educational innovations for children generally, it becomes tempting to consider some ideas articulated by the psychologist David McClelland, and referred to in the previous chapter in our discussion of aptitude tests and competence. Before concluding this present chapter, let us examine some of McClelland's ideas.

ON THE MISUSE OF APTITUDE TESTS AS SELECTION DEVICES

In both this chapter and the previous one, aptitude testing was central to our discussions. We saw in Chapter 3 that aptitude test scores are the raw data that had to be assessed in our attempt to get to the heart of the question of intergroup differences in intelligence. We found that misinterpretations of test scores have resulted in serious exaggerations of the fixedness of current trends in performance. Earlier in the present chapter, we saw that aptitude test scores comprise the raw data that were employed in attempts to assess the efficacy of compensatory educational programs and we found, among other things, that scores change with experience.

As every American student knows well from personal experience, aptitude test scores are also employed in another way that relates to education; aptitude tests are very often employed as selection devices by officers of admission to educational institutions. A potentially great irony is involved in the use of aptitude tests for school admission purposes. The irony resides in the fact that such tests were originally designed for precisely this purpose, that predicting success in school is what such tests do best, yet . . . their employment for this purpose may well be the most unfair practice of all!

This rather startling notion was spelled out by McClelland (1973) in remarks directed to the Educational Testing Service (the same organization that evaluated Sesame Street), which is best known as the institution that administers the College Board and Graduate record examinations. To appreciate McClelland's fears, we must review some of his ideas, already referred to in Chapter 3. There we saw that his interpretation of considerable research led him to assert:

1. that aptitude tests may not assess general ability at all and that the concept of general ability may be a myth;
2. that aptitude tests merely assess acquired competences of the kind reflected in the "games" played both on tests and in school;
3. that aptitude test scores correlate with grades in school but that neither of these quantitative indices can justifiably be interpreted as causing success in life;

4. that the amount of formal schooling completed and other acquired "credentials" *do* correlate with success in life; and
5. that the key to understanding this whole complex of relationships may well be differential access to credentials, with the difference varying across social classes.

If all this is true, then we must consider the possibility that we are not justified in using aptitude tests in selecting applicants for college entrance, because, by so doing, we transform the tests into "instruments of power over the lives of many Americans" (McClelland 1973, p. 1), and this would be an obvious misuse of power if it resulted in unfair discrimination. It would, moreover, be a misuse of *unwarranted* power if it were to perpetuate, as McClelland fears it does, "a mythological meritocracy in which none of the measures bears significant demonstrable validity with respect to any of the measures outside of the charmed circle" (p. 2).

The essence of McClelland's dramatic warning to the testers-cum-selectors appears in the following quote:

> ... why keep the best education for those who are already doing well at the games? This in effect is what the colleges are doing when they select from their applicants those with the highest Scholastic Aptitude Test scores. Isn't this like saying that we will coach especially those who already can play tennis well? One would think that the purpose of education is precisely to improve the performance of those who are not doing very well. So when psychologists predict on the basis of the Scholastic Aptitude Test who is most likely to do well in college, they are suggesting implicitly that these are the "best bets" to admit. But in another sense, if the colleges were interested in proving that they could educate people, high scoring students might be poor bets because they would be less likely to show improvement in performance. To be sure, the teachers want students who will do well in their courses, but should society allow the teachers to determine who deserves to be educated, particularly when the performance of interest to teachers bears so little relation to any other type of life performance? (McClelland, 1973, pp. 2-3)

If current admissions practices do favor those who need education the least and, more significantly, discriminate against those who need it the most, then a bona fide effort at compensatory education must include a thoroughgoing reassessment of the use of aptitude tests for entrance to educational programs. What may require compensation more than anything else is the selection procedure, which has for so long reserved the credentials for the privileged; aptitude tests lie at the heart of that procedure. McClelland sees a continuing legitimate and useful role for tests in education, that of evaluating educational progress; if he is right about the illegitimacy of their use in college entrance selection, this use ought to cease.

In areas other than education one might still be justified in employing tests to screen applicants for particular jobs—a procedure that would be economical. Selecting those persons who display relatively high degrees of job-relevant skills would result in considerable savings in training. But such economic considerations ought not govern selection for places in schools. We ought not select as students those on whom teachers need devote the least amount of effort because the students already have the skills the teachers want them to learn.

It seems to me that one of the most straightforward implications of McClelland's strong but carefully reasoned attack on testing-for-selection-to-be-educated is that access to education must be opened up at all levels. During the late 1960s, open-admission policies were in fact implemented in a few universities and discussed very widely in academic circles and elsewhere. The inevitable difficulties experienced by many minority-group members whose earlier experiences had not included the opportunity to learn the skills required for good performance in college were interpreted by many to demonstrate the folly of this experiment. Not surprisingly, many of the critics of open admissions were quick to express worry about "the lowering of standards." But if McClelland is right, and if the difficulties experienced by the heretofore disadvantaged are not the product of fixed, limited, "general ability," then the real consequence of an open-admissions policy will not be a lowering of standards but a raising of effort expended by teachers.

Open admissions would be folly only if those who are difficult to teach are in fact unteachable because they are really as unintelligent as their test scores make them appear to be. But, as we have seen, and as McClelland once again reminded us, there may not even be any such thing as native intelligence. Even if there is, there is no good evidence that intelligence or aptitude tests measure it!

Hence, in very courageous language, McClelland asserted to his psychologist colleagues, "Psychologists should be ashamed of themselves for promoting a view of general intelligence that has encouraged such a testing program . ." (1973, p. 4).[3]

As I read McClelland's line of argument, it is extremely compatible with views expressed in this chapter: most, if not all, of our children need better education than they are presently receiving; the potential of many children to benefit from education has been grossly underpredicted by tests; access to educational opportunities must be very much expanded so that those who need it are as able to get it as those who don't need it as much; and the specialists whose job it is to provide education must expend more effort and employ better teaching techniques than they have. It is compensatory education in this comprehensive sense that I believe is supported by all the issues discussed in this chapter.

Before leaving the topic of contemporary education, we must consider one more line of argument about what better and more widely available schooling can and cannot be expected to accomplish. It is an argument that has been well researched and widely disseminated, most notably in publications by Coleman *et al.* (1966), Jencks *et al.* (1972) and Mosteller and Moynihan (1972). Taken together, these works make clear that differences among schools in various quality indices are less importantly related to educational achievement and subsequent "success" in life than many advocates of education-as-equalizer may have assumed. These studies show that inequalities in attainments are produced mostly by non-academic, socioeconomic factors that impinge so potently on individuals that it seems impossible for better schooling alone to undo the damage produced by poverty and cultural deprivation. It is abundantly clear, in any case, that schools as presently staffed and constituted are not up to the task, particularly if the task is defined as the realization of the American value of equality of opportunity throughout all arenas of life. The Jencks report in particular makes it explicit that unless our society purposefully embarks on a vigorous, determined income redistribution program, the equal opportunity value of American society will remain a tantalizing and frustrating myth. Ethnic and social class discrimination (because they are prime contributors to income inequities) must also be eliminated before true equality of opportunity may be realized. Without such fundamental changes in American society, enrichment of educational experiences, in the view of these social scientists, will only be of marginal value.

It is impossible to dispute this thesis, although one can challenge any apparent implication that compensatory education efforts should be abandoned. One must acknowledge that equalization and enhancement of classroom experience, brought about in the prevailing societal context of profound inequities in most other aspects of life, would comprise a feeble effort compared to what is needed. Whether what is really needed will be done or not depends on our society's (and its leaders') willingness to do it, and about that there must be profound doubts.

By the same token, and in recognition of the complexities of the total picture, equalization of educational experiences may well be an appropriate initial target.[4] As a strategy for overcoming the complex inequalities of opportunity in America, educational reform may well be the most politically feasible of alternative starting points. As with all vicious cycles, entry must be made at a point of vulnerability. While the immediate effects of better education for the less well off may be small, there will be some effects, some of which may trigger other necessary societal changes. Indeed, if the initial effects are smaller than are widely hoped for, this "failure" could, if properly exploited, induce subsequent efforts in other, more promising directions (such as those advocated by Jencks *et al.*—some form of income maintenance).

For the present, then, this writer is confident, even in the face of these three negative assessments of the role education can play in equalizing opportunity, that continuing improvements in schooling, particularly, but not exclusively, for the socioeconomically disadvantaged, ought to be vigorously pursued. What a child acquires in school may not improve his or her chances for the good life unless what happens to the child at home and in the neighborhood is also positive, but what happens at school may gradually have an impact on what happens elsewhere. Just as it is naive to assume that schooling *per se* can mask the negative impacts of poverty and all that goes with it, it is surely incorrect to expect equality to be attained without the very best possible education for all.

That equality of educational opportunity does *not* prevail in American society, which manifestly proclaims egalitarian values, probably reflects some long-standing prejudices about the differential quality of human groups, some of which prejudices were challenged in Chapter 3. Let us now move to Chapter 5 and examine in greater detail the general phenomenon of prejudice and its many practical consequences—discrimination. The effects of discrimination, one of which has been to impede the realization of the potential of education, transcend the school system and impinge on every arena of social life.

NOTES

[1] The efficacy of computer-assisted instruction was perhaps first demonstrated by Omar Khayam Moore in a fascinating series of experiments in which pre-school children were taught to read and write by interacting with an electric typewriter linked with a display screen. Moore also achieved some success in training brain-damaged persons in these linguistic skills by employing his computerized typewriters (see Moore, 1965). It has long been apparent to psychologists who are knowledgeable about the principles of learning that the reliability and rigor of a computerized dispenser of reinforcements is unmatched by any human teacher. There are, of course, other characteristics of human teachers that make it unlikely that they will be displaced by computers, at least so long as members of the teachers' own species sit on school boards. When the school boards are controlled by computers, it may be an altogether different story!

[2] For detailed accounts of the ETS evaluation, see Ball and Bogatz (1970, 1972) and Bogatz and Ball (1971a, 1971b). A more detailed summary of this evaluation than is given here may be found in the study by Lesser (1974, pp. 212-230).

[3] The particular testing program that prompted this remark by McClelland was a three-hour intelligence test employed by the Massachusetts Civil Service Commission for selection of candidates for training as policemen. Candidates who could define "quell," "pyromaniac," and "lexicon" would be more likely to become police recruits. This is an unusually dramatic instance, perhaps, but McClelland's point holds generally.

[4] Even this requires a form of redistribution of income. See Miner (1963) for a revealing picture of school funding inequities.

5
Intergroup relations: The psychology of prejudice and discrimination

The two preceding chapters of this book, which deal with the intelligence and educability of particular human groups, contain many references to ethnic prejudice. Beliefs about the capabilities of whole groups of people, and the advocacy of particular educational policies relating to them, are, of course, part of a whole network of attitudes and behaviors that comprise intergroup relations. Much interaction among groups, in every arena of social life, involves ethnocentric values and discriminatory practices. It is this broader topic of intergroup relations that will concern us in the present chapter.

By analyzing the general phenomena of intergroup prejudice, perhaps we can better understand why so many people continue to believe that some groups are less educable than others. We shall see how this particular distortion of reality is imbedded in a whole complex of beliefs that affirm that various groups are generally less valuable than others. We shall also discover how the dissemination of ethnocentric beliefs serves to sustain the very social conditions that appear to validate them. Thus, we shall see how prejudice sets in motion the familiar mechanism of the self-fulfilling prophecy, thereby creating a truly vicious cycle, oscillating from prejudice to discrimination and back again.

Before undertaking an analysis of the general phenomena of prejudice and discrimination, let us set the stage by considering one more study that was done in a schoolroom setting. It demonstrates that the relatively poor performance in school that we noted in earlier chapters to be characteristic of many culturally disadvantaged children could in part be due to teachers' expectations that such children would do poorly (Rosenthal and Jacobson, 1968).

The psychologists who performed this study provided teachers in an urban, abilities-tracked primary school with a test that was allegedly capable of measuring their pupils' capacities for intellectual gain. Actually, this "new instrument" was a standard IQ test. In a contrived but casual manner, Rosenthal and Jacobson communicated to the teachers the names of several children, whom, they alleged, the test had revealed as likely to make rather marked gains in the course of the school year. In actuality, these names were selected at random, with five children in each classroom (in six grades and in both fast and slow tracked classes) designated as "academic bloomers." The psychologists, but not the teachers, knew the actual test scores of all the children, including those named as especially promising pupils. Thus, on the basis of subsequent administrations of the tests by the teachers, it was possible for the psychologists (but not the teachers) to determine the real gains in scores made by all children.

In every grade, there were average gains made by both groups of children—those who had been named as promising *and* those who had not been—but the designated children, particularly in the lower grades, showed larger gains. For example, among the children who were in the first grade at the end of the study, the average gain of the alleged "bloomers" was nearly 30 IQ points, while that of their non-designated classmates was about 12 IQ points. It would be hard to find a clearer example of a self-fulfilling prophecy.[1]

Moreover, when the teachers were asked to rate all their pupils along a variety of "personality" dimensions, the designated children were described as more likely to succeed in later life, happier, more curious, more interesting, better adjusted, and less in need of help. The ratings given to the undesignated children were not only lower generally, but the more IQ points such children had actually gained, the *less* favorably they were rated! Finally, the least favorable ratings were given to undesignated children with the highest IQ gains who happened also to be in "slow-track" classrooms.

To account for the differences in average gains in IQ scores between the designated and undesignated children, Rosenthal and Jacobson, with the teachers' ratings in mind, suggested that the teachers probably communicated, in subtle ways, their own expectations to the children, who, in turn, developed consonant expectations and motivations. The teachers' ratings certainly appear to indicate that the teachers were prejudiced. It also seems clear that both the experimenters' intervention and the two-track system operative in the school contributed to the prejudice.[2] Finally, it appears that halo effects compounded the problem for the children for whom there existed no expectation of unusually good performance. Putting all this together, the impression is that children who are not expected to do well in school are subject to subtle pressures that serve to constrain their performance. In those cases in which they nevertheless do well, they are viewed as displaying undesirable behavior! It is as if they are damned if they do and damned if they don't.

Self-fulfilling prophecies, like the one we have just considered, are among the most serious by-products of prejudice and, simultaneously, one of the psychological mechanisms which sustain it. But it is only one of many. Prejudice is the larger phenomenon, and it will require a lengthy analysis.

PREJUDICE AND ITS CAUSES

Introduction

To prejudge is not in itself necessarily wrong. No one ever knows enough, so all of us must sometimes either act on the basis of incomplete information and untested assumptions or not act at all. However, whenever we *claim* to know without really knowing, or whenever we refuse to accept what *is* known and act as if it were not so, then we have gone beyond prejudging. Then we are behaving prejudiciously. When prejudice involves whole categories of human beings, it breeds sociological and psychological pathology and leads to behavior that ranges from unfair discriminatory practices through apartheid to genocide.

Sadly, it must be noted that such behavior patterns are common throughout the world, sometimes with the support of governments. Even in nations where the official rhetoric deplores ethnic prejudice, there is little evidence that people generally understand prejudice or are able to control its costly manifestations.

If intergroup prejudice is poorly understood, it is not for lack of attention by social scientists. The research literature contains many pertinent findings and many theories as to the causes of prejudice. However, the findings are diverse and the theories range rather widely.

They include some facile and misleading notions like the Rodgers and Hammerstein view that children "have to be taught to hate and fear",[3] and a generalized Marxist view that prejudice is deliberately perpetrated by capitalists who need a degraded class of men to exploit. We shall see in this chapter that while there is a germ of truth in these and other theories, they err in at least two ways. They have elevated what may be a particular *feature* of prejudice to the status of its cause and, of more practical import, they have implied solutions that are so utopian that they are, in fact, not solutions at all. We shall therefore attempt to show in this chapter that a better understanding and control of prejudice inheres in the recognition that prejudice and discrimination have multiple causes and that all societies, even those composed of "men of good will," inadvertently produce prejudice to one degree or another as a concomitant of socialization practices.[4]

To recognize this will be to admit the pervasiveness of prejudice and its deep-rootedness in the most basic processes of society. At the same time, to recognize it is the essential prerequisite to dealing with prejudice realistically and effectively. That it must be dealt with realistically perhaps goes without saying. Its social and psychological costs are enormous. It can be shown that no one benefits in the long run from the social products of prejudice and discrimination, for these products constitute heavy burdens, including psychological ones, on the oppressed and oppressor alike.

In response to this pervasive and serious problem, psychologists can suggest remedies worth trying. Among them may be strategies that will permit the political psychologist to succeed where others have thus far failed. We shall conclude this chapter with an examination of some of these strategies. Like all remedies, their prescription depends on diagnoses, so let us turn now to a close examination of alternative ways to conceptualize prejudice and its causes.

Some theories of the causes of prejudice

Like most other behavioral phenomena that have interested scholars for centuries before the emergence of modern psychology, prejudice and discrimination have been considered from a variety of viewpoints. As a result, a number of overlapping theories of prejudice have been generated by scholars in diverse disciplines. These theories are seldom contradictory; rather, they are complimentary, differing from each other primarily in emphasis. As Allport[5] has viewed the contemporary state of affairs that has resulted from the existence of this set of theories, ". . . what we have at our disposal is a ring of keys, each of which opens one gate of understanding" (1954, p. 208).

Unfortunately, however, exponents of one or another theory often treat it as *the* theory of prejudice, and as such they can encourage *mis*-understanding. As Allport's more generous assessment of these theories suggests, it might be better to treat their totality, or at least some combination of parts of all of them, as the basis for a theory of prejudice. Accordingly, what we shall do in this section is examine a number of approaches, then comment, criticize, select, and reject, and by so doing attempt to construct a position that reflects the accumulated wisdom of earlier theorists. In this review of earlier theories we shall be guided primarily by the work of Allport and that of D.T. Campbell.[6]

The numerous theories that have been reviewed by Allport and by LeVine and Campbell all contain true statements about prejudice. However, our concern in this chapter is with the manner in which these theories attempt to *explain* the existence of prejudice. In this regard, each one is in itself inadequate.

Some of the theories argue from an historical perspective, claiming that each instance of prejudice has its unique historical roots. Of course, it does. Every phenomenon has its unique history. But it is most unparsimonious to argue that every phenomenon is caused by a unique chain of historical events. To do so is to fail to look for generalizations without which we would be helpless to predict and control the phenomenon. Historical analysis may help us to understand how a particular ethnic group may have become a target of prejudice at some particular time in some particular place, but it cannot tell us why intergroup prejudice is so widespread a phenomenon, spanning such a multitude of histories.

Some writers with an historical bent have transcended unique history telling to generate one or another kind of theory that is merely historically oriented in the sense that it views prejudice as something handed down over time and across generations. In such theories, the question of *ultimate* origins is ignored but proximal "causes" are implied. Thus, a theory asserting that we have prejudice only because we are ignorant of peoples other than ourselves lays the proximate blame for prejudice on the doorstep of all the educational institutions—the schools, the churches, and all other information-dispensing authorities—which have existence prior to that of any given generation that falls under their influence. It leaves untouched the question of ultimate cause and imples that more and/or better education would eliminate prejudice.

Theories that claim that we have prejudice only because we are raised in certain ways (for example, by authoritarian parents) also have an historical bias. In this instance, the historical emphasis is accompanied by a psychological sophistication which enhances the apparent attractiveness of the theory. But the theory is still faulty to the degree it implies that *if only* history had not produced authoritarian child rearers, there would be no prejudice.

A final example of an historically oriented (and pseudo-psychological) theory is the popular one referred to earlier as the Rodgers and Hammerstein view. It says, in essence, that the present generation becomes prejudiced only because it is taught to be prejudiced by the previous generation . . . which, in turn, presumably, has been taught this by its elders. The implication? *If only* children were not taught to be prejudiced, they would not acquire the habit.

Still other theories, which may or may not contain historical perspectives, maintain that certain classes of people deliberately teach prejudice since they have something to gain from its propagation and maintenance. In general, these theories simply point to villains, evil men of power who indoctrinate the masses in racial, religious, and ethnic prejudice. There is, of course, no doubt that history is replete with demagogues who encourage hatred and whose careers are sustained by its manifestations. However, theories that grant to villains the status of the *cause* of prejudice go well beyond merely noting the sad fact of their common existence. The theories imply that *if only* there were no such people, there would be no prejudice.

Somewhat more sophisticated versions of these bogey-man theories imbed the argument in economic terminology. Thus, some theorists have argued that certain economic systems require prejudice in order that there be availabe an exploitable class of denigrated drones. While it may be true that prejudices at least indirectly accomplish this function, as a theory of the cause of prejudice it would be tenable only if it could be demonstrated that prejudice was unique to, or at least more common in, societies characterized by particular economic systems. Unfortunately for the theory, this has not been demonstrated. Although prejudice may serve to sustain exploitation, there is little reason to believe that if exploitation could somehow be done away with, prejudice would disappear. While it may also be true that individuals who discriminate and oppress sometimes gain short-run economic advantages, there is considerable evidence that prejudice exists among people who are themselves economically and otherwise disadvantaged.

Finally, there are theories that focus on the fact of power differentials between discriminators and those discriminated against. Such power differentials surely exist, but they are probably more accurately viewed as a consequence of prejudice and, once established, a hindrance to its reduction. But there is little reason to believe that intergroup prejudice is not also characteristic of groups with relatively equivalent power, so it would be difficult to argue that power differential is either a necessary or sufficient cause of prejudice.

All of these theories, as we have already acknowledged, are attractive because they have a ring of truth to them. This, however, reflects only the fact that the theories describe very familiar features of prejudice. By elevating one such feature to the status of cause, each theory misleads. Even more seriously, the theories force us to adopt a profoundly pessimistic outlook with regard to the possiblity of reducing prejudice. For all these theories imply that prejudice will not be reduced until and unless some very unlikely, utopian changes are brought about. They say, in essence, that we must continue to endure prejudice until education is greatly improved, or until an economic revolution occurs, or until the world is rid of all its villains. All such changes, it may be stated without testimony, are extremely visionary.

Thus, the various points of view just reviewed must leave us dissatisfied. They are inadequate as explanations of prejudice and depressing when considered as guidelines for ameliorative action. Can we find, in psychological theory, something better?

A theory of prejudice based on ethnocentrism

The point of view around which the rest of this chapter will revolve is that intergroup prejudice derives from ethnocentrism, which, in turn, is a virtually inevitable concomitant of socialization pressures which exist in all societies.

Segall summarized this point of view as follows:

> In any society the young must be taught that "our way of doing things is right." That "our way" is but an arbitrary selection among numerous alternatives is considered a dangerous piece of knowledge, should it become widespread. Rather, "our way" tends to be purposely identified with God's way, or at least the

God-given way for true men to behave. When sooner or later the socialized individual discovers others who don't behave that way, it is usually too late for him to conclude anything except that those others must be less human than he. Conveniently, this conclusion serves also to provide legitimized targets for repressed hostility, or scapegoats.

The essence of socialization is the suppression of impulses— e.g., "Thou shalt not kill" . . . But we all come to understand that the commandment really means that we shouldn't kill anyone like ourselves. And all around us there are people not like us. Sometimes we make them wear yellow armbands so that we may be sure to recognize them. More often, physical or cultural differences make it easy to find them. All too often, we devise discriminatory practices to maintain and exacerbate existing differences, just to be sure that we don't lose sight of our targets. It is no coincidence that the racist admits that what he fears most is the "mongrelization of the races." Think how difficult it would then be to know whom he could hate with impunity!" (1967, p. 45)[7]

There are many parts of this argument that require delineation. We must consider ethnocentrism, socialization, repressed hostility, scapegoating, and several other social psychological mechanisms, one at a time, before the argument may be understood. The various parts of the argument represented by these several concepts derive from the works of many different social scientists, some of the most notable being William Graham Sumner, Sigmund Freud, and John Dollard.

A. *Ethnocentrism:* The concept of ethnocentrism, first used by the turn-of-the-century sociologist, William Graham Sumner, was defined by him as "the view of things in which one's own group is the center of everything, and all others are scaled and rated with reference to it . . ." Employing the term analogously to egocentrism, which connoted individual narcissism or self-love, Sumner asserted for societies that, "Each group nourishes its own pride and vanity, boasts itself superior, exalts its own divinities, and looks with contempt on outsiders. Each group considers its own folkways the only rights ones, and if it observes that other groups have other folkways, these excite its scorn" (1906, p. 13).

The essence of ethnocentrism, thus, is a positive attitude toward the ingroup accompanied by and contrasted with negative attitudes toward one or more outgroups.

Some ideas inherent in Sumner's concept are important for our analysis of prejudice. Particularly so is his stress on the universality of tribal self-love and the implication this has for intertribal (or more generally, intergroup) hostility. For if every tribe considers itself loveable, it must consider other tribes who behave differently as *less* loveable and, in some instances, even despicable. In other words, tribal self-love makes possible and is simultaneously fueled by, intertribal hostility. In still other words, a sense of ingroup requires a consciousness of outgroup; the feelings toward one are the reciprocal of the attitudes toward the other.

Another of Sumner's notions was that ingroup members must suppress any *intragroup* hostility which might arise, in order to be able to take collective action against nature whenever the need arises. Intrasocietal cooperation, Sumner noted, requires the renunciation of individual impluses.[8] This particular idea is an echo of some well-known Freudian views of societal dynamics; in Freud's version, the implications of this idea for our analysis of intergroup relations are even more obvious.

B. Displaced hostility and other Freudian mechanisms: Many of Freud's ideas, slightly modified from their original versions, contribute to the argument we are developing. A central notion of Freud's was that each of us begins life as a narcissist, who must be taught to control his individual impulses. To Freud, socialization, the process which brings this about, is simply a regimen designed to convert the individual narcissist into a civilized being, a person who, as Sumner would have put it, is trained to engage in "antagonistic cooperation" with his ingroup mates (1906, p. 16).

Freud's view of socialization stresses, however, that the civilizing process entails numerous psychic costs, not the least of which is ambivalence toward socializing agents. Freudian theory, as is well known, attributes the negative component of this ambivalence, hostility toward parents, to sexual jealousy, an idea that was most fully developed in the hypothesis of the Oedipus Complex. One can ignore that particular idea, which many contemporary psychologists reject, and still accept Freud's *observation* that children develop, for whatever reason, hostility toward parents and other authority figures.[9]

A likely explanation for this hostility is that it is generated by the fact that such persons force us to suppress our narcissistic impulses. These persons are, of course, the very people who we are also taught most deserve our love. And love them we do, if only because, for a time at least, they indulged us in the exercise of those very same impulses. Thus, we both love and feel hostile toward them. This produces conflict and tension, which demands that somehow the hostile feelings be denied, suppressed, redirected, or otherwise controlled. How is this accomplished? Contributions by the sociologist John Dollard help us to move beyond the germinal ideas of Sumner and Freud and to develop an answer which reveals further the dynamics involved in intergroup relations.

C. *Dollard's extension of Sumner's and Freud's ideas:* Dollard, a sociologist who blended Freudian theory and learning theory in several works written during the 1930s and 1940s at Yale University, put several ideas together in his analysis of intergroup relations (1938). He began by noting the necessity for restraint of impulse in social life everywhere. He acknowledged that hostility would result from this restraint and that the hostility would, in the first instance, be directed toward the source of the restraint—i.e., toward parents and other socializing agents. He then reminded us that the direct expression of such hostility, because it would be a threat to ingroup solidarity, is itself restrained. So, that tabooed hostility is repressed and becomes subject to displacement. Up to this point, Dollard's analysis is essentially a restatement of Sumner and Freud. At this juncture he introduced an important additional point.

Dollard postulated that in every society there is likely to be some kind of institutionalized process which encourages or at least permits the displacement of hostility. Often, if not always, the process involves the designation of an outgroup, some "foreigners" who can be detected, isolated and pointed at as legitimized targets of hostility. Thus, in effect, do societies instill brotherly love through the encouragement of neighborly hate.

Among the many different kinds of evidence one could cite to support this notion is the common practice employed in child-rearing of warning a child not to behave "like one of those people." The use of outgroups as bad examples most surely impresses on children more than merely the idea that it is good to behave the way their parents wish them to.

The legitimization of outgroups as targets of displaced hostility can easily be accomplished, even in societies that profess to hold high moral values (and what society doesn't?). But first there is a minor hurdle to be overcome. Since *we* are, almost by definition, decent, upstanding people, we cannot direct our hostility against others unless it can be shown that they deserve our hostility. To show this, at least two processes may easily be encouraged. One is to note as often as possible the deviations from our own standards of behavior of which they are guilty. The other is (if we are powerful enough to accomplish it) to discriminate against them in ways which will force them to appear deserving of whatever we do to them in ways which will force them to appear deserving of whatever we do to them, including the original discriminatory practices. This last process, of course, is the self-fulfilling prophecy again.

If the ingroup possesses enough power *vis-à-vis* the outgroup to create a social system that makes deviant behavior of the kind we disapprove more likely to occur among outgroup members, the latter will consistently "demonstrate" that they deserve our ill will. And if that were not enough to reinforce ethnic prejudice, there is always at least one more Freudian mechanism—the projection of guilt—which can do the trick. Again, as is well known, Freud argued that id-dominated impulses don't really disappear, they are merely suppressed. From time to time, the socialized individual will, to his distress, sense that he really covets his neighbor's wife. As such impulses surge toward the surface, he will feel guilty for having the impulse and for feeling hostile to the authorities in his own society who prevent him from exercising his impulse.

If he then "admits" to himself that decent people don't behave the way he feels like behaving, he might then project his behavioral dispositions onto others, who, it will turn out, are imbued with all the motives which are taboo in the ingroup, including sexual excess and disrespect for authority. To an even greater extent than before, they become legitimate targets of our hostility.

D. Scapegoating: Once an identifiable group has been imbued with all the characteristics of an outgroup, it can serve a variety of ingroup solidarity functions. One of these is to shoulder the blame when things go wrong for the ingroup. In times of economic stress or whenever other threats to the smooth functioning of the society arise, there will be a tendency to point to the outgroup as being responsible for the difficulties. There will be a readiness on the part of the ingroup members to accept this kind of explanation, for they will already "know" that outgroup members behave maliciously and place their own selfish interest above those of the society.

Scapegoating is one of the most vicious features of the entire phenomenon of prejudice. In Hitler's Germany, it culminated in genocide. More recently in East Africa, it led to the expulsion of thousands of Asians who were blamed for a variety of economic difficulties for which they could not possibly have been solely responsible.[10]

In the light of the theory of ethnocentrism, scapegoating is both a consequence of prejudice and a practice that further reinforces prejudice. Once again we have an example of a vicious cycle in intergroup relations. Persons identified as somehow deviant are legitimized as targets of hostility. In times of stress they are blamed for whatever difficulties the society is undergoing.[11] Once they are labeled responsible for our difficulties, the apparent legitimacy of the hostility directed toward them is enhanced, and it becomes more acceptable than ever to discriminate against them.

On the last few pages, by leaning heavily on the works of Sumner, Freud, and Dollard, we developed the argument that socialization, the acceptable goal of which is ingroup solidarity, also breeds outgroup hostility. We saw that this comes about as the result of the suppression of individual impulses that are projected onto outgroups and by the displacement of hostility in the direction of outgroups. This argument constitutes a diagnosis of prejudice that leads to some specific policy recommendations. Before considering these, however, we need to examine some facts about intergroup relations that have been brought to light by empirical research and to see how these facts both confirm the argument and refine it. Clearly, the argument as presented above provides merely a gross ouline of the process. So let us look at it more closely.

EMPIRICAL FINDINGS AND REFINEMENTS OF ETHNOCENTRISM THEORY

Ethnocentrism theory serves as a source of many predictions about intergroup relations. These predictions encompass such questions as the features of society that correlate with the intensity of ethnocentrism, the kinds of outgroups that are most likely to be chosen as hostility targets, the content of stereotypes that are likely to develop for particular ingroup/outgroup pairs, and many other details. The testing of a number of such predictions has been the focus of some cross-cultural research reviewed by LeVine and Campbell (1972), has been discussed in a theoretical and research review paper by Rosenblatt (1964), and has been undertaken by numerous other psychologists.

Some propositions regarding the content of stereotypes

Since ethnocentrism theory suggests that all groups encourage the outward displacement of hostility, it follows that verbal descriptions of outgroups will be dominated by negatively valued characteristics, so that the groups will be perceived as legitimate targets of hostility. Making outgroups appear deserving of animosity is so important that they will sometimes be imbued with negative characteristics that are totally imaginary. Blatant invention of negative characteristics, however, is seldom necessary. It is generally easy to find genuine characteristics that may be negatively evaluated. In other words, many stereotypes will, in a sense, be "true."

That stereotypes include content that is true does not mean, however, that the stereotype genuinely justifies the ethnocentrism. Quite the reverse, for often the truth of a stereotype is paradoxically a consequence of the ethnocentrism. We have already pointed out that ethnocentrism leads to discrimination which leads to behavior on the part of its victims which further degrades them in the eyes of the discriminators. There is also a more subtle phenomenon which contributes to the "validity" of certain stereotypes. Within any set of mutually ethnocentric groups, each group will perceive that the others are more favorably disposed to themselves and employ different standards in dealing within groups than across groups. Thus, from the point of view of *any* group, it can accurately be said about any *other* group that they love themselves more than they love us, they help each other more than they help us, they take pleasure from outwitting us, and, in short, they tend to treat us with hostility. These will tend to be veridical perceptions. They will be cited as justification for our disliking an outgroup when, in fact, they are really consequences of the fact that the ingroup and outgroup are mutually ethnocentric.

The next point about the content of stereotypes is terribly obvious but often overlooked in analyses of intergroup relations. It is that any differences in customs of which people are aware will tend to be evaluated negatively. (This is a point to which we will return when we are ready to make policy recommendations.) Since all groups vary to some degree in customs, and since ingroup customs are nowhere viewed as arbitrary, but rather as proper, moral, and right, outgroup customs will be seen as correspondingly improper, immoral, and wrong. Otherwise, the propriety of the ingroup's ways would be suspect. To avoid this challenge, it is necessary that observed differences be more than noted. They must be evaluated.

We are referring here both to customary differences and to the evaluation of these differences. The differences, we are stressing, function as a *cause* of ethnocentrism. Their evaluation, we are suggesting, is a *consequence* of ethnocentrism. We would not employ negatively toned words to describe outgroup customs and postively toned adjectives to describe our own, were there not pressure to reinforce the apparent God-given quality of our own ways.

Because any language is rich in evaluative terms, it is a very simple matter to describe any given characteristic in either positive or negative terms. Thus, any noticed difference in typical behavior between "them" and "us" can be evaluated in our favor. For example, if we typically work more than they and they play more than we, we can describe them as lazy. They in turn can describe us as compulsive.

Ethnocentrism theory suggests that this is precisely what we will do. The theory predicts that pairs of interacting groups who share a mutual antagonism will engage in complimentary stereotypes that reflect real differences, but add to the awareness of these differences evaluative judgments.

Moreover, the theory implies that whatever real differences there are to be noted will also be exaggerated, reflecting the pervasive cognitive tendency to produce more orderliness than exists in reality. Either to reduce or avoid cognitive dissonance, outgroups, toward whom our attitudes are negative, will tend to be seen as having even more of a negatively valued characteristic than might in fact be the case. Thus, we should expect that the proportions of outgroup members who possess such a characteristic to be exaggerated, too. We should expect the trait to be attributed to most, if not all, of them.

The result of these dynamics may be illustrated by a set of stereotypes commonly held by Englishmen and Americans:

	Descriptions of	
Descriptions by	Englishmen	Americans
Englishmen	Reserved	Forward
Americans	Snobbish	Outgoing

For purposes of this example, it is assumed that many Americans do initiate social contacts with greater frequency and more ease than do many Englishmen, and that this characteristic difference has been observed. In the example, each group, in referring to the same observed difference, is able to employ a positively toned adjective for its own characteristic and a negatively toned adjective for that of the other group. And to complete the picture and convert the initial observation of difference into a full-blown stereotype, some people would summarize the situation by asserting that, for example, "Most Americans are outgoing and friendly, while English people are snobbish and cold."

Perhaps it should be underscored that this example employed two ethnic groups of very similar culture and a long history of friendly relations. Even in such a case, the stereotyping principles were easily illustrated.

An important implication of the dynamics just shown is that the nature of any perceived behavioral difference between groups is irrelevant; whatever the direction of any difference, it can be and is likely to be evaluated in "our" favor. Thus, if a person predisposed to dislike a particular group were confronted by the fact that members of that group scored higher on the average on some performance measures than did the observer's own group, he could refer to them as shrewd, crafty, tricky, or employ many other such terms which would serve to justify his prejudice.

The central point in all of this, of course, is that for the ethnocentric perceiver, any way in which *they* are believed to differ from *us* can be interpreted as both the cause and justification of our feelings toward them. Of course, this is causal misperception, but it is a kind of misperception that is not easily corrected. As we shall attempt to make clear later on, the only efficacious way to attack this form of stereotyping is to reduce existing differences or, at the very least, avoid situations that bring them into focus.

Another principle relating to the content of stereotypes derives rather directly from some of the Freudian ideas that we incorporated into ethnocentrism theory. You may recall that the theory asserted that everyone, during socialization, is taught to suppress selfish impulses, but nevertheless occasionally experiences the desire to indulge in them. To allay the guilt that will be experienced as these impulses surface, he will be disposed to project his own negatively sanctioned behavioral tendencies onto the despised outgroup. It follows, therefore, that many stereotypes should picture the out-group as immoral, unclean, and deserving of punishment.

Published studies of stereotyping (e.g., Blake and Dennis, 1943; Campbell, 1967; Cauthen, Robinson, and Krauss, 1971; Ehrlich, 1962; Gilbert, 1951; Schoenfeld, 1942; Sherif, 1935; Tajfel, Sheikh, and Gardner, 1964; Vinacke, 1956) and ordinary experience confirm that the content of stereotypes conforms quite well to the pertinent predictions derived from ethnocentrism theory. The fit between the data and the theory is so good, there is little point in prolonging the discussion. But before leaving the topic, I will reiterate that while stereotypes function as justification for ethnocentrism, the theory asserts that the content of stereotypes is really a consequence of ethnocentrism.[1][2]

Some propositions regarding individual differences in prejudice

Up to this point we have stressed general processes to which we are all prone. But certainly some of us are more prejudiced than others. Some of us will be less willing than others to engage in discriminatory behavior or to employ stereotypes. If we add a few additional psychological insights to ethnocentrism theory, what does it have to say about individual differences?

Rosenblatt (1964) has generated a number of propositions about individual motivational and cognitive characteristics that relate to individual levels of ethnocentrism. One such proposition underscores that the relatively weak and frightened individuals within a society would most readily adopt ethnocentric attitudes. They would do this in the course of striving to identify themselves with an ingroup that is necessarily perceived as strong, good, successful, and potentially victorious. While all of us may possess the psychic need to belong to a supra-individual entity in order to mask our fragile mortality in something which will endure, the more threatened, bewildered, or less competent one is, the stronger this need should be.

The central character of a popular American television program,[13] Archie Bunker, personifies this phenomenon. He has been described by the actor who portrays him as "The American White man ... trapped by his own cultural history.... Archie's dilemma is coping with a world that is changing in front of him. He doesn't know what to do, except to lose his temper, mouth his poisons, look elsewhere to fix the blame for his own discomfort ... he won't get to the root of his problem because the root of his problem is himself, and he doesn't know it" (Hano, 1972). As a recent analyst of the television program suggested, "It is not that Archie Bunker is filled with hate so much as he is filled with fear.... The world has changed, but Archie hasn't and he is trapped" (Hano, 1972).

Motivationally, the Archie Bunkers (and there is some Archie in all of us) *need* to simplify the changing world around them. Cognitively, such persons tend to create orderliness to a self-deceptive degree. In Rosenblatt's terms, we "simplify the world by placing the world's innumerable stimuli into a finite number of categories" (1964 p. 135). These are general needs and tendencies, of course, but the thrust of Rosenblatt's argument is that they are more intense for some of us than for others—that is, "greater among the bewildered people experiencing changes from their traditional way of life and relatively uneducated people" (p. 135).

Since stereotyping involves such cognitive processes as oversimplification and the exaggeration of differences, it should be expected that individuals who are, for whatever reasons, more prone to such error tendencies would engage more in stereotyping and hence behave in more ethnocentric ways. Considerable research by psychologists interested in cognitive processes has shown that persons under stress decline in judgmental accuracy, make more wild guesses, and commit other perceptual errors. If failing to reach one's goals (frustration) is stress-inducing, then it follows that generally frustrated individuals ought be more inclined to ethnocentrism.

Early research (see Allport, 1954, p. 434) revealed a negative correlation between degree of education and prejudice. This correlation can, of course, reflect a variety of causal mechanisms. However, it is at least consistent with the present analysis of ethnocentrism and Rosenblatt's propositions concerning individual differences, if one considers education as a complex of experiences which (a) makes it difficult to engage in the cognitive distortions characteristic of stereotyping and (b) reduces the likelihood of at least certain kinds of frustration which can generate the motivational states that feed the flames of prejudice.

Empirical research has also revealed the not very startling fact that children of authoritarian parents are more prejudiced than children of non-authoritarian parents. Since authoritarianism and ethnocentrism are positively correlated, there is good reason to believe that authoritarian parents tend to teach their own prejudices to their children. It is also possible that children who are reared by authoritarian parents, who typically are rather strict disciplinarians, will develop relatively strong, but repressed, hostility toward parents, which becomes transferred onto outgroup members. For either or both of these reasons, we should expect relatively permissively reared children to be less prone to ethnocentrism.

Further implications of the line of argument that has been developed here include the prediction that ingroup members who feel themselves marginal but who want to feel as if they truly "belong" should be more prone to ethnic prejudice than well-integrated ingroup members. By the same logic, persons who, for whatever reason, *choose* to be marginal (e.g., youthful dissidents who question the validity of their own society's prevailing practices) should be less ethnocentric. In either of these two cases, the underlying explanatory concept would be conformity—overzealous conformity in the first instance and nonconformity in the other.

Rosenblatt's propositions thus point out that individual differences in ethnocentrism ought to be correlated with a number of indices of the degree to which individuals are integrated psychologically into their own societies. These propositions may be summarized as follows: The more enculturated individuals, especially those who are either unable (through lack of education or other experience) or unwilling to question the value of ingroup membership will be more prone to outgroup prejudice. When summarized in this fashion, it is clear that these predictions about individual differences are consistent with the Sumner-Freud-Dollard theory of ethnocentrism.

Also consistent with this is a program of research undertaken by one eminent student of race relations in the United States. Pettigrew has presented various findings to support the argument that the basic social-psychological process of conformity underlies much interracial behavior (Pettigrew, 1958, 1959, 1960, 1961). This view assigns greater causal weight to social situations than to profound, internal personality factors, without denying that prejudice for many people is an outward manifestation of deeply rooted personality syndromes, like that identified by research into the so-called authoritarian personality (Adorno et al., 1950). Pettigrew's central point in this regard is that, while generally an individual's degree of authoritarianism may be a good predictor of his level of ethnic prejudice, there are social settings, characterized by popularly accepted, regularly displayed patterns of discriminatory behavior, in which such behavior cannot be attributed to authoritarianism. Such communities simply are not characterized by higher levels of authoritarianism than are communities in which discriminatory behavior is less popular. For example, ". . . the South's heightened prejudice against the Negro cannot be explained in terms of any regional difference in authoritarianism" (Pettigrew, 1961, p. 109) because mean F-scale scores from the South are not significantly higher than mean scores from other regions in the United States (1959).

The striking set of facts which is the departure point of Pettigrew's analysis is that generally high levels of prejudice, unaccompanied by high levels of authoritarianism, are characteristic of certain societies (e.g., South Africa) or regions (e.g., the deep South in the United States) in whch the customs, traditions, and in some cases even the laws positively sanction, condone, and support discrimination.

Many persons who live in such social settings may be guilty not of prejudice anchored in profound personality syndromes, but of a much more superficial, "other-directed" prejudice. To one who is a target of discrimination, the behavior of an "other-directed" discriminator is, of course, just as damaging as the behavior of a confirmed bigot, whose behavior is part of an integrated complex of attitudes and values, but it may be very important to note the possible existence of other-directed prejudice since the behaviors associated with it might well be less resistant to change. It certainly seems reasonable to expect that situationally reinforced discriminatory behavior patterns would be less tenacious than similar behaviors that are external manifestations of deeply rooted personality syndromes. For this reason alone, Pettigrew's analysis is worth considering. It leads to an optimistic policy implication—reduce prejudice by making changes in the social setting—a prescription that will be discussed later in this chapter.

For the present, we are concerned with Pettigrew's notions primarily as they relate to our effort to understand the causes of prejudice. From his basic proposition—that some discriminatory behavior is situationally reinforced so that the behavior should be viewed as an example of conformity—flow some testable predictions. One is that in settings like the deep South, individual differences in prejudice are correlated with individual tendencies to conform. In his own test of this hypothesis, Pettigrew (1959) examined an adult, White, southern American sample and found that, after controlling statistically for age and level of education, persons who could confidently be considered more conformist were more anti-Negro than their comparable age and education mates. A typical finding was that church-goers were more prejudiced than non-church-goers in this setting where going to church is behavior that conforms to community norms. Similar differences in level of anti-Negro prejudice were found to relate to several other social characteristics that qualify as indices of conformity to community standards. Together the findings indicate that the more typical in his general habits the individual white southerner was, the more anti-Negro he was. This kind of relationship between conformity and prejudice does not appear to exist to the same degree in other parts of the United States (Pettigrew, 1961, p. 109).

Another finding that supports Pettigrew's contention that anti-Negro attitudes and behaviors in the South during the 1950s were not expressive of authoritarianism is that anti-Negro prejudice there was not correlated with anti-Semitism (Prothro, 1952). This fact takes on meaning when it is viewed in the context of findings that emerged from research with the F-scale that showed authoritarianism generally to be correlated with prejudice against any and all out-groups (Adorno et al., 1950). It suggests that anti-Negroism in the South cannot be explained as primarily an expression of authoritarianism or of other personality syndromes.

Other psychologists have produced findings which cast doubt on the importance of "personality" in understanding prejudice. In a study done in two societies, the United States and Greece, college students revealed different patterns of outgroup social distance (Triandis and Triandis, 1962). While certain cross-cultural commonalities in outgroup prejudice were discerned in the questionnaire response collected by Triandis and Triandis, the prejudices of Greeks were found to be characteristically different from those of Americans. Although for both groups proximal differences in religion related to social distance, nationality was salient only in Greece and race was salient only in the United States. Triandis and Triandis interpreted this set of findings to mean that different social distance norms prevailed in the two cultures and, that within each of them, social distance reflected more than anything else, "conformity to group norms" (p. 20).

The Pettigrew argument and supporting findings lend additional credence to the proposition developed a few pages earlier to the effect that the more positively individuals value their ingroup membership, accept and act out its values, the more prone they will be to outgroup prejudice. Pettigrew's synthesis of relevant findings helps us to refine that proposition and suggests conformity as a social psychological mechanism underlying the reciprocal relationship between ingroup and outgroup attitudes which the proposition asserts. From Pettigrew's analysis, we are helped to recognize that the conformity-prejudice correlation is most likely to exist in communities where the norms include maltreatment of outgroups. Therefore, the correlation may reflect the simple fact that those who conform . . . conform. They go to church because that is accepted and expected behavior; they mistreat Negroes for the same reason. Or it could mean that persons who conform have to believe that the ways of the society to which they are conforming are good, and, consequently, that the ways of a visible, numerous outgroup, whose members display, for whatever reason, counternormative behaviors, must be bad. The second interpretation is more in keeping with the ethnocentrism-based explanation of prejudice which we have been developing in this chapter, but both interpretations are consistent with it. Moreover, whatever the underlying mechanism, in considering the theory, we have been led to a most important fact—namely, in many situations it is the best integrated members of society—the most upstanding pillars of the community—who are the most likely to be prejudiced. Ethnocentrism theory can clearly incorporate this fact. Indeed, it predicts it.

In the presentation of Pettigrew's arguments, authoritarianism theory may have appeared to be a foil. It should be recalled, therefore, that neither Pettigrew nor this writer denies or ignores what has been learned from research into links between authoritarianism and prejudice. There are links. Interestingly, what we know about these links is also consistent with ethnocentrism theory. Individuals who score high on the F-scale (Adorno *et al.*, 1950) tend to be raised by authoritarian parents, are likely to be chauvinistic, favor law and order, are suspicious of and hostile toward social and political deviants and—as if to get us right back in Pettigrew's camp—are highly conformist. All of these characteristics of the authoritarian suggest that persons whose ethnic prejudice reflects an underlying authoritarianism can equally well be described as ethnocentric in the Sumnerian sense of the term—positively oriented toward their own (but no one else's) society. Such a person, it should be apparent, is maximally subject to the very same psychological processes, including guilt, projection, displacement, etc., that ethnocentrism theory considers fuel for ethnic prejudice and discrimination.

Berkowitz's evidence supporting the displacement hypothesis

Before leaving this topic of individual differences, let us examine a study that relates the topic to one of the core notions in the ethnocentrism-based theory of intergroup behavior—displacement of aggression. The theory could be interpreted to suggest that while *everyone* is subject to the temptation to displace aggression under certain conditions (e.g., when the appropriate target is an authority figure, protected from attack), persons who, for whatever reason, are more prejudiced would be more subject to that temptation. Leonard Berkowitz's reading of the relevant theoretical notions in Adorno *et al.*, (1950) and in Dollard *et al.*, (1939) led him to predict just that. Berkowitz (1959) inquired whether prejudiced individuals were more likely to respond to frustration-induced anger with displaced aggression than were equally angered but less prejudiced individuals. He determined that this was indeed the case.

His study was an experiment, with random assignment of college student subjects (all female) into either a hostility arousal or non-aroused condition. (Under arousal conditions, the experimenter was the villain; he accused each subject of being late, deprecated her performance of the task, and raised doubts about her ability to do college-level work.) Half of the 48 subjects were recruited into the experiment because they had high scores on an anti-Semitism questionnaire administered a month prior to the experiment; the other half were low scorers. The task all subjects performed required working with another girl (actually a confederate of the experimenter). Upon completion of the task, each subject was asked to indicate whether or not she liked the experiment, whether she would like to work again with her partner, and whether she would like to try to get to know her partner better. The first query constituted a general annoyance measure; the other two questions provided opportunities to displace that annoyance.

The key findings were as follows:

1. Annoyance varied across arousal conditions, and was independent of subjects' level of prejudice. Girls who experienced Berkowitz's obnoxious behavior admitted enjoying the experiment less than did girls who served under non-arousal conditions, and this difference held for both prejudiced and non-prejudiced subjects.

2. Under non-arousal conditions, level of prejudice did *not* relate to expressions of liking for the partner, but under arousal conditions —where anger was generated by the experimenter—the prejudiced girls displayed heightened levels of hostility toward partners while the low-prejudiced girls actually showed unchanged friendliness toward partners.

What Berkowitz found, then, is consonant with the following notion: When annoyed, prejudiced persons are more likely than others to displace their hostility away from authority figures and onto less significant others. This interpretation of Berkowitz's findings supports the displacement component of an ethnocentrism-based theory of prejudice and refines our understanding of individual differences.

It leaves unanswered, however, the question of whether some people are more prone to displacement of aggression *because* they are more prejudiced or are more prejudiced because they are more prone to displacement. Perhaps the safest resolution of this dilemma is that these two personal characteristics are both manifestations of ethnocentrism. An individual who possesses either of these behavioral dispositions (to displace aggression or to express ethnic prejudice) is likely to possess the other. Such a person, according to the theory developed in this chapter, is as he is because he is well-socialized, conformist, and respectful of authority.

The real significance of Berkowitz's findings thus might well be that they are consonant with this theory. The theory requires merely that outgroup prejudice and tendency to displace aggression be correlated; the theory does not suggest one as the cause of the other. Rather the theory asserts that the cause of both resides in the personal histories (including socialization) of the individuals.

What we have discovered by considering research on authoritarianism, Pettigrew's studies, and Berkowitz's research, is that ethnic prejudice and allied behaviors like displacement of aggression are likely to be more characteristic of individuals who conform to their ingroup norms, whatever the reasons for their conformity. In the case of the extreme authoritarian, the conformity is rooted in personality dynamics. In the case of the "well-adjusted average guy" who happens to live in a community where discrimination is itself a norm, his prejudice is situationally reinforced and more superficial. But conformity is common to both. Thus, conformity may be the single most potent individual difference variable in ethnic prejudice.

LeVine and Campbell (1972) develop a similar argument at the sociological level of analysis, attributing greater amounts of prejudice to groups that place greater stress on the values of membership. Basing their argument on the sociological concept *reference group*, they derive, among others, the following propositions:

"The more internally unified an ingroup the more outgroups will be rejected and the fewer ingroups will be used as positive reference groups.

"The more internally unified an ingroup the more similar the outgroup must be to the ingroup to be used as a positive reference group.

"Groups offering their members greater rewards for membership will exhibit more ingroup loyalty and solidarity and less tendency to emulate other groups" (pp. 68-69).

Conformity then, according to more than one theory, is a key concept in our attempts to understand differences in levels of prejudice among groups *and* among individuals.

Propositions concerning temporal variations in prejudice
Its enhancement or reduction by leadership

If some anti-group behavior is "merely" conformist, there must exist social forces to encourage that behavior. When we say that people are conforming, we mean that they are behaving in ways consonant with norms which serve as behavior standards. Norms are perpetuated in many ways, but surely these include verbal admonitions by generally respected authorities and other forms of overt behavior by persons who are likely to be emulated.

Most people find it comfortable, psychologically, to believe that they are behaving "decently," "properly," and in accord with the law. Therefore, it must also be that they need to know what behaviors qualify as proper. While the definition of what is legal, decent, or proper is partly determined by the behavior of peers, in any social setting, relatively authoritative persons wield greater influence in establishing norms than do others.

The determinants of influenciality vary, of course, across situations. Sometimes it is perceived technical expertise that grants power to influence; more often it is simply the prestige associated with high status. In most communities, elected or appointed officers in the revered institutions of the community, such as the government or the church, enjoy that kind of prestige, which enables them to wield considerable influence. They can do so at least in situations where it appears reasonable for them to know what is right, and sometimes even in situations where there is no obvious justification.

The behavior of leaders, particularly those who occupy official status, is thus a potentially important influence on prejudice, at least with regard to what we have called (in accord with Pettigrew) "other-directed" prejudice. A leader's behavior can either encourage or constrain discrimination.

In drawing a parallel with findings from the classic social psychological experiment by Asch, which showed that conformity to peer pressures to assert something contrary to the evidence of one's own experiences may be markedly reduced when only one person corroborates the experiential evidence (Asch, 1951), Pettigrew suggested, ". . . when even one respected source—a minister, a newspaper editor, even a college professor—conspicuously breaks the unanimity, *perhaps* a dramatic modification is achieved in the private opinions of many conforming Southerners" (Pettigrew, 1961, p. 110). This hypothesis suggests that changes over time in the prejudice level of a particular community will occur in response to variations in leaders' behavior.

Rosenblatt was also concerned with the waxing and waning of ethnocentrism within a particular society (1964, p. 132). To a considerable degree, variations in intergroup feelings are seen by Rosenblatt as within the control of political leaders. For example, the more leaders demand and reward loyalty and adherence to ingroup standards, the less are positive rewards available for friendly interaction with outgroups. It should be noted that this proposition comes very close to restating the core notion in ethnocentrism theory of a reciprocal relationship between ingroup and outgroup attitudes. A provocative implication of this proposition is that whenever an ingroup is made to feel itself threatened, ethnocentrism will increase. Another implication, which relates also to the question of the selection of targets for intergroup hostility, is that the more threatening a particular outgroup is perceived to be, the more likely it will become the object of prejudice and discrimination. Both the overall degree of threat and the apparent source of threat are manipulable by ingroup leaders; hence the responsiblity of leadership ín either the fanning or dampening of prejudice is underscored by Rosenblatt's analysis.

In yet another way, we have seen that enthnocentrism is the negative reflection of group cohesiveness. The more cohesiveness is encouraged, especially when encouragement involves invoking the specter of subversion from "outside agitators," the more intergroup hostility will result. This particular derivation from ethnocentrism theory as well as Pettigrew's underscoring of the importance of leadership, has an obvious implication for our efforts to prescribe ways to enhance intergroup relations. It shall be made explicit later in this chapter.

Propositions concerning selection of targets

From ethnocentrism theory we may derive a number of predictions about the choice from among outgroups of those that will receive the brunt of displaced hostility. But with regard to this issue, ethnocentrism theory in fact makes too many predictions, some of which are mutually contradictory. For example, on the one hand, the theory seems to suggest that the less well known a particular outgroup is, the more easily it may be stereotyped. On the other hand, the theory implies that for an outgroup to serve as a target for displaced hostility, it ought to be reasonably close at hand and quite visible.

Actually, when a theoretical position leads to a set of incompatible predictions, this may have a positive impact on empirical investigations to resolve the dilemma. Such a study has already been reported (Brewer, 1968) with regard to ethnocentrism theory's embarrassment of riches surrounding the question of the selection of outgroups.

With data collected in Kenya, Uganda, and Tanzania from 50 respondents in each of ten societies that are part of those three new nations, Brewer was able to determine some of the correlates of social distance in East Africa. (Social distance, a measurable aspect of intergroup relations [see Bogardus, 1928] is the reciprocal of the acceptability of a particular outgroup. The greater the social distance at which a group is held, the more it is a target of intergroup prejudice.) Among the findings were: (a) outgroups perceived as *dissimilar* were held at higher degrees of social distance, (b) social distance tended somewhat to vary with physical distance, so that neighboring groups were slightly better liked than *distant* groups, (c) outgroups perceived of as advanced and modern were somewhat better liked, but this was a weak relationship, limited to dissimilar groups. Of all the findings, the only one that revealed a relationship of real magnitude was the first—the relationship between perceived similarity and social distance. But the totality of Brewer's findings provides a picture of the possible dynamics involved in the selection of neighbors either as friends or enemies; this view supports ethnocentrism theory. Those whom we believe behave like us, we like; we *especially* despise those whom we perceive as different and backward.

More research surely is needed on this question of why certain groups bear the brunt of ethnocentrism, but what little has already been done suggests that the selection of targets will tend to be consonant with the preservation of the ingroup's self-esteem. And that idea, of course, is the core of the argument that has been developed in this chapter.

In this section of the chapter, we considered some research and propositions relating to stereotyping and its content, we reviewed some ideas pertaining to individual differences in prejudice, some ideas about variations over time in prejudice, and, finally, some ideas and findings concerning the selection of outgroups as hostility targets. By so doing, it perhaps became apparent that ethnocentrism theory offers a useful conceptual framework for an analysis of intergroup relations.

LeVine and Campbell (1972) present several other theories (e.g., realistic group conflict theory), which depart from and sometimes challenge some of Sumner's notions, including the direction of causality (from ethnocentrism to discrimination) and Sumner's implication that ethnocentrism is a universal phenomenon, possessing similar dynamics everywhere. Clearly, Sumner was not correct in every detail, and competing theories have much to commend them.

In my judgment, however, the policy implications that flow from the Sumnerian ideas presented here are far more promising than those that derive from other theories—e.g., those that make exploitation the cornerstone of the theory. This alone justifies the effort to interpret intergroup relations in sociopsychological rather than economic-conflict terms.

On that assumption, let us look at some well-known facts about intergroup relations and see whether ethnocentrism theory can help us first to understand them, and then by acting as a guide in our search for ways to change them.

INTERGROUP RELATIONS IN THE UNITED STATES— A PARTIAL INVENTORY

Few social phenomena have been as much observed, commented on and argued about as have the relations among ethnic groups in the United States. There is perhaps no issue about which Americans are more self-conscious, nor is there any aspect of American life that has generated more comment by foreign observers of the American scene (cf. Myrdal, 1944). In many respects, the history of the United States is a history of intergroup relations. It is a history marked by both successes and failures, but as of the 1970s, the situation remains grim. Whatever else may be happening currently in the nation, our continuing search for ways to integrate persons of diverse background, to maximize access to opportunities, and to avoid social disintegration remains a highly salient area of concern.

Because questions of intergroup relations have received and continue to receive so much attention, it is impossible in a single book (let alone in a brief chapter) to summarize adequately what has already been described and it is difficult to say anything that has not already been said. Thus, we are limited here to a cursory and partial listing of probably well-known features of intergroup relations as they exist in the United States. My purpose in recalling them is simply to bring them to the reader's attention, so that he/she might then engage in what I believe is the useful intellectual exercise of reconsidering what is known in the light of the conceptual framework that has been developed in this chapter.

The Kerner Report: Black-White relations in the U.S.A. in the sixties

The report of a Commission established by Presidential decree in 1967 (in the wake of race riots in Newark, New Jersey, and Detroit, Michigan), deals with the most obvious problem of intergroup relations that exists in the United States—relations between Blacks and Whites. The Commission dealt with three questions posed by the riots: What really happened? Why did it happen? What can be done to prevent its happening again? In the course of answering these questions, the report revealed much that no concerned citizen can dare ignore. At the very least, one must be aware of the Commission's pessimistic conclusion that "our nation is moving toward two societies, one black, one white—separate and unequal" (Kerner, 1968, p. 1).

In one dramatic sentence, the report summarized the history of Black-White relations in the United States and brought that history up to date: "Discrimination and segregation have long permeated American life; they now threaten the future of every American" (1968, p. 1). Moreover, the Commission members made it clear that the division between the races was actually deepening as of 1967 and that the disintegration of the society into two (or more) hostile parts was inevitable as long as the nation continued on its present course. The Commission further emphasized that massive changes in both public and private policy were required if the nation were to reach its professed goal of equal and common opportunities within a single society.

Although the violence on the streets during the "long, hot summers" of the 1960s galvanized the federal government to convene the Kerner Commission, its report made it very clear that the violence was only a symptom of a far more profound sickness in the society. The Commission warned that were the government to respond to the violence merely by attempting to suppress it, the underlying problems could only be exacerbated. At the same time, the Commission acknowledged that the society could not tolerate for long such outbursts as had occurred in Newark and Detroit, so it identified clearly the only acceptable course of action—to seek out and eliminate the root causes of racial violence, thus preventing further outbursts.

The root causes, said the Commission, are to be found in the discriminatory practices that produced the ghetto and nearly every other feature of the black-American subculture that propels its most frustrated members to violent expression.

The ghetto, said the Kerner Commission, is the *product* of discrimination. "What white Americans have never fully understood . . . is that white society is deeply implicated in the ghetto. White institutions created it, white institutions maintain it, and white society condones it" (p. 2).

In that terse pair of sentences, the Commission accused the dominant core-cultural ingroup of ethnocentrism, discrimination, and the creation of institutional pressures which have made American Blacks the example par excellence of "the outgroup" as ethnocentrism theory defines it. The foci of the Kerner Commission study were consequences of racial discrimination for the total society. In the view of the Commission, those consequences will, unless checked, result in a fundamental weakening of the society.

By emphasizing the ultimate consequences of ethnocentrism, the Commission made explicit what is perhaps implicit in ethnocentrism theory—namely, that discrimination may in the short run sustain the ingroup, but it carries the seeds of its own destruction in the long run.

A brief look at a few details revealed by the Kerner Report can be instructive. The Report discussed conditions in the ghetto which comprised the grievances cited by the rioters. These included charges of police brutality on the one hand, and inadequate police protection on the other. They included being forced to live in substandard housing and having to pay exorbitant rentals. They included unemployment, underemployment, and employment discrimination, as well as poor health and sanitation services. These and similar conditions added up, in the eyes of the Commission, to "a clear pattern of severe disadvantage for Negroes compared with whites."

This disadvantage is the product of White racism. That is the term employed by the Kerner Commission to refer to the "very pervasive discrimination and segregation that as of 1967 was still the dominant feature of American life." But by 1967, some forms of discrimination had become less acceptable (e.g., educational and employment discrimination). Still, in the view of the Commission, enough damage had been done by the practices of earlier generations that the ramifications of those practices were still operative. Moreover, migration patterns influenced by racial prejudice—the fleeing by Blacks from the rural South into northern urban areas, followed by White migration out of those urban areas—has resulted in concentrations of relatively improverished Blacks in precisely those regions of the United States where facilities and services are clearly inadequate —the cities. Thus, conditions which exist in the city ghetto "destroy opportunity and enforce failure."

Another irony of history noted by the Commission is that the media-inspired revolution of rising expectations among Blacks occurred at precisely the moment in history when conditions for success were increasingly limited for ghetto residents. (Even more ironically, the genuine and marked improvement in the lot of a few Blacks—the few who have achieved fame by accomplishments in politics, the arts, the professions, etc.—has accentuated the plight of those still trapped in the ghetto.) According to the Commission, in the ghetto, marked by the vicious cycle of unemployment and family breakdown, poverty in the context of higher than average prices for essentials like food, high crime rates in areas patrolled by a mistrusted police force, and, most serious of all, a genuine inability to get out, the psychological consequences inevitably include "bitterness and resentment, which in turn lead both to anti-social and self-destructive behavior."

To one who is interested in ethnocentrism theory, the import of the Kerner Commission's report resides in its stress on the attitudes and behaviors of *white* Americans as the explanation for the behavior of black Americans.

By laying both the historical and contemporary blame for the ghetto riots of the 1960s on white racist practices, the Commission report implicitly supports ethnocentrism theory. The behavior of black Americans is interpreted as a reaction to discriminatory practices of the white core-cultural ingroup. What the Commission did not go into, however, is why the ingroup behaved, and continues to behave, the way it does. While the Commission report recounted in detail the many barriers constructed by white Americans to frustrate attempts by black Americans to participate as full-fledged members of American society, the report relied only on history to explain the construction of those barriers. (See Chapter 5 of the report.) While the history helps us understand the cumulative impact of discriminatory practices, it does not explain why Negroes became targets of discrimination in the first instance. To answer that question, we might merely have to remember that the United States has been, from its beginnings in colonial times, a European cultural entity. Europe's first encounters with non-European peoples, including, but not only, Africans, were encounters with people whose physical appearance, language, and behavior were markedly different. The mere noticing of such differences is, according to ethnocentrism theory, both necessary and sufficient to establish a sense of ingroup/ outgroup, from which discrimination flows. If one begins with that proposition, then adds to it the historical facts pertaining to differential power, technological development, and economic prowess, the bleak picture of White-Black relations in the United States begins to make sense.

Consistent with this argument is the well-known fact, often misinterpreted, that while Blacks, generally speaking, have not been able to become integrated into American society, European immigrants have succeeded. The Commission dealt competently with this issue, attributing the white American/black American difference to several factors—historical, economic, political, and cultural. But the cornerstone factor might well have been what the Commission termed "the disability of race" (p. 15). From the very beginning, Negroes encountered by Whites have suffered from discrimination far more pervasive, profound, and continuous than that experienced by any European immigrant group (see Chapter 9 of the report). Perhaps only ethnocentrism theory can tell us why that has been so.

The psychology of minority group status:
Some consequences of discrimination

The literature that describes what it has meant to be a Negro in American society is large and still growing. Summarizing it is beyond us, but some of the key concepts that have emerged from attempts to understand the "Black experience" must be considered here.

Perhaps the cornerstone of any attempt to analyze this aspect of intergroup relations—the psychological consequences of discrimination—is the notion of ghetto psychology. Allport, in his classic work, "The Nature of Prejudice" (1954), devoted a chapter to what he called "traits due to discrimination." His list of such traits was lengthy and included obsessive (but not unjustified) expectation of rebuff, tendency to deny or hide membership in a discriminated against group, passivity, withdrawal from potentially unpleasant encounters, protective clowning (often termed "ghetto humor"), cohesiveness (usually termed "clannishness" by dominant ingroup observers), and, perhaps most common of all, self-hatred.

The phenomenon of self-hatred among minority outgroup members has been noted and discussed by many commentators. De Tocqueville saw it in the 19th century among some Negro slaves: "Having been told from the beginning that his race is naturally inferior to that of the whites, he assents to the proposition, and is ashamed of his own nature" (1838, Vol. I, p. 334). In a classic work by Kurt Lewin, an eminent social psychologist who was a Jewish refugee in Nazi Germany, there is a thorough discussion of self-hatred among Jews (1941). In addition, Bruno Bettelheim, also a psychologist and an inmate of a concentration camp, discussed the self-hatred of inmates in terms of their identification with the aggressor—the camp guards (1943). A black-American philosopher, Philip Hollie, writing more recently, has spoken of the "unselfing" of American Blacks as the ultimate cruelty inflicted upon them by their victimizers and has related it to "passive adaptation," "survival through surrender," and, once again, "Identification" (1970, p. 300).

Until at least the 1950s, the predominant behavior patterns of black-Americans were characterized by internalized hostility, submissiveness, overt acceptance of white domination, and emulation of white "ways." There were, of course, exceptions; not every American Negro shuffled and acquiesced as did Hollywood's stereotypic shoeshine boys, chauffeurs, and maids. From the beginnings of slavery through to the beginnings of the Civil Rights movement in the 1950s, there were Blacks whose personal sense of human dignity somehow allowed them to overcome ghetto-psychological pathology. But the dominant behavior patterns were those of a submerged people, hemmed in from all sides by pressures to accept and endure. To the degree that the Negro masses aspired to change, it was to whiteness. According to Guttentag (1970) class distinctions within the American Negro caste were based partly on "degree of whiteness" from Civil War times through 1954. Throughout Negro society, according to Guttentag, there was hopelessness, despair, and alienation, but always a search for acceptance by passing—either by appearing to be white, or by behaving white. In her terms, a "culture of poverty" developed, while included hardly any group cohesiveness but considerable identification with the aggressor.

In the 1960s, a marked change began. There emerged, in the words of one behavioral analyst (Caplan, 1970), a "new ghetto man." For reasons historians may one day illuminate, the "civil rights movement," basically integrationist in character, was transformed into the Black Power movement, which was basically separatist. And where the former movement was exhortative, the latter made "non-negotiable demands," where the one sought legislative reform and law enforcement, the other sometimes advocated defiance of the law and, in some of its offshoots at least, it countenanced violence. If the old ghetto man was alienated, the new one was politically disaffected, prepared to break some laws in order to achieve rights already guaranteed by others (Caplan, 1970). If the old ghetto man aspired to be White, the new ghetto man was expressively proud of being Black. As Caplan summarized, the new ghetto men ". . . have developed a sense of Black consciousness, [and] have abandoned traditional stereotypes that made non-achievement and passive adaptation seem so natural."

Some social scientists understandably see great hope in this development. Not only does it represent a growing out of a ghetto psychology that was self-destructive, it appears also to be likely to enhance social cohesiveness within the American Black subculture. Guttentag (1970) implicitly applauded Black leaders for enhancing this cohesiveness by helping Blacks to perceive "a common external threat," to realize that cooperative action could eliminate that threat, and to recognize that individual mobility within and out of low status groups is severely constrained. Acknowledging that cohesiveness is not an end in itself (and that cohesiveness has some negative implications), Guttentag reviewed some of its positive attributes (e.g., enhanced attraction of membership, better within-group communication, internalization of ingroup norms, the setting and pursuit of group goals, etc.) and suggested that "the lack of ethnic group cohesiveness [as was the case for most Negroes until the Black Power movement emerged] must be weighed against both the positive and negative of strong group cohesiveness forces among poor individuals" (p. 124).

Other social scientists in doing that weighing, have come up with a less enthusiastic reading than did Guttentag (cf., Pettigrew, 1969). They tend to be most impressed by the separatist quality of the movement and to underscore that intragroup cohesiveness based on separatism automatically implies exacerbation of intergroup hostilities. Surely, as Pettigrew noted, separatism is likely to lead to an enhancement of existing diversity in values that characterize the white and black subcultures, to a reduction of intergroup communication, to a diminution in efforts to arrest mutual stereotypes and other conceptual distortion, and to a growth of vested interests for continued separation.

The question of whether the separatist movement which began in the 1960s was, on balance, good or bad is complex. Its answer depends on how one defines the goal of the movement and how one values that goal once it is defined; most important, it depends on evidence that is not yet available. Nonetheless, it may be instructive to grapple with the question, and to consider how it appears when viewed within the conceptual framework of ethnocentrism theory.

Several ideas may be worth considering.

Ethnocentrism theory can encompass both the old and the new ghetto man. Both are easily understandable as products of discrimination. Both involve aggression based on discrimination-induced frustration. The difference is in the direction of the expression of aggression. Indeed, ethnocentrism theory would predict self-hatred only as an early response and would clearly predict externalizing of that aggression sooner or later. Based on the point of view developed in this chapter, it would have to be said, as our point of departure, that outgroup hostility on the part of black Americans was inevitable. Whatever forces have existed to enhance black consciousness (and surely white discrimination against Blacks over 250 years is one of those forces) have also served to create a black ethnocentrism, a feature of which ultimately had to be anti-white attitudes in some form or other.

A second point worth considering is the apparent fact that the new externally directed aggressiveness of black Americans is correlated in time with a noticeable spurt in social, political, and economic progress. (A spurt, yes, but still very little. As late as 1975, the gaps between Whites and Blacks in employment and income were still increasing!) Many commentators would be tempted to conclude that the correlation reflects a causal relationship, with gains reflecting enhanced responsiveness by white society to the demands of Blacks who no longer appear content with the leavings. Thus, in the short run at least, there appears to be positive evidence of a pragmatic kind—the new movement *appears* to be working, at least within constraints that reflect the general economic conditions of the nation as a whole.

Third, there is reason to assume that the new ghetto personality is psychologically healthier than the old one. Surely it is better for a victim to stand up to his aggressor than to direct his aggressions inward. And, to the degree that self-hatred and its allied psychological mechanisms foster behavior that confirms the dominant group's stereotype of the submissive group, the self-fulfilling prophecies anticipated by ethnocentrism theory will continue to be fulfilled. Perhaps the best way to begin to break that vicious cycle is to substitute self-pride for self-hate.

For all this, the fact remains that the dominant thrust of ethnocentrism theory leads to serious doubts about the separatist movement as a long-term strategy for enhancing intergroup relations. As a short-term tactic, it may well be useful, but viewing it in the light of ethnocentrism theory, its flaws become disturbingly evident.

The price of ingroup cohesiveness is, according to the theory, deterioration of intergroup relations, for the one is the reciprocal of the other. The price, for any outgroup—particularly a minority group for whom no amount of rhetoric about power can redress the drastically inequitable power relations which prevail—of drawing attention to its distinctiveness is to maintain its salience as a displaced hostility target. While short-term gains may be real and many, the possibility that in the long term those gains will be wiped out must be taken seriously by those who are in positions wherein they might influence the movement. They must ask themselves whether it is possible to identify some short-term goals (such as an enhancement of self-confidence, a significant increase in educational and occupational achievement) that can perhaps efficiently be met via the black power, black pride, black-is-beautiful *tactic*, and then, those goals achieved, turn the movement away from separatism and back to integration. Perhaps when some critical mass of confident, educated, appropriately employed black Americans are so visible that their presence gives lie to the myth of inferiority, integration can once again become the goal and, for the first time, a goal that is within reach of the generation pursuing it.

If the movement of the Sixties, for all its separatist features (and whether because of or in spite of them), has facilitated educational and occupational openings, it cannot be faulted as a tactic. Nonetheless, if it is permitted to continue on the course it was heading in the late Sixties and early Seventies, it might well insure the coming of the very catastrophe envisioned by the Kerner Commission—a country composed of two societies, more unequal than ever before.

As this is being written, there are signs that the separatist aspects of the movement are being tempered. There are also signs that the short-term gains predicted above are nearing realization. If so, the warnings and doubts expressed here become of academic interest. If not, they ought to be debated earnestly by all who seek to realize the ultimate goal of a single society, unconcerned with superficial differences, providing equal opportunity to all, living in peace with itself, and enjoying the contributions of all of its variously talented members.

PSYCHOLOGY'S POTENTIAL CONTRIBUTION TO AMERICAN RACE RELATIONS

Improving intergroup relations in the United States is a goal that few would fail to endorse. There are, however, many versions of "improved relations" and many alternative approaches that have been advocated for each of them. Furthermore, the problems of prejudice and discrimination are so multidimensional, that various features of those problems suggest a variety of particular solutions rather than a simple sweeping approach. For all the complexity, however, there does appear to be a central thrust that is virtually demanded by what we know to be the core of the problem, a thrust that is also predicted by ethnocentrism theory to be most promising. That thrust involves the *enactment, endorsement, and enforcement of legal statutes prohibiting discriminatory practices.* Since at first glance, this advocacy may appear singularly uninventive, the balance of this chapter will be devoted to amplifying and justifying it.

A restatement of the problem. It has been argued here that some hostility toward outgroups is a virtually inevitable consequence of ingroup socialization and enculturation.[14] Scapegoating, displaced aggression, the perception of threat to the ingroup from people who are different, are all psychological processes that are at least potentially present in all societies and that are almost unavoidably fueled by any efforts at enhancing ingroup solidarity and cohesiveness. Conformity to ingroup norms is another process encouraged by socialization and, as we have seen, it is a process that can be employed either to enhance *or* diminish prejudice and discrimination. We have also seen that leadership is a variable of considerable import. But most important is the fact that any perceived difference—physical or behavioral—that distinguishes one group from another is likely to serve as the basis for mutually negative stereotyping, "justified" discrimination, consequent enhancement of the original differences and subsequent rounds of "justified" discrimination. In short, the problem may be summarized as a vicious behavioral cycle of perception of difference, discrimination, and self-fulfilling prophecy, stemming from fundamental, but often misguided, efforts to sustain a particular society.

Breaking the vicious cycle. The key strategic question, given the afore mentioned analysis of the problem, is where in the cycle to intervene. To many psychologists, one fact stands out—the behaviors within the cycle that are most subject to direct external influence are *overt discriminatory practices.* They can, obviously, be declared illegal. (They can also be positively sanctioned, as in the apartheid laws of South Africa and in the various *separate facilities* laws that for long prevailed in the Unted States.) Clearly, then, it is well within the ability of society to modify the social reinforcements that impinge on overt intergroup behaviors. The one link in the chain that is most vulnerable is discriminatory behaviors.

But is there reason to believe that controlling discrimination will affect prejudice?

The effects of legal action on prejudice. Many years ago, William Graham Sumner, the very person we have credited in this chapter with the core notion around which our theory revolves, insisted that "stateways cannot change folkways" (cited in Allport, 1954, p. 469). His pessimistic view has often been echoed by those who insist that "brotherly love cannot be legislated." Sumner and his echoists are, of course, right, if we interpret their views strictly and narrowly. The position they argue, however, dodges the question we are asking here. We are not advocating the legislative control of attitudes, rather the control of behavior, and the real question is whether such behavioral control would indirectly affect attitudes in the desired direction. Our answer is an emphatic "yes." Our theory and existing facts indicate that this ought to happen, and there is already considerable evidence that it does happen.

Why should anti-discriminatory legislation *reduce intergroup prejudice?*[1][5]

Intergroup prejudice, whatever else may sustain it, requires a target—that is, an outgroup behaving in ways that appear to justify its being a target. Any social program that reduces the salience of an outgroup in these respects should subsequently impact on negative attitudes *vis-à-vis* members of such a group.

All social practices that keep groups apart, that enhance differences in lifestyle, that reinforce preexisting differences in educational and occupational attainment, automatically feed intergroup hostility. There is no reason to doubt the converse of this. Any practices that would make groups more alike and enhance equal status contacts that serve to demonstrate how very much alike they really are, will increasingly make if difficult for either group to view the other with hostility.

The effects of contact. It is necessary to digress a bit in order to discuss intergroup contacts. There is no reason to believe that contact *per se* will enhance intergroup attitudes. Contact between visibly different peoples in fact often has adverse consequences. In the past, and often even today, when Blacks and Whites interact the encounter exacerbates social distance. This is so primarily because such contact merely reinforces preexisting stereotypes. It does this because the contacts are more often than not unequal status contacts. Such contacts can have a most serious impact, particularly on the Whites involved, for they would provide once again "evidence" of the "inferiority" of Blacks, which inferiority "justifies" their being treated as inferior.

It is also likely, as we have already asserted, that mere dissimilarity will be evaluated as "less good." So long as minority ethnic group members are believed to be dissimilar in their value system and beliefs, those perceived differences will reinforce prejudice against them. In accord with the theoretical framework presented in this chapter, Rokeach (1960) sees perceived dissimilarity of belief systems as a major cause of ethnic prejudice. A series of studies has shown that both the ethnicity of a stimulus person *and* his values influence (variously under different conditions) his acceptance or rejection (cf. Rokeach, Smith, and Evans, 1960; Stein, Hardyck, and Smith, 1965; Triandis, 1961). In the most recent of those studies, seemingly contradictory findings of the two earlier ones were shown to be complimentary. Stein *et al.* clarified what was for a time a complex picture of demonstrating that white high school students' acceptance of age peers was influenced *mostly* by apparent congruence of beliefs but *also* by race. When subjects were told that certain stimulus persons were either White or Black and held beliefs that were either consonant or dissonant with the subjects' own beliefs, belief consonance was far more determining of social character than was race. However, race was not ignored by these subjects; some of the data collected by Stein *et al.* revealed that Negro stimulus persons, to whom the experimenters attributed a particular level of consonance of beliefs, were viewed by the subjects as less like themselves in belief than comparable white stimulus persons! When subjects were provided with *no* information about stimulus persons' beliefs, the subjects accepted or rejected on the basis of race. Under those latter conditions, it seems reasonable to speculate that the history of Black-White relations in the United States has fostered *assumptions* on the part of Whites that Blacks will hold different values. As a result, race will, under these conditions, function as a *sign* of different values, which in turn will "justify" maintaining social distance between races. As this study's authors conclude, "The practical implications of these results are obvious. If people of different races encounter one another under conditions favoring the perception of belief congruence (as for example, in equal-status contacts), then racial prejudice should be substantially reduced" (Stein *et al.*, 1965, p. 289).

This analysis says in effect that *equal*-status contacts, because they would tend to disconfirm negatively evaluated differences, should weaken prejudice by destroying its cognitive foundations.

As, increasingly, Whites encounter Blacks in high-status occupations, with credentials, skills, and all the other visible signs of success as defined by the core culture, the underpinnings of prejudice will crumble and the entire edifice will lose the support on which it has for so long depended.

How to maximize equal-status contacts. It ought to be obvious by now that so long as black Americans are discriminated against in the areas of housing, health, education, and occupation, equal-status contacts will remain the exception. Hence, legally enforced anti-discrimination measures constitute a strategy for which an achievable goal is to make such contacts commonplace.

Thus, one good reason for employing the legal strategy advocated here is to enhance the probability of prejudice-weakening equal-status contacts.

The legal strategy and conformity. Earlier in this chapter we saw that prejudice and discrimination are often manifestations of conformity, especially among well-meaning non-bigoted individuals (Pettigrew, 1961). We also know that throughout much of our history in the United States, the overwhelming majority of laws, both federal and state, sanctioned segregation and other forms of discrimination. (Indeed, for nearly one hundred years after 1875, the U.S. Congress did not pass a single federal civil rights law.) The 1954 Supreme Court decision outlawing *de jure* school segregation was an incredibly striking reversal of long-standing traditions, embodied in the law. It is not very far-fetched, then, to argue that the laws as written and interpreted over many generations, actually fostered racial prejudice. It is no more far-fetched to predict that anti-discrimination laws can contribute to its demise. Our most confirmed bigots—the high F-scale types—are, by definition, particularly respectful of the law (although prone to break laws in the pursuit of presumably loftier goals).[16] In any event, they are responsive to authority; if authority demands respect for laws, they will find themselves able to resist such demands only at the cost of profound discomfort. Of greater import are the more numerous groups of people who want to be and perceive themselves as good, clean, decent, humanistic, and, most significantly, law-abiding citizens. These are the kinds of people to whom Pettigrew attributed "other-directed" prejudice. Basically conformist, they are potentially "other-directed" liberals. (Pettigrew spoke of the southern White of the 1950s as "the latent liberal" [1961, p. 110]). It is these people—and they comprise a large segment of our population—who will accept desegregation if it is legally demanded, if those laws are enforced, if the responsible leadership insists that the laws be enforced and respected, and if their peers in the community begin to show signs of compliance. They may not like it, but they will do it. Opinion polls will show opposition to a practice that is counter to tradition, but that practice will be followed (cf. Hyman and Sheatsley, 1956, which reported a survey in which over 80 percent of white southerners polled expressed opposition to desegregation, while most of them expressed the opinion that it was inevitable). And, as we know in 1975, desegregation *has* occurred.[17] Similarly, a 1954 poll in Oklahoma showed overwhelming attitudinal opposition to school desegregation which was nevertheless accomplished throughout that stated by 1957 (Jones, 1957). Once the advocated behavior is performed, we have much good reason to expect that the appropriate attitudes will emerge (cf. Festinger, 1957). Indeed, the strategy here advocated can be defended perhaps best of all by relating it to the psychological principle that attitudes are most easily changed by forcing changes in the behavior to which the attitudes relate. Just as behavior change will follow attitude change, so does a change in attitude follow from a change in behavior. While attitudes cannot be legislated, behavior can.

Our policy prescription, then, is simple. Equalize opportunity by proscribing discriminatory practices which produce inequities. The policy goal is to minimize the kinds of differences that feed ethnocentrism and thereby make it impossible to engage comfortably in intergroup hostility and discrimination.

Even if such a policy should succeed, and a particular people are no longer perceived as an outgroup, would not ingroup solidarity needs lead inexorably to the selection of other targets? After all, the theory developed in this chapter asserted that ethnocentrism is an inevitable consequence of socialization. While that may well be so, it does not seem that mankind is doomed forever to sustain self-love by other hatred. We can learn to vent our aggression against non-human targets. We can try to conquer disease and poverty and other problems which plague all mankind. Thus, our "targets" could be what Sherif and his colleagues have termed "superordinate goals"— problems whose solution require cooperative effort (Sherif *et al.*, 1954).

Won't our advocated policy tend toward cultural homogenization and won't we therefore lose much that is valuable in separate cultural achievements? My answer to this is that cultural homogenization is already underway and progressing rapidly, but that its products will not necessarily be less diverse or less valuable than the products of separate cultures. Individual diversity is itself great, and likely to continue to result in a spawning of new ideas, inventions, and institutions, some of which will work and hence continue man's cultural evolution. We shall continue to borrow and lend ways of life, which will be synthesized and revised. But the resultant distribution of ways of life would no longer be correlated with race and ethnicity to the degree they presently are. In their present form, the differences divide us, so much so that some of us are reluctant to try a behavior which we identify as not "for us."

The objections just considered do not, therefore, seem justification for not advocating the policy of legal constraints against discrimination. It seems not only the logical implication of the analysis of the dynamics of intergroup relations which was the burden of this chapter, it seems also to be the only promising, non-utopian prescription psychologists can offer to this seemingly unending cycle of discrimination and prejudice.

NOTES

[1] The obvious strength of the Rosenthal and Jacobson study lies in the fact that it was an experiment, with random assignment of subjects to treatment and control groups, with the treatment consisting solely of a manipulation of teachers' expectations. However, the alert student will have noticed that the study was prone to at least one external validity threat. The fact that the teachers themselves administered the tests on the later occasions may have allowed their expectations to affect post-test *scores* without affecting the abilities which the tests were designed to measure. However, this demands only a cautious restatement of the study's findings, wherein the effect is limited to teacher-administered test scores. Still the study shows how prejudice can result in a self-fulfilling prophecy with serious consequences for its victims.

[2] The widespread practice of so-called "abilities" tracking constitutes a dilemma. Whatever its pedagogical justification, it also produces de facto segregation *within* racially balanced schools. Since non-Whites are disproportionately represented among the culturally disadvantaged and since, as we saw in our previous two chapters, culturally disadvantaged tend to score low on aptitude tests, non-Whites tend disproportionately to be assigned to "slow-track" classes.

[3] In the musical play *South Pacific* (music by Richard Rodgers, lyrics by Oscar Hammerstein, II, book by Oscar Hammerstein, II and Joshua Logan, adapted from James Mitchener's *Tales of the South Pacific*), a character "explains" racial prejudice, singing, "You've got to be taught to be afraid of people whose eyes are oddly made, and people whose skin is a different shade—You've got to be carefully taught" (Rodgers, Hammerstein, and Logan, 1949, p. 136).

[4] History, both ancient and recent, also contains many examples of purposeful encouragement of ethnic prejudice. Such cases are in some respects easy to understand. More difficult are the more common instances of prejudice in societies whose rhetoric and legal systems stress universal civil rights. For the prevalence of prejudice among "men of good will", an explanatory theory is much needed.

[5] As early as 1950, G.W. Allport showed that scholarship on the causes of prejudice was characterized by different foci—historical, socio-cultural, phenomenological and others—and that these different foci led to the development of different, but not incompatible, theories (see Allport, 1950). Allport summarized a number of these theories in his book *The Nature of Prejudice* (1954).

[6] The relevant works of D.T. Campbell include unpublished lectures given at Northwestern University as well as Campbell (1965), Campbell and LeVine (1961); and LeVine and Campbell (1972).

[7] The article from which this summary is excerpted was published in the East African nation of Uganda, in a magazine whose editor, Rajat Neogy, a Ugandan citizen of Asian origin, was subsequently accused of treason, jailed and acquitted only after public outcry. Later, all of Uganda's Asians, long the target of ethnic hostility, were expelled from the country by its president who, in the course of defending his action in a letter to the Secretary General of the United Nations, compared himself proudly to Adolf Hitler, whose treatment of the Jews he praised.

[8] In LeVine and Campbell (1972, p. 12), may be found a listing of 23 facets of Sumner's theoretical syndrome of ethnocentrism. The listing includes nine ingroup and 14 outgroup attitudes and behaviors which, in the strongest version of Sumner's theory, are hypothesized to be present and interrelated universally. The listing generates 23 x 22/2 pairs, or 253 correlational hypotheses, not all of which, obviously, have empirical support.

[9] Malinowski's observations that among young boys in avuncular societies (tribes in which the mother's brother is the boy's disciplinarian) nightmares often concern uncles rather than fathers have led some psychologists to conclude that Freud erroneously focused on the father's role as mother's lover, rather than on his role as boy's disciplinarian, in speculating as to the cause of hostility toward fathers among Viennese boys (see Campbell, 1961, p. 335).

[10] In the United States, key personnel in the Nixon Administration, including persons with the highest responsibility for law and order, engaged in a series of sordid actions, including suppression of dissent, political espionage, bribery, and other forms of circumvention of the law, partly in the expectation that the nation felt itself so threatened by dissenting rebels that most "patriotic" Americans would accept any behavior from its leaders just so long as the preservation of the society appeared to be its goal. For a time, the Administration succeeded, being checked only after it became painfully apparent that the Administration's own behavior was flagrantly dissonant with American values.

The events that came to be known as the Watergate scandal may suggest that there are limits to scapegoating, since the public ultimately rejected the Administration's arguments. But at the same time, the events suggest how potent the temptation is to try to identify those who dissent and otherwise deviate from the core of the normative behavioral patterns of society as trouble-makers, whose suppression justifies nearly any and all means. If the Administration had limited its attacks to dissenters, there might well have been no national scandal.

[11] Still another example drawn from the sordid history of the Nixon Administration: U.S. government spokesmen during 1972 blamed the prolongation of the Vietnam war on the anti-war movement!

[12] LeVine and Campbell (1972, Chapter 10) distinguish stereotypes held by ethnic groups within a polity from stereotypes about external groups. Regarding the former, differences in socioeconomic roles are seen by LeVine and Campbell as the bases for ethnic images that contrast rural and urban subgroups, occupational subgroups, and groups residing in different regions of a single nation (often along a North-South dimension). Many of the details of this formulation of intranational stereotyping are not strictly derivable from ethnocentrism theory but neither are they incompatible with it.

[13] "All in the Family" was watched each Saturday evening during 1972 by approximately 50 million Americans. Praised by many and criticized by others who questioned its impact on intergroup relations within the United States, the program was, in certain respects, the most straightforward portrayal of bigotry among ostensibly well-intentioned "average guys" that had been presented to date in the mass media.

[14] These socio-cultural forces (socialization and enculturation) may well have been paralleled by biological evolution, as Campbell once suggested in a provoca-

tive essay contributed to a symposium on human motivation (1965). He argued that since outgroup hostility is part of a complex of individual behaviors, all of which have *group* survival value, such hostility may be completely understood only if it is viewed as a manifestation of socioevolutionary pressures. In particular, the causes of such an "altruistic" response as self-sacrificial participation in war seem necessarily rooted in group-level phenomena. While intergenerational teaching and learning may be necessary to develop such an "altruistic" motive, the individual disposition to acquire it probably reflects, in Campbell's view, an evolutionary process whereby the *social* has steadily replaced the *solitary* in all forms of animal life. The altruism of outgroup hostility may, then, be viewed as an evolutionary achievement but, as Campbell warns, even if it is presumed to have a genetic basis it may no longer have the group survival value it once had. "The wisdom produced by evolutionary processes—be they biological or sociocultural—is retrospective" (1965, p. 306). Hence, ethnocentrism, even if once biologically adaptive, may have by now become dysfunctional.

In a revision of his 1965 paper, Campbell (1972) abandoned the notion that individual commitment to group survival has a genetic basis. He stated, ". . . I now believe that these self-sacrificial dispositions, including especially the willingness to risk death in warfare, are in man a product of social indoctrination, which is counter to rather than supported by genetically transmitted behavioral dispositions" (p. 23).

Campbell's later position, which is much more consonant with prevailing social science theory—especially realistic group conflict theory—makes it very clear that altruistic service to the ingroup, which makes "possible tribalism, nationalism, and war, and are thus suicidal for modern man" (p. 23), need not be a feature of human life forever. ". . . that man's termite-and ant-like capacity for military heroism is in culturally transmitted disposition, not genetic ones, makes me more optimistic about the possibilities of social inventions eliminating war . . ." (p. 34).

[15] The argument developed here is very similar to that presented by Allport (1954) in Chapter 29 ("Ought there be a law?") of his book, *The Nature of Prejudice.*

[16] Testimony during the Watergate hearings illustrated this dramatically. Cf. Erlichman's assertions about the ultimate morality justifying the illegal entry and search of files of Ellsberg's psychiatrist.

[17] As of this writing (1975), it must be noted that desegregation of northern, urban school systems is occurring slowly and in the face of much opposition, couched usually in terms of anti-busing attitudes. It must nonetheless be predicted that enforcement of desegregation orders will, ultimately produce desegregation and, once it is a fact, it will be accepted.

6

On relations between the sexes[1]

"Two thousand years ago, we didn't even know who was the ladies and who was the fellas! Sure, ladies were there all the time, but we thought they were just cute, fat guys. . . . Bernie discovered ladies. One morning he got up smiling and said, 'You know? I think there's *ladies* here!' "[2]

To this fanciful account of the "discovery" of half of humanity, it may be added that there were ladies even before there were psychologists. Yet, some students of behavior seem to be waiting for the second coming of Bernie to confirm that fact! For all of psychology's interest in sexual behavior, it has shown little concern either with differences between the sexes or with the relations between males and females. For all we may know about sexuality and sexual behavior, we know almost nothing about behaviors distinguishing one sex from the other. And sometimes, it seems we don't even care.

In a recent 548-page textbook on experimental psychology, a not atypical example of its genre, there is not a single entry in its subject index for sex differences (Insko and Schopler, 1972). Throughout the text, which, incidentally, the authors dedicated to their wives, there appears statement after statement about the effect of one or another environmental manipulation on "people," e.g., ". . . subjects who were led to believe that they won a debate changed their attitudes . . . more than subjects who were led to believe that they had lost" (p. 41). Who were the subjects? Were they male or female?

If representatives of the two sexes were included, did they behave similarly when given the falsified information about the outcome of the debate?

If one were to review the hundreds of experiments reported in that textbook, one would find that sometimes subjects were male, sometimes female and occasionally both, but who they were, and what their sex was, are matters of seemingly little import to the psychologists who reported the studies.

This is not nitpicking. Psychologists' lack of concern with the gender of their research subjects is a serious matter. Of all the characteristics differentiating people from each other, one that is associated with very striking variations in behavior is sex. Consider, for example, this bald fact: Of the five million people arrested for all crimes in the United States in 1966, nearly four and one-half million were male. For certain crimes—vandalism, drunkenness, illegal possession of weapons—males account for approximately 95 percent of the arrests. Put in other words, as matters stood in the 1960s, odds were better than ten-to-one that the perpetrator of any of a variety of criminal behaviors would be a male rather than a female. Talk about events that deviate from chance! Psychologists know few variables that serve as better predictors of behavior than sex. Age might rival sex in importance as a determinant of behavior. To study relation's between age and behavior, there is a specialization known as developmental psychology. But no comparable subfield exists for sex.

For the most part, psychologists have treated sex differences in behavior as a methodological problem rather than a substantive one. In thousands of experiments designed hopefully to discover the experiential antecedents of behavior, sex differences were thought of as bothersome occurrences that muddied the water, as subject characteristics that made stimulus-response, cause-and-effect relationships difficult to discern. Psychology, after all, is the systematic search for *general* principles of behavior. The search is designed to record how *people* respond to a given set of stimulus conditions. If, as was early found to be the case, males and females typically respond differently to the same conditions, how could the psychologist hope ever to pin down the whys and what-fors of human behavior if he/she had to deal with both sexes?

The solution? A popular one was to conduct research with subjects all of one sex, usually male. Surprisingly, this was true even in the case of the study of socialization, a field in which psychologists have necessarily been interested in the acquisition of role-determined behavior, one example of which, of course, is sex role. Hoffman completed a lengthy review (1963) of research findings pertaining to the socialization of "morality"—a diffuse class of behaviors surely not unique to one sex—and was forced to note that the generalizations he could draw "apply mainly to males since most of the studies on which they were based deal only with males." Another popular solution was to use subjects of both sexes but to analyze and report the data provided by each group separately, leaving it to future scholars to make sense out of the between-sex differences if they should be so inclined. Because the latter solution often led to inelegant research reports, with two sets of curves showing one kind of relationship between stimulus and response for males and quite a different one for females, the former solution was more popular. As a result, many psychologists ruled out the possibility of "discovering" still another "sex difference" by employing sexually homogeneous subjects. It was as if those psychologists were saying, "Look, my job is difficult enough. Why should I complicate it further by opening my research to the possibility of two, often contradictory, sets of findings?"

On the other side of this coin, some psychologists must have been tempted to employ subjects of *both* sexes in their experiments, but only as a kind of insurance policy against "negative results." Unsure of finding support for their predictions about stimulus-response relationships, they could at least count on being able to report a statistically significant sex difference, whether interested in it or not.

So, the published psychological research from the beginnings of scientific psychology to the present contains numerous studies done with sexually homogeneous samples and numerous others with reported but unexplained sex differences. The literature contains very few studies of which the *object* was to understand sex differences and how they might have come about.

All of this is changing. The world's largest "minority group"—women—suddenly burst into consciousness as such in the 1960s with the publication of books, pamphlets, and magazine articles pertaining to the "women's liberation movement." This phenomenon has forced psychologists to attend to some very fundamental questions about sex and behavior.

The "problem" of women was thrust into focus by a new kind of self-assertive feminism which developed mainly in the United States during the late 1960s, an era in which other significant social changes were occurring, including, significantly, marked changes in sexual attitudes and behavior. The degree to which sexual liberality and feminine liberation were causally interrelated comprises a fit subject for both speculation and research. Indeed the women's liberation movement itself is a phenomenon which calls for thoughtful analysis, as do all important social movements. Later, we'll examine the movement as one manifestation of a more complex cultural evolution process. We will also analyze its possible impact on relations between the sexes.

For the present, however, we are concerned with the movement primarily because it has brought to the surface a number of long-suppressed questions about behavioral differences between men and women. The movement has forced a recognition that men and women have some unique behavior patterns and problems and it has underscored how poorly we understand the forces which have produced these sex-linked behavioral characteristics.[3]

For the psychologist, this means that the sexes *per se* are worthy of study. There is some irony in the fact that the women's liberation movement is at least partly responsible for the psychologist's new interest in sex differences, since much of the thrust of the movement has been to assert equality. But, as we shall see, the assertion of equality is essentially a demand for equality of opportunity, accompanied by an elimination of long-standing discriminatory practices which *assumed* some differences and *created* others. Accordingly, the existence of the movement underscores the need to recognize and understand sex differences, to determine how they may have been produced, and, most important, to distinguish between those that matter and those that don't. There would have been no need for equality demands if the true nature of, and reasons for, sex differences had not been for so long ignored, misunderstood, or distorted.

As we have already seen in our chapter on racial and ethnic prejudice, exploitative differential treatment justified by alleged but false differences is discrimination. Combatting it successfully demands a genuine understanding of what the real differences are and how they came to be.

For the psychologist, then, the general growth in awareness of the fact that women have long been the victims of discrimination has brought into focus a host of questions pertaining to sex. In the first place there are some simple empirical facts to be ascertained about the kind and extent of differences in behavior between males and females. Such facts are far less numerous than they should be. In the second place, there are the less simple analytic problems pertaining to the *causes* of these differences. Thirdly, there are the quite complex questions about relations between men and women. What is the nature of these relations, how did they develop, and what are their psychological implications for men and women alike?

Before dealing with the simpler questions, we must touch upon the harder ones, those that pertain to male-female relations. For, as many of the most articulate spokeswomen of the movement have suggested, the "simpler" questions of what sex differences there are and how they have come about can best be answered only by taking a good, hard look at the man-woman relationship. To do so means entertaining the hypothesis that the behavior patterns distinguishing women from men not only influence the relations between the sexes, but are also to some degree *the result of those relations.*

Recall how, in Chapter 5, it was shown that many behaviors of minority group members that are cited by majority groups as *justification* for discriminatory treatment are in fact a *product* of the discrimination itself. It is not at all unlikely that a similar process is involved in the relations between the sexes. If they are indeed involved in a majority-minority kind of relationship, characterized by exploitative, discriminatory actions, some characteristically male *and* female behaviors will result. Just as American Blacks and Whites have acquired behavior patterns that are conditioned by race relations, so men and women have acquired behavior patterns conditioned by sex relations. That relations between the sexes have long been character-ized by inequities, discrimination, and exploitation is the key concept of the women's liberation movement. This concept was the cornerstone of Kate Millet's *Sexual Politics* (1970) and of Shulamith Firestone's *The Dialectic of Sex* (1970) to cite only two of several works that traced the centuries-old development of differential power and domination that has placed males in a privileged status *vis-à-vis* females.

Millet, in her book, underscores the analogy drawn earlier between sex relations and race relations by providing an overview of events that, in her words, ". . . have forced us to acknowledge at least that the relationship between the races is indeed a political one . . . and . . . quite in the same manner, . . . the situation between the sexes now, and throughout history, is . . . a relationship of dominance and subordinance" (1970, pp. 24-25).

These events are too numerous to be dealt with adequately in a summary. Let it merely be noted that Millet's review supports the arguments that over time and space, men clearly tend to dominate women. The historical and anthropological evidence can hardly be interpreted otherwise, and hardly anyone has ever tried to do so. Just as few would claim that the tendency in race relations has been for Blacks to dominate Whites, few would claim that women have dominated men, except in isolated cases, and these are indeed exceptions that prove the rule. There may be legitimate arguments about the degree of domination and about the reasons for it, but no arguments about its prevailing direction.

So let us move immediately to matters of more direct relevance to us—Millet's sociopsychological notions, which explicitly or implicitly pervade her discussion of the "patriarchy" which she considers to be the essence of man-woman relations.

Millet argues that many social forces that have been revealed by research in sociology, economics, and anthropology serve to sustain the sexual power differential. At the core of all these discrimination-reinforcing mechanisms, however, is a truly psychological process, the *conditioning* of the basic ideology of patriarchy (p. 26). Through socialization, the attitudes that *produce* "appropriate" sex differences in temperament, role, and status are acquired. What makes the attitudes "appropriate" of course is simply that the attitudes that are learned are those that sustain the political *status quo*.

At the sociological level of analysis, the family is singled out as "patriarchy's chief institution" (p. 33), but, again, there is a psychological point inherent in the argument, since the function of the family in sexual politics is to mediate between society at large and the individual, providing the arena in which the crucial socialization takes place.

Economically, Millet reminds us of the myriad institutions in the marketplace (and in the schools, which provide channels to the marketplace) which discriminated against women. Different admission standards (places in educational institutions as well as occupations) and different reward criteria (as in salary and promotion differentials) are clearly economic forces sustaining the patriarchy. But again, the continuation of such discriminatory practices depends on sociopsychological factors, most notably attitudes about proper roles for men and women. Most significantly, both men and women should hold these attitudes for the system to be sustained. Thus, somehow the system must teach these attitudes to both sexes.

From anthropology, Millet can find evidence that cosmologies, religions, and myths seem almost universally to sustain the patriarchy: "Patriarchy has God on its side" (p. 51). To this, I can only add that since mythology may readily be thought of as a reflection of psychology, with persons creating gods in their own image, then the anthropological facts also underscore the fundamentally psychological nature of the system's lore. If, as anthropology also shows Millet, more taboos apply to women than to men, obviously those who devised the taboos in the first place held certain beliefs about sex differences. And a belief is a psychological thing that must be taught and reinforced.

Millet in fact acknowledges the central importance of psychology in her sexual politics thesis. She sees the ultimate effect of *all* the factors (sociological, economic, etc.) sustaining patriarchy as a *psychological* effect—namely, "the interiorization of patriarchal ideology" (p. 54). This is a truly sociopsychological hypothesis in that it points to a set of social forces that are said to have a psychological impact, which in turn sustains the social forces. In expressing this interaction between society and the individual, this statement amplifies the hypothesis stated earlier to the effect that sex differences in behavior not only *influence* relations between the sexes but also *reflect* them. Both versions of this hypothesis assert that *in some respects* women behave the way they do because they are treated in certain ways by men. The parallel with psychological processes in the ghetto is all too obvious.

Millet pursues this parallel by linking her internalization-of-ideology hypothesis to behavior patterns that reflect the patriarchy's effect on women, an effect she considers fundamentally ego destructive. "The female is continually obliged to seek survival or advancement through the approval of males as those who hold power. . . . When in any group of persons, the ego is subjected to such invidious versions of itself . . . the effect is bound to be pernicious" (p. 55). And she detects "the presence in women of the expected traits of minority status: group self-hatred and self-rejection, a contempt both for herself and for her fellows—the result of that continual, however subtle, reiteration of her inferiority which she eventually accepts as a fact" (p. 56).

Shulamith Firestone, in her book *The Dialectic of Sex* (1970), sees more than a parallel between sexism and racism; to this writer, the two phenomena not only have similar dynamics, they interact with and have an impact on each other. For her, racism is a manifestation of sexism; ". . . the races are no more than the various parents and siblings of the Family of Man; . . . the physiological distinction of race became important culturally only due to the unequal distribution of power [within the family]. Thus, *racism is sexism extended*" (1970, p. 122). American race relations are parallel to sex relations, according to Firestone, not only because the two phenomena involve differential power and exploitation, but also because Whites and

Blacks have been assigned status in society resembling the hierarchically related status that exists in the Western nuclear family. "The white man is father, the white woman, wife and mother, her status dependent on his; the blacks, like children, are his property, their physical differentiation marking them the subservient class, in the same way that children easily become a servile class *vis-à-vis* adults" (pp. 122-123).

However provocative this notion that racism derives from sexism, it must be noted that it is purely speculative; no solid evidence supports it. Moreover, it ignores much material evidence that racism has roots other than those that must exist in the power differentials found in a nuclear family. At the same time, the idea is worthy of consideration, if only for the dramatic way in which it underscores the sociopsychological *parallels* between racism and sexism. Both phenomena, whether one derives from the other or not, clearly seem to reflect the existence of status sets based on differential power, with negative psychological impacts on the less powerful in both cases.

Gunnar Myrdal, in his prescient Appendix 5 of Volume 2 of *The American Dilemma* (1944) may have been the first social scientist to comment pointedly on the similarity of the status of women to that of blacks.

As in the Negro problem, most men have accepted as self evident, until recently, the doctrine that women had inferior endowments in most of those respects which carry prestige, power, and advantages in society, but that they were at the same time, superior in some other respects. The arguments, when arguments were used, have been about the same: smaller brains, scarcity of geniuses and so on. The study of women's intelligence and personality has had broadly the same history as the one we record for Negroes. As in the case of the Negro, women themselves have often been brought to believe in their inferiority of endowment. As the Negro was awarded his "place in society, so there was a "woman's place." In both cases the rationalization was strongly believed that men, in confining them to this place, did not act against the true interest of the subordinate groups. The myth of the "contented women," who did not want to have suffrage or other civil rights and equal opportunities, had the same social function as the myth of the "contented Negro." In both cases there was probably—in a static sense—often some truth behind the myth.

In drawing a parallel between the position of, and feeling toward, women and Negroes we are uncovering a fundamental basis of our culture. Although it is changing, atavistic elements sometimes unexpectedly break through even in the most emancipated individuals. The similarities in the women's and the Negroes' problems are not accidental. They were, as we have pointed out, originally determined in a paternalistic order of society. (pp. 1077-78)

Just as Millet pointed to feminine ego-destructive implications of the patriarchy that resemble psychological reactions in the ghetto, so Firestone detects, among other defensive reactions, identification with the aggressor as a characteristic behavior pattern of many women: ". . . they choose to embrace their oppression, identifying their own interests with those of their men in the vain hope that power may rub off; *their* solution has been to obliterate their own poor egos—often by love—in order to merge completely into the powerful egos of their men" (p. 124).

Thus, these two writers, Millet and Firestone, are concerned with behaviors that are characteristic of women in Western society, behaviors that are ego effacing and that, it is persuasively argued, result from centuries-old institutional arrangements whereby females, having been compelled to play a subservient role, have internalized values consonant with that role.

In seeking an answer to what we earlier designated as our first and simplest question—namely, what are the behaviors distinguishing the sexes—it should now be clear that a potentially useful guideline for our search exists in the hypothesis that relations between the sexes in the form they have taken for so long have *produced* behaviors in women that are consonant with their filling a fundamentally subservient status. (Relations between the sexes obviously has behavioral implications for males, too, and we shall consider these later.)

We should turn, now, to our first question. What in fact, is known about feminine behavior that distinguishes it from masculine behavior? Is what is known consistent with the Millet and Firestone analyses? Millet asserted in 1970 that not much had been empirically determined: ". . . psychology has yet to produce relevant studies on the subject of ego damage to the female which might bear comparison to the excellent work done on the effects of racism . . ." (pp. 55-66). But some very good work has recently been begun.

Matina Horner, a psychologist working at the University of Michigan,[4] prodded by the fact that decades of research on achievement motivation (cf. Atkinson, 1958) had provided practically no information about women's characteristic reactions to challenge,[5] began a program of research on sex differences in achievement motivation (Horner, 1968, 1969).[6]

Dr. Horner provided 90 women and 88 men, all university undergraduates, with a standard stimulus—a sentence that was to be taken as the beginning of a story, one to be completed by each subject as he or she saw fit. For the men who completed this projective test, the stimulus sentence read "*After first-term finals, John finds himself at the top of his medical school class.*" For the women, the stimulus was the same, except that *Anne* replaced *John* and the pronouns were made to agree in gender.

Here, side by side, are excerpts from stories written by a male and by a female, both honor students.

Male	Female
"John is a conscientious young man who worked hard. He is pleased with himself. John has always wanted to go into medicine and is very dedicated. . . . John continues working hard and eventually graduates at the top of his class."	"Anne starts proclaiming her surprise and joy. Her fellow classmates are so disgusted with her behavior that they jump on her in a body and beat her. She is maimed for life."

As Horner viewed the situation illustrated by these two stories, women appear to be no less interested than men in success, but, unlike men, are also threatened by its possibility. Horner (1969) has suggested, "A bright woman is caught in a double-bind. In testing and other achievement oriented situations, she worries not only about failure, but also about success. . . . For women . . . the desire to achieve is often contaminated by what I call the *motive to avoid success*" (p. 38, italics in original).

Stories were scored as expressing this success-avoidance motive if they contained any references to negative consequences of doing well. Of the 90 stories written by women, 59 were so scored; of the 88 by men, only eight expressed the motive to avoid success. From this fact alone, Horner's central hypothesis—that a motive to avoid success is characteristic of females—seems to be clearly supported.

A closer look at the 59 stories which expressed fears about succeeding would reveal that the fears included expectations of social rejection ("She will be a proud and successful but a very lonely doctor"), and doubts about femininity ("Anne no longer feels so certain that she wants to be a doctor. She is worried about herself and wonders if perhaps she isn't normal.") Some stories even appear to be attempts at denial of Anne's success ("It was luck that Anne came out on top because she didn't want to go to medical school anyway.") Clearly, the evidence supports the view that conflict and ambivalence surround many females' reactions to a potential achievement and it appears, from the content of stories told by Horner's subjects, that the source of the conflict resides in societal expectations concerning performance standards on the one hand and the female role on the other. If children of both sexes were taught that to achieve is good, but if girls (and only girls) were also taught that they ought not to appear to be trying to achieve in the same way that boys strive to do so, then the kinds of behaviors found by Horner could clearly be the result. While Horner's research itself did not explore these possible child-rearing patterns, they seem likely antecedents of the behavior she observed.

And if such child-rearing processes are at work, what sustains them, if not a set of stereotyped values about masculinity and femininity which reflect the traditional relations between the sexes?

Findings like Horner's are quite consistent with findings from other studies that have dealt with differences in the ways males and females think of themselves. For example, McDonald and Gynther (1965) employed a sample of 400 high school seniors in southern, urban, segregated schools. The students were both Black and White, and, more significantly, male and female. They all completed a checklist questionnaire in two ways: first, to indicate words they thought were descriptive of themselves (self-ratings) and second, to indicate characteristics they believed to be desirable ones (ideal self-ratings). Males were far more likely than females to check *Dominance* both times—that is, among males, dominance was rated higher than it was by females, both as a self-characteristic and as an ideal characteristic. Of perhaps greater interest psychologically was the fact that for males, the discrepancy between the self and ideal self on dominance was lower than it was for females. Some females thought they were more dominant than they ought, ideally, to be! Few males were plagued by such a concern!

A similar study had the additional feature of having been conducted in two cultures (Peck, 1967). In this research, college students, both males and females, in the University of Mexico and in the University of Texas, were presented with a list of 15 value terms (e.g., "love," "success," "freedom," wealth," etc.) and asked to rank-order them. Analysis of the scales that emerged indicated, not surprisingly, several highly significant differences between the two cultures and, to a considerable extent, the cross-cultural difference in value rankings was independent of sex. For example, in the Texan sample, both males and females ranked *love, freedom*, and *wealth*, 1, 2, 3, respectively. Certainly, as one examines Peck's data, culture was responsible for more differences than was sex. But one sex difference that did show up was quite striking, particularly so because it interacted with culture. The value concept for which a sex and culture interaction occurred was *career success*. Generally, Mexicans ranked it higher than did Texans—but what was most revealing was that while Mexican males and females agreed in this ranking of career success, Texan males and females gave it highly discrepant rankings. Specifically, among the Mexican respondents, career success was ranked *first* by males and *second* by females; among Texan respondents, it was ranked *fourth* by males but *twelfth* by females. What is most provocative about this entire complex of findings is that while both sexes within a given culture seem to acquire similar value orientations, presumably because they are exposed to similar culturally mediated experiences, the value concept *career success* stands out as an exception in American culture but not Mexican! A tenable interpretation of Peck's findings is to consider them evidence that a sex difference in the valence attached to career success is socially conditioned, for such a difference is not universal; it occurs in American culture but obviously not in all cultures. It would, of course, be interesting to extend Peck's research to a large sample of cultures in an attempt to discover where the difference exists and where it does not. Is American society unique? Probably not, but additional research is needed before the question may be answered. What is clear from Peck's study, though, is that a sex difference in attitude toward career success is not a universal; rather, it is culturally linked and that is an important enough fact in itself.

We have now examined three studies concerned with sex differences in aspects of personality pertaining to motives, self-images, and values, and we have seen that among young women in the United States there may be a characteristic tendency to differentiate themselves from young men by (a) experiencing greater fear of success, (b) expressing a desire to appear less dominant and (c) attaching less importance to success in careers. We have also seen, with regard to the last finding, that the sex difference is apparently culturally mediated. Although we have reviewed only three studies, we have seen enough perhaps to conclude that something akin to a ghetto psychology is indeed characteristic of women—American women, at least—just as the Millet and Firestone analyses led us to expect.[7]

But, there is more. Although, as was noted at the outset of this chapter, psychologists have not been very zealous in searching systematically for sex differences and their causes, intriguing differences pepper the literature. Let's look at one more study, this one dealing with the manifest willingness to take risks. Slovic (1966) employed 1047 children of both sexes, ranging in age from six to 16 in a game-like task. The children were volunteer players in a decidedly non-laboratory setting; they encountered Slovic's game at a county fair.

The game involved a sort of free vending machine with ten switches on it. Subjects were told that pushing any but one of the switches, one at a time, would result in their receiving M&M candies. Pushing the non-winning switch, the location of which was a secret, would, in effect, be a "disaster." If pushed, the game would be terminated and the accumulated M&M's would have to be surrendered. With these considerations in mind, it must have been apparent to the kids that the more switches they pushed, the greater the likelihood of disaster, so the key dependent variable in the experiment was number of switches pushed. This was scored by Slovic and analyses were performed on proportions of children of different ages and sexes who stopped short of various numbers of pushes. (Recall that nine pushes would be a rationally maximal risk-taking behavior, given the conditions of the vending machine.)

Several findings are pertinent to our present concerns. First of all, there was a striking sex difference in the number of children who volunteered to play Slovic's game at all; of the 1047 subjects, 735 were boys! We don't know, of course, the sex ratio of children attending the fair, but it is unlikely that it was better than 2:1 male! Secondly, the discrepancy between numbers of males and females volunteering increased as age increased. In other words, among younger children, the male-female ratio of volunteers was not so high but it got steadily higher with higher age groups. The third interesting finding derives from the game itself; among those who did volunteer to play, more girls than boys stopped short of pushing nine switches. By this measure, then, girls appeared generally less willing than boys to take the risk of losing their M&Ms. They would pick up their M&Ms and go home with fewer M&Ms than they *might* win, rather than try to win more at the risk of losing all. The fourth fact is theoretically most intriguing; it concerns an interaction between age and sex in the way the game was played. The general finding, that girls assumed less risk than boys, must be qualified, for among the youngest age group (children from six to eight years of age) there was no such sex difference. It began to appear later, with girls stopping short more often than boys at every subsequent age level and with the difference being statistically significant only for children in two of the higher age groups—those who were 11 years old and 14-16 years old.

Considering all of Slovic's findings, then, it may be speculated that American children acquire different risk-taking orientations depending on their sex, and the relevant experiences that produce this sex difference in risk-taking occur well into childhood, at a time when sex differentiation in child-rearing has already been introduced.

SEX DIFFERENTIATION IN CHILD-REARING PRACTICES

We have completed our examination of several studies that describe rather marked differences in behavior between the sexes, which differences, we suggested, are products of differential socialization of children depending on their sex. Let us turn now to research that focuses directly on socialization and that therefore can show us whether or not sex differentiation is, as we have suggested, characteristic of socialization practices.

The Barry, Bacon and Child study

One of the most significant studies in this regard is a cross-cultural research project that has become a minor classic (Barry, Bacon, and Child, 1957). Employing data contained in the Human Relations Area Files, these psychologists examined ethnographic reports for 110 societies and found that in varying numbers of them it was possible to determine with some confidence the degree of emphasis placed on training of children to be nurturant, responsible, obedient, achievement-oriented, and self-reliant. The particular concern of Barry, Bacon, and Child was whether or not each society differentiated between the sexes in its training of these behavior patterns and, if so, the direction of the difference. With regard to self-reliance, the investigators found enough information to make reliable judgments for 82 societies. Among these 82 societies, 85 percent of them were judged to emphasize self-reliance training more for boys than for girls. The remaining 15 percent provided no evidence of a sexual differentiation in self-reliance training. In not a single society was self-reliance found to be emphasized more for girls. Conversely, among 33 societies for which the judges could assess sex differentiation in nurturance training, no societies emphasized nurturance training more for boys than for girls. In 82 percent of these cases, girls were given more nurturance training than boys and in the remaining 18 percent there appeared to be no sex difference.

Responsibility and obedience training were also found to be more likely emphases in socialization practices for girls and achievement training was found to be a male emphasis in socialization. Although a few deviant cases could be found with regard to responsibility, obedience, and achievement training, the overall picture was quite clear. There was rather striking cross-cultural consistency in sex role differentiation, with boys more likely to be trained to be self-reliant and achievement oriented, while girls were more likely to be trained to be nurturant, responsible, and obedient.

Given the cross-cultural generality of sex differentiation in socialization that Barry, Bacon, and Child discovered, it might be tempting to conclude that societies everywhere have through the accumulation of folk wisdom merely "discovered" that little boys are different from little girls and that they ought therefore be subject to differential training. Clearly, such a conclusion is not demanded by Barry, Bacon, and Child's findings, nor is it a conclusion that they themselves drew from their findings. Rather, they attempted to explain the nearly universal tendencies to differentiate between the sexes in socialization as appropriate preparation for adult roles which themselves are socially defined. In a sense, of course, this merely pushes the problem back one step; we must now ask why societies have defined adult roles in such a way that there *is* a division of labor by sex. (As early as 1937, Murdoch provided considerable evidence that sex-based division of labor exists very widely around the world and that the sexual divisions are very consistent from society to society.) Barry, Bacon, and Child, in accord with numerous anthropologists who dealt with this problem before them, suggested that sex role differentiation is at base a set of solutions that societies have come up with to deal with problems that arise from genuinely biological differences across the two sexes including especially differences in physical strength and the child-bearing function of the female. Granting that this is a bow in the direction of biological determination of differences in behavior across the two sexes, it must be noted that Barry, Bacon, and Child are *not* asserting that female nurturance on the one hand or male self-reliance on the other are themselves biologically caused behaviors. They are merely saying that in response to what must have been obvious anatomical and physiological differences between the sexes, societies have devised different economic roles for the two sexes which in turn have made it functional to differentially socialize the two sexes.

A related question has recently been examined very closely by V. Mary Stewart,[8] a Canadian psychologist specializing in culture and behavior studies. Her concern is with (a) behavioral differences across the sexes, (b) how these differences reflect sexual distinctions made during socialization, and (c) how these socialization distinctions reflect ecological press, mediated by economic forces.

Various measures of psychological differentiation,[9] or field independence, at the perceptual and cognitive levels especially, have revealed a fairly consistent pattern of sex differences in North American core-cultural groups, but the pattern is far less consistent among other groups. As Stewart summarizes the North American findings, it is clear that from early adolescence, very reliably, males exceed females in field independence (Stewart, 1974; Witkin and Berry, 1975). From studies that have also employed masculinity-femininity assessments (e.g., Crutchfield, Woodworth, and Albrecht, 1958; Fink, 1959; Miller, 1953; all reviewed by Stewart, 1974), we know also that masculine orientation is correlated positively with differentiation. In non-Western samples (which might better be designated, following Stewart, as non-WASP-American), while the sex differences in field independence that occur are almost always in favor of males, the more interesting fact is that often the difference is very much smaller than is typical for WASP-American samples, and sometimes it is nonexistent.

As Stewart has asserted, the most provocative feature of aggregate findings derived from Western and non-Western societies is the *variation in the extent of the sex differences*. It is this feature to which Stewart would have us properly direct our attention.

What ecocultural differences might be responsible for this variation? Certainly, we would think first of dimensions of child-rearing practices along which societies vary. From Witkin's own work (1967, (1969), three salient ones have emerged: conformity/self-assertiveness, protectiveness/curiosity-encouragement, and consistency and moderateness of discipline. When children are rewarded for asserting themselves, for exploring and experimenting, and are not subject to inconsistent outburst of parental coercion, they tend to acquire the kinds of skills that earn them high scores in tests of psychological differentiation.

What is critical for our present discussion is that while individual parents within particular cultures vary along these (and other) socialization dimensions, so do societies. In other words, modal tendencies vary from society to society. And this cross-societal variation is not willy-nilly; it relates systematically to other ecocultural variables. The latter set of variables includes degree of food accumulation, population mobility, the perceptual complexity of the environment, population density, and degree of political and social integration. Essentially, the same ecocultural variables that relate to psychological differentiation *per se* relate also to the likelihood of sex differences in psychological differentiation, although the latter set of relationships are somewhat more complex and demand more complex interpretations.

To grasp the key features of this complex story, it is well to recall the work reported in 1957 by Barry, Bacon, and Child, which has been reviewed above. That Barry, Bacon and Child found that the different socialization practices across the two sexes do not vary willy-nilly from culture to culture but instead show essentially the same pattern from society to society makes it clear that we must reject a *tabula rasa* theory of sex role differentiation in socialization. In other words, we cannot say that societies have *arbitrarily* decided to teach girls to behave in one way and boys to behave in another. Like any content of culture, socialization practices are related to other cultural elements. The striking aspect of the Barry, Bacon, and Child study is their demonstration of systematic relationships between sex role differentiation during socialization and other cultural elements. For example, not every society in the sample studied by Barry, Bacon, and Child had sex differences to the same degree. In some societies there is much more sex differentiation during socialization than in other societies. It was found that large sex differentiations tended more often to occur in those societies with "an economy that places a high premium on superior strength, superior development of motor skills requiring strength" (p. 330).

A later study by the same team (Barry, Child, and Bacon, 1959), showed that achievement, self-reliance, and independence training were most likely to be stressed in hunting and fishing societies as compared with agricultural and pastoral societies. That fact, however, takes no note of the sex of the children being socialized. A second, more immediately relevant fact is that in *both* classes of societies (low and high food accumulating groups) whatever is stressed (nurturance, obedience, and responsibility in the case of high food accumulating groups and self-assertiveness, achievement, and independence in low food accumulating groups) there is a relationship with sex. *If* sex distinctions are made, girls almost always receive *more* nurturance, obedience, and responsibility training and *less* assertiveness, achievement, and independence training than boys. The next fact is that the *degree* to which societies actually distinguish between males and females in applying these socialization emphases is predictable in terms of ecocultural variables. Societies are more likely to distinguish the sexes during socialization (stressing compliance more for girls and independence more for boys) if the subsistence mode is cultivation of grain crops or large animal husbandry, large animal hunting, if polygyny prevails, and if the society is composed of nomadic hunters, provided they don't fish. Indeed, from the 1959 study we learn that "maximum sex differentiation was found in nomadic non-fishing societies, and minimum sex differentiation in nomadic fishing societies." As Stewart points out, sedentary farmers on the one hand and herders on the other, whether sedentary or nomadic, are intermediate in degree of sexual distinction during socialization and should also be intermediate in degree of sex difference in psychological differentiation, which is a personality product of socialization.

Available data are consistent with this argument. John Berry's work (1966, 1971) shows minimal sex differences in field dependence/independence among nomadic and fishing societies (e.g., Eskimos and several Canadian Indian groups) and larger differences among agricultural societies (e.g., Temne, Zulu, and New Guinea Indigine).

Stewart (1974) was induced by this whole set of findings to generate an economic model (as well as some partially competing and complementary models) to explain how sex role differentiation might derive ultimately from ecology and subsistence mode. Her economic model takes into account two biological factors cited by Barry, Bacon, and Child (1957)—namely, the superior physical strength of males and the child-bearing function of females, as relevant to sexual division of labor during adulthood. Where the subsistence economy involves especially large grain crops or large animal herding, the sexual division of labor will find women tending home and children. To prepare males and females for their respective tasks, boys and girls will be differentially socialized with, as we have already seen, males encouraged more in the direction of independence and females taught more to be nurturant and compliant.

Further, in sedentary groups, while both males and females will tend to be less independent and more conformist and otherwise more socially responsive than nomads, the density and stability of sedentary communities will provide both more roles and more role specialization. Because women will tend to be assigned the child and home care roles, which demand interpersonal sensitivity, nurturance, and social responsiveness, the pressures toward field dependence will be especially strong for females.

Stewart's economic model also suggests that sedentary high food accumulating societies differ from nomadic low food accumulating societies in the value placed on women's work. First of all, in the latter groups, there is less division of labor by sex, but, further, where women do perform specialized tasks, they are often important contributors to the primary subsistence activity. As an example, Stewart cites Eskimo women's fishing while their men hunt. Since such contributions by women are integrated with and crucial to the success of men's activity, they will be valued by the men who will then not be inclined to denigrate women nor to demand subservience from them. In sedentary, high food accumulating societies, on the other hand, even when women participate in farming or animal husbandry, their tasks, like hauling water and weeding the fields, will tend to be regarded with contempt. In such settings, men can be expected to encourage socialization practices that will produce women whose behavior appears, to the men at least, to make the women worthy of contempt. Female subservience ought to be a product then of socialization.

Still other ideas are part of this economic model. Role specialization in sedentary societies is often accompanied by frequent father absence or exclusive mother-son sleeping arrangements, or both. But since either factor could produce young males with less than maximally masculine identities, while role specialization requires just that, in such societies there will be particular pressures to distinguish between males and females throughout socialization, with the process culminating, as Burton and Whiting (1961) have shown, in male initiation ceremonies. Where all of these factors are operative, men will value manhood, denigrate female activity, and dominate women, demanding subservience and conformity from them.

This economic model of Stewart, as well as other of her ideas, is well worth further elucidation, but we have seen enough perhaps to suggest some possible behavioral consequences of sedentarization in particular and modernization generally. Quite simply, it appears that as groups become more sedentary, more food accumulating, and develop more specialization of labor by sex, they will become generally more conformist, less autonomous and innovative, and all of these tendencies will be manifest by females more than by males, since socialization distinctions by sex will increase, with the females targeted for the heaviest doses of obedience, nurturance, and responsibility training. Two consequences of sedentarization suggested by the psychological literature, thus, are a general decrease in psychological differentiation and an enhancement of sex differences in psychological differentiation. The reasons for this may be any or all of the mechanisms discussed by Stewart (1974).

As Stewart notes, we cannot conclude that field independence is superior (or inferior) to field dependence, nor, I would add, can we conclude that sex differentiation in socialization is inferior (or superior) to no sex differentiation. On the other hand, from the perspective of our own culture's value system, I would expect that many of us would assign higher marks to a culture that maximizes field independence and minimizes sexual differentiation in both adult roles and child rearing. If that is so, we must either wish for a renaissance of nomadic societies that subsist via hunting and fishing (which is, as we all know, a vain wish), or we must accept sedentarization and much, but not all, that goes with it. When a high food accumulating economy works well, and as technology advances, we could let those developments free us from some of the practices of the past. Certainly under such conditions the child-rearing function and relative lack of physical strength of women are less important facts than they may have been historically. We might still find it desirable to have a high degree of role specialization, but there would be little reason to link that specialization to sex. Also, as labor-saving devices proliferate, we all could spend less time at work—and, consequently, more time at home—so despite role specialization, we would all be involved in our special roles for a smaller portion of each day and during fewer days. With more leisure time to fill, we could both do more common things together and more specialized activities as individuals. Who knows, we might *all* become more highly differentiated psychologically. It would not be a case merely of women becoming more like men, but of men and women both becoming more like persons.

Is sex differentiation applied arbitrarily?

It is interesting to note in this regard that Shulamith Firestone in her recent call for a feminist revolution, asks her readers to consider the "likely possibility that the fundamental dualism (the fact that men and women throughout history have existed as separate classes in the Marxian sense) springs from sex itself" (Firestone, 1970, p. 8). Firestone develops "an analysis in which biology itself—procreation—is at the origin of the dualism" (p. 8). She even asserts: "The immediate assumption of the layman that the unequal division of the sexes is 'natural' may be well founded. We need not immediately look beyond this" (p. 8). Further, she states, "Men and women were created different" (p. 8). However, Firestone goes on to make it very clear that just because a sex-class system may have sprung from a biological reality, the biological difference cannot justify the domination of one group by another. She points out that humans are unlike other animals in that they have culture; in that sense, they have "begun to outgrow nature" (p. 10).

Firestone's point of view is thus very similar to that of Barry, Bacon, and Child. Of course, males and females are biologically different, and superimposed upon this difference is a tremendous complex of culturally determined differentiation. Much of it is unfair and possibly even socially maladaptive. Considerable evidence, some of which we have already reviewed in this chapter, makes it clear that differential treatment of the sexes has at least produced damaging psychological consequences. Certainly there is nothing in Barry, Bacon, and Child's study which denies this; indeed, the study provides some of the best evidence we have that the sexes generally are differentially treated.

It is too bad, therefore, that Millet in her well-known work on sexual politics should have misrepresented the Barry, Bacon, and Child position. She stated, "The implication forced upon the reader [of a statement by Barry, Bacon, and Child, '*many of the adjustment problems of women in our society today may be partly traced to conflicts growing out of inadequate childhood preparation for their adult role*'] is that a university education is quite appropriate for the male yet damaging to the female since it is likely to produce 'adjustment problems' or cases of arrested development (inadequate preparation for adulthood). . . . The logical outcome of their suggestion is an end to higher education for women" (1970, p. 228). This is, of course, utter nonsense. Their quoted observation merely reflects discovery by Barry, Bacon, and Child that sexual differentiation in socialization often relates to preparation for specialized adult roles. They were not justifying sexual differentiation in adult roles.

Be that as it may, we have now seen that it ·is probable that in most, if not all, cultures, socialization practices vary across the sexes. Thus, we are all on firm ground when we hypothesize that behavioral differences that characterize the sexes are themselves cultural products mediated largely by differential socialization practices. With evidence like that provided by Barry, Bacon, and Child, it is at least easy to dismiss two alternative explanations of why there are sex differences in behavior—we can consider it quite unlikely that cultures merely apply arbitrarily different socialization practices to the two sexes, and we consider it quite unlikely that behavioral differences across the sexes must reflect only different instinctive predispositions of the two sexes.

As the anthropologist, Roy D'Andrade has put it, "Sex differences are not simply characteristics of individuals; they are also culturally transmitted patterns of behavior determined in part by the functioning of society" (D'Andrade, 1967). D'Andrade points out that one of the best documented findings in anthropology, as noted earlier in this chapter, is that there is a fairly consistent pattern of division of labor by sex. In his chapter, D'Andrade relates how the sexual division of labor is accompanied by sexual distinctions in social structure with the most common arrangement being a combination of patrilocal residence and patrilineal descent. However much these cultural phenomena may relate back to anatomical and physiological differences between the sexes, the fact remains that they are cultural phenomena.

Thus, in most places in the world and probably over long periods of human history, social systems have existed in which men were the breadwinners and women the housekeepers and child-rearers. Differential power, differential privilege, and concomitant differences in behavior patterns have resulted. On the basis of the facts revealed by Barry, Bacon, and Child's research, it seems a most reasonable hypothesis that in ages past societies took biological differentiation (most notably those relating to reproduction) into account when devising specialized labor-roles and then developed differentiated socialization practices to prepare males and females to play those roles. Assuming this to be so, it follows that in modern technologically sophisticated societies, where labor roles need no longer be differentiated on the basis of sex, sexual differentiation in socialization has become anachronistic.

If this analysis is correct, we should predict that a blurring of sexual differentiation in socialization should occur first in industrialized societies while such differentiation should be most tenacious in societies in which the subsistence economies involve jobs for which child-bearing generally would interfere with their efficient conduct. In this regard it is noteworthy that the United States is a society in which sexual differentiation in socialization is not only diminishing (albeit over the protests of many traditionalists), it was already of lesser magnitude than in most societies in the Barry, Bacon, and Child study done in the 1950s (p. 331).

We should expect, therefore, that in Western, industrialized societies, the trend should be toward decreasing socialization differences and decreasing differences in behavior between the sexes. What differences remain, we ought view as products of differential socialization that has historicocultural roots but that are less functional than they may once have been.

The significance of family structure

A provocative finding of Barry, Bacon, and Child (1957) was that sex differentiation was *less* likely in societies with nuclear families (as in the United States) as compared with polygamous, extended family societies. This finding might well reflect the fact that the smaller and more isolated the family group, the more likely it is that any member of it, regardless of sex, will at some time play any role. In such a setting, then, children of both sexes should have very similar training and experience with adult role models who help to blur sex-role distinctions. That the contemporary American family structure is markedly nuclear may be a second reason (along with our industrialized economy) for our *relatively* low degree of sexual differentiation in socialization.

In this regard, it is ironic that early theorists of the feminine liberation movement (e.g., Millet) singled out the nuclear family as a target, blaming that institution for supporting the patriarchy. The irony resides in the very real possibility that the nuclear family is one of the features of our society that permitted the feminist movement to take root by creating social conditions that encouraged the blurring of sex roles.

If the feminist theorists erred in laying blame at the feet of the nuclear family, their error perhaps was caused by their lack of a cross-cultural perspective. By concentrating on their own culture and stressing the sexual inequities that exist without considering the relative level of inequity in comparison with the levels extant in other cultures, they may have attacked an institution that actually ought be praised.

This possibility, admittedly the product of a speculative analysis on my part, is reminiscent of the state of affairs that characterized the larger "counter-cultural movement" of the late 1960s. One of that movement's major targets was the university, precisely the institution *par excellence* for the birth and sustenance of a counter-cultural movement! Few other settings in our society permit withdrawal from the marketplace for a period of years to analyze, criticize, challenge, and be skeptical. Is there a generalization to be drawn from these two cases—the feminists' attack on the nuclear family and the counter-culturalists' attack on the university? I think there is. It may be characteristic of all social movements in their early stages to direct their attacks on the institutions that are closest at hand, even if they are the very institutions that nurture the movement. Such institutions will tend to be misperceived as contributing to the problem rather than as aiding in its solution.

This error tendency will be exacerbated whenever the movement's ideological leaders spawn conspiracy theories, a simple-minded and all too popular temptation.[10] To the degree that Millet perceived the nuclear family as an invention of males to maintain women in a status of oppression and subjugation, locked into supportive, nurturant roles, she may have fallen prey to this temptation. By so doing, Millet may have inadvertently caused us to overlook a force in our society that actually is moving us toward sexual equality.[11]

Whether the nuclear family structure will propel us toward sexual equality, of course, depends on the willingness of both males and females to share both breadwinning and homemaking responsibilities. But, the burden of the argument developed in this section is that such willingness is more likely to occur in societies built on nuclear families than in societies composed of extended families. At least, this is what the Barry, Bacon, and Child findings suggest.

Before leaving this argument, it ought be noted that even a nuclear family society might find it functional to maintain at least a small degree of sex-role distinction in adulthood (and hence in socialization practices) in response to the procreational role differences of the sexes. In any event, in our own society today, however much we are moving toward a blurring of sex-role distinctions, those distinctions persist and concomitant behavioral differences are still characteristic of the sexes.

A further look at behavior differences

Earlier, we looked at a few of the behavioral differences that distinguish males from females, after having asserted that few psychologists had dealt systematically with these behavioral differences. At this juncture, it is appropriate to qualify that accusation somewhat and say a little bit more about what is actually known concerning sex differences in behavior. The work of Eleanor Maccoby and several colleagues must be cited as an important exception to the allegation concerning psychology's lack of concern with sex differences. Dr. Maccoby, in 1967, edited a highly informative volume dealing with the development of sex differences. In it she summarized several hundred studies in which sex differences were reported. Maccoby's classified summary of research in sex differences (1967, pp. 323-351) is the best single resource of its kind.[12] Among the facts that stand out in every summary are that males appear to be more overtly aggressive than females, that girls are somewhat more dependent than boys, that some studies show females to be more susceptible to social suggestion than boys (although many studies show no sex difference), that girls are more nurturant and affiliative than boys, that girls display more anxiety than boys on a variety of paper and pencil tests, and that girls show superiority over boys in verbal ability while boys show superiority over girls in spatial and quantitative abilities.[13] (Other findings are also reported by Maccoby.) In fact, then, we do know quite a bit already about sex differences in behavior, and we do have pretty good reason to believe that these sex differences are largely cultural products. In a chapter in the Maccoby volume (Hamburg and Lunde, 1967), the authors reviewed several lines of research into the role of sex hormones in the development of sex differences in human behavior and were forced to conclude that there is little evidence relating to the nature or extent of sex hormone effects on human behavioral development. While no one goes so far as to assert that there are *no* direct links between biological differences between the sexes and behavioral differences between the sexes, the import of culture simply cannot be denied.

Nonetheless, as has long been the case with "racial" differences, sex differences in ability and personality have, with depressing regularity, been attributed, by scientists of stature, to nature.

Thus, writing at the beginning of the 20th century, one German scientist, Moebius, "explained" the "inferiority" of women as a reflection of their smaller brains. More recently, Lionel Tiger (1970) asserted ". . . there is considerable evidence that differences between males and females . . . are directly related to our evolution as an animal . . ." Two noted geneticists, Darlington and Mather, in a textbook published in 1969, stated, "Genetically, the two sexes differ, perhaps, much as two species differ. They are mutually adapted for purposes of reproduction. But each is also adapted to its special cultural activities" (p. 384). Early in his career as a student of sexual behavior, Kinsey wondered, too, whether, because males and females behaved so differently in sexual intercourse, a taxonomist should classify the two sexes as different species. (He later reversed himself, after studying feminine sexual behavior.) Aristotle regarded "the female nature as affected with a natural defectiveness" and, in *On Politics*, concluded that "it is a general law that there should be naturally ruling elements and elements naturally ruled . . . the rule of the freeman over the slave is one trend of rule; that of the male over the female another . . ."

Freud, who seemed to regard women as mutilated, incomplete males, was an admirer of J.S. Mill, yet found his essay *On the Subjugation of Women*, "prudish and ethereal." Thus, even a psychologist who contributed to the overthrow of many long-standing prejudices regarding human behavior, was himself unable to break free from the tradition of viewing the two sexes as naturally different and unequal, with the female doomed to perpetual inferiority.

So, despite the lack of evidence to support it, the view of naturally based superiority of the males *vis-à-vis* females persists. Despite the reasons to believe that cultural forces are responsible for the ways things are—and hence that they need not remain that way—authoritative voices may be found to bless reactionary efforts to maintain the status quo. And, as sex differentiations continue, so will sex differences, suggesting to the naive that sex differences are, as the traditional authorities said, nature's way.

THE IMPACT OF SEX DIFFERENTIATION ON MALES

Throughout most of this chapter we have focused on the impact on females of relations between the sexes. We ought not conclude the chapter without at least mentioning the impact on males. There are psychological consequences of being cast into a role characterized by "superiority." Not the least of these difficulties is the pressure that some males must feel in living up to the demands of this role. If psychologists today had the self-confidence of a Freud, one of them might have invented "the machismo" complex. I will leave it to the reader to think for himself (or herself) of examples of male behavior patterns that might reflect the pressures on males to behave in "masculine" ways. The reader might also wish to speculate on some of the social implications of such "masculine" behavior. The crime statistics cited earlier in this chapter might be a case in point. So might mankind's long and continuing history of warfare. Congresswoman Bella Abzug, another leading spokeswoman for the women's liberation movement, may have been right on the mark when she stated, as was reported in the newspapers in September 1972, that we need not only a women's liberation movement but a male liberation movement as well.

The prevailing myth of instinctive, sex-linked aggressiveness, which we will examine in Chapter 7, might well contribute to self-doubts among males regarding their masculinity. In cultures in which maleness and aggression are conceptually linked, males whose sexual identity is, for whatever reason, a matter of concern to themselves are likely to be more than normally motivated to engage in aggressive behavior. This motivation could derive directly from felt needs to demonstrate masculinity or indirectly from frustrations experienced in teasing, taunting, and embarrassing encounters with peers or elders.

The particularly striking set of facts pertaining to criminal behavior, which was mentioned earlier in the present chapter, bears quite directly on this argument. The first fact in this set is simply that in most societies, including complex, large, industrial societies, most crimes are committed by men. By itself, this fact, as suggestive as it may be, says little about the antecedent conditions of crime. Indeed, the fact is subject to diverse interpretations, including biological determination of criminal proclivities. Other facts in this set reveal which males contribute most to the crime statistics, and these facts suggest that those males who are relatively insecure in their sex-role identification are disproportionately likely to commit criminal acts!

In a cross-cultural study of the correlates of crime, Bacon, Child, and Barry (1963) tested the hypothesis that criminal behavior can occur as a defensive reaction to initial feminine identification by correlating frequency of crime with household structure, where households varied in degree to which the father is present to permit male-male intergenerational contact, and, hence, masculine identification for young boys. The study revealed, in a sample of about 40 societies, that as the opportunity for contact with the father decreased, the frequency of crime—both crimes against property and personal attacks—increased.

Bacon, Child and Barry reviewed several studies done in the United States which yielded findings consistent with their own cross-cultural finding. These findings included evidence that adolescent crime is disproportionately committed by boys from fatherless households. Studies in the United States of adolescent gangs also contain observations such as the following: joining a gang "springs from a little boy's search for a masculinity he cannot find at home" and it is "first a protest against femininity and then an assertion of hypervirility" (Rohrer and Edmonson, 1960, cited by Bacon, Child, and Barry, 1963).

Other cross-cultural findings that relate to this argument include a positive correlation between prolonged exclusive mother-child sleeping arrangements (as found in polygamous societies) and the frequency of personal crime (Bacon, Child, and Barry, 1963).

On the basis of such findings,[14] it seems reasonable to expect males, particularly those who suffer from any degree of doubt about their own masculinity, to be strongly disposed to the performance of aggressive behavior. We might also expect such persons to be rather defensive about their rights to aggress, to gather about them various symbols and accouterments of aggressiveness (such as guns and powerful cars), and to be attitudinally supportive of warfare and other aggressive solutions to human conflicts. In short, such persons should come close to personifying the stereotyped male.

Before leaving this topic, it might be well to raise a question about the paradoxical relationship between sexual behavior and violence, which is observed for example, in rape. This peculiar pairing of sex and violence might be understood partly as an action by a culturally conditioned male, who, for whatever reason, feels a strong need to demonstrate his masculinity. For such a person, rape may well be the most "functional" of all actions, for his masculinity is thereby doubly demonstrated—via simultaneous manifestations of sexual prowess and aggressiveness. Moreover, the omission of tenderness from the act saves him from any feelings that could serve to challenge his sense of masculine identity.

Thus, just as Whites pay a psychological price for their social dominance over Blacks, males may be hurting by their continued participation in a patriarchy. The women's liberation movement, therefore, may serve to liberate us all.

ANOTHER LOOK AT THE WOMEN'S LIBERATION MOVEMENT

As this book is being written, the women's liberation movement is being confronted by what appears to be a backlash. Not only are many males acting defensively *vis-à-vis* the movement, so are many females. Of course, some women reacted negatively to the more theatrical and sensational aspects of the movement from the very beginning.

During the off-year elections in November, 1975, voters in some states, including the usually "liberal" state of New York, rather soundly defeated Equal Rights Amendment propositions. Apparently, opponents of the Women's Liberation Movement successfully exploited latent fears among women that legislation designed to guarantee equal treatment under the law would in fact do ill-defined damaged to the status-quo "privileges" of women in American society. The anti-ERA campaign pointed to such unrealistic prospects as integrated public toilets, a military draft for women, and a sweeping loss of alimony benefits.

Perhaps more critical in the unwillingness of many voters—especially women—to approve equal rights was a mechanism like the fear-of-success motive that was revealed by Horner's research (1968, 1969) reviewed earlier in this chapter. Apparently, many women are still more comfortable with the traditional, subservient "feminine" role than with the kind of autonomous, self-actualized identity that ERA and the movement encourage.

Rejection by women of some of the arguments of feminine liberation leaders could properly be described as underscoring the necessity for a women's liberation movement in which consciousness raising is a necessary first step. It follows from fundamental premises of writers like Millet, Firestone, and others that many women, in true ghetto-psychology fashion, will have accepted and become "comfortable" with their socially defined subservient roles, and hence would be discomforted by attempts to dislodge them from those roles. At the same time, it probably ought to be acknowledged that there are some legitimate bases for opposition, if not to the movement itself to some of its separatist manifestations. As is the case with any human problem, relations between the sexes is a very touchy business indeed. As we have seen in the recent history of Black/White relations in the United States, there may come a time when it is temporarily functional for a subservient group to cry "enough," to assert not only that it deserves equal opportunities but that it has unique characteristics that ought to be a source of pride to its members. During such a period, the prevalent tendency will be separatist, since the short-term goal will be the redefinition of identity, a process that is quite personal and has to be achieved without interference from the outgroup which was largely responsible in the first place for the faulty identity that must be displaced. On the other hand, people have to live together, be they Black and White or male and female. Self-assertion and separatism thus can help create conditions under which human relations become more positive, but alarms must be sounded if and when the separatist tendencies appear dangerously to push people further apart.

Just as Blacks ultimately need Whites, women need men (and vice-versa, of course). For Blacks to treat Whites as enemies and for women to behave similarly toward men, may be a desirable short-term tactic which permits escape from self-denigration, but it is a tactic that could, if allowed to persist, push the goal of a redefined relationship further from reach. Since the nature of the relationship between the sexes is the key to the rest of the story of sex and behavior, it would be tragic if that relationship were not improved.

Fortunately, there are many processes at work in society today that make it likely that the women's liberation movement will both enhance human relations and diminish sex discrimination. As noted earlier in this chapter, it is perhaps no accident that the women's liberation movement developed when it did. Other revolutions in values, others seeking after new lifestyles, were concomitants of the women's liberation movement. Included among these were some very marked and significant blurrings of traditional distinctions between males and females. Some of these concern sexual behavior itself, wherein females discovered that they too could enjoy sex, and males discovered that it was delightful that women had discovered this. Other blurrings of distinctions between the sexes occurred in hair style and clothing and entry into educational institutions and careers, to mention only a few. The list could be extended considerably. In view of what we have already seen about the interrelationship of various cultural forces, we can only predict that sexual differentiation in childhood and socialization will diminish even further, particularly in industrialized societies.

If sex role differentiation in socialization is being minimized, then sex differences in behavior should be reduced in number and degree. Whether the women's liberation movement *per se* will be able to claim responsibility for this success may be a moot point. It may well be that the women's liberation movement, emerging as it did in the 1960s, served to underscore a problem for which there was already a solution.

Be that as it may, everything we seem to know about sex differences in behavior, the etiology of sex differences in behavior, and the nature of relations between the sexes, supports the proposition that any social policy that points in the direction of maximizing sex differences ought be rejected while social policies that encourage a blurring of sex differences ought be advocated. Then, some day, Mel Brooks' Bernie might rise up and announce, "You know? I think there's *persons* here!"

NOTES

[1] This chapter was written with assistance from Ms. Geri Kenyon, Ph.D. candidate in Psychology at Syracuse University, who searched and critically reviewed some of the relevant literature discussed herein.

[2] These words, slightly reordered, are those of comedian-writer-producer Mel Brooks, who, with Carl Reiner, created the comedy routine, *The Two-Thousand-Year-Old Man*, issued by Capitol Records. The context is a satirical interview with the alleged old man who nostalgically recalls the significant discoveries and inventions of two millenia.

[3] Misunderstandings may reflect unquestioned prejudices. Psychologists, like other people, have probably been asking some wrong questions about the sexes (by starting from erroneous assumptions), in addition to failing to ask the right ones. For a good discussion of this kind of "unconscious sexism" see Bem and Bem (1970).

[4] Horner, after earning her Ph.D. at Michigan, joined the faculty at Harvard University and, in 1972, was appointed President of Radcliffe College.

[5] See French and Lesser (1964) for an exception.

[6] A good account may be found in Gornick (1971).

[7] Examples of ghetto-psychological behavior among American women are so numerous, it may be unnecessary to cite any here. One sticks in my mind, however.
   Some years ago one popular NBC morning show visited Rumania. In the course of that visit, the show's host conducted an interview with an American business executive who had spent three years developing and managing a glass factory there. He described a variety of topics relating to political and technological issues, while his wife sat primly by, on camera, smiling, but saying nothing. After some ten minutes, the host turned to her and asked, "Mrs. Blank, tell us, what is it like living here in Rumania?" Giggling, she replied, "Oh, your

audience is going to be so jealous when I tell them that I have full-time maid service for $65 a month." The point was not pursued; the host turned back to her husband and resumed the discussion of technological progress in Eastern Europe.

Can it be that real people discuss "ring-around-the-collar?" Apparently so— and so they will continue to do, as long as we expect them to and as long as they are taught that we expect them to. In this regard, the reader should recall the findings of the Rosenthal and Jacobson experiment on teacher expectations, which was discussed in Chapter 5.

[8] Stewart's review, not yet published, was initially presented in a symposium on "Cross-cultural Studies of Psychological Differentiation" at the Second International Conference of the International Association for Cross-Cultural Psychology, held at Queens University in Kingston, Ontario, in August 1974.

[9] The concept *differentiation* (Witkin, 1967), in its generic sense, refers to a skill to discriminate parts from the whole field in which they are imbedded. Applied to perception, a high level of differentiation would be reflected in ease of isolating a simple figure from a complex figure which includes it, as in the Embedded Figures Test. Regarding cognitive style, the concept denotes skill in shifting problem-solving strategies. The concept also includes manifest social autonomy, freedom from conformity, high self-regard and individualism, all of which facets of differentiation have been found to be intercorrelated.

[10] Recall how in Chapter 4 in our discussion of theories of prejudice, we rejected conspiratorial theories—those that seek to explain prejudice as the deliberate practices of "evil" people—as naive. Male oppression of females has been far too prevalent to attribute it to male devils alone. Moreover, to argue that women have been kept down *because* men have chosen to keep them down is to attribute to women a weakness—or to men a strength—that comprises a burden they hardly need to bear.

[11] For another defense of the nuclear family as a social-structure variable that potentially contributed to a minimization of sex differentiation during socialization, see Barry (1969).

[12] A second edition, edited by Maccoby and Jacklin was published in 1974 and comprises an updated, more complete account of what is currently known about sex differences. The second edition confirms that what is known about sex differences in behavior does *not* support the view that males and females are genetically programmed to function differently.

[13] For the most part, the studies that have shown these differences were conducted in the United States.

[14] These findings are correlational; caution must be exercised in interpreting them causally. For instance, the factor of family structure, *viz.*, "fatherless homes," is confounded with socioeconomic status and with other variables of possible causal import.

7
The etiology and control of violent behavior

"Don't fight, children; play nice." . . . My mother, and probably
   yours.
"Make love, not war." . . . An anti-war slogan popular in the
   United States during the 1960s.
"Kill the pigs." . . . ditto.
"Electrocute hijackers and castrate the rapists." . . . A well-
   known American religious leader, counsellor to Richard
   Nixon.

* * * * * * * *

There are likely no aspects of human behavior about which more
confusion abounds than hostility, aggression, and violence. Through
time, all civilizations have both condemned and condoned violence,
often simultaneously. Men have argued over when it is justified, with
only a minority saying "Never." Violence is sometimes advocated by
those who would overthrow governments and by those who would
preserve them. Each group almost always condemns aggression when
it is committed by the other.

At some level of consciousness, everyone "knows" that to aggress
is to behave in a generally disapproved manner, yet aggression often
seems justified, is encouraged, and sometimes rewarded.

The word *aggress* and its derivatives, *aggressive, aggression,* and
aggressor, have been variously defined. In this chapter, we follow

Dollard, Doob, Miller, Mowrer, and Sears (1939) who, in their classic work, *Frustration and Aggression*, defined aggression as "a sequence of behavior, the goal-response of which is the injury of the person toward whom it is directed" (p. 9). We will not be concerned with the antecedents to such a behavior sequence until later in this chapter. Our definition is satisfied if the behavior involves interpersonal harm, whether physical or psychological. Thus, we are not presently distinguishing between a harm-inflicting act in response to an aggression committed by another person from similar action which lacks a prior attack. Whatever the *instigation*, if it leads to a response designed to inflict personal injury, that response is, by definition, aggressive. Although we will later be very much concerned with instigations to aggression, it is useful to define aggression independently of its antecedents. The issue of what provokes aggressive behavior is better treated as a substantive question than a definitional one.

There are problems with the definition employed here. Among them is the difficulty inherent in the concept of intent that is embedded in the definition. It is certainly not always possible to discern whether a harm-inflicting action was committed purposely. However, since accidentally produced injury is clearly outside our present topic, it seems preferable to live with the ambiguity relating to *purpose* and consider aggression to be overt behavior, likely to inflict harm on another person, and committed for that purpose.

In everyday American-English, to be "aggressive" often means to be outgoing, energetic, non-reticent, and in other ways active. Interpersonal harm is not part of the meaning in that popular usage. It should be clearly understood, however, that this second meaning of *aggressive* makes it an entirely different concept from the one that is the subject of the present chapter. That aggressiveness has these two meanings may itself contribute to the ambivalence many people feel about harm-inducing aggressive behavior.

As if to illustrate our profound ambivalence about aggressiveness, our socially sanctioned institutional violence is usually wrapped in the rhetoric of non-violence. Thus, our armies fight their wars in the name of peace ("the war to end all wars," "the search for a generation of peace," etc.) and our police employ force so that they may maintain order. The supremely ironic example of this double-talk is the advocacy of the death penalty on the grounds of its alleged efficacy in deterring the commission of crimes that result in the loss of life.

Much confusion also abounds over *why* people aggress. Most

appear to act out of hate, but many claim humanistic motivation for their hostile acts. We have even witnessed anti-war activists detonating bombs to punctuate the ardency of their yearnings for peace. Not surprisingly, therefore, we wonder if it is not a primal feature of the human condition to feel hostile and express aggression. Does not the pervasiveness of human aggression constitute adequate proof that aggression is fundamental to human nature?

We seem to encounter aggression everywhere. One sunny morning on a street bordering a university campus, a bearded and obviously benign professor in a rusting Volkswagen found himself blocked in the wrong lane of traffic. Eager to make a left turn, he noted beside and to the left of his own car, a VW bus, bedecked with peace symbols. Inside it were two long haired, love-beaded young men. Fancying himself a sympathizer of the counter-cultural movement, the professor smilingly called to them. They looked his way and surely must have sensed, he thought, that he was a friend and ally. "I'm afraid I'm in the wrong lane," he said. "Since the traffic is stopped, would you let me pull out to make a left turn?" They looked first at each other, then turned to him and, as one, jabbed aloft the middle fingers of their right hands. In spite of the scenery and costumes, the gesture's meaning was immediately transmitted. Relegated to the over-30 ash heap, the professor could only think, "Hostility rides again, even in a psychedelic VW bus."

So we wonder. Is aggression inevitable? Is it instinctive? Surely violence, the threat of violence, and the fear of violence are nearly constant features of social life in many societies today, the lofty goals of the love generation notwithstanding. At every moment, somewhere, violence finds its victims. No day passes that is free of violent acts, committed either by mad men or sane, by villains or heroes, acting either in passion or with cold, grim determination.

Bombs rain from the sky over villages and cities. Machine-guns and hand grenades decimate a band of religious pilgrims debarking from a plane in the Holy Land. A team of athletes leaves the Olympic Games in caskets and a hundred tourists have their civilian aircraft shot out from under them. A campaigning politician, reaching to grasp an outstretched hand, receives instead five blasts from a hand gun. A squalling infant is beaten by its mother to still its strident cries. A pseudo-religious band of kids kill (for thrills) a group of glamorous celebrities. On a late-night television talk show, a retired CIA officer, currently a life insurance salesman, confesses killing an associate in Vietnam he believed to have been a double, or perhaps triple, agent. Some in the audience applaud his candor. Dozens of unarmed peasants in a Vietnamese village are cold-bloodedly murdered and a nation is divided in its judgment of the morality of the act.

And if the real world is not violent enough, prime-time television entertainments are dominated by scenes of violence that surpass those that appear on the televised newscasts. For those who prefer to pay money to be entertained, the screens of movie theaters around the world show more of the same, in vivid color and even larger than life.[1]

Needless to say, we live in an age of violence. Perhaps more to the point, however, is that all ages so far have been violent ones. Thus, the most overriding question about human aggression must be whether man can ever achieve a non-violent lifestyle. Two centuries ago, Voltaire's fictional philosopher, Dr. Pangloss, thought not. Confronted by one hostile act after another, this wise man could only resignedly suggest, "This is the best of all possible worlds" (Voltaire, 1759).

Voltaire's *Candide* reads, as do our daily newspapers, like an inventory of man's capacity and ingenuity for violence. The devastation of natural catastrophe, also detailed in this 18th-century novel, pales in contrast with the pain and destruction inflicted on man by his fellows. Slappings, kickings, and beatings are commonplace and justified by some characters in the novel as character building. On a larger canvas, religious trials and wars impinge on masses of people, burning and tearing them to pieces. In one vivid scene that is quite characteristic of Voltaire's novel, Candide "clambered over heaps of dead and dying men and reached a neighboring village, which was now in ashes; it was an Abare village which the Bulgarians had burned in accordance with international law. Here, old men dazed with blows watched the dying agonies of their murdered wives who clutched their children to their bleeding breasts; there, disembowelled girls who had been made to satisfy the natural appetites of heroes gasped their last sighs; others, half-burned, begged to be put to death." (Voltaire, 1759, pp. 68-69). Wondering why, Candide learns only that "this is the best of all possible worlds."

Little wonder that the mild-mannered hero, this "young man to whom nature had given the sweetest of dispositions," kills two men in the course of the novel, and intends to murder the brother of his sweetheart, saying, ". . . as I have now begun to dip my hands in blood, I will kill away" (p. 91).

Whatever else this story may tell us, it makes clear that violence is pervasive not only in our own time. Violence has been so long a part of human experience that many are tempted to say, in accord with Dr. Pangloss, that there is nothing to do but to learn to live with it. Most psychologists, however, disagree.

Since the early 1930s, with the emergence of the post-Freudian and post-MacDougallian learning theorists, considerable attention has been devoted to systematic research into the causes of aggression. As a result, considerable understanding of this phenomenon has resulted. The complex picture that is coming into focus is one with many encouraging implications. In essence it says that we need not accept the widespread belief that aggression is inevitable, because it is a form of behavior which, like any other learned behavior, is subject to modification and control. Aggressive responding can be replaced by learnable alternatives.

In the course of this chapter, some of the evidence that over-whelmingly supports this environmentalistic view of aggression will be discussed. First, however, it is necessary to acknowledge that the Panglossian view, although rejected by several generations of modern psychologists, remains a popular view among lay persons. Moreover, the view that aggression is a part of human nature has been supported by some highly touted professionals, who, for one reason or another, enjoy the status of authority on the subject. Accordingly, before we proceed to look at the scientific evidence bearing on the question of aggression, we shall examine some of the writings of those who espouse the archaic instinctivist position. Then we shall speculate as to why the temptation to consider aggression instinctive remains so strong and so popular.

ON AGGRESSION AS AN INSTINCT

Konrad Lorenz, a renowned and respected student of animal behavior is one of a group of writers who, during the 1960s, argued that aggressive behavior in man is an expression of "an aggressive instinct" (1963). (Others include Ardrey [1966], Morris [1967], and Storr [1968]. All of them received considerable coverage in the popular press, much of it uncritically accepting of their views.) In one characteristic statement, Lorenz alleged, "Aggression, the effects of which are frequently equated with those of the death wish, is an instinct like any other ..." (1963, Introduction, p. x), and in another, he claimed it a "fact that aggression is a true, primarily species-preserving instinct ..." (p. 49).

In an effort to support his allegations, Lorenz offered arguments so weak that ordinarily a psychology textbook would simply ignore them. But because Lorenz and his followers have managed to attract so much popular attention, we ought to expose them here. Although they in fact tell us practically nothing about aggression, they reveal what many people seem to want to believe. That is worth knowing, and it is important, once we know it, to inquire why it is so.

Let us look first at what is perhaps the single most curious argument in Lorenz's book. It involves, oddly enough, a concern with culture, something that an instinct theorist like Lorenz usually cares little about. To support his instinctivist position, Lorenz cited allegedly permissive child-rearing practices in the United States, claiming that they ". . . showed that the aggressive drive, like many other instincts, springs spontaneously from the inner human being and the results of this method of upbringing were countless un-bearably rude children who were anything but non-aggressive" (p. 50). (One wonders what Lorenz, himself a product of a pre-Hitler Germanic upbringing, would say about *its* products. One wonders also how a believer in the instinctiveness of aggression speaks at all of "the *results* of" a "method of upbringing.")

It would, of course, be ridiculous to deny the existence of some number of "rude" children in the United States, or anywhere else for that matter, even though rudeness is hard to measure, involving, as it obviously does, some culturally determined values that affect its definition. Assuming that "rude children" could be identified satis-factorily, whether their number would turn out to be "countless" is another matter. In any event, counting, a basic activity in all sciences, is one in which Lorenz has certainly not engaged as part of his attempt to understand human aggression.

Dismissing, then, the ludicrous argument just cited, let us turn to a somewhat more sophisticated one employed by Lorenz. In it, he attempts to make his views appear compatible with contemporary evolutionary theory and knowledge. He says, ". . . as good Dar-winians we must inquire into the species-preserving functions, which, under natural—or rather precultural—conditions is fulfilled by fights within the species, and which, by the process of selection has caused the advanced development of intra-specific fighting behavior in so many higher animals" (p. 30). With these words, fighting within species was branded functional in the evolutionary sense. And, lest it be thought that Lorenz excluded man from the implications of this verbal sleight-of-hand, note that he added, ". . . it is not only fishes that fight their own species;[2] the majority of vertebrates do so, too, man included" (p. 30).

That men, as well as fish, fight among themselves is beyond dispute. That most behaviors of either fish or men tend to be somehow adaptive and conducive to species survival is also indisputable. However, putting together these two indisputable facts in no way forces the conclusion that man's aggressive behavior is either instinctive *or* species-preserving. It could well be neither.

After all, the victims of human aggression are seldom naturally selected; more often they are chosen as targets by their aggressors. Even if it could be argued that, in some "long run," human aggression tends to weed out the weaker members of the species (a dubious proposition at best), there would still be no contingent necessity to conclude that because it served that function, aggression must be instinctive.

It is perhaps noteworthy that in Lorenz's own statement about the alleged species-preserving function of aggression there is a hint that since man is a *cultural* animal, so-called "natural" functions might be less significant for men than they are for animals without culture. Curiously, Lorenz more than hints at the importance of culture with regard to aggression; he seems actually to *deplore* culture's intervention. Thus, he states, ". . . the aggression drive has become *derailed* under conditions of civilization . . ." (p. 30, italics added).

In another statement, Lorenz reveals what appears to be a felt need to defend aggression against those who question its contribution to the quality of human life. After acknowledging that "the aggressive impulse often has destructive results," Lorenz announces, "But, so, too, do other instincts, if in a less dramatic way" (Introduction, p. x). It is as if Lorenz wants us not only to accept aggression as instinctive, but to like it as well!

Of course, Lorenz is not alone in postulating an instinctive basis for human aggression. He has been singled out and his views exposed to rather unrestrained criticism because he seems to have succeeded more than anyone else in making instinctivism once more a seemingly respectable position. Although Lorenz really did little more than restate old, outmoded doctrines,[3] his work has been popularly well received. This reception perhaps was due to his reputation as a competent ethologist, which reputation may have produced a halo effect on his psychological pronouncements.

Among psychologists, Lorenz's accounts of the behavior of numerous animal species in nature are considered genuine contributions to science, while his views on the causes of human aggressive behavior have not been taken seriously. Particularly among psychologists specializing in the study of aggression, Lorenz's fame as an ethologist counts not at all.

One leading specialist in the study of aggression, Leonard Berkowitz, has carefully examined the writings of Lorenz and those of three of his followers (Ardrey, 1966; Morris, 1967; Storrs, 1968). Berkowitz found these not only to be based on a highly over-simplified conception of the causes of aggression, but full of errors of reasoning and fact (Berkowitz, 1969). Among the faults detailed by Berkowitz was an unforgivable "neglect of the role of learning in human aggression" (p. 373).

Although their works are concerned mostly with *human* aggression, the Lorenzians, rather than studying directly human aggressive behavior, merely attempt to explain it by drawing what Berkowitz has termed "gross analogies" with superficially similar response patterns among other species of animals. One such argument by analogy, found in Ardrey's book, was noted by Berkowitz to encompass "Madagascar lemurs, herring gull colonies, certain groups of gibbons, and Italy and France" (p. 375). This surely matches any example of ethnocentrism included above in Chapter 5; no further comment, I assume, is necessary!

The instinctivists' tendency to argue by analogy, Berkowitz noted, is often buttressed in these books about aggression by a labeling trick that could make almost any behavior seem to be a manifestation of a putative aggressive instinct. Thus, it has become common practice for Lorenzians to assert, almost in passing, that a smile is an "appease-ment gesture." For an unwary reader, swept along by such semantic body-English, the implication that aggression underlies even expres-sions of affection is difficult to avoid. If that is so, must not aggression be a very primary phenomenon indeed? It matters little to the unwary that no evidence is offered by the Lorenzians that a smile *is* a gesture of appeasement. The Lorenzians' use of such "word magic" would, perhaps, score debaters' points, but science does not advance by debate.

In what is perhaps the most telling aspect of Berkowitz's critique of the instinctivist position on aggression, he spotlights their postula-tion of a supply of "aggressive energy flowing from one channel of behavior to another" (p. 381). Berkowitz is correct in reminding us that a long time ago it was common for psychologists to invent such conceptions of "psychic energy." Freud, of course, was the best-known inventor of hypothetical fluid forces pulsing through the psyche, sometimes becoming pent-up, diverted, "sublimated," and ultimately released in some disguised fashion. But psychologists long ago abandoned this highly poetic style of theorizing for it is not only unparsimonious, it also has theoretical implications that evidence has shown are simply untenable. In short, those who build a psychological system around hypothetical psychic energies are simply wrong.

In the particular case of aggression, the postulation of a hypothetical packet of aggressive energy implies that some finite amount of potential-to-aggress will either be manifest in an aggressive act *or* be subject to "cathartic release." (Indeed, Freudian psychologists themselves drew this implication for aggression.) As we shall see later in this chapter, most recent evidence of the effect of vicarious aggression shows that it is hardly cathartic. The effect, in fact, is often quite the opposite. Witnessing aggression does not "dissipate aggressive energy"; it often elicits aggressive behavior that might not otherwise take place.

For these and other reasons discussed by Berkowitz, the instinctivist position with regard to human aggressive behavior does not deserve the attention it has received in recent years. Most biological and psychological specialists, like those represented in a volume on *Man and Aggression* edited by Montagu (1968), are in accord with Berkowitz. They find it both necessary and easy to dismiss the instinct "explanation" of human aggression.

Nonetheless, it must be acknowledged that among non-specialists the temptation to conclude that aggression is instinctive remains very strong. It is therefore of some use to inquire about the reasons for the widespread willingness to attribute aggression to instinct.

First of all, there is, of course, the sheer pervasiveness of human aggression—from the village of Abare to the village of My Lai. This alone makes many wonder how aggressive behavior could be anything but instinctive. Since most of us know few, if any, persons who never aggress, we have reason to believe that aggressive behavior possesses one of the essential defining characteristics of an instinct—universality of occurrence within an entire species. When we are confronted with an alleged exception—a Gandhi, a Martin Luther King, or an entire tribe as described by an anthropologist—we either doubt the validity of the allegation or dismiss its subject as an exception that somehow proves the rule. Of course to do so is not cricket, since for a response to be properly considered an instinct it must truly be a universally occurring response. Therefore, if we insist on ducking that constraint, there must be some other, perhaps more profound, reason why so many people continue to insist that aggressive behavior is instinctive.

The fundamental reason may reside, paradoxically, in the very fact that it is a whole complex of social forces, and not instinct, that governs aggressive behavior! Later in this chapter, we shall consider in detail what some of these forces are and how they probably operate. For the present, it is only necessary to recognize that in all societies, people are rewarded *both* for aggressing (under certain conditions) *and* for inhibiting their tendencies to aggress (under other conditions). As a consequence of this complex reinforcement schedule, with the "same" response only sometimes being rewarded, felt needs to aggress would be accompanied by guilt feelings, of a type that some psychologists have termed *aggression-anxiety*, by threats to self-esteem, or by some other distressing state of mind. To alleviate these sorts of psychological discomfort, what better argument is there than the one that says, "I just can't help myself from wanting to aggress because my aggression is instinctive?" And, of course, "if I should succeed in suppressing my aggression, what an accomplishment, what a triumph of free will over nature, . . . how much I deserve praise!"

The belief that aggression is instinctive *also* provides a rationale for the vast numbers of humans who, for whatever reason, look upon the world as an arena in which competitive, self-serving behavior is demanded. After all, if the human species is assumed to be composed of instinctively aggressive individuals, we must be confronted on all sides by persons who are out to get *us*—even though they approach us with arms outstretched and "appeasement gestures" on their faces. Ergo, our hostile reaction to them can always be seen as self-defensive. Moreover, our preparedness, our need to bear arms, to maintain a strong defensive posture, to remain vigilant, and the like (all of which is likely to encourage *them* to do likewise) all find their ultimate justification in the belief in the inevitability of aggression by everybody else.

Thus, reasons abound for the popularity of the instinctivist "explanation" of aggression. The ultimate paradox which resides in the belief that aggression is instinctive is, of course, that the belief serves as a self-fulfilling prophecy. If enough people believe that aggression is inevitable, that alone could serve to make it so.

We find, therefore, that fostering the belief in the inevitability of human aggression actually sustains the kinds of intergroup ethnocentrisms that we examined in the previous chapter. In a later chapter, we will see how this same belief has hampered efforts to make war a less frequent instrument of foreign policy. And fostering the belief may have many other anti-social implications. This, in the opinion of this political psychologist, may be the single most damning aspect of the work of the Lorenzians. As Berkowitz has put it, "In the end, the Lorenzian analyses must be questioned because of their policy implications. . ." (1969, p. 383). As he and many other psychologists have noted, man's capacity for violence demands careful and sophisticated consideration. The simplistic allegations of the instinctivists must not be permitted to mask the complex processes whereby man learns to be aggressive, nor to hide the sad fact that presently most societies provide numerous forms of instigation to aggression. Those instigations are controllable. The instinctivists divert us from these facts and would damn us to dwell forever in this "best of all possible worlds."

THE ROLE OF SOCIAL FORCES IN HUMAN AGGRESSION

Any attempt to explain human aggression must take into account many diverse facts. The instinct doctrine handles only one of these facts quite well—the fact that aggression is so pervasive. An alternative explanation must do better than that, but it must at the same time include aggression's pervasiveness among the phenomena it explains. The following line of argument, gleaned and adapted from various writings by Freud, by Dollard *et al.*, and by Berkowitz, is an attempt to do this.

The argument to be developed here places great emphasis on learning, particularly the learning that occurs during socialization. However, the argument avoids the trap of taking sides in an artificial, exaggerated, and oversimplified nature-*vs.*-nurture controversy. To ask whether aggression is instinctive *or* learned is to accept a false dichotomy. As the following argument unfolds, it should become clear that aggressive *behavior* is learned, while the potential for its being learned has much to do with the biological predispositions of the human animal.

Those behaviors that we define as aggressive—responses resulting in intentional harm to others—are, like any other behaviors emitted by an organism, subject to environmental control. In other words, they are learnable and, by implication, extinguishable. Like any other response, an aggressive response is likely to be strengthened when rewarded, and weakened when not. This is, of course, a very basic psychological statement, the validity of which is known by those who have taken only one course in psychology. But it bears reiteration.

Having stated this basic principle, however, we have merely begun the argument. The next step must be to consider how aggressive responses come to occur and get rewarded in the first place. What accounts for the very high probability of occurrence which in turn allows it to be rewarded? Since we know that aggression is an extremely common class of behavior, it seems very likely that it has a high probability of occurrence in advance of its being rewarded.

This is indeed the case. During early childhood in every society, responses with aggressive components are very likely to occur *and* very likely to be rewarded. Basing my argument on this premise, I shall assert that the two keys to understanding human aggression, both of which are essential, are (1) its prepotency during infancy and (2) its socialization during childhood.

1. *The prepotency of human aggression*
The human infant starts life with an incredibly wide behavioral potential, but it can actually produce a very narrow repertory of responses. Everything it ultimately comes to do is, of course, the end product of a complex, continuous interaction between what it can do in the beginning and what environmental forces, mainly socially mediated rewards, selectively shape. Obviously, though, it can't be rewarded for a response it doesn't make. Those responses that it can and does make, are the only ones subject to reinforcement. Are aggressive responses among those few that the infant can make?

In a sense, yes. Among the limited repertory of responses at birth are actions that possess, in a primitive way, some of the basic attributes of what later in life are recognizable as aggressive responses. The infant can cry, push, pull, thrash about wildly, and struggle. It does so whenever it needs something. (Later in life, as we shall see, the child may come to emit similar responses whenever it *wants* something, whether it is needed or not, but for the moment we are not concerned with *want*, a concept, that is difficult to define but with *need*, an intuitively obvious concept.)

When in *need*, then, the infant responds in one of the very few ways it can respond; these ways just happen to possess features of aggressiveness—especially, *intensity* and an emotional state similar to what, in everyday language is labeled *anger*. These responses further possess, albeit unknown to the infant who emits them, very strong social demand characteristics. In other words, the infant's responses serve as compelling stimuli for certain classes of responses by his caretakers. A very likely outcome of the infant's behavior is that someone will respond sooner or later by satisfying the need. It is of little or no import that the infant is unaware in the beginning that this will be the outcome. It matters not that the struggling lacks intentionality. In short order, it will acquire that property. What does matter is that in the beginning the behavior that possesses the basic features of aggressive responding is there.

It is in this sense that aggression is considered to be *prepotent* in the human organism. The infant responds to needs in the only ways it can, and these ways involve behaviors that are precursors of aggression. Let us label these behaviors *proto-aggression.*

It is very important to note that we are *not* here stating that the human infant starts life with an aggressive *instinct*, nor even with an aggressive *drive*. Rather, it begins life with recurrent needs, the satisfaction of which requires signaling of distress. The signals it can emit involve the basic components of aggressive behavior.

It probably matters greatly that the infant responds the way it does when in need since this affects what it is likely to learn to do later as it comes to develop more complex responses to states of need. If the infant smiled when hungry, or emitted a three-word sentence when soiled, the story we are about to tell would be a very different one indeed. If smiling and making polite requests were prepotent responses, we would be about to account for the pervasiveness of gentility, rather than the pervasiveness of aggression.

2. *The socialization of aggression. Part I*

We have just seen that there is very little that a human infant can do when in need except to emit rather diffuse but intense responses. Consequently, whenever a caretaker responds to these need-signaling behaviors of an infant, not only are the needs attended to (which has an immediate impact), the behaviors are reinforced (which has a long-range impact). During all those months before the baby matures sufficiently to acquire linguistic competence, it thus receives considerable reinforcement for its primitive, proto-aggressive behaviors.

If the Freudians and learning theorists who say that early experience is crucial in shaping the psychological development of the organism are correct even only in broad outline, then there is good enough reason to predict that all humans will acquire a strong and continuing disposition to respond "aggressively" whenever in some state of need. Such responses, albeit in primitive form, are the ones that not only occurred most frequently early in life, but were also most frequently rewarded.

Furthermore, the proto-aggression of the infant is subject to precisely the kind of reinforcement schedule that produces exceedingly strong response dispositions or habits. Because few caretakers are able to reward *every* need-signaling response of a discomforted infant, such responses are subject to a partial reinforcement schedule, just the kind that has long been known to make a response highly resistant to extinction (cf. Humphreys, 1939; Skinner, 1938). Not only that, in the intervals of delay between the first distress call and the response of the caretaker, the infant's responses are likely to increase in intensity, so that it is often a very strong response that receives the reward.

Of course, as socialization proceeds, caretakers become increasingly demanding with regard to the behavior of their children. As a child becomes increasingly able to signal and specify the nature of its need linguistically, caretakers elicit and reward these more sophisticated responses and endeavor not to reward the more primitive ones. Still, there is a long and difficult period of learning the more socially acceptable ways of signaling need, during which the child often regresses to earlier response patterns, which the caretaker sometimes in desperation reinforces. So, even while learning to behave in a "more civilized" manner, the child is inadvertently being taught that if all else fails he can get what he needs by making a fuss.

As he acquires linguistic skills, which enable him to label his needs, the concept of "want" is gradually acquired. In English, at least, and probably in many other languages, children are seldom asked, "What do you need?" nor are they expected to say "I need . . . ." Instead, the child is asked, "What do you want?" and he replies in kind. Whatever distinction there is between want and need, it becomes blurred, and all the behaviors associated with need-reduction generalize to want-satisfaction. And these behaviors must surely include the proto-aggressive responses originally linked to need-signaling.

If a child always gets what he wants by asking politely for it, he never need do anything but ask. But that's not the way it is at all. For one reason or another, asking often fails to produce the wanted object. When this is the case, the likely alternative to asking will be an earlier reinforced response. Another way to say this is that, when frustrated, the child will regress to earlier behavior. Since that earlier behavior is proto-aggressive behavior, it turns out that a highly probable response to frustration is proto-aggression.

Moreover, what was once a diffuse proto-aggressive response will subsequently become a directed, bona fide aggressive response, focused on another human being. Whereas earlier, the frustrated child responded by flailing aimlessly about, complaining, as it were, to no one in particular, the discovery that the ability to satisfy his wants resides in persons serves to sharpen his complaints so that they are directed to persons. The mere direction of a vigorous movement toward a person can, without possessing intent to harm, inflict harm if contact is made. An occasional success in getting what is wanted following such a response would be enough to reward and thereby strengthen a form of behavior that is now clearly recognizable as aggression.

In the first instance, the persons most likely to be the targets of such responses are the child's caretakers, whom he perceives as capable of satisfying his wants. One of the basic "insights" that must be acquired during socialization is an awareness that our caretakers have immense power either to satisfy or frustrate our wants. As a concomitant of this awareness, we learn first to direct our strivings toward them.

As the child comes into contact with more and more people, particularly with other children, he is likely to encounter other persons who from time to time stand between him and his satisfaction. Other children especially are likely to have something he wants—or want to take from him something he has. The interaction that is likely to ensue under such conditions will almost inevitably involve interpersonal struggling, because one or both of the actors will previously have struggled under similar, frustrating circumstances. Regardless of the outcome of the struggle, no matter who wins, the child will learn from it that aggression has a payoff. The message will be clear enough; occasionally, harm has to be inflicted or at least threatened in order to secure one's wants.

The learning of this particular lesson is further facilitated by the simple fact that the child will probably often find himself in the company of other children who learned it before he did. He will therefore witness many models whose successful aggressive behavior he will come to emulate. Thus, his learning by direct reinforcement will be buttressed by what he learns by imitation.[4]

The careful reader will recognize that, according to this account, what the child will have learned thus far in his development is simply to respond in an aggressive manner in order to get what he wants (and not because he "wants" to hurt anybody). This kind of aggressive responding is what some psychologists (Aronson, 1972, p. 144) term *instrumental* aggression. Often, this is distinguished by psychologists from *intentional* aggression—a response in which the infliction of harm is a desired end. Aronson, for example, reserves the label "aggression" for "behavior *aimed* at causing harm or pain" (p. 143); at the outset of the present chapter, I defined aggression as "a response *designed* to inflict personal injury." These definitions are in accord with what most psychologists mean by aggression. Thus, it should be clear that what has so far been described is a class of behavior that does not completely satisfy this definition.

To complete our theoretical account of how learning to be aggressive is a likely outcome of socialization, we must consider how a child learns to inflict harm intentionally. But first, let us recognize that writers, like Aronson, who distinguish between instrumental and intentional aggression are correct. (Aronson employs different terminology than is used here. He distinguishes two kinds of "intentional aggression," one of which he calls "instrumental," the other "aggression as an end in itself." Because the *intent* to harm is not an aspect of instrumental aggression, it seems clearer to speak of "instrumental aggression" on the one hand and "intentional aggression" on the other.) This distinction needs to be made. Men do commit both kinds of actions, and the underlying psychologies of these two kinds of actions must not be confused. Aronson provides a good example (p. 144), contrasting an injuring tackle of a quarterback by a defensive football player who wants to win a game (in my terms, this is instrumental aggression) and an identical act motivated solely by a desire to retaliate for a real or imagined insult (which would be intentional aggression).

But however useful and necessary this distinction may be, it must be understood that the two kinds of aggression are developmentally related. Instrumental aggression will be learned earlier, and the probability is high that intentional aggression will be an outgrowth of instrumental aggression.

Any instrumental response can become "an end in itself." Simply because a particular response has more than occasionally led to reinforcement, that response can come, via conditioning, to be intrinsically rewarding. Psychologists have described this particular conditioning phenomenon in a variety of terms—e.g., via *secondary reinforcement* ("a stimulus that occasions or accompanies a reinforcement acquires thereby reinforcing value of its own," Keller and Schoenfeld, 1950) and via *functional autonomy* (Allport, 1937). This mechanism applies to any response. As applied to instrumental aggressive responses, children who learn to make them successfully can learn also to make them for no reason other than to make them, because, as it were, it "feels good" to make them! Of course, it feels good because some subtle learned motives are also satisfied, like a drive for a sense of mastery, self-esteem, and the like. Therefore, in one sense, even what we have called intentional aggression does not totally lack instrumentality. But the distinction between intentional and instrumental aggression is still worth making provided that we do not lose sight of the fact that the one is merely an outgrowth and refinement of the other.

To recapitulate: To this point we have followed the infant from a helpless being who can only struggle aimlessly in an effort to satisfy his needs, through an intermediate stage where he learns to seek want-satisfaction by attacking others, through to a subsequent stage where he learns to inflict harm apparently for the sole sake of doing so. Without postulating either an aggressive drive or an aggressive instinct (and with no talk at all of any mythical "aggressive energy"), we have seen how society acts upon biologically programmed response dispositions to shape behavior patterns that are finally and in all respects aggressive.

We need go no further in order to demonstrate that the etiology of human aggression may be accounted for in social learning terms and that the instinct postulate is excess baggage to the psychologist. But, in fact, the story of the development of aggression is not yet finished and the rest of it is rather complex. For there comes a time during the socialization process, when socializing agents attempt to deal directly with aggression *per se*. Let us consider this next chapter in the story.

3. *The socialization of aggression. Part II*

Sooner or later, every caretaker "decides" that he or she will no longer tolerate certain behaviors from the child, particularly aggressive behaviors directed against the caretaker. Many cross-cultural surveys (e.g., Lambert, 1971) have shown that quite generally around the world, one of the most intolerable behaviors is aggression against a parent. It is typically punished. So, often, is peer aggression, especially in societies where, according to Lambert, there is reason to fear that peer aggression will generalize to aggression against other adults (pp. 53, 59). So most parents, at least some of the time, will either withhold rewards for behavior in older children that appears aggressive or they will punish that behavior. Punishment, has, among other consequences, the enhancement of frustration. If, as we have already seen, frustration is likely to lead to still more aggression, a vicious cycle has now been set in motion. Wants will be felt, expressed, and sometimes unfulfilled. Frustration will be felt and aggression expressed. Aggression will be punished and the frustration is enhanced, thereby increasing the probability of occurrence of subsequent aggression.

By this point, the socialization of aggression becomes an exercise in discrimination learning. Attention is focused on teaching the child when, where, and against whom he may not aggress (and, by implication, when, where, and against whom he may do so with relative impunity). A most likely outcome of this process is that the child will acquire two incompatible behavioral dispositions. One is the cognition that persons resembling parents are frequent sources of frustration toward whom he will be disposed to aggress. The other is that the more a person resembles a parent, the less free the child is to attack him. Because he can't, he will be in conflict; he will feel urges to aggress against authority figures and he will sense strong inhibitions against doing so. The conflict itself can produce still more frustration, the most likely outcome of which will be manifest aggression against less appropriate, but more permitted, targets. The vicious cycle thus becomes even more vicious, since the stage has now been set for the development of displaced aggression.

There are, of course, all sorts of constraints on this process which parents will differentially introduce. Some may try to teach their children a morality embodied in a set of values that preclude "picking on the weak." But this morality must compete with considerable prior experience, the clearest implications of which are that one is ill-advised to aggress against the strong!

There are also cultural factors impinging on the process. The cross-cultural study referred to earlier, for example, found United States mothers to be the most permissive of the six societies studied (the others were in India, Mexico, Kenya, the Philippines, and Okinawa) with regard to peer aggression by their children. This fact Lambert interpreted as a reflection of the American practice of living apart from relatives, a situation that does not prevail in the other societies included in the study. "In the American town, where almost no relatives live nearby, the child can fight anyone he wishes without getting in the parents' way" (Lambert, 1971, p. 51). American mothers were not, by the way, particularly permissive with regard to their children's aggression toward mothers.

Whatever the details of the process in any given society, and whatever the reasons for the cross-cultural differences in those details, it seems very likely that children in the course of growing up anywhere will acquire a mixed bag of conflicting response tendencies relating to frustration and aggression, and they will suffer, to varying degrees, from aggression-anxiety. This is surely not a pretty picture of one of the costly consequences of socialization, but it is a picture that fits much of what we know. Most of us do become angry when frustrated, and most of us experience anxiety when we become angry with someone whom we are not supposed to feel angry with.

Primed to attack, but constrained from doing so, we nevertheless do attack from time to time, often after all other alternative courses of action have failed. With shame and guilt, some of us regress to earlier learned modes of reacting to aggression. (Others aggress without experiencing those psychological costs.)

The foregoing analysis also leads to the prediction that aggression is more likely when the target is seen as one unlikely to aggress back. The analysis also suggests that aggression will be more likely when authorities appear to sanction it. And, the analysis allows for individual and cultural differences. All of these factors are part of the picture, and none of them are predicted by an instinct theory. Hence, most psychologists blame aggression on socialization.

To summarize, the essence of the speculations presented above on the role of social forces in human aggression is that our tendencies to aggress are an end product of a socialization process in which our prepotent proto-aggressive reactions to frustration are reinforced in ways that make bona fide aggressive actions likely to occur under some conditions and less likely under others. The analysis denied the existence of an aggressive instinct. It also avoided the postulation of aggressive energy. Further, it did not allege, as did some earlier psychologists, that aggression is a biologically programmed response to frustration.

At the same time, we did not say that humans are taught to be aggressive. We said they almost unavoidably learn to be aggressive because they are rewarded for prototypical aggressive responding during the helpless days of infancy.

But just as they learn to aggress, they can learn not to aggress. Proto-aggression need not be transformed into aggression. If the key to aggression lies in the socialization process, so does the key to non-aggression.

Before considering how this "best of all possible worlds" might be made better, let us examine some of the psychological research on which the foregoing analysis was based. The additional details that will be revealed will help us suggest some policy considerations.

THE LINK BETWEEN FRUSTRATION AND AGGRESSION

One of the ideas developed in the preceding analysis of how humans learn to be aggressive was the notion that aggression *becomes* a likely response to frustration. That there is a link between frustration and aggression is an old idea in psychology. A most thorough discussion of the frustration-aggression hypothesis appeared in a classic volume by a team of learning theorists (Dollard *et al.*, 1939) who acknowledged that Freud had earlier asserted that aggression was a "primordial reaction . . . whenever pleasure-seeking or pain-avoiding behavior was blocked" (p. 21). The Dollard team reexpressed this notion as follows: ". . . the occurrence of aggressive behavior always presupposes the existence of frustration, and, contrariwise, . . . the existence of frustration always leads to some form of aggression" (p. 1).

Subsequently, this badly stated proposition underwent considerable modification, with even its own authors (e.g., Miller, 1941) qualifying it by noting that frustration sometimes has consequences other than aggression. Accordingly, Miller (p. 338) suggested rephrasing the second part of the frustration-aggression hypothesis so that it read, "Frustration produces instigations to a number of different types of response, one of which is an instigation to some form of aggression."

In its amended form, the hypothesis has continued to enjoy strong support from students of aggressive behavior (cf. Berkowitz, 1958) and many derivatives of this hypothesis have received empirical support.

For example, there is evidence, gathered a long time ago, that the likelihood of crying by an infant (a response which in our analysis would be considered proto-aggressive) is related to milk deprivation. If this link ever needed documentation, it was provided by R.R. Sears and P.J. Sears in a study reported in the Dollard *et al.* volume (1939). This simple relationship provides clear support for the basic postulate that frustration increases the likelihood of occurrence of proto- or bona fide aggression. Other early studies, reviewed in detail by Berkowitz (1958) showed that the strength of aggressive tendencies varied positively with the degree of interference imposed and the history of frustration that an individual has experienced. The hypothesized link between frustration and aggression must be considered one of the best documented in psychology.

The particular part of the refined hypothesis that says that the actual occurrence of frustration-induced aggression depends on intervening factors also has empirical support. Such intervening variables as expectation of punishment, beliefs concerning sanctions, and characteristic individual differences have all been found to play a part (see Berkowitz, 1958, for a review of pertinent research).

Furthermore, there is considerable evidence that when frustration occurs, aggression is, under some circumstances, predictably displaced. The classic supporting study was done by Miller and Bugelski (1948) who found ethnic scapegoating to be facilitated by experimentally induced frustration. Another, somewhat later, study—a cross-cultural analysis of folk tales—revealed that in cultures in which children are more severely punished for aggression and restrained from aggressing, aggression targets in children's stories were more distinct from the tale's hero (more displaced, as it were) (Wright, 1954).

In more recent research on aggression, the link between frustration and aggression and the allied notion that experiential factors intervene to determine whether or not an aggressive response actually occurs (and, if so, whether it is displaced or not) have been pretty much taken for granted. Modern researchers considered these notions established and have progressed to more subtle questions, a few of which we shall shortly consider. So the frustration-aggression hypothesis, appropriately amended and refined, now enjoys the status of a psychological principle.

With confidence, it is generally acknowledged that frustration sets the stage for the occurrence of aggression. However, we must not lose sight of the fact that aggression is neither the *inevitable* outcome of frustration, nor as Freud suggested, "the primordial reaction" to it. In the analysis in the preceding section of this chapter, aggression was described as a *likely* reaction on the part of a frustrated person, but the likelihood was not due to any biological link between frustration and aggression. Rather, it was asserted that when frustrated, we engage in behaviors which we have learned are likely to satisfy needs and wants. *Among* these behaviors are proto-aggressive and aggressive responses; under certain conditions we regress to them. So, whether we aggress or not when frustrated depends on other things that we have learned.

For all this, however, frustration must be considered a key variable in human aggression. We shall have to include it in our thoughts for a recipe for a less aggressive world.

RESEARCH ON THE PROCESS OF LEARNING TO AGGRESS

In our analysis, much stress was placed on learning. That we learn to respond in ways that lead to reinforcement and that aggression is a way of responding that is often reinforced require no further amplification. But our analysis also suggested that much of our learning to aggress involves imitation and vicarious reinforcement. This statement calls for some discussion. The research supporting it also can enhance our understanding of the mediating factors that control our reactions to frustration.

For many classes of behavior, there is evidence that learning results from the observation of the behavior of others. This is particularly true when the observation includes witnessing the reinforcement contingencies of the others' behavior (vicarious reinforcement).

However, we apparently learn much merely by observing, regardless of the outcomes of the observed behavior (Bandura, 1971a). Moreover, we can learn both to perform old responses in new settings and to acquire new responses.

An early, now classic, study of imitation was done by Miller and Dollard in 1941. The emphasis in this study was on conditions likely to elicit the occurrence of "matching behavior" involving responses already in a child's repertory. Later work focused on the learning of new responses via imitation (e.g., Bandura and Walters, 1963; Mussen and Parker, 1965) and much of it has been concerned with the effects on the observer of the outcomes contingent on the behavior of the model.[5]

Although some disagreement prevails over the mechanisms involved in learning by observation, all these studies have shown that opportunity to observe someone engage in some behavior results, under a variety of conditions, in the observer's acquiring the potential for similar behavior. Whether or not he *performs* it may depend both on the consequences impinging on the model and on the inducements applied to the observer (Bandura, 1965b).

There is no reason to doubt that aggressive behavior, like any other kind of behavior, is learnable by observation. In fact, considerable experimental evidence shows that it is; many of the aforementioned studies of imitation have employed aggressive responses as the behavior to be observed. Some typical studies were those by Bandura and various co-workers, performed as social psychological experiments with children.

In a number of these experiments, children were exposed to one or another example of aggressive behavior and were subsequently provided with an opportunity to commit an aggressive response themselves. The nature of the model available for emulation and the kind of aggression witnessed varied from experiment to experiment, but the general finding that emerged from the series of experiments was that exposure to aggressive models was followed by aggression, significantly more than was the case without such exposure (e.g., Bandura and Huston, 1961; Bandura, Ross, and Ross, 1961; Bandura, Ross, and Ross, 1963).

Some of the resultant aggressive behavior on the part of the observers in these studies involved newly learned responses, learned via imitation. More important, however, is Bandura's interpretation of these research findings. He sees them as demonstrating that exposure to aggressive behavior on the part of relatively prestigious models (e.g., adults observed by children) creates the impression that aggressive behavior (involving new or old responses) is acceptable. Hence, such observations have the primary effect of weakening previously learned inhibitions of aggression, making a given instigation to aggression more likely to result in overt aggressive behavior.

As early as the mid-1950s, it was demonstrated in a real-world "field experiment" that persons were more likely to commit a traffic violation in imitation of a previous violator, the more the model person appeared to be a high-status individual (Lefkowitz, Blake, and Mouton, 1955). The authors of this study attributed the differential effectiveness of transgressing models, who were either well- or sloppily groomed, to a difference in the degree to which they reduced the inhibitions of the observers. It is possible, as the authors speculated, that when we view a transgression committed by a high status person whom we consider, rightly or not, as unlikely to be punished (or less severely than would be a low-status person), we not only identify with him but are more likely to emulate him, in the hope that we too might escape negative sanction. In any event, inhibition release as the mechanism underlying imitation of transgressors is supported by this study. The same mechanism seems likely to affect the imitation of aggressive models.

A basic test of the notion that observation of aggression diminishes one's own aggression-inhibitions would consist of assigning subjects (randomly, or by some appropriate matching technique) to two groups, one of which observed aggressive models while the other did not Subsequently, both groups would be made to experience some identical frustration. If the first group were to respond to the frustration with more aggression than the second group, evidence would have been provided that observing an aggressive model results in overt aggression. If the model's behavior were not novel—if it were behavior that the observers already had in their repertory—then the weakening of inhibition notion would be a preferred explanation. If it were novel, then some learning by imitation would be involved. (Of course, both processes work in the same direction—they induce manifest aggression in observers—so from a practical point of view, it doesn't matter very much which process is dominant.)

One such experiment was performed by Bandura, Ross, and Ross (1961) with nursery school children, an adult model, and a five-foot high inflated Bobo doll, on whom the model sat, pummelled, kicked, and spewed verbal attacks. Compared with a control group not exposed to this model/Bobo encounter, children in the experimental group later performed considerably more imitative acts, after being frustrated by being invited to play with some highly attractive toys and then prohibited from doing so as soon as they evinced interest. The control group, of course, was similarly frustrated.

It was reported in this study that some of the children in the experimental group became "carbon copies" of the models, displaying behavior that was virtually identical to that displayed by the models. However, the children also displayed aggressive behavior that had not been anticipated by the models, suggesting that in this situation there was both learning by imitation and a release of aggression-inhibition.[6]

In a later experiment by the same researchers (Bandura, Ross, and Ross, 1963), it was found that both live and cartoon film models were generally as effective in producing aggressive responses to frustration as were live, in-person models. Indeed, children who observed live *film* models earned aggression scores that were the most consistently different from control-group scores, a fact that has implications to be discussed below when we consider the impact of media-transmitted violence. For the present, let it be noted that the two studies just described support the proposition that observing aggression can result both in the learning of new aggressive responses and the reduction of aggression-inhibition.

The student who wonders how learning to aggress by observation comes about—what other variables modify it—should go a step further and consider another study by Bandura (1965b, reprinted in 1971a). In this experiment, children witnessed one of three TV performances involving aggression against a Bobo doll. The performances varied only with regard to the consequences for the model-aggressor, who, in one version was rewarded, in another was punished, and in the third suffered no consequences. When given a subsequent opportunity to imitate the model, children did so to varying degrees, depending on the consequences they had seen applied to the model's behavior. The differences occurred mainly between those who saw the model punished, on the one hand, and all the other children on the other. Moreover, this difference occurred primarily among girls; the boys' level of imitative aggressiveness was both higher than the girls' and unaffected by the observed consequences to the model (who was a male). But the experiment didn't stop here.

After the more or less free response tests of imitative performance, the children were all induced by promises of treats and pictures to show and tell what the model had done. In *this* test of what they had learned by observation, *all* groups, both boys and girls, performed equally well. The contingencies attached to the model's behavior *no longer made any difference.* By its two separate tests, this experiment showed that reinforcements administered to the model influenced observers' performances, but not their acquisition of matching response dispositions.

Considering various aspects of this experiment,[7] it appears that (a) the necessary and possibly sufficient condition for learning by observation is simply the opportunity to observe, (b) knowledge of the outcomes of the model's behavior influence the observer's probability of overtly imitating, but not his learning how to do so, (c) overt occurrence of responses already learned can be elicited by inducing the potential performer to anticipate rewards for doing so. The original sex differences reported by Bandura (1965b) and their subsequent elimination in that same experiment are particularly interesting in this regard, for obviously the two findings together reveal that the girls learned as much as the boys did, but their original performance was more subject to vicarious reinforcement control. In other words, the girls had more aggression-inhibition to overcome, and it took only the inducement of small rewards to overcome it.[8]

To the degree then that any culture provides opportunities for the observation of aggressive behavior, it should be expected that observers will learn—and feel freer—to aggress themselves. This simple mechanism, learning by imitation, must be counted among the cultural forces that increase the likelihood of the occurrence of aggression. Thus, we learn to aggress overtly not only when our own aggression is reinforced, but also when somebody else's is!

But isn't it widely believed that watching someone else aggress has a cathartic effect, making the watcher less likely to aggress? And isn't watching make-believe violence fun and games, which makes us feel better and thus makes us less likely to aggress? On the basis of what we have just seen, it seems hardly likely that we can say yes to these questions. Let's take a look at some obviously pertinent research.

THE IMPACT OF TELEVISED VIOLENCE
ON HUMAN AGGRESSION

By 1973, more than enough evidence had been accumulated to sustain the unhappy conclusion that television audiences, particularly in the United States, are regularly exposed to leisure-time stimulation that bears a direct causal relationship to overt aggressive behavior. This straightforward and unavoidable conclusion emerged from investigations sponsored by the Television and Social Behavior Program of the United States National Institute of Mental Health.

The report of this massive study may be found in a not altogether adequate summary by the Surgeon General's Advisory Committee, and in a series of five volumes, separately authored, which provides comprehensive details. The summary is entitled *Television and growing up: The impact of televised violence.* The five volumes appear under the general title, *Television and social behavior.* All of these reports are available from the United States Government Printing Office. The total report and the history of the project which produced it has been reviewed by Lee Bogart (1972-1973).

The research reported in these volumes is of interest to us here primarily for its substantive findings. On the other hand, Bogart's review examined the Surgeon General's report "as the product of a three-way process of interaction between government, powerful business interests, and social science" (p. 492). As such, it is also a fascinating document. To Bogart, "what was studied and why becomes more interesting than what was learned" (p. 492). Certainly, as Bogart shows, the Television and Social Behavior program constitutes an instructive case study of the snares and traps threatening applied social psychology. Among the most interesting features of this case study are the following: the three major television networks and the National Association of Broadcasters were permitted by the government to blackball candidates for the Advisory Committee; among the social scientists who were black-balled were Albert Bandura and Leonard Berkowitz (whose work, as we have already seen, is central to the issue); the purified committee which drafted the summary included two network executives, one former network executive and two network consultants, as well as several social scientists; the summary emphasized (properly) the caution that must always be exercised in interpreting research into causal relationships but it created the impression that less was established than was actually the case; the press, which based its reports on the summary, seriously misinterpreted the findings. It may also have been the case, as Bogart argues, that enough knowledge existed *before* this $1,000,000 crash program was undertaken, to conclude that televised (and filmed) violence subsequently contributes to overt aggression by those who view it. Thus, the mere act of opening up the question once more in the manner in which it was done, implied that more doubt existed than was actually the case.

For the political psychologist, then, the Television and Social Behavior project is must reading and Bogart's report of its history serves to place it in context.

Liebert, Neale, and Davidson (1973) have presented a cogent review of the large series of investigations undertaken under the auspices of this federal government agency. Although initial journalistic reports of the NIMH investigations were ambiguous, as Liebert *et al.* aptly show, the evidence that TV programming contributes to aggressive behavior is overwhelmingly positive.

There are, of course, three possibilities with regard to a link between violent content TV programming and overt aggressiveness on the part of TV viewers. The link may be positive, negative, or non-existent. Numerous case histories, anecdotes and considerable research[9] have for long suggested that the link is positive. But many persons responsible for TV programming have suggested regularly that there is no link at all, that, in fact, violence on TV does nothing more to the viewer than entertain him. Some Freudian and otherwise clinically oriented psychologists have even suggested that the link is negative—that the viewing of violence has a cathartic effect.

The catharsis point of view has, of course, a very long history. In one of the earliest extant commentaries on drama, Aristotle suggested that the act of witnessing a drama purges the witness of whatever extreme feelings are being expressed on the stage. A modern version of this Aristotelian hypothesis involves an elaboration of the frustration-aggression hypothesis. This elaboration has suggested that when an individual is frustrated, his aggressive "drive" increases, which leads to feelings of discomfort that are reducible through fantasy aggression. A statement of this line of reasoning may be found in Feshbach (1955). Feshbach's notion that a heightened aggressive drive state may be reduced by fantasy aggression led him to predict that viewing violence would serve to minimize overt aggression.

At least two studies done during the past two decades cast serious doubts on Feshbach's 1955 hypothesis (Mussen and Rutherford, 1961; Siegel, 1956). In the 1956 study, experimental evidence was gathered which showed that young children, interacting in pairs, displayed more aggression toward each other after viewing a Woody Woodpecker cartoon (which had numerous aggressive incidents) than they did after seeing an otherwise comparable but non-aggressive film. Challenging studies like these induced Feshbach and a collaborator, Singer, to offer a modified version of the catharsis theory (Feshbach and Singer, 1971).

The revised version of the catharsis hypothesis proposed two kinds of dynamics whereby a fantasy aggression might result in the reduction of overt aggression. In the first, fantasy aggression was seen as leading to a reduction in drive level (a process like that suggested in the 1955 version) with the immediate result being a sense of well-being on the part of the fantasy aggressor, which reinforces his fantasying. As a result of this reinforcement, the probability of future occurrence of fantasy (as opposed to overt) aggression would be enhanced. The second dynamic involved an *increase* in aggressive drive level reaching such a heightened state that the individual in effect frightens himself by the very thought of the consequences that would stem from his expressing his aggressions overtly. Hence, the ultimate effect would be to inhibit overt aggression. Thus, in one version, drive level is hypothesized to be reduced, in the other it is increased; in either case, the end result is expected to be cathartic.

With this somewhat more sophisticated (and two-pronged) hypothesis as background, Feshbach and Singer undertook a large-scale experimental field study in which they searched for evidence to support the catharsis prediction. And, in contrast to the Siegel (1956) and the Mussen and Rutherford (1961) studies, Feshbach and Singer's study obtained results that at first glance seemed to support the catharsis hypothesis.[10]

Feshbach and Singer employed 400 young boys as subjects in their experiment, all of them either in correctional or custodial institutions or in private schools. The private school boys were drawn from middle-class (or higher) backgrounds, while the others were of lower socioeconomic origins. All the boys in the study were assigned lists of TV programs to watch, and their assignments included six hours per week of regularly scheduled TV programs over a six-week period. The experimental manipulation in this study involved random assignment of boys to two groups, for one of which the television diet consisted of shows with much violent content, while for the other group the programming was essentially non-violent. Among the dependent measures obtained in this study were ratings by teachers and other institutional staff members of overt aggressive actions by the boys. These behavioral ratings were made once each day for each boy in the study.

Two major findings stand out. The first is that generally the boys who had witnessed the violent programs earned *less* aggressive ratings than the boys who had watched the other programs (although this finding must be qualified since the only statistically significant difference across viewing groups was obtained for the institutional-ized boys). The second finding was that over time the boys who had viewed the violent programs showed a decrease in their aggression scores, while those who viewed the control set of non-violent programs actually showed an increase. (Again, significant differences occurred only among the institutionalized boys, so this finding, too, must be qualified.) Taken at face value, these two findings offer seemingly impressive support for the catharsis hypothesis.

However, the Feshbach and Singer study has not withstood either attempts at replication or careful reanalysis. At least two critiques, one by Chaffee and McCleod (1971) and another by Liebert, Sobol, and Davidson (1972) have presented very serious challenges to the original interpretation of the Feshbach and Singer findings. The critics have called attention to the fact that the boys in the study who were assigned to watch the non-violent programs indicated plainly that they resented being put on such a bland diet! Their resentment could well have generated the overt aggression that was so characteristic of this group during the six weeks of the study. It has also been pointed out that the institutionalized boys assigned to watch non-violent shows complained so much that the authorities relented and inserted *Batman* into their list of approved programs. Clearly, then, the boys in the supposedly non-violent program group did watch one highly violent program. Thus, the high (and increas-ingly so) level of overt aggression on the part of this so-called control group is subject to diverse interpretation, which in turn casts doubt on the value of this study as a test of the catharsis hypothesis.

More important even than these critiques is an attempt by Wells (1972) to replicate the Feshbach and Singer study with improve-ments in design as dictated by the critiques. When Wells did this, he obtained data that sustained the opposite conclusion—that watching aggression has an instigating, rather than an inhibiting, effect, at least on boys with some degree of aggressive predispositions. Wells could produce no evidence for catharsis in his well-designed study.

Indeed, the weight of evidence is in the same direction as Wells' finding. As is shown by Liebert, Neale, and Davidson (1973), there have been several field studies and many experiments that sub-stantiate the incitement hypothesis, and only the internally invalid Feshbach and Singer study to give false comfort to the catharsis believer.

One of the most interesting sets of experiments conducted to date were also field studies, because they were performed not in a psychological laboratory but in real-world settings such as TV preview theaters and under home viewing circumstances. Lacking some of the features of bona fide experiments, these studies are more realistic than most experiments and therefore deserve special attention. Milgram and Shotland (1973), with cooperation from the CBS Office of Social Research, designed and conducted several field experiments, most of which employed as stimulus material three versions of an episode of a popular network program, *Medical Center*; one involved a punished anti-social act, another an un-punished anti-social act, the third a pro-social act, plus an entirely different episode devoid of any anti-social behavior. The anti-social act in the program consisted of the breaking into a charity collection box (while the pro-social act was inserting money into the box).

In one study, some 600 people were recruited via newspaper ads and street contacts to report to a preview theater in New York City where they saw one or another version of the *Medical Center* program. At the showing, they were given a gift certificate to be redeemed some time later at a gift distribution center. Those who appeared there (342 people in this particular study) found an unoccupied office, a terse note telling them that the gifts were no longer available, and a collection box with money in it, including an enticing dollar dangling from it. The redemption center was, of course, designed by the experimenters as the test situation wherein the subjects' behavior *vis-a-vis* the collection box could be monitored unobtrusively.

In this study, a few subjects did perform anti-social acts that resembled the act shown in two of the four *Medical Center* versions, but no significant differences in the frequency of such acts occurred across the various versions of the program seen.

In another, very similar study, the presumably frustrating experi-ence of learning that no gift was forthcoming was softened by revising the message so that it required a short trip to another office in the same building in order to obtain the promised gift. This modification in the experiment depressed the overall rate of anti-social acts committed, but, again, the theft rate was unrelated to program version.

One study in the series that employed actual broadcasts was conducted in New York City, where over a million sets were tuned to the punished anti-social version of the *Medical Center* episode while the rest of the country was watching a neutral episode that had been shown in New York a week earlier. Some 3500 persons in New York were contacted by mail and asked to watch the earlier of the two broadcasts and another 3500 were similarly contacted regarding the anti-social version. All of these persons were also invited to the gift distribution center (236 actually appeared) where the test situation yielded very few anti-social acts nor any significant differences across the two groups of viewers.

The foregoing descriptions of portions of the Milgram and Shotland research program serve not only to convey the innovative nature of this cleverly blended quasi-experimental methodology, but also to indicate that the research program—the few studies reviewed here and the others in the series—did not produce any evidence of imitative effects. The psychologists concluded, "We did our best to find imitative effects, but all told, our search yielded negative results" (1973, p. 66). From this series of studies, then, the allegation that viewing anti-social acts on television enhances the probability of the viewers' performing similar acts, would have to be considered unproven. But as Milgram and Shotland themselves point out, neither do their negative results prove that television programming as it currently prevails does *not* stimulate anti-social behavior. The findings (or, the lack thereof) of their quasi-experiments perhaps ought not to be generalized beyond the very particular combination of events, subject recruitment, subject self-selection, etc. that characterized the studies. Numerous factors make the studies very different from the circumstances to which one would like to generalize, this despite the unusual degree of realism in the research. It is probable, too, that the single act employed in the experimental stimulus was inadequate to stimulate an imitative response; several different violent and anti-social acts, such as are available any night of the week on network television, might have cumulative effects that simply could not be detected in the research done by Milgram and Shotland.

Of course, as the authors point out, negative results may always be explained away by an infinitude of *ex post facto* excuses that are purely speculative so that there is no avoiding the fact that their studies, for whatever reasons, yielded no intergroup differences in the commission of imitative anti-social acts.

However, the Milgram and Shotland story contrasts with that told by Lefkowitz, Eron, Walder, and Husemann (1972, 1975). This study, not an experiment but a field study, spanned a ten-year period and employed as subjects 460 19-year olds who at the outset of the study had been part of a group of 875 third-grade youngsters, all of whom were at that time rated by their peers on aggressiveness. (Incidentally, at that point it was found that aggression ratings for boys correlated positively with watching violent TV programs. The TV watching behavior was assessed by mothers' reports. This finding did not hold for girls.) At the second point, a most interesting finding emerged, and again it held only for boys. This time, the subjects themselves reported on their viewing habits but, again, contemporary peer ratings of aggressive behavior were obtained. It was found that there was a significant positive correlation between TV violence watching while in the third grade and aggressive behavior at age 19. The relationship between rated aggressiveness in the third grade and violence viewing at the age of 19, however, was *not* significant. (Thus the data do not support an alternative hypothesis that persons who seek out violence on TV are, to begin with, more aggressive.) The total set of data clearly supports the hypothesis that a diet of violent TV is related causally to subsequent overt aggressive behavior.

We could present additional evidence. Instead, the reader is directed to Bogart's review (1972-1973), to the Liebert, Neale, and Davidson volume (1973) and to the Lefkowitz *et al.* volume (1975) for additional evidence.[11] These three excellent sources also reveal just how pervasive violent programming is on American television. As Liebert *et al.* put it, "the best documented fact about television is that it is violent." They presented data showing that in each year from 1967 through 1971, more than 80 percent of all programs on American television channels had at least one violent episode included. Moreover, they presented data to show that the average number of violent episodes *per hour* on American television during those same years was 7.5 episodes. As Milgram and Shotland (1973) put it, "The prevalence of violent acts on commercial television in the United States is undisputed" (p. 1). So the amount of such stimulation impinging on children is not trivial. Recognizing that by 1970 nearly all American homes had at least one TV set and that the average set is on several hours per day, with average primary and secondary schoolchildren watching more than 15 hours per week, it is strikingly obvious that exposure to a potent series of instigations to aggression is considerable.[12]

There are, not surprisingly, individual differences in reaction to televised instigations to aggression. (See Bogart [1972-1973], for a very thoughtful discussion of the interactions that exist between aggressive predispositions, social background factors, TV watching, and subsequent overt aggression. Lefkowitz *et al.* [1975] also discuss such complexities.) But the fact of individual differences does not dilute the impact of the evidence that TV programs serve as instigations to aggression for at least some people under certain circumstances. In practical terms, it is a real problem that cries out for action, even though not every child who watches commits an aggression. Milgram and Shotland, despite the negative results of their own research, remind their readers (1972, p. 42) that if an anti-social TV program were to influence only one-tenth of one percent of its viewers, one thousand people would be affected by a program watched by only one million.

As if the influence of television weren't enough in itself to create a very high potential for aggressive behavior, we are also blessed in the United States and in many other nations with widely held *ideas* about aggression (ideas that are related to the old instinct notion), which serve to provide us with a superabundance of aggressive models. There is more aggressiveness to be emulated than would be the case if these ideas were less popular than they are. That we hold these ideas results in some most unfortunate self-fulfilling prophecies.

SELF-FULFILLING PROPHECIES AND AGGRESSION

Human social life is replete with examples of myths being converted to reality simply because the myth is so tenacious. In the case of aggression, there is the myth that males are naturally more aggressive than females. This belief, it can easily be shown, functions as a self-fulfilling prophecy that results in males behaving more aggressively than females. That they do, constitutes a temptation for the uncritical to conclude that aggressive behavior is, just as the instinct theorists maintain, biologically determined. And round and round we go.

That the myth *produces* the reality rather than reflecting the reality is a simple argument. As children display certain behavior, they will be reacted to by adults and their peers in ways determined partly by shared values that apply to the behavior. If, in a given culture, aggressive behavior is considered natural, normal, or other-wise appropriate when it is performed by males but not when it is performed by females, then the same behavior when emitted by the two sexes will be differentially reinforced. In effect, aggression among boys will be encouraged. The end result, of course, will be for boys to aggress more than girls, thereby sustaining the myth of biologically determined sex differences *and* boys will aggress more than they might otherwise.

Furthermore, more male models will themselves emit aggressive responses than will female models and, since same-sex emulation is more likely than cross-sex emulation (recall the findings of Bandura, Ross, and Ross [1961, 1963] reported above), still more forces will exist for the enhancement of male aggressiveness in succeeding generations.

To carry the argument a step further, it seems likely that an additional result of imbibing the myth that relates (and in the extreme *equates*) aggressiveness and masculinity, males will be less subject to aggression-inhibition than will females (which we earlier saw is another documented fact). This would serve as still another factor making manifest aggression more likely among males.

What we have just seen about the myth of natural male aggressiveness may be recapped as follows: Males are more likely than females to be rewarded for aggression, to be exposed to same-sex models who aggress, and are less likely than females to acquire aggression-inhibition. All of these phenomena contribute to sex differences in aggression and sustain the very myth that in the first instance creates the conditions that convert the myth to "reality." This self-fulfilling prophecy is one of several mechanisms whereby aggressive behavior is encouraged by prevalent cultural forces. With such forces at work, and with media violence to stimulate and instigate aggression, there is clearly no longer any need to attach credence to aggressive instincts.

In addition to learning processes, which contribute to overt aggression—socialization, learning by imitation, sex-role identification, and the like—there are in society many conditions that set the stage for its occurrence and many cues that trigger it.

CONDITIONS AND CUES FOR AGGRESSION

Within limits and with some qualifications, the greater the frustration, the more the stage is set for overt aggression. The more frustrating life is within a society, the more aggression instigation is to be expected. Individuals who are more subject to frustration are likely to be driven to aggress more often than individuals who are less often frustrated. But since no society is free of frustration, and since no individual lives a totally frustration-free existence, everyone experiences it. No one escapes sibling rivalry, or intergenerational conflict, or competition for scarce resources, all of which engender frustration. Hence, instigations to aggression are everywhere a part of every man's environment. Thus, there is little to say about instigations to aggression beyond noting their very pervasive existence.

What requires some attention, however, is the parallel topic of cues to aggression. When frustrated, one may or may not aggress. What helps determine whether or not aggression occurs are the stimuli present in the environment when the instigation to aggression has occurred. These stimuli may be called cues to aggression. Many contemporary environments, it is sad to note, also contain many of these.

The aggressions of others

As we have already seen, the observation of aggression by others, even when it is not directed against ourselves, makes it more likely that we will aggress. Thus, one major category of experience that serves as a cue to aggression is the aggression that goes on around us. We have also seen that the impact of others' aggression is greater the more it goes unpunished. And, surely in the world in which we live, unpunished (even rewarded) aggression is common.

Even as children, we regularly witness at home, in school, and on the playground, aggressive acts that gain rewards. Throughout life, on our playing fields and battlefields, men are cheered, praised, and decorated for aggressive actions. In the media, conflicts are regularly resolved violently; TV's most frequent cliche is the good guy destroying the bad.

Over the long range, the effect of such experience is the learning to become aggressive, with the primary underlying mechanism being the reduction of aggression-inhibition. The same experiences probably serve in the short run to trigger an aggressive response, particularly when we happen to be frustrated. Thus, these experiences serve as aggression cues. Many studies have demonstrated this, including those by Bandura and his colleagues, which were cited earlier in this chapter in another connection.

The clearest support for this principle may be found in research reported by Berkowitz (1970). In an experimental task, students were subjected to ridicule and punishment and made to believe it had come from a student partner. Then some of them were shown a violent scene from a Hollywood movie, while others watched a film of a footrace. After this, they were given an opportunity to administer electric shocks to their partners. Those who had witnessed the violent film expressed more aggression via the shocks against their supposed tormenters.

A provocative finding in this particular experiment was that students who had been told that the violence in the film was justified were the subjects who responded most aggressively. This is particularly interesting in view of the fact that much of the violence presented in films and on TV is accompanied by information that implies justification. In this respect, media violence appears to be governed by a seriously misplaced morality. It is often violence committed in pursuit of a socially sanctioned goal, like punishment of villains. But, as Berkowitz has noted, ". . . justified aggression is precisely the kind that seems likeliest to encourage the expression of aggression by members of the audience" (1970, p. 92).

To exacerbate this particular difficulty, as some psychiatrists have pointed out (cf. Gilula and Daniels, 1969), our society not only sanctions many forms of violence, it also simultaneously condemns it both in reality and in the media, thereby enhancing aggression-anxiety. This in turn may motivate us to rationalize our aggressive tendencies and actions by inventing all sorts of justifications, only some of which we will ourselves believe.[13] For some, this state of affairs could well be the beginning of a life-long pattern of compulsive aggressiveness.

Clearly then, efforts by television producers to distinguish between sanctioned and non-sanctioned violence do nothing to reduce the negative impact of media violence. All of it, sanctioned or not, contributes to the problem by serving as cues to aggression.

Objects that trigger aggression

Those who would arm themselves (or others) justify weapons as peacekeeping. But it has been shown, again by Berkowitz (1970), that the mere presence of a weapon can stimulate aggressive behavior. The mere sight of a gun can be an aggression-inducing stimulus.

In an experiment conducted with students in a large American university, subjects in an experimental group were given a particular task to perform, during which they were humiliated and punished by seven electric shocks which they were led to believe were administered by a student partner. Control group subjects received only one shock. Then, all subjects were given an opportunity to evaluate their partner's performance, which also included the possibility of shocking him. As subjects took their places for this phase of the experiment, they did so either at an empty table or at one containing some items ostensibly "left over from another experiment." These items were either some sporting equipment or a pair of guns, which the experimenter pushed aside nonchalantly. The finding? The angry subjects (those who had received seven shocks) who saw the guns were the ones who gave the most shocks to their partners. Berkowitz interpreted this result as showing that the stimulus of the guns triggered aggression in the already angry men, on the basis of which he warned that we had better recognize that the interaction of hostility with such a cue is likely to result in overt aggression.

Even more disturbing is the possibility that a stimulus like a gun can trigger aggression in non-angry people. Although this was clearly not the case in the experiment just described, it *was* in another performed with young children. In this, children were allowed to play with an older child who had been primed by the experimenter to play in a friendly manner. Then, some of the young children were given toy guns to play with, while others were not. Subsequently, all of them were given an opportunity to push a button, the alleged outcome of which would be the toppling of a block tower built by the older child. More of the children who had played with the gun pushed the button (Berkowitz, 1970, p. 90). Here, the stimulus of the gun not only cued aggressiveness; it actually seemed to elicit it, bringing it about under conditions in which neither frustration nor anger were present.

This last finding, that the mere presence of a gun serves as a stimulus to aggression even in the absence of instigation to aggression, should be thought of next time one reads statistics like those from the United States for recent years which showed an annual frequency of gun involvement in 55,000 cases of assault, 71,000 cases of robbery, 100,000 gun-inflicted injuries, and about 8,000 murders, most of them involving family members and friends (Gilula and Daniels, 1969). Much violence, Berkowitz has argued, is impulsive rather than premeditated, and the mere availability of a gun may provide the critical impulse.

Explicit instructions to aggress

While most of us, most of the time, are taught not to aggress, there are times when any one of us may actually be told to do so. When those who tell us are authority figures, we are remarkably prone to comply. We need not, and certainly don't, condone the behavior of an Eichmann or a Calley by admitting that there is some Eichmann/ Calley in all of us. But admit it, we must, if Milgram's research (1963, 1965) is to be properly digested.[1][4]

Milgram's goal was to discover the conditions under which a person will comply with an order to hurt another person. Milgram was hard pressed to find conditions under which the average person would not! In his laboratory, hundreds of adults were recruited, mostly of middle- and working-class background, and placed in a simulated, but very realistic teaching laboratory where they were to "teach" someone else by punishing him for every error he made. The punishment consisted of electric shocks, the voltage of which "had to be" increased with each successive error. Although no shocks were ever actually delivered, it certainly appeared to the subject that he was delivering them for he heard moans, groans, screams, and calls for mercy from his "victim" in a pre arranged, highly dramatic fashion. Milgram characterized the situation as it must have appeared to the subject. "He may continue to follow the orders of the experimenter, or he may refuse to follow the orders of the experimenter and heed the learner's pleas." In other words, the situation was one in which the experimenter's demands that the experiment continue conflicted with the victim's pleas that it be stopped.

The results include many findings that illuminate the variables that influence the resolution of such conflicts. For example, it was found that the more physically remote the victim was, the more likely it was that the subject continued to inflict shocks. Also, the more surveillance by the experimenter, the more he was obeyed. There were other findings that illuminate some of the processes that seem to influence obedience, including how the subjects perceive the status of the experimenter, his institution, and the setting of the experiment. But for our present purposes, the most important fact of all is that under *all* conditions of the experiment there were some people who were *fully* obedient. They administered shocks, moving step by step to "450 volts," long after hearing cries to the effect that the pain was unendurable, and considerably after the learner had ceased to show any signs of life! Although the proportion of subjects who went that far varied with experimental conditions, there were always some who did. And, it is sad to report, such persons were considerably easier to find than a person who refused to give a single shock!

The high level of obedience that appeared over so many different conditions of Milgram's experiment was striking. Although many subjects expressed disapproval over what they had been told to do, they did it nevertheless. And these were not persons selected for characteristic sadism. In Milgram's words, "With numbing regularity, good people were seen to knuckle under the demands of authority and perform actions that were callous and severe. Men who are in everyday life responsible and decent were seduced by the trappings of authority, by the control of their perceptions, and by the uncritical acceptance of the experimenter's definition of the situation into performing harsh acts" (1965, p. 75).

What a chilling prospect Milgram's findings suggest! Are most of us likely to do as we are told, even when we are told to inflict harm, just so long as the instruction comes from what is perceived as a legitimate authoritative source? So it appears.

Indeed, it may even be worse. Via socialization, we seem to learn to respect authority so well that we are not only prone to obey, we even tend to claim authoritative sanction as justification for aggression when none exists. Because our socialization engenders much conflict over aggression, when we actually have aggressed, we seem strongly motivated to find an excuse for having done so. Psychologists label this kind of behavior *dissonance reduction*.

DISSONANCE REDUCTION AND THE JUSTIFICATION OF AGGRESSION

For reasons we have already covered, any instigation to aggression is likely to place the individual in a conflict. To aggress or not to aggress will be the question. The relative strengths of competing responses, the magnitude of the instigation, the presence of cues, the perceived sanctions, all of these factors will influence the outcome of the conflict. If it is resolved by the commission of an overt act of aggression, the actor should find himself in a state of post-decision distress. "I have hurt someone" and "I know I ought not to have done so" are incompatible cognitions. Following aggression, then, we should expect an aggressor to be in a state of cognitive dissonance (Festinger, 1957) and, hence, likely to engage in behaviors that serve to reduce the dissonance. A number of laboratory experiments have focused on this phenomenon—the reduction of post-aggression dissonance—and by so doing have both illuminated and underscored the notion that socialization imparts both inducements *and* inhibitions to aggression.

In these studies, the typical paradigm resembles the Milgram situation in that it involves the use of an experimenter's confederate against whom a naive subject, known initially to oppose aggressive behavior, is induced to administer shocks or otherwise punish for errorful performance (cf. Buss, 1961). However, in these studies, unlike the Milgram experiment, the inducement is of minimal intensity, with the subject made to understand that he does indeed have a choice; he can refuse to aggress. For those subjects who do aggress, then, the basic condition for post-aggression dissonance, theoretically, exists. The subject would know that he had aggressed and, by so doing, had violated a social value to which he himself subscribed.

According to cognitive dissonance theory, the magnitude of post-aggression dissonance should depend upon the degree to which the aggressor believed he had a choice at the time he aggressed, as well as upon the intensity of the aggressive act committed. Also, the less justification for aggression offered by the experimenter, the more dissonance the aggressor should experience. Finally, the greater the aggressor's characteristic level of self-esteem, the more cognitive dissonance he should experience (since the better he regards himself, the more the aggressor should be discomforted by knowledge of his value-contradicting behavior).

In a series of experiments by Brock and Buss, these independent variables were shown to influence the amount of dissonance as manifested in a variety of behaviors which the researchers interpreted as dissonance reduction mechanisms. It is these behaviors that are of interest here. They are *consequences* of behaving aggressively, but they also serve to reveal what our socialization techniques have armed us with to alleviate our aggression anxieties. Again, it is not a pretty picture.

In one study (Buss, 1961) subjects were induced to punish a "learner" with whom they did not expect subsequently to interact. The magnitude of punishment (electric shocks) was made to vary from subject to subject. After the training phase of the experiment, subjects were given an opportunity to evaluate the learner. The greater the shock, the more the subject *devalued* his victim.

In another, (Brock & Buss, 1962) subjects were led to believe that they had either high or low degrees of choice and were then asked to evaluate the pain they had administered. The greater the perceived choice, the more they *minimized* the pain they had inflicted.

Two studies by the same authors employed a postaggression measure of the subject's *perception* of the degree to which they were obliged to aggress. One study (Brock and Buss, 1962) showed that the greater the shock administered, the more subjects reported obligation. Another (Brock and Buss, 1964) showed that subjects who had been provided with no justification by the experimenter for aggression reported more obligation than did subjects who had been provided with justification.

There were still other findings, but enough have been reviewed here to make it clear that the committing of aggression can motivate much distortion of reality in an effort to maintain self-respect. This in turn underscores that we have conflicting tendencies with regard to aggression in the first place and reminds us how easy it is to resolve the conflict by aggressing. These experiments support the proposition that for many of us aggression produces psychological discomfort which can only be reduced by denying the magnitude of pain we have caused, by denigrating our victim, by claiming that we acted under duress, or by some other distortional process that removes the onus from ourselves.

Lest the reader conclude that such perceptual distortions occur only in the laboratory, he/she ought to recall the defense arguments offered by the My Lai massacre participants or the account by the former Green Beret officer of his shooting of the so-called triple agent. In his telling of that story, he stressed such features as his use of a dulling chemical on the victim prior to shooting him (minimizing the pain inflicted?), the alleged oriental stoicism concerning individual life (devaluing the victim?) and the existence of an official order to dispose of his long-time associate (enhancing the perceived obligation?).

From this line of research on the cognitive consequences of aggressive behavior, we have learned two important facts. Most of us cannot commit aggression without feeling a need to "justify" it. And it is apparently not difficult to perceive justification.

Sometimes, we are provided with an excuse for our aggressive acts. Otherwise, we invent one.

THE REDUCTION AND CONTROL
OF AGGRESSIVE BEHAVIOR

We have now seen enough about how aggression becomes pervasive in human social behavior to begin our consideration of how to make it less common. Questions pertaining to the prevention and control of aggression are difficult ones. However, there is reason to believe that ways to prevent overt aggression can be found. The instinctivist position, which we have rejected, would obviously provide *no* basis for optimism. The social learning approach which was delineated in this chapter, on the other hand, does offer some hope. Even the studies reviewed in the last two sections, which revealed a pervasive tendency to follow orders and which showed a willingness to perceive obligation to aggress where none exists, paradoxically constitute reasons to be optimistic. For such studies really show us how our tendencies to aggress are dependent on external control. "Human nature," in the classical sense of the term, may be relatively immutable, but the social environment may be changed; as it changes, so will the nature of men who inhabit it.

If, as we have concluded from our examination of various findings and theories, aggressive behavior is (a) instigated by frustration, (b) inhibited by aggression-anxiety, and (c) triggered by the presence of cues that signal its apparent legitimacy, then the frequency of occurrence of overt aggressive responses should be reducible through policies and programs which (a) minimize frustration, (b) maintain or enhance inhibitions of aggression, and (c) remove from the environment aggression-legitimizing cues. Berkowitz (1970), acknowledging that these prescriptions are more easily articulated than implemented, nevertheless asserted, "A society that wants fewer violent outbursts should reduce frustrations, leave inhibitions intact, and remove immediate cues that can set off aggressive acts" (p. 93).

FRUSTRATION REDUCTION

Frustration, we have seen, does not inevitably produce aggression but it is extremely likely to serve as an instigation to it. Accordingly, eliminating from the social environment some of the sources of frustration should decrease the probability of occurrence of aggressive behavior.

The reduction of frustration is, of course, a long-term and difficult task. But the difficulties ought not deter us from making a start, for as frustrations mount, their reduction becomes increasingly difficult. Nor should we be deterred by the fact that not all sources of frustration can ever be eliminated. It is true that no society could permit every person to satisfy all of his wants all of the time. Inherent in social order is constraint of goal-seeking behavior whenever the attainment of one man's goals interferes with the attainment of another's. Moreover, there is no such thing as the ultimate satiation of need, for as one goal is reached, a new one is acquired to tantalize. Indeed, in many societies, the invention of new needs and goals is an institutionalized activity, exemplified by industries that build in "obsolescence," create a continuing array of "improved" products, and devote a staggering portion of their wealth to eliciting and rewarding acquisitive behavior. It is unlikely that many persons reared in such a consumption-oriented environment can escape a nagging sense of failure in attaining goals, no matter how many have been reached. But does this mean that we must accept things as they are and live lives marked by successive waves of frustration, or does it mean, on the contrary, that we are already armed with the knowledge of where to begin to reverse the tide? For those who have what they need, might it not be easier than we think to show them that they don't need what they think they want?

Perhaps frustration-reduction can be achieved among the relatively well-off. But for the relatively poor in affluent societies, and for the great masses of people in the more numerous poverty-stricken societies around the world, the problem is surely more difficult. For them, the vast majority of mankind, there is the two-pronged goal of failure to satisfy life's basic needs and increasing awareness of the discrepancy between what is and what could be. Hence, there exists in the world, a profound sense of frustration exacerbated by what has come to be labeled, somewhat blithely perhaps, as the revolution of rising expectations.

Social inequities and frustration

An analysis of rioting in ghettos in American cities from 1964 through 1968 led some observers to conclude "that the continued exclusion of Negroes from American economic and social life is the fundamental cause of riots" (Caplan and Paige, 1968, p. 9). This conclusion was based on a variety of findings that are pertinent to our present discussion of frustration and the possibility of its reduction.

The focus of the inquiry by Caplan and Paige was a series of comparisons between rioters and non-rioters, with both groups drawn from census tracts in two U.S. cities (Detroit, Michigan, and Newark, New Jersey) in which extensive violence had occurred. The compared groups shared many characteristics, including age, income level, experiences with unemployment, regularity of church attendance, and verbal acceptance of certain social values. On the other hand, the groups differed in some very interesting ways. For example, the rioters were better educated than the non-rioters. "Although it is true that the rioter is likely to be a high school dropout, his non-rioting neighbor is more likely to be an elementary school dropout" (Caplan and Paige, 1968, p. 5). Also, rioters were more likely to have been long-time residents in the ghettos, more aware of a gap in incomes among Blacks, and significantly, much more likely to report personal experiences of unfair discrimination, both in school and on the job market. Of special importance is that the rioters, compared with non-rioters, were more likely to reject traditional stereotypes of Negro inferiority and, thus, were more able to externalize blame for their current plight.

Fundamentally, all these differences suggest that the rioter was a relatively *aware* person, holding higher expectations, which he believed were unreachable through no fault of his own. In short, he was frustrated, felt helpless, and was angry. As Caplan and Paige interpreted their findings, the rioters were those who more clearly sensed that their exclusion from the mainstream of American life was "a result of arbitrary racial barriers" (p. 9).

Perceiving this exclusion as arbitrary and unjust is, of course, galling and frustrating. In essence, the level of frustration reached the explosive proportions it did among the rioters because, as Caplan and Paige put it, "their conception of their lives and their potential had changed without commensurate improvement in their chances for a better life" (p. 9).

If we accept this analysis, there are two quite distinct prescriptive implications we can draw from it. One is to slow the rise in expectations (the policy of benign neglect?), the other is to revise the institutions and policies that currently prevent the realization of expectations. With regard to the particular problem on which Caplan and Paige were working—the plight of urban Blacks in contemporary America—it is quite obviously movement toward equality of opportunity that must occur, however politically unpopular that may be in the short run. It is obviously too late (not to say immoral) to reduce aspirations.

The frustrations of the poor everywhere must be reduced, and there is no acceptable alternative to reducing them by attempting to meet legitimate aspirations. "But," the realists will cry, "that is impossible. Some level of frustration is unavoidable in any society." So it is, but it is surely not clear that present levels of frustration must be accepted. While it is true, as Berkowitz has put it (1970, p. 93), that ". . . for many people, expectations are likely to outstrip reality for a long time to come, " efforts must be made to improve reality. Indeed, while expectations cannot be reversed, except perhaps in the short run and at considerable social cost, real improvements in the quality of life are feasible. Moreover, they can occur in ways that will produce long-term benefits to the "haves" that exceed their costs. Of course, to embark on a farsighted social program calls for a degree of enlightenment in political leadership that history shows us is rare. So, once again, we see that the political psychologist acting in the role of policy advocate has his work cut out for him.

He must demonstrate that frustrations can be reduced by providing equal opportunities. That is not, after all, a new value in democratic ideology. Steps toward realizing it will become politically more acceptable if it can be shown that such steps serve also to eliminate some instigations to aggression.

Inhibition maintenance

If sources of frustration are, as we have just argued, potentially removable, it must nevertheless be admitted that history offers little hope of rapid progress in this regard. Rather, it is likely that for some time to come, despite even our best efforts, instigations to aggression will be very much with us. Accordingly, an attack on sources of frustration must be accompanied by efforts to control aggression by reinforcing aggression-inhibition.

Imbedded in the findings of nearly all the studies of aggression we considered in this chapter is evidence of internal conflict over aggressive tendencies. The disposition to commit an aggressive act is often accompanied by a counter tendency. Hence it is promising to search for ways to encourage responses that are incompatible with aggression.

All normal, intact human beings, having been more or less socialized, should have acquired alternative responses to frustration that compete with aggressiveness, such as withdrawal, friendly attempts to persuade, cheerfully turning to a substitute set of goals, and the like. All of these are classes of responses that will have been rewarded from time to time in most persons' socialization histories. But, as we surely know by now, all of us will also have been rewarded for aggressive reactions to frustration, particularly during earlier stages of life, before alternative responses are even possible. Periodically we will find that the strength of an aggressive response exceeds the strength of an alternative response, with the result that an aggressive response will be the one that will actually occur. When this happens after the child's parents have come to expect him to make an alternative response, they will react negatively to the manifest aggression. The consequence of this, as we have seen, is that the aggressor will come to anticipate adverse reactions to his aggression, which will serve to inhibit future overt aggression.

As a theoretical argument, this is fine. But it does not follow from this that, to enhance inhibition of aggression, socialization agents need merely react negatively to manifest aggression. Since negative reactions are likely to be punishing, and since punishment enhances frustration, it is critical that would-be aggressors also be taught to make satisfying alternative responses. It is surely not enough to punish aggression.

Two prescriptions follow from this line of argument. The first pertains to the socialization of aggression during childhood. It should be expected, given the prepotency of aggression, that children will, from time to time, be frustrated and aggressive. Techniques that will elicit and reward alternative responses need to be put into more widespread practice. The most effective aggression-inhibition may well be a well-learned incompatible response.

Secondly, with already socialized individuals, it should be expected that the tendency to aggress will exist at considerable strength in the hierarchy of responses to frustration. Hence, strenuous efforts must be made to avoid conveying the impression that earlier learned inhibitions against aggression no longer apply. In other words, the impresion must not be allowed to exist that aggression is sanctioned. This, in essence, is what Berkowitz meant by "leaving inhibitions intact."

In this regard, the entertainment media comprise an arena in which much can be done. After reviewing some of the evidence concerning TV programming presented earlier in this chapter, Berkowitz argued that the widespread tendency to employ violence as "entertainment" serves to weaken existing inhibitions against aggression. Can we not, he therefore asked, arrange to have more entertainment that is as absorbing but less violent? And might not more of the characters who people the "make-believe" world of television provide examples of behavior worth emulating?

If aggressive models are so readily imitated, as Bandura's and Berkowitz's research has shown, might not non-aggressive models be as readily imitated, if more of them were available and apparently successful? Surely nothing that we saw in this chapter forces us to conclude that aggressive behavior is intrinsically more imitatable than non-aggressive behavior.

Perhaps it is also necessary to demonstrate more convincingly that behaviors other than aggressing ones can have a payoff. With this thought in mind, let us take a brief look at another ongoing research area within social psychology that might offer some interesting insights.

Game theory and responses incompatible with aggression

The theory of games inspired a number of psychologists to conduct experiments employing situations in which both cooperative and competitive responses are possible in a search for the conditions favoring one or the other. Such situations are common in the real world. Often, striving together and striving against are two possibilities in cases where limited, attractive resources are available to more than one person. There are, of course, many variables, which together serve to determine whether cooperation or competition will predominate. In real-world settings the complex interactions among these variables make it difficult to predict what will happen in a particular instance, but experimental research and resultant theories allow us to list the variables and make some predictions about the ways in which they interact. As early as 1950, Martin Deutsch reviewed earlier theoretical efforts and incorporated them into a theory of his own.

Among the variables that Deutsch identified as influencing the choice between cooperation and competition are the scarcity of the resource being striven for, the existence of rules governing the struggle, the degree and nature of pre-existing affiliations among the strivers, and many others (Deutsch, 1950). Because the variables are many and the resultant interactions complex, it has been very useful to examine their operation in the admittedly artificial setting of the psychological laboratory.

A frequently employed experimental situation is the two-person, non-zero-sum game that is one or another variation of the so-called Prisoner's Dilemma (Luce and Raiffa, 1957). In this situation, each of two players must choose one of two moves, with the payoffs to each determined by the combination of moves. If both players make a cooperative move, both players receive a moderate prize. If one player makes a competitive move, this results in a big payoff for the mover, but only if it is not reciprocated. If both players make the competitive move, both suffer. In the long run, the cooperative response is the rational behavior. See Fig. 3 for a sample payoff matrix in a game such as this.

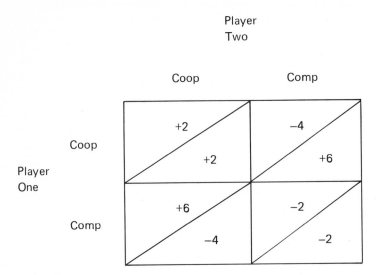

Note: In each of the four cells in this matrix the number above the diagonal is the outcome for Player One, while the number below the diagonal is the outcome for Player Two. Thus, if Player One makes a cooperative response, while Player Two makes a competitive response, Player One would *lose* 4, while Player Two would *gain* 6, as is seen in the upper right cell of the matrix.

Fig. 3

In most experiments involving this situation, however, players are more likely to make the competitive response. Over a wide variety of experimental conditions, it has been found that the frequency of cooperative responses is well below 50 percent, and the proportion of competitive responses even increases over trials (see Gallo and McClintock, 1965, for a review of many empirical studies).

This general finding holds over a broad range of payoff matrices, and it holds for players of both sexes and with a variety of personality profiles. At first glance, then, the findings from research into how people play this kind of game offer little encouragement to those who seek ways to make men less aggressive and more cooperative. It appears as if people generally are out to get as much as they can for themselves while assuming that others will occasionally attempt cooperation and thus lose.

Indeed, if one considers a variation of the basic experiment, the situation appears grim. In studies in which one player is really an experimenter's confederate, primed to make a high proportion of cooperative responses, the real player typically produces a barrage of competitive responses, thereby taking advantage of the situation, and of his opponent.

But there is some hope. For the same research has shown that if one player continues long enough to make cooperative responses, the other player eventually does so, too. Perhaps his dominant motive changes from greed to guilt, but the fact remains that here is an environmental condition under which cooperative behavior may successfully be elicited. Might the prescription be as simple as "do unto others as ye would have them do unto you"?

There are other bases for hope as well. For example, despite the fact that the predominance of competitive responding holds over a variety of personality types, there *are* individual differences; less authoritarian persons, and people who hold internationalistic as opposed to chauvinistic attitudes are among the kinds of people who seem more prone to cooperate in two-person games. Moreover, if players are communicated to in ways that encourage mutual trust (either by the experimenter or by other players) cooperation is increased. Under certain conditions, if players, for whatever reason, like each other, they are more likely to cooperate.

One fascinating study demonstrates the last-cited principle, along with its contradiction. Because of the way the contradiction may be resolved, the study is worth looking at. Oskamp and Perlman (1966) employed a game with cash payoffs to American college students paired on the basis of degree of acquaintance and friendship. Male students from a small, coeducational liberal arts college and male students from a nearby college that stressed business training played against college mates, who were either best friends, acquaintances, non-acquaintances, or disliked persons. These relationships had been determined independently of the experiment proper, and several weeks earlier by a sociometric questionnaire. The results? Friendship was positively related to cooperation in one group, but not in the other.

Among the liberal arts students, a majority of all responses (an average of about 17 out of 30 trials) were cooperative and, more importantly, cooperation was more frequent the closer the pair members were sociometrically. Pairs composed of best friends made, on the average, about 22 cooperative responses, acquaintances made 20, non-acquaintances 14, and pairs composed of a player and someone he disliked made only 11. On the other hand, among the business students, practically the reverse occurred. All kinds of pairs *except* those composed of best friends made about 14 cooperative responses, while the best friend pairs averaged only six! As the authors put it, "under some circumstances friendship may lead to high cooperation and disliking to low cooperation, but under other circumstances very close friendship may allow a strongly competitive rivalry to develop" (Oskamp and Perlman, 1966, p. 225).

So, we find once again that situational factors are crucial in determining behavior. The behavior of best friends in this study varied tremendously across colleges. Why it may have done so is of prime importance as we consider ways to encourage responses that are incompatible with aggression.

The fact that the liking/cooperation relationship held in one college but not in another suggests that something like "cultural values" affect the basic tendency to cooperate or compete. Perhaps the effect of friendship is to accentuate the predominant response, with predominance determined by the cultural setting. In settings in which competition is positively valued or justified as leading to some "greater good" like "economic progress," there is perhaps little reason to expect cooperation, especially when people are interacting with persons whose approval they value.

From this study we might conclude that in societies in which competitiveness is encouraged, cooperation is not likely to emerge. Since many societies in which there is need to encourage behaviors that are incompatible with aggression are societies which traditionally encourage competition, attempting to encourage adults to cooperate is probably not a very promising strategy. In such societies, unless one is prepared to encourage a revolution in economic values, attention might better be focused on children (who might in turn produce a revolution!). In any event, there is empirical evidence, none of it very surprising, that children can be taught to cooperate without their even being exhorted to do so. The teaching of cooperative behavior is simply a matter, as the reader should by now expect, of establishing contingencies between reinforcing stimuli and cooperative responding.

In a classic study by Azrin and Lindsley (1956), ten two-person, same-sex teams of children between the ages of seven and 12 years played a game in which each player had to choose one of three holes into which to place a stylus. Children sat opposite each other and saw that they each confronted identical situations. However, no instruction was ever given that they behave identically.

During some phases of the game, if both children placed their stylii in opposite (identical) holes within .04 seconds of each other, a light would go on and a jelly bean would be dispensed into a cup accessible to both. The first 15 minutes of the experiment comprised such a phase, but that it did was never revealed verbally to the children. This phase was followed by an "extinction period" of at least 15 minutes during which no reinforcements were provided no matter what the children did. After a steady rate of responding without reinforcement was observed by the experimenters, they reintroduced reinforcement (again with no word to the children about changing conditions) and this was continued until another steady rate of responding was reached. In short, the children were exposed to a typical operant conditioning procedure involving reinforcement, extinction, and more reinforcement.

The clearest summary of the resultant behaviors may be expressed by the median number of cooperative responses per minute during four critical three-minute periods: During the first three minutes of the first reinforcement period, the median was 5.5. During the last three minutes of that period, it was 17.5. During the last three minutes of the extinction period, it was 1.5, and during the last three minutes of the second reinforcement period, it was back up to 17.5. This experiment convincingly demonstrated that operant conditioning can be employed to control cooperation between children without verbally instructing them. Cooperation, like any other response, is subject to environmental control. If we really wish to teach behaviors incompatible with aggression, the techniques are surely at hand.

Removal of cues that trigger aggression

There remains one more efficacious policy that is called for by our analysis of the causes and supports of aggression. The stimuli that trigger it will have to be made far less common than they presently are. We do not yet have a comprehensive inventory of stimuli that function as triggers to aggression but weapons (real and toy) are surely among them.

While the real weapon may be impossible to eliminate, since law enforcement may require the use of some weapons, their numbers and their general availability to the public surely can be better controlled. (And there are, of course, police forces in the world which very effectively carry out their responsibilities without carrying firearms.)

With regard to toy weapons, there is little that need be said. There is simply *no* justification for their production and promotion. In this regard, it is perhaps a hopeful sign that American toy manufacturers by 1973 seemed to have curtailed their production of toy guns, perhaps in response to public outcry.

Such outcries ought continue, for as Berkowitz has argued, ". . . reducing the number of aggressive stimuli people encounter from day to day is probably the easiest way of reducing violence to effect, and the fastest" (1970, p. 93). What are we waiting for?

Similar outcries might be directed with effect toward the controllers of the media. As we saw when we considered the impact of TV, the villain is not the medium, but the message. Television can clearly have either anti-social or pro-social effects, and in the last analysis the power to determine which of these impacts TV will have rests with the public. It is the responsibility of the political psychologist to arm that public with the facts it needs.

A CONCLUSION

There is much that need and can be done to make aggression a less familiar experience. Instigations need to be reduced both in frequency and intensity. This requires fundamental social changes that will eliminate some of the frustration impinging on us all. Since some frustration will always occur, additional strategies are called for in order to reduce the likelihood that overt aggressive acts will be the reaction to frustration. These strategies include moving toward the elimination of cues that appear to legitimize aggression, and socialization practices that reinforce responses incompatible with aggression.

Whether or not the prescriptions suggested in the latter part of this chapter are the best possible ones, the implication of all the research we examined is clearly that we are justified in insisting that this is not yet the best of all possible worlds, and we are justified in searching for ways to reduce the violence that pervades it. Aggression is neither instinctive nor an inevitable consequence of frustration. Rather, it is aggression that breeds aggression. So might cooperation breed cooperation, if only environmental contingencies were made conducive to *it* instead of to aggression. The pessimist may still argue that aggression and counter-aggression have been so long with us, that the vicious cycle cannot be broken. But it is not an impossible dream.

NOTES

[1] As we shall see later in this chapter, the violent content of our prepackaged popular entertainment is not only an increment in the violence that engulfs us. Nor is it merely a reflection of a reality that predates its production. Filmed and television violence can be also a stimulus and instigation for those who are "entertained" by it to commit aggressive acts for themselves.

[2] Lorenz's observations of the fighting behavior of certain tropical fishes are extremely interesting and worthy of any social scientist's attention. As an observer, Lorenz has made many significant contributions. It is his interpretations of those observations which must be questioned vigorously.

[3] Instinctivism as a form of psychological theorizing reached its zenith in the work of MacDougall (1908) and was severely damaged by attacks mounted by several generations of learning theorists. It was dealt what should have been the *coup de grace* by Beach in 1955, in his famous paper, *The Descent of Instinct.*

[4] The situation just described also involves learning via *vicarious reinforcement.* This mechanism is discussed in some detail, later in this chapter.

[5] There is a voluminous literature on these topics—e.g., Bandura (1965a, 1969, 1971a,b,c), Bandura and Huston (1961), Bandura and McDonald (1963), Bandura, Ross and Ross (1963), Campbell (1961), Gewirtz and Stingle (1968), Kanfer (1965), Kanfer and Marston (1963), Lewis and Duncan (1958), Rosenbaum and Bruning (1966), Rosenbaum, Chalmers, and Potts (1971).

[6] Two additional findings from this study are of interest: boys were more influenced by the models than were girls, male models generally produced more aggressive responses in observers, and male-male model-observer pairings produced more aggression than female-female pairings. These facts are particularly relevant to our understanding of why aggression seems to be predominantly a masculine trait, an issue we shall discuss later in this chapter under the heading of sex differences.

[7] Other studies, dealing with behavior other than aggression, support the same propositions (see, for example, Rosenbaum and Bruning, 1966).

[8] Another sex difference to be kept in mind for our later discussion.

[9] See Atkin, Murray, and Nayman (1971) for a bibliography of 550 published works, many of them social psychological experiments, whose evidence "supports the thesis that exposure to filmed or televised violence tends to lead young children to a state of heightened excitability and to an increase in subsequent displays of aggression" (Bogart, 1972-1973, p. 494).

[10] Bogart (1972-1973) called attention to the fact that this is the *only* published study that does so.

[11] For a well-reasoned assessment of the evidence by a psychologist who doubts that the portrayal of violence in TV programs is as critical in inducing violence as many other factors, see Singer (1971, Chapter Two).

[12] As this chapter was being written (1975), the major television networks were reported to be revising their prime time schedules in ways that would markedly reduce the violent content on programs likely to be viewed by children.

[13] A series of studies on reactions to one's own aggression demonstrates this dramatically. Some of these studies will be discussed later in this chapter.

[14] This research, in which persons are encouraged to believe that they are actually harming other persons, has been criticized for employing deceptions that brought to bear upon its subjects a rather horrendous experience (cf. Baumrind, 1964). Readers will find the debate concerning the ethics of the use of deception in social psychological experimentation very thought provoking. It is especially so because much of the debate focuses on Milgram's research, which was designed to investigate how "normal" people accept orders to administer pain to others by being led to believe that the pain is being administered in the pursuit of a higher goal—scientific understanding. The irony is all too obvious, since Milgram himself was inflicting psychological discomfort (which, of course, he took great pains to eliminate after the experiment was completed) in the pursuit of scientific knowledge. Should Milgram be criticized for throwing light on the manner in which all of us, including social psychologists, sometimes justify inflicting harm?

8
Psychological contributions to the search for a warless world

In this less-than-best of all possible worlds, can we at least find ways to make wars less likely?

When intergroup conflicts are between whole nations, failures to resolve these conflicts peacefully can have cataclysmic consequences. Wars and genocide involve ruthless, mass violence that maims and kills indiscriminately. Such acts—sanctioned massacres, as Kelman (1973) labels them—may be more easily understood and, consequently, avoided if subjected to psychological analyses. These acts seem to require a particular kind of psychological environment in which a society's usual restraining forces against violence become inoperative. Such an environment, in Kelman's view, can result from such psychological processes as perception of authorization to commit violence, perceived dehumanization of the victim, and other processes that were examined earlier in this book, especially in the discussion on prejudice in Chapter 5 and the discussion on aggression in Chapter 7.

But does knowing how sanctioned violence can be triggered move us any closer to a warless world? Can we effectively apply psychology in the international arena, where diplomats and statesmen have struggled for centuries, with only sometimes success?

Some psychologists believe that just as "wars are made in the minds of man," so can peace. While most would acknowledge the inevitability of human conflict, they would hold out hope that war as a way to resolve conflict would become an archaic institution.

To the surprise of many who find such thoughts visionary, Americans generally are coming to view the abolition of war as not only necessary, but possible! A Gallup poll conducted in 1971, even while the U.S.A. was engaged in armed conflict in Southeast Asia, found 46 percent of those surveyed agreeing that war is an outmoded means for resolving conflict; only 43 percent agreed that war under any conditions is "necessary," with most of those citing "survival" as the only condition necessitating war.

While the Gallup poll results may be encouraging, they merely tell us that many people wish that effective means to avoid war could be found, and believe that such a search is worth undertaking. To date, the search has not yet been undertaken with much optimism or vigor. It might, therefore, be valuable to look at some avenues that psychological considerations suggest are worth exploring.

ENHANCED COMMUNICATION

There are two versions of the communication argument; one calls for better communication between potential adversaries, and the other calls for the psychological education of international negotiators.

The most often advocated policy for enhancing positive international relations has been "communication." In an otherwise sophisticated discussion of the psychological approaches to world peace, Amitai Etzioni revived this very old notion by advocating increased and improved communication between adversaries. He argued, for example, that "Communication can be increased by visits of Americans to Russia and Russians to America, exchanges of newspapers, publication of American columns in Soviet newspapers and vice versa, by summit conferences and the like" (1967, p. 362). Unfortunately, there is little evidence from psychological research that intergroup communication *per se* improves intergroup relations.

Some psychologists also look to better communication as something that would serve the interests of peace, but they have in mind stepped-up communication between psychologists on the one hand and policy makers in their own country on the other hand. For example, what R.K. White would like communicated are psychological phenomena that many psychologists take for granted, but that policy makers regularly ignore (1970). The goal of such communication, obviously, is the education of policy makers. White has discussed some obvious applied psychological principles that are widely acknowledged but commonly ignored, and some non-obvious principles that until recently were relatively unfamiliar. In the first category, White listed the necessity for empathy in international interactions, the dangers of black and white, or good guy/bad guy thinking, and the ease with which self-fulfilling prophecies influence international behavior. These notions are, White believes, easy to understand and even likely to be paid lip service by policy makers. But, he argues, ". . . our most important task is to . . . communicate them in such a way that they become really familiar and really used . . ." (White, 1970, p. 345). As matters presently stand, few policy makers behave as if they knew these principles.

The second category of principles consists of provocative ideas that could, if attended to, stimulate some novel behaviors. One such idea is Osgood's GRIT proposal, which we will examine in some detail below. Others include an application of a well-established finding from experimental social psychology to the effect that a two-sided presentation of an argument is more persuasive than a one-sided presentation when dealing with an audience that initially is opposed to one's own point of view. The application is found in a proposition that either side in an international encounter should publicly accept as much of the other side's point of view as possible. To do so, of course, would be to ignore the political rule of thumb that one must never appear to be soft or yielding. However, such rules of thumb might best be ignored. If Side A really seeks a rapprochement with Side B, the former ought to be prepared to acknowledge the validity of at least some of Side B's positions before attempting to solicit a similar acknowledgement from B.

Two other propositions discussed by White deal with perceptual distortions that seem characteristic of many situations that lead to war—the tendency to view territorial conflicts as if they were threats to one's own "person" (in White's view a dangerous but avoidable practice), and the tendency to exaggerate the degree to which others, especially the masses under our "enemy's" control, favor *our* policy (a form of wishful thinking that engenders the kind of foreign policy adventures that led the United States into the Bay of Pigs in Cuba and into "pacification" efforts in Vietnam).

Bronfenbrenner, a social psychologist who happened to be in the Soviet Union in 1960 shortly after Soviet-American relations were seriously strained and exacerbated by the U-2 spy plane flight, did an analysis of mutually held views in each nation. One was, just as White suggests, that the masses were really not as sympathetic to the regime as their leaders claimed. Thus, the American view was that many Russians secretly despised Communism, while the Russian view was that few Americans really liked capitalism.

This perceptual distortion, Bronfenbrenner argued, was accompanied by other, mutually reinforcing misperceptions—e.g., their government deludes them, especially by telling lies about us; they are potential aggressors against us, because they don't like us, or deal honestly with us, nor can they be rational in their dealings with us (Bronfenbrenner, 1961).

These kinds of distortions, sustained perhaps by a need for cognitive consistency once a state of conflict between nations is acknowledged to exist, can serve, obviously, to exacerbate the conflict, and make its peaceful resolution less likely.

In White's view, each nation's foreign policy makers must be made vigilant with regard to these perceptual distortions. Thus, better communication can contribute to peace, but the targets of the communication are those who presently conduct foreign policy as if such ideas were totally unknown to them.

TENSION REDUCTION BY UNILATERAL INITIATIVE

A very promising direction that might be more vigorously pursued in the search for peace is obviously grounded in psychology and may be labeled the *initiatives approach*. This approach is best exemplified by a theory of international relations linked with a model for rational behavior in the international arena called Graduated Reciprocation in Tension-Reduction. Formulated by the psychologist Charles F. Osgood (1962), this approach has been echoed by other writers (cf. Etzioni, 1962) and has been exemplified by a series of events in 1963 that have come to be known as the Kennedy experiment (Etzioni, 1967) and by actions of Egypt and Israel during the summer of 1975, including the reopening of the Suez Canal and a pullback of Israeli troops from the Sinai peninsula.

The "Kennedy experiment" began with a speech by the late American president announcing unilateral stoppage of atmospheric nuclear tests. The speech turned out to be the first in a series of *detente*-producing actions by both the Soviet Union and the United States, which, according to one observer, were brought to a halt because the U.S. "administration felt that . . . hopes and expectations for more Soviet-American measures [were] running too high" (Etzioni, 1967, p. 367). The Egyptian and Israeli actions were both announced in advance as unilateral tension-reduction steps. To appreciate the significance of these events, Osgood's ideas must be examined carefully.

Osgood's approach, Graduated Reciprocation in Tension-Reduction, or GRIT, has as its key the notion that wars result ultimately from mutual distrust between adversaries. Hence, the avoidance of war requires the creation of an atmosphere of mutual trust (Osgood, 1962, p. 6). It should be obvious from the statement above that Osgood's views constitute a *psychological* theory of international relations, since, however trust is defined, it is obviously a psychological variable.

To argue that the likelihood of war depends on trust, Osgood must be willing to make the assumption that the behavior of nations parallels in some significant ways the behavior of individuals. Indeed, he does assume this, as he tells us, ". . . the problems we face today are primarily matters of human nature and human relationships" (p. 21). A further assumption is that ". . . what little we do know about the psychology of individual behavior may provide us with at least a model and perhaps a few good leads for understanding the behavior of nations" (p. 21). Applying these assumptions specifically to the problem of war, Osgood in effect endorses the UNESCO doctrine born in the aftermath of World War II, that "war begins in the minds of man."

This view is not unique to Osgood. We have seen it expressed by White and by Bronfenbrenner. Etzioni echoed it when he suggested that nations in conflict, like individuals in conflict, become trapped in a spiral of misperceptions and behaviors that result in self-fulfilling prophecies. In Etzioni's words, "the hostility of one as perceived by the other evokes his hostility; which in turn is perceived by the first side, further increasing *his* hostility" (1967, p. 361).

Probably few students of international behavior are impressed by the psychological approach, but Etzioni argues that it is good enough "to stand among the major hypotheses" (1967, p. 361). His own version has it that as tension builds in the relationship between two states, each state behaves as an actor in a two-person conflict and becomes subject to psychological processes that distort reality. Among these are a *"rigid* adherence" to earlier established (and often outmoded) stances, repression of possible devastating consequences of one's own moves, selection of facts that validate policy commitments and blockage of facts that challenge them, and paranoia resulting in failure to see anything but treachery in what might be genuine concessions (1967, p. 362).[1]

Osgood's version of this same argument is that men, whether

acting on their own or on behalf of a nation-state, often react to stress—including that induced by competition—with a variety of reality-distorting perceptions and behaviors that serve only to enhance the stress in an upward spiraling fashion.

Thus, Osgood points to such reactions as *denial*, where the likely consequences of an action literally become unthinkable; *projection* of our own hostile tendencies onto our adversary, because his ultimate intentions are perceived as evil, while ours can only be good; and *psychologic*, the use of compelling, but illogical pseudo-syllogistic reasoning, where false conclusions result from faulty premises, all in the interest of cognitive consistency.

Osgood sees these and other processes propelling men into escalating conflicts, as manifest during the Fifties in the United States-Soviet arms race and during the Sixties in the hostilities in Southeast Asia, to mention only two of a multitude of examples.

Devised by Osgood early in the 1960s, his plan reflected the then current concern over the arms race, the concept of a nuclear deterrent, the prospects of nuclear holocaust and other features of the then salient "cold war." During that period, some soon-to-be-forgotten demagogue coined the phrase "better dead than red" to rally nationalist forces in the United States to a policy exemplified best by an ever-mounting arms race justified by the concept of deterrence. Accordingly, Osgood's efforts must first be viewed as a psychologist's response to those forces that provided the context for his efforts.

In that context, Osgood argued that the choice was surely not limited to surrender or Armegeddon and that the deterrence argument was not only specious, but psychologically unsound.[2] The concept of deterrence, which was regularly cited as the humane justification for the arms race, is, Osgood pointed out, a psychological argument and must be recognized as such. Whether employed to justify an arms race, or capital punishment, the concept of deterrence is based on assumptions about the behavioral reaction of those confronted by the possibility of weapons being used or punishments being applied.

Thus, in the case of the arms race, "An opponent is assumed to be deterred from initiating a nuclear attack by his expectation of unacceptable retaliation" (Osgood, 1962, p. 54). But, Osgood went on to point out that the effectiveness of a threatened retaliation as a deterrent depends on its credibility. This in turn depends on the adversary's ability to perceive, conceptualize, and evaluate it objectively and rationally. These abilities are precisely the psychological processes that are in short supply under conditions of stress and tension. Instead, as we saw above, these conditions breed *denial*, which makes the possible retaliation appear incredible, a decline in ability to evaluate an opponent's intentions, a tendency to worry about improbable events rather than to consider likely possibilities, and other processes apt to reduce the chances that deterrence will result.

Thus, the arms race, rather than reducing the likelihood of outbreak of hostilities actually increases it. This, of course, is not the only psychological argument we can mount agaist the arms race. Etzioni reminded us that "even if armaments were initially ordered to serve a psychological motive, once available they generate motives of their own to propel hostile postures and wars" (1967, p. 363).[3] But, from Osgood's point of view, the crucial argument is that an arms race will not deter hostility because the initial tensions that engendered it will not be reduced by it. If anything, they will be exacerbated.

Therefore, Osgood argues that it is a misplaced effort to attempt to control the use of arms through an arms race, and a vain effort to attempt to control arms through negotiation (particularly since in negotiation each side is strongly motivated to negotiate from strength, with strength defined as some advantage over one's opponent). In other words, arms races and peace conferences and treaty deliberations *per se* do nothing to reduce tension. Without tension-reduction, all such policies are likely to fail. What, then, is likely to work? Somehow, the thrust of the effort must be to reduce tension.

GRIT is Osgood's answer to the question of how international tension may be reduced. The essence of GRIT is (a) unilateral execution of small (but increasingly larger) steps away from confrontation, (b) with each step announced in advance, (c) with no conditions attached, (d) carried out as promised, and (e) accompanied by explicit challenges to the other side to take comparable steps. In his words, "We would have to move very carefully and gradually, but by taking consistent tension reduction steps we might be able to create an atmosphere of mutual trust" (p. 6).

In presenting his plan, Osgood emphasized that he was not proposing abrupt and complete disarmament. Indeed, he was suggesting that the giving up of nuclear arms—the ultimate "deterrents" —be done last, only after all lesser concessions had been made and reciprocated. Obviously, only by reducing the tension level to the point at which neither side feels a need for any deterrent could such a step be expected to be taken.[4]

In an attempt to characterize his GRIT proposal, Osgood has said, "It is perhaps best viewed as a kind of international (rather than interpersonal) communicating and learning situation, where the communication is more by deeds than words and where what is learned—hopefully and gradually—is increased mutual understanding and trust" (p. 88).

Perhaps the most important point to be stressed is that the policy is designed to reduce tension, since tension is the prime force underlying irrational interaction between players in the game of international competition. Since the reduction of tension, according to Osgood, "is independent of its sources" (p. 61), it can be accomplished by steps that have nothing directly to do with those sources. Thus, the initiator of a tension-reduction step can choose any arena in which to make it, whether that arena is or is not a particularly salient one. The requirements are merely that the step be one that can be interpreted only as a movement away from confrontation, that it be sincere, that it be announced and identified as part of a deliberate peace-seeking policy, that it be accompanied by a public invitation to the adversary to reciprocate and, finally, that it be executed as promised, whether or not reciprocity results. Of course, if it is not reciprocated, then the exercise terminates.

If it is reciprocated, and the response of the adversary contains, as it is likely to, a counter-challenge provoking a second step, there would be set in motion a process that resembles an arms race in form but that is opposite to it in substance and effect. Instead of tension spiraling upward, it would spiral downward.

To carry out a GRIT plan successfully, Osgood noted that flexibility and improvisation would be required, elicited, and rewarded. The improvisation, of course, would be guided by some principle, just as improvisation in jazz is constrained by adherence to a theme or set of chords or some other structure. For example, a basic theme in a GRIT program could be to make successive initiatives graduated in risk, with each increment proportional to the degree of reciprocation obtained. The importance of the improvisation notion, of course, is that each step along the way would in some way have to be determined by the response that had occurred to the previous step.

The ultimate benefit of learning how to improve tension-reduction steps could, of course, transcend the success of a particular GRIT program. Initiating improvised strategies is a style of foreign policy behavior that must surely be an attractive posture for policy makers. It is a position in which they seldom find themselves when involved in tension-heightening confrontations. Perhaps, then, the execution of a GRIT exercise would reinforce that unfamiliar response tendency.

Be that as it may, GRIT seems worth trying. It may already have been tried. At least, Etzioni has described the Kennedy experiment of 1963 as a partial application of a psychological theory which, though unnamed by Etzioni, resembles GRIT in many respects. As Etzioni put it, "The Kennedy experiment can be viewed as a test of a moderate version of the psychological theory that seeks to use symbolic gestures as unilateral initiatives to reduce tension to get at other factors, . . ." (1967, p. 365). Etzioni's paper should be consulted for a comprehensive account of the "experiment," but a very brief summary is in order here.

Some eight months after the Cuban confrontation between the United States and the USSR, President Kennedy, in the context of a strong conciliatory speech, announced that the U.S. was unconditionally halting atmospheric nuclear tests and would not resume them unless another nation did so. Within five days, Soviet actions included a removal in the United Nations of a long-standing objection to a U.S.-backed proposal pertaining to the Middle East, the cessation of jamming of Voice of America broadcasts to the Soviet Union so that recordings of the Kennedy Speech might be heard, and an announcement by Soviet Premier Krushchev welcoming the Kennedy speech and revealing that the production of strategic bombers by the USSR had been halted. Over the next few months, from July to November of 1962, events included the signing of a negotiated treaty on atmospheric testing, a Soviet call for a pact between NATO and the Warsaw Pact nations, a suggestion by President Kennedy that the U.S. and the USSR cooperate in space research, and speeches calling for expansion of consulates, direct air travel between New York and Moscow, and other forms of peaceful contact. There was also a step by the United States to reduce trade barriers by legalizing the sale of wheat to the USSR, another step by the Soviet Union whereby it suggested that the two sides agree not to orbit nuclear bombs, and the release by both sides of captured spies.

Reviewing these events, Etzioni concluded that, "For each move that was made, the Soviets reciprocated" (1967, p. 368). Etzioni also noted, "The Russians showed no difficulties in understanding the gestures and in responding to psychological initiatives; and they participated in a 'you move—I move' sequence rather than waiting for simultaneous, negotiated, agreed-upon moves . . . [Furthermore] it seems that the Russian reciprocations were "proportional" to the

American ones. . . . the Russians responded not just by reciprocating American initiatives but by offering some initiatives of their own" (1967, pp. 368-369).

After analyzing changes in tone of press reports and changes in measured public opinion during the months of the Kennedy experiment, Etzioni argued that the central hypotheses of this psychological theory, including a practical impact on public opinion, were supported by these events. In an evaluative summary he described the events in the following words:

"(a)   unilateral gestures were reciprocated;
 (b)   reciprocations were proportional;
 (c)   unilaterally reciprocated gestures reduced tensions;
 (d)   unilaterally reciprocated gestures were followed by multi-lateral-simultaneous measures, which further reduced tensions;
 (e)   initiatives were 'suspected,' but, when continued, they 'got across;'
 (f)   the gestures and responses created a psychological momentum that pressured for more measures, a reversal of the cold war or hostility spiral; [and]
 (g)   when measures were stopped, tension reduction ceased. . . ."
       (1967, pp. 371-372)

All of these occurrences were compatible with GRIT.

However, it must be admitted that the series of events known as the Kennedy experiment do not constitute a rigorous test of Osgood's theory. (The so-called experiment obviously lacked a control group!) Moreover, the steps taken were not accompanied by the kinds of rhetoric Osgood would have suggested. Efforts to communicate a desire for peace were often accompanied by arguments stressing security and other self-serving purposes. Nonetheless, there was much that happened in 1962 that served to make Osgood's arguments appear considerably more realistic than many "practical men of affairs" would be willing to grant.

Given the existence of a theory like GRIT and some evidence dating from the Kennedy years that processes like those suggested by Osgood can indeed be set in motion, we are perhaps entitled to offer the proposition that psychological factors do indeed appear in international relations. Both leaders and masses, at least when public opinion is allowed to influence policy makers, are persons who are subject to consistency needs and other cognitive and emotional forces influencing decision making in the international arena.

However promising the Osgood approach may appear to be, it

does not deal with a number of factors that contribute to the probability of international conflict. While this may be obvious, we ought to note that the reduction of tension does not necessarily remove economic, social, and political differences of opinion, which often comprise the substantive essence of conflicts among states. Thus there are continuing, if not continuous, disagreements over the legitimacy of governments, the location of boundaries, and other seemingly intractable conflicts. While an approach like GRIT might reduce tensions engendered by such conflicts, it cannot by itself resolve the conflicts per se. Happily, though, there may be some other insights derived from psychology that pertain more directly to conflict resolution.

CONFLICT RESOLUTION

If international relations are, as many psychologists have suggested (cf. White, 1966), characterized by misperceptions, then many international conflicts may appear to be more intractable than they really are. Actors in the conflict may, for example, fail to see why "the other side" holds the position it does, or may exaggerate the difference between each side's positions. Also, it is possible that conflicts persist longer than they need to because each side becomes committed to a position no longer justified by current conditions. These and similar possibilities suggest that certain kinds of therapeutic interactions among adversaries might result in redefinitions of conflicts that would result in novel solutions to them.

This form of psychological approach to international relations is nicely illustrated by efforts undertaken in the late 1960s by two teams of scholars, with support from various agencies concerned with the search for peace, including the United Nations Institute for Training and Research. UNITAR's first published research report (UNITAR, 1970) provides a discussion of social psychological technique applied to the settlement of international disputes. Two case studies were discussed in the UNITAR report—one from the Center for the Analysis of Conflict in the University of London (see Burton, 1969) and the other from an attempt by three Yale University professors led by Leonard Doob,[5] concerned with a border dispute in Africa. A brief summary of the Yale effort can serve to illustrate the general approach.

The techniques employed by Doob and his colleagues are small group interaction techniques, which originated mainly in the United

States and which traditionally have been employed by industrial firms to improve their own functioning. The techniques are known collectively as "human relations training" or "sensitivity training"; they have as their goal the learning of communication skills. Participants are placed in what have come to be known as T-groups, with *T* denoting *training*. The T-groups, assisted by trainers or "facilitators," are assembled in what is known as a "workshop," usually in an isolated setting.

The essence of the technique is an effort to change problem-solving attitudes and orientations among persons involved in conflict. It is an attempt to apply sensitivity training, role-playing, and similar experiences developed originally in clinical and management psychology to the international arena. The hope is that such experiences will change mutual perceptions, enhance communication, and produce new solutions among persons directly concerned with international disputes.

Solutions are not imposed; rather, conditions are created which, it is hoped, would permit participants in the dispute to discover their own solutions. These conditions also are intended to make the participants aware of the psychological bias that impeded the discovery of solutions and the possiblity of removing them. In short, the technique is an effort to establish conditions that promote the process of genuine seeking of conflict resolution.

One of the few attempts to conduct such a workshop with an international conflict as its focus was the one recently reported by Doob (1970). It consisted of a meeting of 18 African scholars for two weeks in a resort hotel (Fermeda) in the Tyrolean Alps to discuss border disputes that had been plaguing their home countries—Somalia, Ethiopia, and Kenya—for a decade.

Actually, there was a pair of related border disputes involving the northeastern African nation of Somalia. In one of these, Somalia confronted Kenya, its neighbor to the south; in the other, the antagonist was Ethiopia. Risking oversimplification, one could state the essence of these disputes in terms of a conflict between two principles, both valued by all disputants: one, the right of peoples to self-determination; the other, the sanctity of national sovereignty. However, in these instances, since the disputed territories were respectively within the borders of Kenya and Ethiopia, while the peoples inhabiting them were culturally Somalis, nationals of Kenya and Ethiopia tended to consider the sovereignty principle as most relevant, while the Somalis considered self-determination as the paramount value.

For ten years, the inability to be flexible in the application of these principles had been reflected in intermittent warfare and other forms of human misery. Could not a workshop based on sensitivity-training foster, among a carefully selected group of influential, nongovernmental nationals of the three countries, mutual insights, understandings, and possibly even some novel workable solutions? This thought prompted Doob and two colleagues, William J. Foltz, a political scientist, and Robert B. Stevens, a lawyer, to endure three years of frustration of efforts to realize what they themselves dubbed "the wild idea." The efforts culminated in the two-week experiment on a Tyrolean mountaintop.

The outcome can only be described as mixed. In a revealing report (Doob, 1970), the professional sensitivity T-group trainers offered the most favorable assessments, but even these were not without qualifications and revelations of mistakes. Three participants—an Ethiopian philosopher, a Kenyan political scientist, and a Somalian lawyer and journalist—were far less favorable, but even their contributions to the report of the workshop's accomplishments revealed potentially valuable insights that might well be attributed to the workshop experience. Thus, while one, who was from a nation for whom territorial sovereignty was the dominant principle, asserted, "one became convinced ... that no immediate or permanent solution was possible other than persuading each nation involved ... earnestly to accept the permanency of the present boundaries ... [p. 68]," another said in retrospect, "I learned that we—the African participants—had imbibed uncritically so much of Whiteman's concepts of social and political organizations that we spent all our time parroting outdated and mischievous nineteenth century European fictions, like sovereignty, without being original or even intelligent about them [p. 54]."

The three Yale professors who conceived the experiment offered a variety of observations. Some of them were surprising. For example, an expectation was that nationality would be a salient basis of association at the outset, and then it would decline. The reverse was apparently the case. "Rather than decreasing in strength ... nationality became more salient at the end than at the beginning of the workshop" (p. 107). This phenomenon may in part have reflected the growing frustration participants felt in their efforts to find mutually acceptable solutions and in part the felt needs of participants to reidentify nationally as time to leave the workshop and return home approached.

Another observation by the academics very much to the basic

point was, if not surprising, disappointing: ". . . the main objective of the workshop, at least on the surface, was certainly not achieved. No original solution to the dispute was evolved that won the instant acclaim of all the participants" (p. 120).

To assess longer term impacts of the Fermeda workshop, Doob (1971) interviewed 13 of the 18 participants some 11 months later, following publication of his 1970 book, which some of those interviewed had read. Although during the months following Fermeda the border dispute remained unresolved, many of the participants apparently had been affected in interesting ways by the experience, coming to appreciate the intensely emotional values attached by persons on all sides of the dispute to the lands in question. If no fundamental attitudes were changed, at least an increase in tolerance for, and insight into, opponents' views could be detected in the interview. One clear, positive finding concerned the proposition that the governments of the countries involved would learn about the workshop; ". . . while policy makers have not been influenced by the workshop . . . some of them knew at least that the three groups of Africans came together at Fermeda" (1971, p. 93). Doob's followup study also revealed a strengthening of bonds among participants within each country and even some sense of community across national lines. While some participants expressed complaints or disappointments concerning the workshop, several subscribed to the view that had been promoted by the workshop organizers that formal parliamentary procedures do not provide the best atmosphere for dispute settlement.

All told, however, more questions than answers emerged from the Fermeda workshop and its followup study. About all that could be concluded was that the Fermeda workshop was a significant first attempt which should provoke additional efforts. For surely the "failure" of Fermeda is just as inexplicable and inconclusive as a "success" would have been.[6] That no clear-cut resolution of conflict resulted may say more about the conflict, or the participants, or the setting, than about the method employed. Given the well-documented history of failure of conventional approaches to conflict resolution, there is good reason to continue exploring novel approaches. From the Fermeda experience, it became clear that more experience was needed with variations of these less conventional approaches to determine which work and why, and which don't and why not.

Subsequent to Fermeda, there have been two more attempts at applying the workshop approach to international . disputes—the

Northern Ireland troubles (Doob and Foltz, 1973, 1974) and the Cyprus conflict. The latter attempt was abortive because the Turkish invasion of Cyprus occurred just as the workshop was scheduled to take place (see Doob, 1974 for a detailed personalized report of this "failure," which could prove instructive). The Northern Ireland effort, on the other hand, resulted in a most interesting workshop that yielded some important observations.

Fifty-six Catholic and Protestant residents of Belfast were recruited in the summer of 1972 to participate in an intensive nine-day effort to learn more about their own behavior in groups and to develop insights into their opponents' points of view. Despite the prevalence and intensity of violent conflict in Belfast at the time, this considerable number of persons, most of them leaders or active members of various organizations in Belfast, was persuaded, with the help of two Belfast deputies, to travel by ferryboat to a workshop site in Scotland to explore ways of improving Catholic-Protestant relations.

In contrast to the Fermeda effort, the organizers here did not expect the workshop to yield a plan to resolve the central conflict, which would have been an unrealistic goal considering its complexity and intensity. Rather, they set out to bring together persons of influence and to help them learn about each other and establish a degree of mutual trust to permit the development of initial plans for incremental improvements in intergroup relations. The stress in this workshop, thus, was on process rather than on substantive product. The workshop, described in detail by Doob and Foltz (1973), employed a Tavistock version of sensitivity training (with an emphasis on understanding authority and power) during its first half, while the second half was devoted to the Bethel approach to group dynamics and included an effort to plan some cooperative under-takings that might be attempted in Belfast at some future date.

Insofar as the goal of the workshop was to learn about each other, the workshop appeared to be quite successful.

Although few definitive conclusions may be drawn, an assessment of the Belfast effort, completed nine months later, led Doob and Foltz to assert, " ... for everyone the Workshop itself was an impressive event. Many reported that they had been helped as persons. For some but not all of the participants the Workshop facilitated elaborations or subsequent carrying out of plans of their own devising in spite of intimidation and of the difficulties inherent within Northern Ireland" (1974, p. 237).

The difficulties referred to included some sensationalist journalism

about the workshop and withdrawal from the project by the two
deputies who had earlier helped to set it up (on the grounds that
informed consent of participants had not properly been obtained for
an experience that involved more personal stress than anyone had
expected). Despite these difficulties, Doob and Foltz were able to
interview 40 of the 56 participants, and 22 of them attended a tea
party in Belfast where they informally discussed the conflict and
planned further meetings. For this and other reasons, Doob and
Foltz judged that some form of workshop "intervention, even in the
most bitter of quarrels, is worth making [because] learning and
motivation can be facilitated when interested parties are obliged to
interact continuously over a week or more in an isolated setting
where for the moment they feel relatively detached from the reality
they would improve; subsequently they can more effectively
influence the real-life situation back home" (1974, p. 256).

As to which approach might work best, following Belfast, Doob
and Foltz could say only, "We are convinced that no single
approach—Tavistock, NTL, or any of the other encounter or group
dynamics techniques—is universally applicable to all social situations
..." but it is clear they consider any or all worth continued
experimental application.

In a recent UNITAR conference devoted to these approaches
(UNITAR, 1970), it was concluded that considerable research is
called for before we can even claim to know the potential effectiveness of the human relations approach, much less to know the
variables determining its effectiveness. For example, there may well
be certain preconditions that favor the use of such an approach and
others that preclude it. There are as yet unanswered questions
pertaining to the nature of the participants. Should they be men of
power, men with access to power, or private citizens? Other
questions concern the possibility of long-term as opposed to
immediate effects. Might not both an apparent failure as Fermeda
and a limited success as Belfast set in motion forces leading to a
solution of the disputes some months, or even years, after the
conclusion of the workshops, through diffusion of ideas from
participants to policy makers in their own countries?

In advance of such multi-faceted research, it is difficult to assess
the real promise of a human relations approach to the resolution of
international conflict. Nonetheless, we can hazard a prediction that
wherever the resolution of a conflict requires an increase in empathy,
a change in perceptions, or a new understanding of the other side's
perceptions, a workshop approach like Fermeda and Belfast should

have at least a marginally positive impact. As a device for complementing and facilitating conventional diplomacy, it has considerable promise and must be considered a potentially valuable line of approach for dealing with the resolution of international conflict.

If full-blown workshops like Fermeda and Belfast should prove too expensive or otherwise unfeasible, as happened in Cyprus, perhaps some of the features of the workshop approach might become part of more conventional diplomatic encounters. Indeed, should the day come when sensitivity training workshops are no longer convened because their essential features have been absorbed into standard diplomatic procedures, psychology may have made its most significant contribution to the search for peace.

In 1973, Professor Doob was instrumental in convening, at the Bellagio Conference Center in Italy, a conference of international scholars and international relations practitioners from 11 nations to consider the workshop approach along with other approaches to international conflict resolution. The conferees considered three categories of questions:

1. What courses have past disputes followed with what successes or failures, and why?
2. How can future disputes be prevented or resolved?
3. What kinds of information are needed to answer the first two questions?

Despite the fact that Doob had to report (1974) skepticism on the part of the practitioners of the applicability of existing psychological knowledge and techniques to real-world conflict resolution, the conferees seemed willing to consider alternatives to traditional diplomacy.

Perhaps the most provocative outcome of the Bellagio conference is Doob's own prescriptions that resulted from his consideration of the conference transcripts.

> ... forget broad terms, forget organizations for the moment, and concentrate upon specifiable human beings. ... first delineate the cast of characters within a country potentially or actually participating in an international dispute, ... leaders, followers, negotiators or diplomats, and communicators ... conflicts are not conflicts between vague entities called nations but between and among men belonging to the groupings. [One must identify] the psychological concepts or variables which can subsume

the behavior of men in conflict. . . . goals, knowledge, attitudes, and skills. . . . men in conflict possess the attribute of perfectability. [Hence] the attributes of Homo Pacificus:
- Maximum attainment of goals involving a minimum interference with the goals of others.
- Valid, relevant information concerning all major aspects of conflicts or disputes, and ways of avoiding them.
- Favorable or at least tolerant attitudes toward actual or potential antagonists; rejection of the use of force and of war; favorable attitudes toward negotiation and other peaceful ways of settling disputes.
- Ability to interact constructively with other persons. (1974, pp. 325, 326)

Whether *Homo Pacificus* as defined by Doob is indeed a possibility is still unsure, but Doob's efforts must be numbered among the most ambitious, determined, and promising of any psychologist who has tried to intervene in the international arena.

TOWARD THE REDUCTION OF NATIONALIST SENTIMENT

The three topics discussed thus far in this chapter constitute ways to deal with international conflict once it exists. Throughout modern history, humankind has lived continuously with international conflict in a world that is organized into a set of sovereign nations to which primary allegiance has been encouraged. Moreover, each nation has its own goals, which often conflict with those of other nations. Hence, stronger efforts have been advocated to bring about a world in which the nation-state is deemphasized. Some of the more visionary students of international peace have urged that we look beyond such "practical solutions" as the United Nations to a world without nations. Perhaps a world in which nationalism is no longer the psychological force it has been so long is the only kind of world that can be free of war. But nationalism is surely a tenacious force. Is there any basis in psychological knowledge for a possible dampening of nationalism?

In 1964, writing in the *Journal of Conflict Resolution*, the psychologist Paul Rosenblatt assembled much provocative thought on psychological factors relating to nationalism.[7] Included were numerous hypotheses concerning individual psychological need-states, both motivational and cognitive in origin, that may well be sustained by nationalist values. It was one of Rosenblatt's basic premises that nationalism serves some very fundamental psychic needs, one of the most basic of which is a need to identify one's self in terms of something supraindividual. Historically, of course, (in the western world, at least) the nation-state has been a supraindividual entity that has served this function well. Knowing that one's nation is enduring, relatively powerful, and (thanks to ethnocentric perceptions) located at the center of the universe (or, alternatively, at the apex of "the free world") surely compensates for the unwanted knowledge of one's own fragility. Other psychic needs linked by Rosenblatt to nationalism include *need for cognitive simplicity* (which fuels categorizing the world into good/bad, us/them, our nation/foreigners, etc.), the *need for affiliation*, (which translates into a need for friends, with the likely candidate for friendship drawn from those who share nationality and other characteristics), and a *need for ego gratification and defense*. Identification with a nation-state that is perceived as strong, and ethnocentric focusing on foreign scapegoats can obviously serve all of these needs—and then some.

In considering how nationalism might be diluted, it might be instructive to consider how it is fanned. National leaders are often guilty of doing just that, demagogically stirring national feelings, especially because a manifestation of an activated sense of nationalism is an enhanced respect for the nation's leaders. Rosenblatt's paper is replete with hypotheses concerning the self-serving behavior of national leaders who engage in rhetoric designed to enhance pride in the nation's accomplishments and vigilance with regard to the nation's putative enemies. To the degree that leadership instead focuses on worldwide concerns,[8] leadership could move a population away from nationalism.

Moreover, all of the psychic needs that Rosenblatt's analysis suggests are served by nationalism could perhaps equally well be served by internationalism. The policy recommendation flowing from this analysis would be a call to leadership to modify the rhetoric by stressing ever-larger units of mankind as the supraindividual entity with which we ought identify.

Since there are no psychological data to support the proposition that a national identity is some primordial state of mind, there is nothing but historical inertia to explain the continued prevalence of nationalistic sentiment. Perhaps as a consciousness of "spaceship Earth" grows as a concomitant of increased awareness of the interdependence of mankind, facing such problems as a growing scarcity of resources relative to increasing population—a problem that transcends national boundaries—this policy will become more feasible than it has thus far been.

Just as the famous Sherif *et al.* study demonstrated that confronting a superordinate goal was the only condition which overcame intergroup hostility in a boys' camp (Sherif *et al.*, 1961), perhaps events in coming years will show us that only when nations are forced to cooperate in order for all to survive will nationalism—and the international conflicts it has continuously bred—become a thing of the past.

Is there a contribution that psychology can make in this regard? I believe there is. The truly difficult problems confronting mankind all have psychological components. Hence, the solution of these problems demands an international effort by psychologists to do the applied research that will delineate procedures for dealing with these psychological components. The problems that call for such an effort include, for example, the need to modify consumption habits in a world threatened by misuse and maldistribution of food supplies and energy resources, and the need to modify age-old attitudes pertaining to procreation—attitudes that dangerously reinforce high population growth rates.

The kinds of research projects necessary to make a dent in these seemingly intractable problems have hardly been designed, let alone carried out. Hence, as we near the end of this chapter and of this book, we must confront the single most salient challenge to political psychology. It is that there are universal human problems of a staggering magnitude to which the psychologist, along with other scientists, social scientists, and policy makers, must lend their expertise as research scholars. A by no means inconsequential by-product of this, can be an enhanced public awareness of the intertwined nature of the fates of all nations and a concomitant decline in nationalism.

CONCLUSION

In this chapter we have reviewed several ways in which psychology may participate in the search for a world without war. These included communicating to diplomats what we already know about the mutual distortions of perception to which adversary nations are prey (White), experimental application of tension-reduction techniques (Osgood), training in conflict-resolution techniques (Doob), and reduction of nationalistic ideology by the encouragement of, and participation in, international projects designed to enhance the quality of life on our planet. While none of these approaches has yet adequately been tested, it might be tragic to assume that they will not work. As one American psychologist recently put it, ". . . a good many psychologists feel that the bungling that got us into the Vietnam war, and could get us into a nuclear war, consists largely of ignoring certain fundamental *psychological truths*" (White, 1970, p. 344). Is it too much to hope that truths already known will be made impossible to ignore, and that those as yet undiscovered truths will be sought by psychologists applying the very best research skills they possess?

There have been few psychologists more worth emulating than William James. It was three-quarters of a century ago that James, one of the founding fathers of psychology, sought "a moral equivalent to war" (James, 1911). Perhaps the present generation will move us closer to finding it.

NOTES

[1] These phenomena do indeed bear similarities to the behavior of persons who persist in making competitive moves in non-zero sum games, as described in the previous chapter.

[2] It may also be of some interest that Osgood regularly informed his readers that whatever else he was advocating, he continued to hope that the U.S. would win the cold war (1962, p. 41). To a degree, then, he saw himself as offering an alternative to war or surrender that would result in some kind of victory. It is this writer's conviction that Osgood's suggestions should be viewed as promising even by those whose ultimate desire is a world without war, in which neither "side" wins a competition, but in which both sides optimize the total gain accruing to all. It may be easier to express such a "non-patriotic" view in 1975 than it was in 1962. Thus, Osgood's "patriotism" ought not be held against him.

[3] See the discussion in the preceding chapter on the "triggering" effect of the presence of weapons on the behavior of frustrated persons.

[4] It will be noted that this recommendation is the reverse of one popularly offered, *viz.*, to first negotiate an agreement on the abolition of the most devastating nuclear weapons while retaining the wherewithal for "conventional" warfare.

[5] For some years Leonard Doob, the eminent social psychologist, has given

careful thought to applying psychology to issues relating to war and peace. He has contributed classical analyses of propaganda and psychological warfare (Doob, 1948) and has examined the phenomena of patriotism and nationalism (Doob, 1964).

[6] Once again, this "experiment" lacked control groups.

[7] Rosenblatt's ideas as applied to ethnocentrism were discussed earlier in this book in Chapter 5.

[8] See discussion in Chapter 9 of malnutrition, an instance of a global problem on which leadership might focus.

9

A design for research: Political psychology's unfinished business

It has been the central effort of this book to demonstrate that psychology can be relevant to the real world. In the several chapters that are now behind us, we tried to present some of the insights latent in the *findings* of scientific psychology which can serve to enhance general understanding of social problems and guide the formulation and implementation of policies to ameliorate them. The problems we chose to consider included the need to understand the reasons for differential performance of various human groups and the search for ways to maximize the impact of education for those who need it most, to enhance intergroup relations, to control violence, and to improve the chances for international peace. We could have chosen other problems of social import, but surely those we dealt with are among the most pressing ones confronting us as we near the end of psychology's first century as a science. We saw, I believe, that some promising guidelines for the solution of such problems may be derived from what psychological research has already found to be true about human behavior.

It would be misleading, however, to conclude this book with the impression that we know all we need to know. Although there is considerable information to be conveyed by psychologically expert witnesses, there is much that remains to be done by psychologists serving as researchers. There are, as was noted at the end of the preceding chapter, numerous, seemingly intractable problems confronting mankind, including population and resource dilemmas, that cry out for attention from psychologists. It seems appropriate, therefore, that this final chapter be devoted primarily to a *design* for research rather than an additional report of existing findings. Thus, this chapter can serve to underscore the continuing need to consider real-world problems and apply to them whatever creative research design skills we can muster.

There is a second reason for concluding this book with a design for research. From a pedagogical point of view, it may well be that discovering how we frame questions is even more valuable to the student than finding out what is already known.

Thus, we turn now to an example of a design for research on a problem of growing magnitude and obvious significance, for which little information is presently available—the relationship of diet to psychological development and the search for ways to improve nutritional status in a world confronted by a potential shortage of food.

The research design we shall consider is a proposal that was framed by the present writer in collaboration with colleagues at his own university and others in the United States and in Africa, with many of them in disciplines other than psychology. It is a proposal that could be carried out almost anywhere in the world, but was in fact designed to be implemented in the East African nation of Tanzania, where several political and intellectual leaders contributed significantly to its formulation. Thus the proposal, is cross-cultural, interdisciplinary, and is the joint product of researchers and policy makers. As such, it is a most appropriate example of political-psychological planning.

ON THE DEVELOPMENTAL
CONSEQUENCES OF MALNUTRITION

**What is already known and believed: The alleged
causal relation of malnutrition to human development.**

An editorial in *Science* recently asserted that the tendency of children reared in poverty to do poorly on tests of intelligence "to an important extent . . . is a *result* of malnutrition early in childhood" (Abelson, 1969). The editorialist also said, "It seems likely that millions of children in developing countries are experiencing some degree of retardation in learning *because* of inadequate nutrition, and

that this phenomenon may also occur in the United States"
[emphasis mine].

Are these statements justified? Do we know that inadequate
nutrition permanently retards human mental development causing
lower intelligence and learning ability? A review of the relevant
literature reveals a growing consensus that the evidence, albeit
impressive, is far from conclusive. As Abelson correctly notes,
"because of complex social and psychological factors associated with
malnutrition, it is not easy to assess the effects of dietary deficiencies
in man" (1969). On the other hand, research with animals, which can
be experimental in design, can produce conclusive evidence of causal
relationships if the experiments are carefully conceived; causal
relationships do, in fact, exist. Such research has amassed considerable evidence of causal links between nutrition and growth and, more
to the point, between nutrition and behavior.

The available evidence: Animal studies

A number of studies based on experimentally manipulated
nourishment of laboratory animals (rats, pigs, and dogs) have sought
anatomical, neurological, and physiological effects of dietary deficiencies experienced during early life. Frequently reported findings
include the retardation of physical growth. If the experimental
deprivation was produced early enough, the animals matured to
subnormal size even when nutritionally adequate feeding followed
the deprivation period (e.g., Dickerson, Dobbing, and McCance,
1967; Jackson and Stewart, 1920).

A number of studies have shown that biochemical developments
parallel the suppressed physical development caused by malnutrition
(e.g., Dobbing, 1968). Another generalization one can derive from
animal studies is that the earlier the nutritional deprivation, the more
serious (and probably irreversible) are its physical and biochemical
effects.

Neurological effects, as indexed by abnormal EEG patterns, have
been demonstrated in some studies (e.g., Platt, Heard and Stewart,
1964). The severity of these effects (in dogs, particularly) has been
shown to increase as a function of the degree of protein deprivation
and of the age at which the deprivation is introduced.

Clearly, then, animals deprived of protein for a time after weaning
show adverse anatomical, neurological, and biochemical effects particularly in the brain and spinal cord.

Given malnutrition's marked effects on the nervous systems of animals deprived of nutrients, findings that suggest that it produces behavioral effects in animals are not surprising.

Behavioral effects in animals.

Research by different investigators over 35 years on the learning ability of animals (mostly white rats) deprived of protein after weaning has yielded moderately consistent results. Recently, Cowley and Griesel (1959) found marked differences in problem solving across two groups of rats—one that had been maintained on a low protein diet and another that had been fed regular laboratory food. In 1963, the same investigators reported similar findings in a second filial generation of low protein animals. Significantly impaired performance on the Hebb-Williams closed field test was, for these animals, accompanied by other behavioral abnormalities, including depressed amounts of bodily activity, "less coordinated" exploratory behavior, and longer reaction times to auditory stimulation (Cowley and Griesel, 1963).

Experiments with pigs at Cornell University (Barnes *et al.*, 1966) have shown dietary effects (including, specifically, the effects of protein deficiency, a condition imposed on one experimental group) on the acquisition of conditioned avoidance responses. In the same laboratory, malnourishment was shown to have detrimental effects on rats' performance in a water maze learning experiment (Barnes *et al.*, 1966). The most severely deprived group of rats in that study also performed relatively poorly on a new discrimination learning problem given them eight months after being taken off a protein-deficient diet.

Current investigators seem justified, then, in considering as plausible the hypothesis that protein malnutrition during early human development has long-range debilitative effects on learning ability. However, the small number of animal studies that bear directly on the problem of behavioral consequences of malnutrition urge further research. Moreover, because species-specific effects possibly exist, it is clearly desirable that the question of malnutrition's long-term effects on human beings be investigated directly by examining human subjects.

Effects of malnutrition on children.

In a review and discussion of research needed to clarify the relationship between nutrition and psychological development, Read

(1969) reiterated, "In contrast to animal investigations, it is very difficult in human studies to extract social-environmental effects from the consequences of malnutrition, particularly since these often accompany one another." A schematically summarized diagram of the complex possibilities follows:

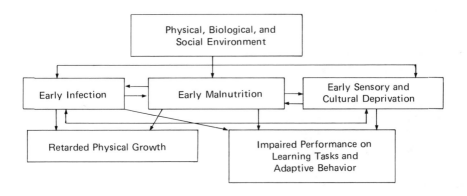

Research completed to date testifies to the existence of these relationships but provides little basis for determining the direction of causality.

Physical effects.

As had been shown in the case of other animals, malnutrition in humans is associated with various anatomical, biochemical, and neurological deficits. All such deficits may have behavioral implications, direct or indirect. Thus, one study (Cravioto and Robles, 1965) suggested that a relation between stature and intellectual attainment reflects the impact of malnutrition on both characteristics.

In a paper dealing with health standards for Ugandan children (Dean, 1954), the researcher cited the "association of kwashiorkor[1] with growth failure and . . . the slowness of growth during treatment of the disease . . ." Coles (1957) also found general deficits in both height and body weight among Ugandan patients.

In followup studies of Guatemalan children recovering from malnutrition (Cravioto, DeLicardie and Birch, 1966), rapid physical growth was found, but the once-malnourished child appears never to catch up completely with his healthy age peers. Head circumference is one of several dimensions which remain subnormal.

Numerous investigators have found biochemical defects in malnourished children (Coursin, 1967; Cravioto, 1962; Dean and Whitehead, 1963). Neuroanatomical studies (Brown, 1966; Winick and Rosso, 1969) revealed for the malnourished individual findings of lesser brain size and cell count, which have obvious implications for the hypothesis that malnutrition leads to behavioral deficits.

Finally, research using electroencephalographic measurements of children (Nelson, 1959; Nelson and Dean, 1959) reported localized disturbances of EEG similar to those found in malnourished animals. Valenzuela and his co-workers (Valenzuela, Peniche, and Macias, 1959) found that the electrical activity of the brain in malnourished children shows consistent abnormalities in the form, frequency, and amplitude of activity. However, upon recovery, these children exhibit a wave form that tends to conform more closely to that of healthy children of the same age. Similarly, research in Algiers and Ceylon [Sri Lanka] (Engel, 1956) found EEG abnormalities in malnourished children that seemed not to persist after cure. Still, any occurrence of EEG abnormalities suggests that malnutrition may affect neurological maturation, consequently affecting psychological functioning.

Behavioral effects.

Recent research offers clear evidence of behavioral effects *accompanying* a state of malnutrition, and less clear evidence suggesting *residual* behavioral effects long after recovery.

Apathy, lowered responsiveness, and depressed intellectual performance are well-documented concomitants of protein malnutrition (e.g., Cravioto, DeLicardie, and Birch, 1966). Although recovery from malnutrition is usually accompanied by a return to normal responsiveness, several studies (e.g., Cabak and Najdanvic, 1965; Robles, Ramos-Galavan, and Cravioto, 1959) show that intellectual attainments of children who have recovered from a clinically severe episode of protein-calorie malnutrition are consistently lower than those of children who enjoyed adequate nutrition in infancy.

Stoch and Smythe (1963) also studied the question of intellectual development. The 21 malnourished South African children in this longitudinal study had a lower mean IQ score than the matched control children. Though this study, like others, was marred by the absence of an adequate control group (the probands, who were illegitimate children drawn mostly from broken homes in which alcoholism and other social pathologies were common; the controls all enjoyed comfortable homes and attended a nursery school), it clearly supports the hypothesis that malnutrition leads to long-range intellectual deficits mediated by neurological malfunction.

Champakam, Srikantia, and Gopalan (1968), working in India, compared IQ test results of two groups of children: nineteen 8-11-year-old children who had had kwashiorkor between ages 18 and 36 months and had recovered, and a group of controls matched with the experimental subjects for age, sex, religion, caste, socio-economic status, family size, birth order, and educational level of parents and subjects. The performance of the control and experimental subjects on intelligence tests differed significantly, particularly in the younger age group (8-9); it tended to diminish in the older age group (10-11 years). The retardation was noticeable mainly with regard to perceptual and abstract abilities.

Measures of cognitive development other than IQ tests have figured in some recent studies, and these also show nutrition-related deficits. In the research done in Guatemala by Cravioto, DeLicardie, and Birch (1966), rural, apparently malnourished, children exhibited depressed performances on tests of intersensory organization (e.g., visual-haptic integration).

Thus, Cravioto (1966) may have been justified in concluding that insufficient intake of protein during infancy, when most neural development occurs, probably affects cognitive development. This theme has recurred often during the past two years in review articles (e.g., Eichenwald and Fry, 1969; Osofsky, 1969). Osofsky concluded that, while the animal data "clearly indicate that malnutrition affects both physiologic and psychologic development," the human data are more difficult to interpret. The present review of the literature leads to a similar conclusion. The available human data are difficult to interpret, and the problem clearly requires more field research.

Recent field studies have been reported involving comparisons between malnourished and (relatively) well-nourished children, matched for a variety of socioeconomic variables (e.g., Klein, 1969). In the first study, the well-nourished group performed significantly better on four of six tests. Klein attributed the lower performance of the malnourished children (rehabilitated at the time of testing) either to lower cognitive proficiency or to greater difficulty in paying attention to the task. In the second study, Klein attempted to replicate the results of the first and to discriminate between the cognitive and attentional interpretation of the first study's results. He used 15 tests, including two new short-term memory tasks and the four short-term memory tests that had earlier produced significant differences. Paradoxically, the four original short-term memory tasks did not produce significant differences in the second study, while the two new ones did. So did two other measures ("embedded figures" and "matching familiar figures"). Taking into account the failure to replicate and the pattern of responses to the various tests used in the second study, Klein concluded that "task difficulty" rather than specific cognitive capacity determined performance. Therefore, he reasoned the effect of early malnutrition may be upon the individual's motivational-attentional disposition rather than upon his intellectual capacity *per se*. The idea should serve to guide future research, whether this reasoning is valid or not, particularly in selecting the behavior to be measured. IQ tests may not be the best measures in studying the psychological effects of malnutrition, as Klein's argument (if not his findings) strongly suggests.

A study done in Colombia (McKay and McKay, 1969) investigated the permanence of the psychological defects found to be correlated with early nutritional status and, less directly, asked whether the correlation reflects a causal relation. These investigators provided one group of malnourished children with daily dietary supplements for six months and another group of malnourished children with the same supplements plus daily nursery school activity for the same period. A variety of simple tests were administered twice, once at the outset and again at the end of the six-month period. Significant improvement in performance was found only for the group that had been both nutritionally *and* psychologically rehabilitated. This finding suggests that depressed performance among malnourished children can, on some tasks at least, be improved, but that the therapy must include psychological enrichment as well as protein. This last point may also imply that the malnutrition's depressing effects reflect psychological deprivation as well as dietary deficiencies.

For this proposal, the value of the field research studies lies primarily in the guidance they offer to research design and the selection of tests and measures. Our design takes into account the various methodological issues that affect research on the behavioral consequences of malnutrition.

The proposed core longitudinal study

In order to assess the long-term consequences of malnutrition, and to isolate nutritional status from the numerous sociocultural variables that also have behavioral consequences, it is deemed essential to build the research around a core longitudinal study. This study will be conducted in an ethnically homogeneous area in the Republic of Tanzania, an area that will have been selected on the basis of preliminary research. The principal criterion for area selection will be prevalence of protein-calorie malnutrition, including kwashiorkor, among children under age five.

Design of the core study.

The format of the core study will be longitudinal, with repeated observations from infancy through early adolescence of at least 100 sibling pairs. One member of each pair will be recruited into the study upon detection of signs of malnutrition, while the other member will be prevented from developing malnutrition through a program of supervised dietary supplementation.

Subjects.

The technique of proband[2] recruitment will depend on the prior selection of a defined area within which a medical team will perform intensive clinical examinations every six months of all children who are under one year of age when the study begins. When clinical signs of malnutrition appear at any of these semi-annual examinations, a child displaying them will be nutritionally (and otherwise) rehabilitated; he will enter the proband sample. Through this process, the proband sample will be composed of children who vary along several dimensions—including age at detection, severity of malnutrition, and intensity and duration of therapy (although all will have experienced *some* malnutrition).

Control recruitment depends on the high probability of subsequent pregnancies among the mothers of proband members. As soon as a child enters the proband sample, his household will become the locus of dietary supplementation and other preventive measures. If he already has a younger sibling who has shown no signs of malnutrition, the sibling will become a member of the control group. If no younger sibling exists at the time supplementation is introduced into the household, the mother will be the object of nutritional care and her next baby will enter the control sample at birth (and, in a sense, prenatally). This technique ensures that the control sample will be composed of children who vary in age at the onset of nutritional supplementation (although none will have experienced malnutrition). Within this control group, comparisons are possible between children who entered it prenatally and those who were weanlings when first contacted.

Thus, this study's basic comparison will be of children who experienced some malnutrition early in childhood with their next younger siblings who experienced none.

A subsidiary control will also be recruited from older siblings— some known to have been malnourished, others with no record of malnutrition, insofar as such children can be found and their prior nutritional status reliably determined.

As noted above, probands will be drawn from children in the first year of age cohort only. It should be understood that these children might not actually enter the study until well after their first birthday, since malnutrition typically develops in the second year of life. In our design, proband recruitment is not restricted to one-year-olds, but to all children who are in the first year of life *at the time the study is commenced.* Children older than age one at the time the study begins cannot serve in this study, unless they happen to be older sibs of probands, in which case they might serve in the subsidiary control group. However, all children in the defined area between ages one and five years who develop signs of malnutrition severe enough to warrant care will receive it from medical personnel associated with this project. These children may also participate in other studies ancillary to the core study that may become appropriate as preliminary results emerge from the core study. Several scientific and ethical criteria will be met.

1. Since all control subjects will be siblings of probands, the basic comparison groups will be subject to similar familial influences. Variables such as socioeconomic status, parental education, family size, interval between siblings and, ordinal birth positions, all of which could affect cognitive and emotional development enough to mask the effects of (or to be confounded with) protein malnutrition, will be controlled to the greatest possible extent. One cannot say that probands and controls will be truly equivalent in all respects other than nutritional history; that is simply impossible. For example, the controls must occupy ordinal birth positions on the average one degree lower than those of the probands. But the ranges of OBPs covered in both samples, and the variability, are likely to be highly similar.[3]

2. Since both probands and controls will receive continuing, intensive medical attention (from detection of malnutrition in the case of the probands and from a prevulnerability age level in the case of the controls), any "Hawthorne effect" of attention *per se* applies nearly equally to both samples. Again, complete equality is impossible. Control subjects will inevitably be younger when attention first focuses on them. For this reason we have introduced the subsidiary control group composed of older siblings.

3. To the extent that parental behavior is changed by a child's inclusion in the proband sample, every proband is potentially subject to an indirect, or mediated, Hawthorne effect. However, since probands and controls share parents, this potential confounding is minimized. Of course, control children might benefit from parental concern that begins earlier, but this is unavoidable and less serious than the problem that would exist were probands and controls recruited from different families.

4. Although the research design requires children who display signs of malnutrition, this design does not compromise the principle of providing maximal therapeutic and preventive care where knowledge, techniques, and personnel are available. On the contrary, the provision of medical care in the defined area is enhanced. The presence of a combined research and clinical team will create a level of prevention and care that should markedly exceed the level available in comparable regions outside the study area. By virtue of the present research design, special medical attention will be given all children in the area up to the age of five years, and beyond in the case of probands and controls. As noted above:

a. From the outset of the study, all children who are between the ages of 1 and 5 years and who develop clinical signs will be treated, even though they will not be employed as research subjects in the core study. In comparable regions, malnutrition often goes untreated or is detected relatively late in its course due to lack of facilities and personnel or to local ignorance of available treatment.

b. All children in the defined area who are under one year of age when the study begins will be carefully scrutinized as soon as signs of malnutrition are detected, and therapeutic measures that virtually insure rehabilitation will begin. Thus, the probands, like all other malnutrition victims in the defined area, will receive a degree of care far higher than· that available in regions outside the defined area.

c. Younger siblings of probands will receive preventive care of a higher order than is available anywhere else in kwashiorkor-prone areas of East Africa.

There is another way in which the proposed research honors the ethics that must accompany any study of the effects of any disease that is (potentially) easy to cure and prevent. In the defined area for the longitudinal study, a study of the prevention of malnutrition will also go forward. Prevention studies will, in fact, derive from the logitudinal study since preventive measures must be applied to each proband's siblings. Once the full complement of probands is assembled, the full-scale studies of prevention will be launched. The defined area will then become the locus of an intensive coordinated campaign to eliminate malnutrition by modifying dietary practices.

Ancillary control studies.

As the core longitudinal study proceeds and comparisons of siblings reveal performance differences attributable to differential nutritional status, it would be instructive and feasible to apply selected behavioral assessments to several additional control groups. These various ancillary controls would assist in the interpretation of findings from the core study.

One of these control groups would be composed of children living in the villages that match those in the defined area from which the basic proband sample is drawn. Children would be selected into this new group on the same basis as the probands. Like them, they would be identified by clinical examination as malnourished and would require and receive treatment. However, this group's treatment would consist only of initial rehabilitation; they would receive no additional intervention other than measurement and testing. The inclusion of this group would permit assessment of the effects on a family of initial rehabilitation and testing of a single malnourished child as distinct from the total intervention applied to families in the basic proband-control study.

Another ancillary control group would be composed of children of the same ages and socioeconomic backgrounds as the control siblings in the core study. These children would be tested only twice during the project—once near its beginning and once near its end—in order to evaluate the effect of the attention focused on children in the core study who are to be subjected to repeated testing.

Another group of relatively well-nourished children will be found and followed throughout the life of the project. They will be tested regularly but not subjected to any other intervention.

Finally, another group of "normals," representing every age group for which testing will be done in the core study, will be tested once only. The performance of previously untested normals will provide evidence for practice efforts that might influence the performance of children in the core study.

AN ACTION PROGRAM TO MODIFY DIETARY BEHAVIOR

Although the long-term consequences of malnutrition during early childhood are unknown, few would disagree that, even in advance of such knowledge, an attempt to eliminate malnutrition is desirable. Therefore, it is proposed to embark on implementation research in Tanzania as soon as preliminary nutritional surveys have been completed. The present section describes research designed to discover the most efficient, effective ways to bring about changes in this behavior so that nutritional status may be improved. Unless research into the causes of protein-calorie malnutrition is conducted hand-in-hand with research into its prevention, nutrition research is difficult to justify in a country where malnutrition is acute. Accordingly, experimental measures which, *a priori*, seem likely to result in malnutrition's prevention will be introduced and evaluated as part of the overall project.

The need to evaluate applied nutrition programs

In various parts of Africa, applied nutrition programs have been designed to encourage the diffusion of innovations in dietary practices, but few have been adequately evaluated (Latham, 1967). Latham has argued, "If applied nutrition programs are to be properly planned and evaluated, then there is a need for much thought and study . . . experimentation and for greatly increased use of social science . . . It would be helpful if universities . . . and bodies which provide funds for research could look with as much favor on this type of investigation as they currently do on biochemical and biomedical nutrition research" (1967, p. 193). Jelliffe (1968) also has pointed to evaluation of nutrition education in developing countries as "much neglected."

Some guidelines for the design of preventive measures pertinent to

Tanzania are available in the literature. Latham has provided a review of deficiencies to be corrected in East Africa (1964a) and some hints as to feasible solutions to nutritional problems prevailing there (1963). He has also described the structure of planned nutrition service programs in Tanzania (1964b).

Examples of teaching manuals—a communication device which the proposed project might employ—are also available; some of these have been designed especially for use in East Africa (e.g., Burgess and Burgess, 1970; Ebrahim, 1968; Latham and Baker-Jones, 1966).

Guides to communication techniques that are likely to be effective in rural Tanzanian settings are also available (e.g., Fugelsang, 1969) and considerable research has been completed on cultural influences on visual perception in East Africa (Segall, Campbell, and Herskovits, 1966).

Other materials too numerous to list here are available from the contiguous countries of Zambia and Uganda and can be adapted easily for use in Tanzania. Available, too, are descriptions of various techniques employed in those countries to teach mothers how to improve child-feeding practices; these techniques can be adapted to and evaluated in Tanzania. Many have been described by Jelliffe (1968), including discussion-demonstrations, the use of non-nutritional incentives, and the use of audio-visual aids. The various techniques and materials used compose an educational program whose goal will be to encourage the diffusion of innovations in dietary behavior. Field experimentation will evaluate this educational program as part of our research. Results of the evaluation will be fed back into the program to guide its subsequent modification and improvement.

Evaluation of the diverse aspects of a campaign such as this presents many methodological difficulties. Fortunately, some excellent models of evaluation research exist. Most employ an experimental design involving comparisons of villages or regions, randomly selected to receive one or another treatment, with comparable units which serve as control groups (e.g., Berelsen and Freedman, 1964; Dodd, 1934; Mathur and Neurath, 1959; Menefee and Menefee, 1963).

A recent study done simultaneously in Costa Rica and India (Roy, Waisanen and Rogers, 1969) had many features similar to the proposed research. It too was a field experiment, employing matched villages, with different treatments applied selectively and with controls. The treatments included various formats for the presentation of educational materials urging a variety of behavioral innovations, including health practices. A before-and-after measurement procedure was employed (termed "benchmark" and "followup" respectively), and the measurements bracketed year-long treatments. The dependent variables were measures of (a) respondents' knowledge of the innovations, (b) their evaluations of the innovations, and (c) how many actually adopted the innovations.

The basic data analysis technique involved the calculation of "net change" scores—the difference between followup and benchmark scores for a treatment village, minus the same difference for its control village. These scores were subjected to an analysis of variance to determine the significance of the treatments' impacts.

In addition, correlational and regression analyses were performed in order to seek the relationships among various village characteristics to scores on both benchmark and followup measures.

This combination of correlational and experimental techniques has much to recommend it. Although infrequently used in social science research, the field experiment is often urged by students of research (Campbell and Stanley, 1963). Free from the artificiality of the laboratory, it nonetheless embodies the essential rigor of experimental control, a *sine qua non* for the discovery of causal relationships. It is clearly preferred for research on the diffusion of innovations (Rogers, 1962).

Theory to guide the design of the evaluation studies will be derived primarily from social psychology. Two substantive subareas of the discipline are extremely pertinent—research on behavioral modification and research on communication and persuasion.

These two categories embrace a number of research techniques and theoretical issues that will influence the design of the research to be undertaken in Tanzania. Thus, in addition to its practical significance, the research will have theoretical implications, particularly with regard to attitudinal and behavioral change. It will provide tests of various propositions that have been derived from research already completed, and it will test the cross-cultural applicability of existing research findings. In designing the research, the kinds of theoretical issues that will be taken into consideration include the following:

1. Since behavior reflects attitudes and since attitudes support behavior, is it more effective to attempt to change attitudes, expecting that behavior change will follow? Or is it more effective to attempt to modify behavior, expecting that new attitudes will automatically become consonant with new behaviors? With regard to dietary practices, one could first try to modify people's attitudes and beliefs concerning the foods they eat, and then trust that they will

translate their new beliefs into appropriate behavior. Alternatively, one could devise certain behavioral modification techniques and let the attitudes take care of themselves. As part of the proposed research, these two general approaches will be compared by employing an attitude-change approach with one group and a behavioral-modification approach with a comparable group.

2. With regard to communications designed to change attitudes about dietary practices, a number of variables could be built into experimental communications. One of these variables has to do with the credibility of the communicator. In the East African setting of our research, it would be of considerable interest to present the same message to a number of equivalent groups, while varying the attributed source of the message along one or more dimensions. For example, one could vary the *role* of the attributed source. It is conceivable that a communication designed to change attitudes about dietary practices might be more effective if it were thought to emanate from medical or nutritional personnel. On the other hand, persons who occupy traditional leadership roles in various communities might prove to be the more effective communicators of dietary information. A study might be designed to reveal a "sleeper effect," were it to exist: though high-prestige communicators have a more potent *immediate* effect, long-term attitude change often occurs to a significant degree in response to communications presented by low-prestige (even negatively evaluated) communicators (the "sleepers"). It is as if the source of the communication is forgotten though its content is remembered. Short-term and long-term effects on dietary behavior might prove to be differentially produced by communicators of varying prestige. This is of particular interest, since attitude change of an enduring nature is clearly the goal of the action portion of our research.

3. Since, presumably, deeply ingrained attitudes underlie dietary behavior, it would be of interest to compare the efficacy of rational and emotional appeals. Are *information* campaigns as effective as campaigns designed to convince people to behave in a certain way, without making any effort to get them to understand why they should behave that way? It is apparent that present efforts to modify dietary practices in East Africa heavily stress education. It would be worth contrasting this "cognitive" approach with a more emotional one. In this regard, we might also investigate the effect of fear appeals. Is it possibly effective to try to change behavior by stressing the negative consequences

of foods that are presently highly valued, or would it be better to stress the positive consequences of foods that are not yet positively valued?

4. Related is the basic theoretical issue of negative vs. positive reinforcement. In any attempt to modify existing behavior directly, one could try to induce particular responses and to offer positive rewards whenever such responses occur, merely ignoring all other responses. Alternatively, one could deal directly with instances of unwanted behavior by punishing them. For various theoretical reasons, most studies of behavioral modification urge the presentation and withholding of positive reinforcement rather than the administration of punishment as a device for shaping behavior. Still, the particular complex of factors surrounding dietary practices might call for an approach that uses negative reinforcement. In the setting presently under consideration, for example, it would be worthwhile to determine the effects of stressing the damaging consequences of low-protein staple foods. Campaigns designed to discourage people from smoking cigarettes would serve as a model for such an approach. Alternatively, one could assess the consequences of providing positive reinforcements for the adoption of other foods as a supplement to the staple diet, on the grounds that the staple is so highly valued that an attempt to eliminate it completely would be impractical.

5. The whole question of the nature of adequate reinforcements would require systematic investigation. It is very likely that what is a reinforcement for some people would not be a reinforcement for others. Considerable research is needed to discover the appropriate reinforcements for various target groups. In this regard, it would be interesting to attempt to link certain desired new behaviors to already existing values. For example, large segments of the target population are found to maintain and express a value of "modernism"; one might try to identify particular diets as part of the behaviors that are labeled "modern" in this setting.

6. Social support for innovative attempts, via group discussions and public decision-making, is known to be facilitating (as in the classic group-dynamics studies of changing dietary practices). Particularly in the Tanzanian context, it would be instructive to investigate variations on group involvement strategies for inducing behavioral change.

These, then, are some of the theoretical issues that would guide the design of research on the most effective means to prevent protein-calorie malnutrition.

The locus and orientation of preventive research

The locus of the studies of prevention techniques will be the defined area in which the rest of the project is conducted. There, a variety of efforts to modify dietary practices will be mounted, and their effects contrasted. These efforts will be directed to various target groups, including mothers, fathers, and various potentially influential men and women. For each target group, prevailing behavior will be ascertained; then, different approaches to modify those behaviors will be undertaken. These would include lectures, discussion groups, documentary films, poster campaigns, and the like, all designed to support the kinds of theoretical issues referred to above.

It will be impossible to investigate all of the researchable questions in a single study. Accordingly, a number of separate experiments will be conducted sequentially over a period of years, with each study yielding data of independent significance that can also provide guidelines for the design of subsequent experiments.

We could, for example, prepare and distribute a series of films, which mobile film units would show in selected communities. The films' content and style would vary according to the dictates of certain theoretical considerations. Behavioral observations would be conducted in selected households and at intervals, following the film showings. Similar observations, for control purposes, would be made in communities not yet exposed to the film program. Those films shown to be the most effective might later be employed on a large scale, even nationally, in a campaign to obliterate protein-calorie malnutrition.

Other approaches—including school-based campaigns, the use of radio, the subsidized distribution of certain foodstuffs, and other techniques that various concerned agencies might wish to use experimentally—could be incorporated into this stream of the overall research project.

Some might argue that the way to eliminate malnutrition is simply to seek the development of protein-enriched varieties of popular staples. It is the fundamental premise of the present proposal that the essence of the problem of malnutrition is cultural and (by extension) psychological. Even when protein-rich foods are available, the problem remains of convincing people to consume them. Hence, the emphasis in the proposed project is to learn how diets can most effectively be changed. Over a period of three to four years, several dietary change experiments, each self-contained but sequentially related, could be completed; with their results in hand, knowledge of how best to attempt to eliminate protein-calorie malnutrition in Tanzania should be available to ministries and agencies for implementation.

CONCLUDING COMMENTS

We have considered in detail a proposed action-oriented research program that would both investigate the hypothesis that malnutrition retards psychological development and evaluate programs to reduce malnutrition. The proposed project also bears on the problem of population growth, surely one of mankind's most critical ecological crises, since attitudes toward family size, particularly in developing countries, are conditioned by the expectations of prospective parents regarding the survival of their offspring. These expectations, in turn, reflect a people's experience with infant mortality, a consequence, albeit often indirect, of the quality of diet. Thus, enhanced understanding and potential control of population growth rates is a possible by-product of research that focuses on the consequences and prevention of malnutrition.[4]

Clearly then, the project plan described here is an example of psychological research applied to problems that confront us as we seek not only to survive, but to enhance the quality of life of those who will inherit this planet from us.

For the political psychologist, there is likely no greater objective than to bequeath to future generations a world in which peace is more probable than it has been, and in which all persons, regardless of sex or ethnicity, are provided with equal opportunity to realize their potential.

In this book, we have tried to show how psychologists might have something—however small—to contribute to this future.

This book is now complete. The task documented by the book has only begun.

NOTES

[1] *Kwashiorkor* is a protein-calorie malnutrition syndrome, whose name derives from a West African word meaning "that which happens to children when their mothers are pregnant again." That very concept suggests that post-weaning malnutrition is traditionally thought of as a "normal" condition!

[2] In biomedical research, the term *proband* is widely used to designate clinical subjects who are both treated and studied.

[3] The use of a subsidiary control group of older siblings will, in any case, allow for some assessment of the effect of individual birth position. Also, if in early returns, first-born children appear in any significant way to be different, the study could be limited to later-born children.

[4] This proposition, and related arguments, may be found at several places in a special issue of the *Journal of Social Issues* edited by Back and Fawcett (1974) devoted to applications of psychology to population policy issues. See especially articles by Kastenbaum on possible links between fear of death and fertility attitudes and by Miller and Inkeles who report empirical links in developing countries between valuations of modern, scientific (especially medical) practices and attitudes toward family planning.

References

Abelson, P.H. Malnutrition, learning and behavior. *Science*, April 4, 1969, **164** (3875), 17.

Adorno, T.W., Frenkel-Brunswick, E., Levinson, D.J., and Sanford, N. *The Authoritarian Personality*. New York: Harper, 1950.

Allport, G. *Personality*. New York: Holt, 1937

Allport, G.W. Prejudice: A problem in psychological causation. *Journal of Social Issues*, 1950, Supplemental Series No. 4.

Allport, G.W. *The Nature of Prejudice*. Cambridge, Mass.: Addison-Wesley, 1954.

Archibald, K. Alternative orientations to social science utilization. *Social Science Information*, 1970, 9, 7-34.

Ardrey, R. *The Territorial Imperative*. New York: Atheneum, 1966.

Aronson, E. *The Social Animal*. San Francisco: Freeman, 1972.

Asch, S.E. Effects of group pressure upon the modification and distortion of judgments. In H. Guetzkow (Ed.), *Groups, Leadership and Men*. Pittsburgh: Carnegie, 1951.

Atkin, C.K., Murray, J.P., and Nayman, O.B. (Eds.) *Television and Social Behavior*. Washington, D.C.: National Institute of Mental Health, 1971.

Atkinson, J.W. (Ed.) *Motives in Fantasy, Action, and Society: A Method of Assessment and Study*. New York: Van Nostrand, 1958.

Azrin, N.A., and Lindsley, O.R., The reinforcement of cooperation between children. *Journal of Abnormal and Social Psychology*, 1956, 52, 100-102.

Back, K.W., and Fawcett, J.T. (Eds.) Population Policy and the Person: Congruence or conflict? *Journal of Social Issues*, 1974, **30**, Whole no. 4.

Bacon, M.K., Child, I.L., and Barry, H., III. A cross-cultural study of correlates of crime. *Journal of Abnormal and Social Psychology*, 1963, **66**, 291-300.

Ball, S., and Bogatz, G.A. *The First Year of "Sesame Street": An Evaluation*. Princeton, N.J.: Educational Testing Service, 1970.

Ball, S., and Bogatz, G.A. Summative research of Sesame Street: Implications for the study of preschool children. In Anne D. Pick (Ed.), *Minnesota Symposia on Child Psychology, Vol. 6*. Minneapolis: University of Minnesota Press, 1972.

Bandura, A. Behavioral modifications through modeling procedure. In L. Krasner and L.P. Ullman (Eds.), *Research in Behavior Modification*. New York: Holt, Rinehart & Winston, 1965a. Pp. 310-340.

Bandura, A. Influence of models' reinforcement contingencies on the acquisition of imitative responses. *Journal of Personality and Social Psychology*, 1965b, **1**, 589-595. (See also Bandura, 1971a.)

Bandura, A. *Principles of Behavior Modification*. New York: Holt, Rinehart & Winston, 1969.

Bandura, A. Influence of models' reinforcement contingencies on the acquisition of imitative responses. In A. Bandura (Ed.), *Psychological Modelling: Conflicting Theories*. Chicago: Aldine-Atherton, 1971a.

Bandura, A. *Social Learning Theory*. New York: General Learning Press, 1971b.

Bandura, A. Vicarious and self-reinforcement processes. In R. Glaser (Ed.), *The Nature of Reinforcement*. Columbus, Ohio: Merrill, 1971c.

Bandura, A. Behavior theory and the models of man. *American Psychologist*, 1974, **29**, 859-869.

Bandura, A., and Huston, A.C. Identification as a process of incidental learning. *Journal of Abnormal and Social Psychology*, 1961, **63**, 311-318.

Bandura, A., and McDonald, F.J. The influence of social reinforcement and the behavior of models in shaping children's moral judgments. *Journal of Abnormal and Social Psychology*, 1963, **67**, 274-281.

Bandura, A., Ross, D., and Ross, S.A. Transmission of aggression through imitation of aggression models. *Journal of Abnormal and Social Psychology*, 1961, **63**, 575-582.

Bandura, A., Ross, D., and Ross, S.A. Imitation of film-mediated aggressive models. *Journal of Abnormal and Social Psychology*, 1963, 66, 3-11.

Bandura, A., and Walters, R.H. *Social Learning and Personality Development.* New York: Holt, Rinehart & Winston, 1963.

Barnes, R.H., Cunnold, S.R., Zimmermann, R.R., Simmons, H., MacLeod, R.B., and Krook, L. Influence of nutritional deprivations in early life on learning behavior of rats as measured by performance in a water maze. *Journal of Nutrition*, 1966, 89, 399-410.

Barry, H., III. *Cross-cultural perspectives on how to minimize the adverse effects of sex differentiation.* Pittsburgh: Know Press, 1969.

Barry, H., III, Bacon, M.K., and Child, I.L. A cross-cultural survey of some sex differences in socialization. *Journal of Abnormal and Social Psychology*, 1957, 55, 327-332.

Barry, H., III, Child, I.L., and Bacon, M.K. Relation of child training to subsistence economy. *American Anthropologist*, 1959, 61, 51-63.

Bass, B.M. The substance and the shadow. *American Psychologist*, 1974, 29, 870-886.

Baumrin, B. The immorality of irrelevance: The social role of science. In F.F. Korten, S.W. Cook, and J.I. Lacey (Eds.), *Psychology and the Problems of Society.* Washington, D.C.: American Psychological Association, 1970, Pp. 73-83.

Baumrind, D. Some thoughts on ethics of research: After reading Milgram's behavioral study of obedience. *American Psychologist*, 1964, 19, 421-423.

Beach, F. The descent of instinct. *Psychological Review*, 1955, 62, 401-410.

Becker, H.S. Whose side are we on? *Social Problems*, 1967, 14, 239-247.

Bem, S.L., and Bem, D. We're all unconscious sexists. *Psychology Today*, November, 1970.

Berelson, B., and Freedman, R. A study in birth control. *Scientific American*, 1964, 210, 29-37.

Berkowitz, L. The expression and reduction of hostility. *Psychological Bulletin*, 1958, 55, 257-283.

Berkowitz, L. Anti-Semitism and the displacement of aggression. *Journal of Abnormal and Social Psychology*, 1959, 59, 182-187.

Berkowitz, L. Simple views of aggression: An essay review. *American Scientist*, 1969, 57, 372-383.

Berkowitz, L. Social Responsibility, Empathy, and Altruism. Paper presented at the annual meeting of the American Psychological Association, Washing, D.C., September 1969.

Berkowitz, L. Impulse, aggression and the gun. In J.V. McConnell (Ed.), *Readings in Social Psychology Today.* Del Mar, Calif.: CRM Books, 1970, Pp. 89-93.

Bernstein, B. Social class and linguistic development: A theory of social learning. In A.H. Halsey, J. Floud, and C.A. Anderson (Eds.), *Education, Economy and Society.* New York: Free Press of Glencoe, 1961.

Berry, J.W. Temne and Eskimo perceptual skills. *International Journal of Psychology,* 1966, 1, 207-229.

Berry, J.W. Ecological and cultural factors in spatial perceptual development. *Canadian Journal of Behavioural Science,* 1971, 3, 324-336.

Bettelheim, B. Individual and mass behavior in extreme situations. *Journal of Abnormal and Social Psychology,* 1943, 38, 417-452.

Biesheuvel, S. Psychological tests and their application to non-European peoples. In G.B. Jeffrey (Ed.), *The Yearbook of Education.* Evans, 1949. Excerpted in D.R. Price-Williams (Ed.), *Cross-cultural Studies: Selected Readings.* Middlesex, England: Penguin, 1969.

Binet and Simon. *A Method of Measuring the Development of the Intelligence of Young Children.* Lincoln, Ill.: Courien, 1912.

Birch, H., and Gussow, J. *Disadvantaged Children: Health, Nutrition and School Failure.* New York: Harcourt, Brace & World, 1970.

Blake, R., and Dennis, W. Development of stereotypes concerning the Negro. *Journal of Abnormal and Social Psychology,* 1943, 38, 525-531.

Bloom, B.S. *Stability and Change in Human Characteristics.* New York: Wiley, 1964.

Bogardus, E.S. *Immigration and Race Attitudes.* Boston: Heath, 1928.

Bogart, L. Warning: The Surgeon General has determined that TV violence is moderately dangerous to your child's mental health. *Public Opinion Quarterly,* 1972-1973, 36, 491-521.

Bogatz, G.A., and Ball, S. *The Second Year of "Sesame Street": A Continuing Evaluation.* Princeton, N.J.: Educational Testing Service, 1971a.

Bogatz, G.A., and Ball, S. Some things you've wanted to know about Sesame Street. *American Education,* 1971b (April), 11-15.

Box, G.E.P., and Tiao, G.C. A change in level of a non-stationary time series. *Biometrika*, 1965, **52**, 181-192.

Brewer, M. Determinants of social distance among East African tribal groups. *Journal of Personality and Social Psychology*, 1968, **10**, 279-289.

Brock, T.C., and Buss, A.H. Dissonance, aggression and evaluation of pain. *Journal of Abnormal and Social Psychology*, 1962, **65**, 197-202.

Brock, T.C., and Buss, A.H. Effects of justification for aggression and communication with the victim on post-aggression dissonance. *Journal of Abnormal and Social Psychology*, 1964, **68**, 403-412.

Bronfenbrenner, U. The mirror image in Soviet-American relations: A social psychological report. *Journal of Social Issues*, 1961, **17**, 45-56.

Brooks, Mel, and Reiner, Carl. *The 2,000-year-old Man.* Capitol Records (Pickwick International), SPC-3279.

Brown, R.E. Organ weight in malnutrition with special reference to brain weight. *Developmental Medical and Child Neurology*, 1966, **8**, 512.

Burgess, H.J.L., and Burgess, A.P. *P.C.M.* Lusaka, Zambia: National Food and Nutrition Commission, 1970.

Burton, J.W. *Conflict and Communication.* London: Macmillan, 1969.

Burton, R., and Whiting, J.W.M. The absent father and cross-sex identity. *Merrill-Palmer Quarterly*, 1961, **7**, 85-95.

Buss, A.H. *The Psychology of Aggression.* New York: Wiley, 1961.

Cabak, V., and Najdanvic, R. Effects of undernutrition in early life on physical and mental development. *Arch. Dis. Children*, 1965, **40**, 532-534.

Campbell, D.T. Factors relevant to the validity of experiments in social settings. *Psychological Bulletin*, 1957, **54**, 297-312.

Campbell, D.T. Conformity in psychology's theories of acquired behavioral dispositions. In I.A. Berg and B.M. Bass (Eds.), *Conformity and Deviation.* New York: Harper, 1961 pp. 101-142.

Campbell, D.T. The mutual methodological relevance of anthropology and psychology. In Francis L.K. Hsu (Ed.), *Psychological Anthropology.* Homewood, Ill.: Dorsey, 1961.

Campbell, D.T. From description to experimentation: Interpreting trends as quasi-experiments. In C.W. Harris (Ed.), *Problems in Measuring Change.* Madison: University of Wisconsin Press, 1963.

Campbell, D.T. Ethnocentric and other altruistic motives. In M.R. Jones (Ed.), *Nebraska Symposium on Motivation: 1965.* Lincoln: University of Nebraska Press, 1965. Pp. 283-310.

Campbell, D.T. Stereotypes and the perception of group differences. *American Psychologist*, 1967, 22, 817-829.

Campbell, D.T. Reforms as experiments. *American. Psychologist*, 1969, 24, 409-429.

Campbell, D.T. Methods for the Experimenting Society. Preliminary draft of a paper delivered to the American Psychological Association, September 15, 1972. (To appear, revised, in *American Psychologist.*)

Campbell, D.T. On the genetics of altruism and the counter-hedonic components in human culture. *Journal of Social Issues*, 1972, 28, 21-37.

Campbell, D.T., and Erlebacher, A. How regression artifacts in quasi-experimental evaluations can mistakenly make compensatory education look harmful. In J. Hellmuth (Ed.), *Compensatory Education: A National Debate, Vol. 3, Disadvantaged Child.* New York: Brunner/Mazel, 1970.

Campbell, D.T. and LeVine, R.A. A proposal for cooperative cross-cultural research on ethnocentrism. *Journal of Conflict Resolution*, 1961, 5, 82-108.

Campbell, D.T., and Ross, H.L. The Connecticut crackdown on speeding: Time-series data in quasi-experimental analysis. *Law and Society Review*, 1968, 3(1), 33-53.

Campbell, D.T., and Stanley, J.C. Experimental and quasi-experimental designs for research on teaching. In N.L. Gage (Ed.), *Handbook of Research on Teaching.* Chicago: Rand McNally, 1963. (Reprinted as *Experimental and Quasi-experimental Design for Research.* Chicago: Rand McNally, 1966.)

Caplan, N. The new ghetto man: A review of recent empirical findings. *Journal of Social Issues*, 1970, 26, 59-73.

Caplan, N., and Nelson, S.D. On being useful: The nature and consequences of psychological research on social problems. *American Psychologist*, 1973, 28, 199-211.

Caplan, N.S., and Paige, J.M. A study of ghetto rioters. *Scientific American*, 1968, 219(2), 15-21.

Carnegie Corporation. The street where letters live and children learn. *Carnegie Corporation of New York Quarterly*, 1971.

Cauthen, N.R., Robinson, I.E., and Krauss, H.H. Stereotypes: A review of the literature 1926-1968. *Journal of Social Psychology*, 1971, 84, 103-125.

Chaffee, S.H., and McLeod, J.M. Adolescents, Parents and Television Violence. Paper presented at the American Psychological Association Meetings, Washington, D.C., September 1971.

Champakam, S., Srikantia, S.G., and Gopalan, C. Kwashiorkor and mental development. *American Journal of Clinical Nutrition*, 1968, 21, 844-852.

Chapanis, N., and Chapanis, A. Cognitive dissonance: Five years later. *Psychological Bulletin*, 1964, 61, 1-22.

Clark, K.B. The pathos of power: A psychological perspective. *American Psychologist*, 1971, 26, 1047-1957.

Clark, K.B., and Clark, M.P., Racial identification and preference in Negro children. In E. Maccoby, T.M. Newcomb, and E.L. Hartley (Eds.), *Readings in Social Psychology*. (3rd edition). New York: Holt, Rinehart & Winston, 1958. Pp. 602-611.

Cole, M., and Bruner, J.S. Cultural differences and inferences about psychological processes. *American Psychologist*, 1971, 26, 867-876.

Coleman, J.S. *Policy Research in the Social Sciences.* Morristown, N.J.: General Learning Corporation, 1972.

Coleman, J.S. et al., *Equality of Educational Opportunity.* Washington, D.C.: Government Printing Office, 1966.

Coles, R.M. The relation of height and body weight of Uganda African patients. *East. African Medical Journal*, 1957.

Coursin, D.B. Relationship of nutrition to central nervous system development and function. Overview., *Federal Proceedings*, 1967, 26, 134-138.

Cowley, J.J., and Griesel, R.D. Some effects of a low protein diet on a first filial generation of white rats. *Journal of Genetic Psychology*, December 1959, 95, 187-201.

Cowley, J.J., and Griesel, R.D. The development of second generation low protein rats. *Journal of Genetic Psychology*, 1963, 103, 233-242.

Cravioto, J. Appraisal of the effect of nutrition of biochemical maturation. *American Journal of Clinical Nutrition*, 1962, 11, 484-492.

Cravioto, J. *Pre-School Child Nutrition.* Washington: National Academy of Science, Nutrition Research, Publ. No. 1282, 1966.

Cravioto, J., and Robles, B. Evolution of adaptive and motor behavior during rehabilitation from kwashiorkor. *American Journal of Orthopsychiatry*, 1965, 35, 449-464.

Cravioto, J., DeLicardie, E.R., and Birch, H.G. Nutrition, growth, neurointegrative development: An experimental and ecologic study. *Pediatrics*, 1966 supplement, Part II, 38, 319-372.

Crutchfield, R.S., Woodworth, D.G., and Albrecht, R.E. *Perceptual performance and the effective person.* Lackland Air Force Base,

Texas: Personnel Laboratory, Wright Air Development Center, Air Research and Development Command, 1958. (Cited in Stewart, 1974.)

D'Andrade, R.G. Sex differences and cultural institutions. In E. Maccoby (Ed.), *The Development of Sex Differences.* London: Tavistock, 1967. Pp. 174-204.

Darlington, C.D., and Mather, K. *Elements of Genetics.* London: Shocken, 1969.

Dawson, E. The protection of human subjects: The Tuskegee study. *Maxwell Review*, 1974, **10**(2), 49-56.

Dean, R.F.A. Standards for African children and the influence of nutrition. *Journal of Tropical Medicine and Hygiene*, 1954, **57**, 288-289.

Dean, R.F.A., and Whitehead, R.G. The metabolism of aromatic aminoacidity in kwashiorkor. *Lancet*, 1963, **26**, 188-191.

De Tocqueville, A. *Democracy in America.* New York: Dearborn, 1838.

Deutsch, M. A theory of cooperation and competition. *Human Relations*, 1950, **2**, 129-152.

Deutsch, M. Organizational and conceptual barriers to social change. In F.F. Korten, S. Cook, and J. Lacey (Eds.), *Psychology and the Problems of Society.* Washington, D.C.: American Psychological Association, 1970. Pp. 47-57.

Deutsch, M., Katz, I., and Jensen, A. (Eds.) *Social Class, Race and Psychological Development.* New York: Holt, Rinehart & Winston, 1968.

DeVos, G., and Hippler, A. Cultural psychology: Comparative studies of human behavior. In G. Lindzey and E. Aronson (Eds.), *Handbook of Social Psychology, Vol. IV.* Cambridge, Mass.: Addison-Wesley, 1969.

Dickerson, J.W.T., Dobbing, J., and McCance, R.A. The effect of undernutrition on the post-natal development of the brain and cord in pigs. *Proceedings of the Royal Society of London Biologists*, 1967, **166**, 396-407.

Dobbing, J. Effects of experimental undernutrition on development of the nervous system. In N.S. Scrimshaw and J.E. Gordon (Eds.), *Malnutrition, Learning and Behavior*, 1968. Pp. 181-202.

Dodd, S.C. *A Controlled Experiment on Rural Hygiene in Syria.* New York: Oxford University Press, 1934.

Dollard, J. Hostility and fear in social life. *Social Forces*, 1938, **17**, 15-26.

Dollard J., Doob, L., Miller, N., Mowrer, O., and Sears, R. *Frustra-*

tion and Aggression. New Haven: Yale University Press, 1939.

Doob, L.W. *Public Opinion and Propaganda.* New York: Holt, 1948.

Doob, L.W. *Patriotism and Nationalism.* New Haven: Yale University Press, 1964.

Doob, L.W. (Ed.) *Resolving Conflict in Africa: The Fermeda workshop.* New Haven: Yale University Press, 1970.

Doob, L.W. The impact of the Fermeda workshop on the conflicts in the Horn of Africa. *International Journal of Group Tensions,* 1971, **1**, 91-101.

Doob, L.W. The analysis and resolution of international disputes. *Journal of Psychology,* 1974, **86**, 313-326.

Doob, L.W. A Cyprus workshop: An exercise in intervention methodology. *Journal of Social Psychology,* 1974, **94**, 161-178.

Doob, L.W., and Foltz, W.J. The Belfast workshop. *Journal of Conflict Resolution,* 1973, **17**, 489-512.

Doob, L.W., and Foltz, W.J. The impact of a workshop upon grass-roots leaders in Belfast. *Journal of Conflict Resolution,* 1974, **18**, 237-256.

Ebrahim, G.R. (Ed.) *Practical Maternal and Child Health Problems in Tropical Africa.* Dar es Salaam: East African Literature Bureau, 1968.

Ehrlich, H.J. Stereotyping and Negro-Jewish stereotypes. *Social Forces,* 1962, **41**, 171-176.

Eichenwald, H.F., and Fry, P.C. Nutrition and learning. *Science,* 1969, **163**, 644-648.

Engel, R. Abnormal brain wave patterns in kwashiorkor. *Electroenceph. Clinical Neurophysiology,* 1956, **8**, 489.

Erlich, D., Guttman, I., Schenback, R., and Mills, J. Post-decision exposure to relevant information. *Journal of Abnormal and Social Psychology,* 1957, **54**, 98-102.

Etzioni, A. *The Hard Way to Peace.* New York: Collier, 1962.

Etzioni, A. The Kennedy experiment. *Western Political Quarterly,* 1967, **20**(2), 361-380.

Feather, N.T. Cognitive dissonance, sensitivity and evaluation. *Journal of Abnormal and Social Psychology,* 1963, **66**, 157-163.

Feshbach, S. The drive-reducing function of fantasy behavior. *Journal of Abnormal and Social Psychology,* 1955, **50**, 3-11.

Feshbach, S., and Singer, R. *Television and Aggression.* San Francisco: Jossey-Bass, 1971.

Festinger, L. *A Theory of Cognitive Dissonance.* Stanford, Calif.: Stanford University Press, 1957.

Fink, D.M. Sex differences in perceptual tasks in relation to selected personality variables. Unpublished doctoral dissertation, Rutgers University, 1959. (Cited in Stewart, 1974.)

Firestone, S. *The Dialectic of Sex: The Case for Feminist Revolution.* New York: Morrow, 1970.

Foster, J., and Long, D. (Eds.) *Student Activism in America.* New York: Morrow, 1970.

Freedman, J.L., and Sears, D.O. Warning, distraction and resistance to influence. *Journal of Personality and Social Psychology*, 1965, 1, 262-266.

French, E.G., and Lesser, G.S. Some characteristics of the achievement motive in women. *Journal of Abnormal and Social Psychology*, 1964, 68, 119-128.

Fugelsang, A. *Communication with Illiterates.* Lusaka, Zambia: The National Food and Nutrition Commission, 1969.

Gallo, P.S., Jr., and McClintock, C.G. Cooperative and competitive behavior in mixed-motive games. *Journal of Conflict Resolution*, 1965, 9, 68-78.

Gewirtz, J.L., and Stingle, K.C. Learning of generalized imitation as the basis for identification. *Psychological Review*, 1968, 75, 374-397.

Gilbert, G.M. Stereotypes persistence and change among college students. *Journal of Abnormal and Social Psychology*, 1951, 46, 245-254.

Gilula, M.F., and Daniels, D.N. Violence and man's strength to adapt. *Science*, 1969, 164, 396-405.

Glass, G.V. Analysis of data on the Connecticut speeding crackdown as a time-series quasi-experiment. *Law and Society Review*, 1968, 3(1), 55-76.

Gornick, V. Why women fear success. *New York*, 1971, 4, No. 51, 50-53.

Guttentag, M. Evaluation of social legislation. In F.F. Korten, S.W. Cook, and J.I. Lacey (Eds.), *Psychology and the Problems of Society.* Washington, D.C.: American Psychological Association, 1970. Pp. 40-46.

Guttentag, M. Group cohesiveness, ethnic organization, and poverty. *Journal of Social Issues*, 1970, 26(2), 105-132.

Hamburg, D.A., and Lunde, D.T. Sex hormones in the development of sex differences in human behavior. In E.E. Maccoby (Ed.), *The Development of Sex Differences.* London: Tavistock, 1967. Pp. 1-24.

Hano, A. Can Archie Bunker give bigotry a bad name? *New York Times Magazine*, March 12, 1972, pp. 32-33, 119, 124-126, 129.

Hawkes, G.R. Strategy for basic-applied research interaction. *American Psychologist*, 1973, **28**, 269.

Herrnstein, R.J. I.Q. *Atlantic*, 1971, **228**, 44-64.

Herskovits, M.J. *The Negro and Intelligence tests.* Hanover, New Hampshire: Sociological Press, 1927.

Hoffman, M.L. Childrearing practices and moral development: Generalizations from empirical research. *Child Development*, 1963, **34**, 295-318.

Hollie, P. Sadean and institutional cruelty. In F.F. Korten, S.W. Cook, and J.I. Lacey (Eds.), *Psychology and the Problems of Society.* Washington, D.C.: American Psychological Association, 1970, Pp. 295-303.

Horner, M.S. Sex Differences in Achievement Motivation and Performance in Competitive and Non-Competitive Situations. Unpublished doctoral dissertation, University of Michigan, 1968.

Horner, M.S. Fail: Bright women. *Psychology Today*, 1969, **3**, 36-38, 62.

Hovland, C.I. Reconciling conflicting results derived from experimental and survey studies of attitude change. *American Psychologist*, 1959, **14**, 8-17.

Humphreys, L.G. The effect of random alternation of reinforcement on the acquisition and extinction of conditioned eyelid reactions. *Journal of Experimental Psychology*, 1939, **25**, 141-158.

Husen, T. *International Study of Achievement in Mathematics: A Comparison of Twelve Countries, Vol. I.* New York: Wiley, 1967.

Hyman, H.H., and Sheatsley, P.B. Attitudes toward desegregation. *Scientific American*, 1956, **195**, 35-39.

Insko, C.A., and Schopler, J. *Experimental Social Psychology.* New York: Academic Press, 1972.

Jackson, C.M., and Stewart, C.A. The effects of inanition in the young upon the ultimate size of the body and of the various organs in the albino rat. *Journal of Experimental Zoology*, 1920, **30**, 87-128.

James, W. *Memoirs and Studies.* New York: Longmans, Green, 1911.

Jelliffe, D.B. *Child Nutrition in Developing Countries: A Handbook for Field-Workers.* Washington, D.C.: U.S. Department of State, Agency for International Development, 1968. (Public Health Service Publication No. 1882).

Jencks, C. (with Smith, M., Acland, H., Bane, M.J., Cohen, D., Gintis, H., Heynes, B., and Michelson, S.) *Inequality; A Reassessment of the Effect of Family and Schooling in America.* New York: Basic Books, 1972.

Jensen, A. How much can we boost IQ and scholastic achievement? *Harvard Educational Review*, 1969, **39**, 1-123. Reprinted in Environment, Heredity and Intelligence. *Harvard Educational Review Reprint Series*, 1969, No. 2.

Jones, E. City limits. In D. Shoemaker (Ed.), *With All Deliberate Speed*. New York: Harper, 1957.

Kamin, L.J. Heredity, Intelligence, Politics and Society. Address at the Eastern Psychological Association, 1973.

Kamin, L.J. *The Science and Politics of IQ*. Potomac, Maryland: Earlbaum, 1974.

Kanfer, F.H. Vicarious human reinforcement: A glimpse into the black box. In L. Krasner and L.P. Ullmann (Eds.), *Research in Behavior Modification*. New York: Holt, Rinehart & Winston, 1965.

Kanfer, F.H., and Marston, A.R. Human reinforcement: Vicarious and direct. *Journal of Experimental Psychology*, 1963, **65**, 292-296.

Kastenbaum, R. Fertility and the fear of death. *Journal of Conflict Resolution*, 1974, **30** (4), 63-78.

Kaufman, H., and Zenar, I. Helper's resentment in help-giving situations. Unpublished paper, Hunter College, 1968.

Keller, F., and Schoenfeld, W.N. *Principles of Behavior*. New York: Appleton-Century-Crofts, 1950.

Kelman, H.G. Violence without moral restraint: Reflections on the dehumanization of victims and victimizers. *Journal of Social Issues*, 1973, **29**(4), 25-61.

Kenniston, K. *The Uncommitted*. New York: Harcourt, Brace and World, 1965.

Kenniston, K. The sources of student dissent. *Journal of Social Issues*, 1967, **23**, 108-137.

Kerner, O. *United States National Advisory Commission on Civil Disorders*. New York: Dutton, 1968.

Kessen, W. Early learning and compensatory education: Contributions of basic research. In F.F. Korten, S.W. Cook, and J.I. Lacey (Eds.), *Psychology and the Problems of Society* Washington, D.C.: American Psychological Association, 1970. pp. 200-203.

Klein, R.E. Performance of Malnourished in Comparison with Adequately Nourished Children (Guatemala). Paper presented at AAAS meetings, Boston, 1969.

Klineberg, O. *Negro Intelligence and Selective Migration*. New York: Columbia University Press, 1935.

Klineberg, O. Negro-white differences in intelligence test performance: A new look at an old problem. *American Psychologist*, 1963, 18, 198-203.

Klineberg, O. Black and White in international perspective. *American Psychologist*, 1971, 26, 119-128.

Koch, S. (Ed.) *Psychology: A Study of a Science.* New York: McGraw-Hill, 1959-1963 (six volumes).

Kramer, J.R. The social relevance of the psychologist. In F.F. Korten, S.W. Cook, and J.I. Lacey (Eds.), *Psychology and the Problems of Society.* Washington, D.C.: American Psychological Association, 1970. pp. 32-39.

Lambert, W.W. Cross-cultural backgrounds to personality development and the socialization of aggression: Findings from the six culture study. In W.W. Lambert and R.Weisbrod (Eds.), *Comparative Perspectives on Social Psychology.* Boston: Little, Brown, 1971. pp. 49-61.

Latham, M.C. *Some Practical Suggestions for Solutions to Nutritional Problems.* FAO/UNICEF, 1963.

Latham, M.C. *Deficiencies to be Corrected in East Africa.* FAO, 1964a.

Latham, M.C. A clinical nutrition survey of certain areas of Dodoma and Kondoa districts. *East. African Medical Journal*, 1964b, 41, 69.

Latham, M.C. Some observations relating to applied nutrition programs supported by the U.N. agencies. *Nutrition Review*, 1967, 25, 193-197.

Latham, M.C., and Baker-Jones, E. *Nutrition Manual for East Africa.* London: Longmans Green, 1966.

Lee, E.S. Negro intelligence and selective migration: A Philadelphia test of the Klineberg hypothesis. *American Sociological Review*, 1951, 16, 227-233.

Lefkowitz, M., Blake, R.R., and Mouton, J.S. Status factors in pedistrian violation of traffic signals. *Journal of Abnormal and Social Psychology*, 1955, 51, 704-705.

Lefkowitz, M.M., Eron, L.D., Walder, L.W., and Husemann, L.R. Television violence and child aggression: A follow-up study. In G.A. Comstock and E.A. Rubenstein (Eds.), *Television and Social Behavior, Vol. III: Television and Adolescent Aggressiveness.* Washington, D.C.: U.S. Government Printing Office, 1972.

Lefkowitz, M.M., Eron, L.D., Walder, L.W., and Husemann, L.R. *Growing Up to be Violent: A Longitudinal Study of the Development of Aggression.* Elmsford, N.Y.: Pergamon Press, in press.

Lesser, G.S. Designing a program for broadcast television. In F.F. Korten, S.W. Cook, and J.I. Lacey (Eds.), *Psychology and the Problems of Society*. Washington, D.C.: American Psychological Association, 1970. pp. 208-214.

Lesser, G.S. *Children and Television: Lessons from Sesame Street*. New York: Vantage, 1974.

Lesser, G.S., Fifer, G., and Clark, D.H. Mental abilities of children from different social-class and cultural groups. *Monographs of the Society for Research in Child Development*, 1965, **30**, (4, Serial No. 102), 1-115.

LeVine, R.A. Cross-cultural study in child psychology. In P.H. Mussen (Ed.), *Carmichael's Manual of Child Psychology*, Vol. 2 (3rd ed.) New York: Wiley, 1970.

LeVine, R.A., and Campbell, D.T. *Ethnocentrism: Theories of conflict, ethnic attitudes, and group behavior*. New York: Wiley, 1972.

Lewin, K. Self-hatred among Jews. *Contemporary Jewish Record*, 1941, 4 219-232.

Lewis, D.J., and Duncan, C.P. Vicarious experience and partial reinforcement. *Journal of Abnormal and Social Psychology*, 1958, **57**, 321-326.

Liebert, R.M., Neale, J.M., and Davidson, E.S. *The Early Window: Effects of TV on Children and Youth*. Elmsford, N.Y.: Pergamon Press, 1973.

Liebert, R.M., Sobol, M.P., and Davidson, E.S. Catharsis of aggression among institutionalized boys: Fact or anti-fact? In G.A. Comstock, E.A. Rubenstein, and J.P. Murray (Eds.), *Television and Social Behavior, Vol. V: Television's Effects: Further Explorations*. Washington, D.C.: U.S. Government Printing Office, 1972.

Loeblin, J.C., Lindzey, G., and Spuhler, J.N. *Race Differences in Intelligence*. San Francisco: Freeman, 1975.

London, P. The end of ideology in behavior modification. *American Psychologist*, 1972, **27**, 913-919.

Lorenz, K. *On Aggression*. New York: Harcourt, Brace and World, 1963.

Luce, R.D., and Raiffa, H. *Games and Decisions*. New York: Wiley, 1957.

Maccoby, E.E. (Ed.) *The Development of Sex Differences*. London: Tavistock, 1967.

MacDougall, W. *An Introduction to Social Psychology*. London: Methuen, 1908.

Mather, J.C., and Neurath, P.M. *An Indian Experiment in Farm Radio Forums*. Paris: UNESCO, 1959.

McClelland, D.C. Testing for competence rather than for "intelligence." *American Psychologist*, 1973, **28**, 1-14.

McDill, E.L., McDill, M.S., and Spreke, J. *Strategies for Success in Compensatory Education: An Appraisal of Evaluation Research.* Baltimore: Johns Hopkins Press, 1969.

McDonald, R.L., and Gynther, M.D. Relationship of self and ideal-self descriptions with sex, race and class in southern adolescents. *Journal of Personality and Social Psychology*, 1965, **1**, 85-88.

McFie, J. The effect of education on African performance on a group of intellectual tests. *British Journal of Educational Psychology*, 1961, **31**, 232-240.

McKay, H., and McKay, A. Behavioral Effects of Nutritional Rehabilitation in Preschool Children (Colombia). Paper presented at AAAS meetings, Boston, December 1969.

Menefee, S., and Menefee, A. An experiment in communications in four Indian villages. *Indian Journal of Social Research*, 1963, **6**, 148-158.

Miles, M.W. *The Radical Probe: The Logic of Student Rebellion.* New York: Atheneum, 1971.

Milgram, S. Behavioral study of obedience. *Journal of Abnormal and Social Psychology*, 1963, **67**, 371-378.

Milgram, S., and Shotland, R.L. *Television and Anti-Social Behavior.* New York: Academic Press, 1973.

Milgram, S. Some conditions of obedience and disobedience to authority. *Human Relations*, 1965, **18**, 57-76.

Miller, A.S., An investigation of some hypothetical relationships of rigidity and strength and speed and perceptual closure. Unpublished doctoral dissertation, University of California, 1953 (Cited in Stewart, 1974.)

Miller, G.A. Psychology as a means of promoting human welfare. *American Psychologist*, 1969, **24**, 1063-1075. Reprinted in F.F. Korten, S.W. Cook, and J.I. Lacey (Eds.), *Psychology and the Problems of Society.* Washington, D.C.: American Psychological Association, 1970. pp. 5-21.

Miller, J.O. Disadvantaged families: Despair to hope. In F.F. Korten, S.W. Cook, and J.I. Lacey (Eds.), *Psychology and the Problems of Society.* Washington, D.C.: American Psychological Association, 1970.

Miller, K.A., and Inkeles, A. Modernity and acceptance of family limitation in four developing countries. *Journal of Social Issues*, 1974, **30**(4), 167-188.

Miller, N.E. The frustration-aggression hypothesis. *Psychological Review*, 1941, **48**, 337-342.

Miller, N.E., and Bugelski, R. Minor studies in aggression: The influence of frustrations imposed by the in-group on attitudes expressed toward out-groups. *Journal of Psychology*, 1948, **25**, 437-442.

Miller, N.E., and Dollard, J. *Social Learning and Imitation.* New Haven: Yale University Press, 1941.

Millett, K. *Sexual Politics.* New York: Doubleday, 1970. London: Rupert Hart-Davis.

Miner, J. *Social and Economic Factors in Spending for Public Education.* Syracuse, N.Y.: Syracuse University Press, 1963.

Montagu, M.F.A. (Ed.) *Man and Aggression.* New York: Oxford University Press, 1968.

Moore, O.K. The responsive environments project and the deaf. *American Annals of the Deaf*, 1965, **110**, 604-614.

Morris, D. *The Naked Ape.* New York: McGraw-Hill, 1967.

Mosteller, F., and Moynihan, D.P. (Eds.) *On Equality of Educational Opportunity.* New York: Random House, 1972.

Mussen, P.H., and Parker, A.L. Mother nurturance and girls' incidental imitative learning. *Journal of Personality and Social Psychology*, 1965, **2**, 94-97.

Mussen, P.H., and Rutherford, E. Effects of aggressive cartoons on children's aggressive play. *Journal of Abnormal and Social Psychology*, 1961, **62**, 461-464.

Myrdal, G. *An American Dilemma: The Negro Problem and Modern Democracy.* New York: Harper, 1944.

Myrdal, G. How scientific are the social sciences? *Bulletin of the Atomic Scientists*, 1973, **28**, 31-37.

Nelson, G.K. The electroencephalogram in kwashiorkor. *Electroenceph. Clinical Neurophysiology*, 1959, **11**, 73.

Nelson, G.K., and Dean, R.F.P. The electroencephalogram in African children: Effects of kwashiorkor and a note on the newborn. *WHO Bulletin*, 1959, **21**, 779-782.

Orne, M.T. On the social psychology of the psychological experiment: With particular reference to demand characteristics and their implications. *American Psychologist*, 1962, **17**, 776-783.

Osgood, C.E. *An Alternative to War or Surrender.* Urbana: University of Illinois Press, 1962.

Oskamp, S., and Perlman, D. Effects of friendship and disliking on cooperation in a mixed-motive game. *Journal of Conflict Resolution*, 1966, **10**, 221-226.

Osofsky, H.J. Fetal Malnutrition: Its Relationship to Subsequent Infant and Child Development. Unpublished Manuscript, SUNY Upstate Medical Center, Syracuse, New York, 1969.

Peck, R.F. A comparison of the value systems of Mexican and American youth. *Interamerican Journal of Psychology*, 1967, **1**, 41-50.

Pepitone, A. Redistributing Wealth Unfairly Gained. Paper presented at the annual meeting of the American Psychological Association, Washington, D.C., September 1969.

Pepitone, A. Social science and social issues. *SPSSI Newsletter*, 1974, **138**, 1, 8.

Peterson, R.E., and Bilorvsky, J.A. *May, 1970: The Campus Aftermath of Cambodia and Kent State.* New York: Carnegie Commission on Higher Education, 1970.

Pettigrew, T.F. Personality and socio-cultural factors in inter-group attitudes: A cross-national comparison. *Journal of Conflict Resolution*, 1958, **2**, 29-42.

Pettigrew, T.J. Regional differences in anti-Negro prejudice. *Journal of Abnormal and Social Psychology*, 1959, **59**, 28-36.

Pettigrew, T.F. Social distance attitudes of South African students. *Social Forces*, 1960, **38**, 246-253.

Pettigrew, T.F. Social psychology and desegregation research. *American Psychologist*, 1961, **16**, 105-112.

Pettigrew, T.F. Racially separate or together? *Journal of Social Issues*, 1969, **25**, 43-69.

Platt, D.C., Heard, C.R.C., and Stewart, R.J.C. Experimental protein-calorie deficiency. In H.N. Munro and J.B. Allison (Eds.), *Mammalian Protein Metabolism*, Vol. 2. New York: Academic Press, 1964.

Price-Williams, D.R. A study concerning concepts of conservation of quantities among primitive children. *Acta Psychologica*, 1961, **18**, 297-305. Reprinted in D.R. Price-Williams (Ed.), *Cross-cultural Studies: Selected Readings.* Middlesex, England: Penguin, 1969.

Prothro, E.T. Ethnocentrism and anti-Negro attitudes in the deep South. *Journal of Abnormal and Social Psychology*, 1952, **47**, 105-108.

Read, M.S. Malnutrition and Mental Development: Needed Research to Clarify Critical Questions. U.S. Public Health Service, N.I.H., 1969, mimeo.

Rhine, R.J. The 1964 presidential election and curves of informative seeking and avoiding. *Journal of Personality and Social Psychology*, 1967, **5**, 516-523.

Riecken, H.W., and Boruch, R. (Eds.) *Social Experimentation.* New York: Academic Press, 1974.

Robles, B., Ramos-Galavan, R., and Cravioto, J. Education of the behavior of the child with advanced malnutrition and of its modification during recovery (Preliminary report). *Bol. Med. Hosp. Infant Mexico*, 1959, **16**, 317-341.

Rodgers, R., Hammerstein, O. II, and Logan, J. *South Pacific.* New York: Random House, 1949.

Rogers, E.M. *Diffusion of Innovations.* New York: Free Press, 1962.

Rohrer, J.H., and Edmonson, M.E. (Eds.) *The Eighth Generation: Cultures and Personalities of New Orleans Negroes.* New York: Harper, 1960.

Rokeach, M. (Ed.) *The Open and Closed Mind.* New York: Basic Books, 1960.

Rokeach, M., Smith, P.W., and Evans, R.I. Two kinds of prejudice or one? In M. Rokeach (Ed.), *The Open and Closed Mind.* New York: Basic Books, 1960. pp. 132-168.

Rosenbaum, M.E., and Bruning, J.L. Direct and vicarious effects of variations in percentage of reinforcement on performance. *Child Development*, 1966, **37**, 959-966.

Rosenbaum, M.E., Chalmers, D.K., and Potts, G.T. Vicarious Reinforcement: A Critical Re-evaluation. Unpublished manuscript, 1971.

Rosenblatt, P. Origins and effects of group ethnocentrism and nationalism. *Journal of Conflict Resolution*, 1964, **8**, 131-145.

Rosenthal, R., and Jacobson, L.F. Teacher expectations for the disadvantaged. *Scientific American*, 1968, **218**, No. 4, 19-23.

Ross, E.A. *Social Psychology: An Outline and a Source Book.* New York: Macmillan, 1908.

Ross, H.L., and Campbell, D.T. The Connecticut speed crackdown. A study of the effects of legal change. In H.L. Ross (Ed.), *Perspectives on the Social Order: Readings in Sociology.* New York: McGraw-Hill, 1968.

Roy, P., Waisanen, F.B., and Rodgers, E.M. *The Impact of Communication on Rural Development.* Paris: UNESCO, 1969.

Scarr-Salapatek, S. Unknowns in the IQ equation, *Science*, 1971a, **174**, 1223-1228.

Scarr-Salapatek, S. Race, social class, and IQ. *Science*, 1971b, **174**, 1285-1295.

Schoenfeld, N. An experimental study of some problems relating to stereotypes. *Archives of Psychology*, 1942, **38**, Whole No. 270.

Segall, M.H. A primer on prejudice. *Transition*, 1967, **7**, 45.

Segall, M.H., Campbell, D.T., and Herskovits, M.J. *The Influence of Culture on Visual Perception.* Indianapolis: Bobbs-Merrill, 1966.

Sherif, M. An experimental study of stereotypes. *Journal of Abnormal and Social Psychology*, 1935, 29, 371-375.

Sherif, M., Harvey, O.J., White, B.J., Hood, W.R., and Sherif, C.W. *Experimental Study of Positive and Negative Intergroup Attitudes between Experimentally Produced Groups.* Norman, Oklahoma: University of Oklahoma, 1954 (multilithed).

Sherif, M., Harvey, O.J., White, B.J., Hood, W.R., and Sherif, C. *Intergroup Conflict and Cooperation: The Robbers Cave Experiment.* Norman, Oklahoma: University Book Exchange, 1961.

Sherwood, J.J., and Nataupsky, M. Predicting the conclusions of Negro-White intelligence research from biographical characteristics of the investigator. *Journal of Personality and Social Psychology*, 1968, 8.

Shuey, A.M. *The Testing of Negro Intelligence.* Lynchburg, Virginia: Bell, 1958.

Siegel, A.E. Film-mediated fantasy aggression and strength of aggressive drive. *Child Development*, 1956, 27, 365-378.

Singer, J.L. *The Control of Aggression and Violence.* New York: Academic Press, 1971.

Skinner, B.F. *The Behavior of Organisms.* New York: Appleton-Century-Crofts, 1938.

Skinner, B.F. *Beyond Freedom and Dignity.* New York: Knopf, 1971.

Skinner, B.F. *About Behaviorism.* New York: Knopf, 1974.

Skinner, B.F., and Ferster, C.B. *Schedules of Reinforcement.* New York: Appleton-Century-Crofts, 1957.

Skinner, B.F., and Rogers, C. Some issues concerning the control of human behavior: A symposium. *Science*, 1956, 124, 1057-1066.

Slovic, P. Risk-taking in children; Age and sex differences. *Child Development*, 1966, 37, 169-176.

Stein, D.D., Hardyck, J.A., and Smith, M.B. Race *and* belief—an open and shut case. *Journal of Personality and Social Psychology*, 1965, 1, 281-289.

Stewart, V.M. Sex and temperament revisited: A cross-cultural look at psychological differentiation in males and females. Paper presented at the Second International Conference of the International Association for Cross-cultural Psychology, Kingston, Ontario, 1974. Mimeographed.

Stoch, M.B., and Smythe, P.M. Does undernutrition during infancy inhibit brain growth and subsequent intellectual development? *Arch. Dis. Childhood*, 1963, 38, 546-552.

Storr, A. *Human Aggression.* New York: Atheneum, 1968.

Sumner, W. G. *Folkways.* Boston: Ginn, 1906.

Suppes, P., and Morningstar, M. Technological innovations: Computer-assisted instruction and compensatory education. In F.F. Korten, S.W. Cook, and J.I. Lacey (Eds.), *Psychology and the Problems of Society.* Washington, D.C.: American Psychological Association, 1970.

Tajfel, H., Sheikh, A.A., and Gardner, R.C. Content of stereotypes and the inference of similarity between members of stereotyped groups. *Acta Psychologica,* 1964, **22,** 191-201.

Terrel, G., Jr., Kurkin, K., and Wiesley, M. Social class and the nature of the incentive in discrimination learning. *Journal of Abnormal and Social Psychology,* 1959, **59,** 270-272.

Thorndike, E.L. Animal intelligence. An experimental study of the associative process in animals. *Psychological Monographs,* 1898, 2(8).

Thorndike, E.L. An experimental study of rewards. *Teachers College Contributions to Education,* 1933, whole No. 580.

Tiger, L. Male dominance? Yes, alas. A sexist plot? No. *New York Times Magazine,* October 25, 1970.

Triandis, H.C. A note on Rokeach's theory of prejudice. *Journal of Abnormal and Social Psychology,* 1961, **62,** 184-186.

Triandis, H.C., and Triandis, L.M. A cross-cultural study of social distance. *Psychological Monographs,* 1962, **76,** Whole No. 540.

UNESCO preamble to the constitution in Editors, *The Europa Year Book 1973: A world Survey.* London: Europa Publications Limited, 1973, I, 59.

UNITAR. *Social Psychological Techniques and the Peaceful Settlement of International Disputes.* New York, UNITAR, 1970, No. 1.

Valenzuela, R.H., Peniche, J.H., and Macias, R. Clinical electro-encephalographic and psychological aspects of recuperations of the undernourished child. *Gaceta Med. Mex.,* 1959, **89,** 651-656.

Vernon, P.E. Environmental handicaps and intellectual development. *British Journal of Educational Psychology,* 1965, **35,** 1-12, 117-126.

Vernon, P.E. Abilities and educational achievements in an East African environment. *Journal of Special Education,* 1967, **1,** 335-345. Reprinted in D.R. Price-Williams (Ed.), *Cross-cultural Studies: Selected Readings.* Middlesex, England: Penguin, 1969.

Vinacke, W.E. Explorations in the dynamic processes of stereotyping. *Journal of Social Psychology,* 1956, **43,** 105-132.

Viteles, M.S. Psychology today: Fact and foible. *American Psychologist,* 1972, **27,** 601-607.

Voltaire. *Candide.* Originally published 1759. In E.R. Durieni (Ed. and Transl.), *The Works of Voltaire.* New York: The St. Hubert Guild, 1901.

Weisner, J.B. The need for social engineering. In F.F. Korten, S.W. Cook, and J.I. Lacey (Eds.), *Psychology and the Problems of Society.* Washington, D.C.: American Psychological Association, 1970. pp. 85-94.

Weissman, M., and Rosenthal, A. The psychological prism: Neither freedom nor dignity. *Maxwell Review,* 1974, **10**(2), 19-32.

Wells, W.D. Television and Aggression: A Replication of an Experimental Field Study. University of Chicago, 1972. (mimeographed abstract, cited in Liebert, Neale and Davidson, 1973).

White, R.K. Misperception and the Vietnam war. *Journal of Social Issues,* 1966, **22,** 1-164.

White, R.K. Three not-so-obvious contributions of psychology to peace. In F. Korten, S.W. Cook, and J.I. Lacy (Eds.), *Psychology and the Problems of Society.* Washington, D.C.: American Psychological Association, Inc., 1970. pp. 344-355.

Winick, M., and Rosso, P. The effect of severe early malnutrition on cellular growth of the human brain. *Pediatric Research,* 1969, **3,** 181.

Witkin, H.A. A cognitive style approach to cross-cultural research. *International Journal of Psychology,* 1967, **2,** 233-250.

Witkin, H.A. Social influences in the development of cognitive style. In Goslin, D.A. (Ed.), *Handbook of Socialization Theory and Research.* New York: Rand-McNally, 1969.

Witkin, H.A., and Berry, J.W. Psychological differentiation across cultures: A theoretical and empirical integration. *Journal of Cross-cultural Psychology,* 1975, **6,** 4-87.

Wright, G.O. Projection and displacement: A cross-cultural study of folk-tale aggression. *Journal of Abnormal and Social Psychology,* 1954, **49,** 523-528.

Zigler, E., and de Labrey, J. Concept-switching in middle-class, lower-class and retarded children. *Journal of Abnormal and Social Psychology,* 1962, **65,** 267-273.

Zimbardo, P.G. The tactics and ethics of persuasion. In B.T. King and E. McGinnies (Eds.), *Attitudes, Conflicts and Social Change.* New York: Academic Press, 1972. Pp. 81-99.

Zimbardo, P.G., and Ebbeson, E.B. *Influencing Attitudes and Changing Behavior.* Reading Mass.: Addison-Wesley, 1969.

Author Index

Subject Index

Ability, 45, 105 (*See also* Intelligence)
Abilities-tracking, 112-113, 151
Abzug, B., 181
Achievement motivation, 58, 81, 163-165
Achievement orientation, 168-169 (*See also* Achievement motivation)
Admissions practices, 106, 160
Admissions tests, 59, 105-107
Africa & Africans, 254-256, 266, 277
   European prejudice toward, 140
Aggression (aggressiveness), xi, 12, 73, 179, 181, 189-242
   alternatives to, 234, 235-239
   and anxiety, 206, 224, 228
   cathartic effects of, 215-217
   cues for, 222-227, 230, 239-240
   cultural differences in, 206-207, 209
   definitions of, 190
   displaced, 206, 209
   and dissonance reduction, 227-229
   as a drive, 201, 215-216
   viewed as energy, 197, 205, 215-217
   and fantasy, 215-216
   and frustration, 207-209, 230-233
   guns, as cues to, 224-225
   individual differences in, 208
   inevitability of, 191-199, 209

   inhibition of, 211-213, 216, 222, 223-224, 227, 230, 233-235
   instigations to, 190, 208, 211, 217, 221, 223
   alleged instinctual basis of, 193-199, 201, 207, 229-230
   instructions to aggress, 225-227
   instrumental vs. intentional, 203-204
   role of learning in, 196-198, 199-213, 230
   and obedience, 225-227
   against parents, 205-206
   against peers, 205
   pervasiveness of, 191-193, 201, 229
   prepotency of, 200-201, 234
   proto-aggression, 201-202, 207, 209
   reduction & control of, 229-241
   and self-fulfilling prophecies, 221-222
   sex differences in, 212-213, 221-222, 241
   socialization of, 201-207
   impact of television on, 214-221, 224, 234, 240, 241, 242
Agriculture, 172
Alcoholism, 271
"All in the Family," 153
Allport, F., xiii
Altruism, 154

312